STUDIES IN ISLAMIC AND JUDAIC TRADITIONS

The publication of this volume
was made possible through a subvention provided by the

Rabbi Charles Eliezer Hillel Kauvar
Publications Fund,
Center for Judaic Studies,
University of Denver,
The Max Richter Foundation of Rhode Island,
and
Friends of the Program in Judaic Studies at
Brown University

Number 110

STUDIES IN ISLAMIC AND JUDAIC TRADITIONS
Edited by
William M. Brinner
and
Stephen D. Ricks

STUDIES IN ISLAMIC AND JUDAIC TRADITIONS

Papers Presented at the Institute for Islamic-Judaic Studies

Center for Judaic Studies
University of Denver

edited by

William M. Brinner

and

Stephen D. Ricks

Scholars Press
Atlanta, Georgia

STUDIES IN ISLAMIC AND JUDAIC TRADITIONS

Edited by
William M. Brinner
and
Stephen D. Ricks

The University of Denver

Library of Congress Cataloging in Publication Data

Studies in Islamic and Judaic traditions.

(Brown Judaic studies ; no. 110)
Includes indexes.
1. Islam--Relations--Judaism. 2. Judaism--Relations--Islam.
3. Islamic law. 4. Jewish law. 5. Maimonides, Moses, 1135-1204.
6. Philosophy, Islamic. 7. Philosophy, Jewish. 8. Philosophy, Medieval.
I. Brinner, William M. II. Ricks, Stephen David. III. Series.
BP173.J8S78 1986 296.1 86-15552
ISBN 1-55540-047-7 (alk. paper)
ISBN 1-55540-048-5 (pbk. : alk. paper)

Printed in the United States of America
on acid-free paper

TABLE OF CONTENTS

Foreword

The great scholar of Islam and Judaism, S. D. Goitein, in his classic work, *Jews and Arabs*, writes of the "great Jewish-Arab symbiosis" and the "vital contributions made by the cultural elements inherent in one civilization to the autonomous spiritual life of the other."[1] He attempted, in a number of his books and papers, to describe this fruitful relationship, thus greatly enhancing our understanding of each civilization. Other scholars have made similar contributions. Nevertheless, this field still remains inadequately cultivated.

In response to this scholarly vacuum, the University of Denver's Center for Judaic Studies established in 1981 an Institute for Islamic/Judaic Studies and has brought together some of America's leading scholars of Judaism and Islam for a series of conferences at which seminal papers were read and discussed. This volume is a by-product of those conferences and we are pleased to bring these excellent articles into print.

The funding of the Institute, and of this volume, was made possible largely through a generous grant of the Phillips Foundation of Minneapolis at the recommendation of Dr. Paula Bernstein, a Trustee of the Center for Judaic Studies. We are grateful to Dr. Bernstein for assisting us to create many exemplary academic forums in which Muslim, Christian, and Jewish scholars share their expertise in the areas of history, religion, law, philosophy, languages, literature, and the arts. We also express our appreciation to the Kennedy Center for International and Area Studies of Brigham Young University, the Max Richter Foundation of Rhode Island, and Friends of the Program in Judaic Studies at Brown University for their special allocation for this publication.

Although the reader of this volume will miss the excitement and dynamics of the interactions of scholars at a conference, our editors, Drs. William M. Brinner and Stephen D. Ricks, have done a most creditable job in making available to us the impressive contributions of some of the most authoritative academicians in the field of Islamic/Judaic Studies. As the beneficiaries of their diligence, we are in their debt.

In an age when Muslims and Jews are either the uncomfortable spectators of, or the unfortunate participants in, the Middle East conflict, it is all the more important to provide a scholarly forum, free of political overtones, in which Muslims, Jews, and Christians can amicably pursue and share their research in Islamic/Judaic Studies. Our Institute is committed to that objective, and the University of Denver is to be commended for encouraging us and sustaining us in this endeavor.

Dr. Stanley M. Wagner
Director
Center for Judaic Studies
University of Denver

[1] S. D. Goitein, *Jew and Arabs* (New York: Schocken Books, 1974), 127.

Introduction

William M. Brinner

Any approach to the question of what has been called the symbiosis, or the mutual influence, of Muslim and Judaic religious civilizations, must make its way with extreme caution through minefields of suspicion, misunderstanding, and hubris on both sides. This is true whether we look to the work of Abraham Geiger written in 1833—so typical of nineteenth-century European scholarship on Islam—with its provocative title *What Did Muhammad Borrow from Judaism?*—or to a fifty-year old work by Muḥammad Jamīl Bayhum, *Arabism and Jewry in Syria* with its also regrettably typical rewriting of Jewish history inspired by newspaper headlines of the day. On both sides we find those who were and are ready to belittle the originality of the other and to exhibit wounds—real or imaginary—inflicted by the other.

As scholarly fashion has changed, the tendency of Western scholars to find Jewish or Christian origins and influences in early Islam has shifted to a more sophisticated realization of the complexity of historical development leading to a new appreciation of the profound influence of Islam on Jewish thought and practice in the medieval and pre-modern periods. It is becoming increasingly clear that these two religious civilizations have interacted on a number of levels, from that of folklore and folk-religion to the realms of theological and philosophical speculation. It is also becoming more apparent that, for a variety of reasons, this interaction was probably more profound than that which existed between Islam and Christianity. Yet, because the meeting between the latter two has always been more dramatic, as the clash between military powers must inevitably be, this Muslim-Christian interaction has always elicited greater literary and scholarly response. From the beginning of the spread of an Islamic state, its armies faced Christian forces: in the wars against Byzantium, during the Crusades, and down to the European confrontation with the Ottoman and Moghul empires that accompanied the rise of European imperialism. The interaction with Judaism, on the other hand, perhaps because of the lack of Jewish political identity and military capacity since the collapse of statehood, has been more muted and hence largely ignored. Only the "Golden Age" of Jewish life in Spain—brief as it was—has been singled out and magnified for reasons which were not always of purely scholarly concern. In recent decades, with the reestablishement of a Jewish political identity, there has been a mutual rediscovery, not always of a friendly or disinterested nature.

The Institute of Islamic/Judaic Studies was founded at the University of Denver by Dr. Stanley M. Wagner under the aegis of the Center for Judaic Studies. One of its primary aims was to provide a nonpolitical, neutral scholarly ground for the examination by scholars, predominantly but not exclusively from the Judaic and Islamic traditions, of the historical and ideational affinities, similarities, and mutual influences all too often overlooked or simply unknown. Beginning in 1982, four annual meetings have been held in Denver to bring scholars together to hear and discuss the results of each other's research. Regrettably, not all of the papers presented at the four meetings could be accommodated in this volume, which contains only a sample of the varying approaches and interests of the contributing scholars.

This volume has been divided into three sections in order to bring together papers on broadly similar—though hardly identical—topics, which give a broad representation of the central themes of the last three meetings. From the first, founding meeting organized by Drs. Charles Geddes and Raphael Jospe, we have chosen only one paper, that of the late George F. Hourani. That meeting, more loosely structured than succeeding conferences, represented a hopeful beginning, giving impetus to the succeeding ones. The second conference in 1983, organized by Drs. Richard Freund and William M. Brinner, centered on scripture, while the conferences of 1984 and 1985, organized by Drs. Raphael Jospe and Lenn E. Goodman, had as their themes law and philosophy respectively. In all of the sessions we sought, at times successfully, to encourage comparative studies, to enable representatives of different backgrounds and disciplines to engage one another in meaningful dialogue, ignorant though they often professed to be of the "other" tradition or discipline.

In this volume, the papers have been assigned, at times rather arbitrarily, to three major divisions: Narrative and Exegesis, Religion and Law, and Philosophy and the Role of Maimonides. These divisions attempt to render the central coordinating themes of the conferences sponsored by the Institute in 1983, 1984, and 1985, although certain papers, placed under one heading, were actually presented at a conference with one of the other central themes.

The easiest and probably most traditional way of approaching the interaction of Judaism and Islam is through an examination of their respective scriptures, especially through a study of those characters and narratives that occur in the sacred books of both faiths. Patriarchs, kings, and other personages found in biblical accounts appear as prophets or divine messengers in the Qur'an. Over a century and a half have passed since the heyday of German studies on the Jewish "sources" of Qur'anic narratives that mention these biblical figures. The papers in this section of our volume generally avoid that approach and explore more fruitful ways of dealing with these narratives, even to the extent—as we find in one paper—of denying any need to search for any borrowing or mutual influence.

The section entitled "Religion and Law" contains papers read at three of the conferences and represents the widest range of topics. These include a study of a purely Islamic legal usage, a comparison of laws governing kinship and marriage prohibitions, as well as of the concept of supererogation in the two traditions. Further, there are studies on the rubrics of religious renewal in Islam and a comparison of the presentation of a moral code within the framework of the lives of the central prophets of Judaism and Islam.

The final group of papers that deals with philosophy contains three papers where Maimonides, the great Jewish thinker of the twelfth century, is a central figure, hence his inclusion in the title of this subsection. Two of those papers, presented at conferences three years apart, deal with somewhat similar themes on the attitutde of Maimonides towards Islam. This is a striking instance of a feature that will be noticed in several of the papers: the continual recurrence of themes and motifs throughout the long history of Islamic/Judaic symbiosis.

Other participants in the conferences, whose contributions at one or another of them are not published in this volume, or who came as observers or discussants, include: (1982) Frederick M. Denny (Colorado); Charles L. Geddes (Denver); Abraham Katsh (Dropsie); Herbert H. Paper (Hebrew Union College—Jewish Institute of Religion, Cincinnati); Abdulaziz Sachedina (Virginia); (1983) Richard Freund (Denver); Lenn E. Goodman (Hawaii); Frederick E. Greenspahn (Denver); Richard Martin (Arizona State); Azim Nanji (Oklahoma State); (1984) Shlomo Deshen (Bar Ilan); Gregory Kozlowski (DePaul); Daniel Lasker (Ben Gurion); John Makdisi (Cleveland State), Seth Ward (Yale); (1985) Lawrence V. Berman (Stanford); Pierre Cachia (Columbia); Dina Dahbany-Miraglia (City University of New York); Vera Moreen (Dropsie); Stephen Pastner (Vermont); Tamara Sonn (Iowa); Rafael Talmon (Haifa).

When giving thanks and recognition for contributions to the success of the venture to date, one must begin with the vision, determination, and effort of Dr. Stanley Wagner, without whom the Institute, its conferences, and this volume would not have come into existence. The devoted efforts of Dr. Raphael Jospe, formerly of the Center for Judaic Studies at the University of Denver, as well as of Dr. Lenn E. Goodman were essential to the success of the meetings. Dr. Goodman also participated in the early editing of these papers. Its must be stressed, however, that without the dedication and labor of Dr. Stephen D. Ricks and his staff at Brigham Young University it would have been impossible to produce this volume.

Above all, one must take into consideration the concern for scholarship and the search for truth that motivated those who participated in these meetings. Despite the present political situtation in the area of the world with which these fields of scholarship are concerned, as well as the atmosphere of tension that too often prevails at scholarly gatherings on the Middle East, these meetings were not only intellectually rewarding but were pleasant social occasions as well. Believers and secularists, Muslims—Shī'ite as well as Sunnī—Christians and Jews came together under the banner of scholarship to shed light on the past in the hope that the future, too, might be brighter as a result.

Guide to Transliteration and Usage

In general, the transliteration of Arabic and Hebrew words and names in this volume follows the rules outlined in the *Encyclopedia Judaica*.[1] The following exceptions and usages should, however, be noted:

1. The original transliteration of Arabic and Hebrew words and names given in quotations and in the titles of works cited will be retained.

2. In Hebrew, the letter *ṣade* will be transliterated *ṣ*, except in the words *matzah* and *mitzvah* (*mitzvot*). Further, the letter *'ayin* will generally be represented by ' at the beginning of transliterated words.

3. As is also the custom in the *Encyclopedia Judaica*, certain widely known Hebrew names will not be transliterated but will be given in their common forms, e.g., Moses.

4. Certain common Arabic names will be given without diacritic marks, e.g., Allah, Islam, Qur'an, Muhammad (the Prophet—note that this name is given with diacritics when it refers to another person). All other Arabic names and words will be transliterated with diacritic marks.

1 "Transliteration Rules," in *Encyclopedia Judaica*, 16 vols. (Jerusalem: Keter Publishing House, 1972), 1:90-91.

Part One:

Narrative and Exegesis

ʿUzayr in the Qur'an and Muslim Tradition

Mahmoud Ayoub

Long before the rise of Islam, Arabia was permeated with Jewish and Christian ideas. In general, the relationship of the Arabs to Christianity and Christians was a cultic one. Both nomadic Bedouins and town dwellers sought blessings and healing from Christian holy men in their desert hermitages. When they accepted the Christian faith, they did so more because of its concern for piety than its theological niceties.[1] This special relationship continued after Islam, when early Muslim ascetics sought the same monks for mystical knowledge.[2]

Arab-Jewish relations were both cultural and social. Before Islam there were Jews in Yemen and Madīna who continued to play an important role in forming the Islamic faith and world view. The formative period of early Islam was particularly crucial because it set the tone for a symbiotic relationship between Jews and Arabs that was to last for many centuries. It produced the golden age of Jewish learning and greatly aided in the development of Muslim philosophy, science, and religious thought.[3]

Muhammad's attitude toward the People of the Book, and notably the Jews, was ambivalent, and remained so in spite of the sharp conflicts between the two communities in Madīna. This ambivalence, moreover, tended to be benign. The Qur'an generally distinguishes between the Jews (*al-Yahūd*) of Madīna and the children of Israel. It presents Muslim history as continuous with the prophetic history of the children of Israel, the house (*āl*) of Abraham. Yet even the Jews of Madīna were necessary witnesses to the Qur'anic claims to scriptural authenticity and the claims of Muhammad to be "the gentile prophet whom they find written for them in the Torah and the Gospel."[4]

It is, I believe, in this context that the Qur'anic passages dealing with Muslim-Jewish relations must be read. This essay first examines some of the verses reflecting the Qur'anic attitude toward the children of Israel and toward the Jews of the Prophet's society. Then it will be possible to study in some detail the personality of 'Uzayr (Ezra) in the Qur'an and Muslim *ḥadīth* and hagiographical tradition. It will become clear that the Qur'anic assertion that the Jews considered 'Uzayr to be the son of God is not an isolated claim, but one of a number made concerning the Jews of Madīna. Whatever juristic and theological significance this accusation came to have, it was the result of Muslim-Jewish interaction and the gradual crystallization of Islamic lay theology and popular piety with its tales and legends.

In reconstucting the personality of 'Uzayr, several genres of literature will be used. The most important sources are, of course, the works of *tafsīr* that deal directly with the subject. Within this vast literature, we will distinguish between Shīʻī and Sunnī tradition and between classical and more recent *tafsīr* works. Another genre which to some extent comes out of the hagiographical *tafsīr* tradition, but which is far less bound by the rules of this science,[5] is that generally known as "tales of the prophets." One Sunnī and one Shī'ī example of this genre will be used in this study.

The Children of Israel and the Jews in the Qur'an

The Qur'anic attitude toward the ancient Hebrews is not substantially different from the position of the biblical prophets. They were a covenant people whom God favored over the rest of mankind.[6] However, while the biblical prophets, and especially those of the Exile, looked forward to a time of reconciliation and covenant renewal, the Qur'an generally holds that the descendants of the prophets had forfeited their covenant privileges through their own stubborn resistance to God's messages by slaying prophets unjustly and disobeying the laws of their own Torah.[7] The Qur'an takes with the utmost seriousness the biblical saga of the wandering in the wilderness with Moses, because this was the covenant period *par excellence*. That the ancient Israelites worshipped the calf when Moses left them for only forty days, that they demanded to see God openly before they would believe, that they chose the meaner food over the better, demonstrates from the point of view of the Qur'an more than mere human frailty. It indicates a willful attitude of disobedience and transgression against God's covenant.[8]

The Qur'an never makes categorical statements in its judgment of the People of the Book. Rather, it always qualifies its praise or condemnation with such phrases as, i.e., "a group of . . ." Islam sees society as an integral whole made up of many individuals. Rights and responsibilities, praise and blame, and rewards and punishment are all viewed on both the social as well as the individual plane. Thus we read concerning those who transgressed on the Sabbath that they were simply a people, while neither the time nor place of their sin and punishment is specified. An even more general commentary on the story concludes, "then We divided those in the earth into communities; among them are some who are righteous and others who are less so. We tested them with both good and evil things that perhaps they might return."[9] In another Qur'anic statement we are told that "there are among the people of Moses a community which guides to the truth and dispenses justice by means of it."[10]

An important factor in Jewish-Muslim relations has been the Qur'anic insistence on the continuity and universality of revelation from Adam to Muhammad, and the Jewish counterclaim that God spoke only to His chosen people, the house of Jacob. I am convinced that the Jewish refusal to accept Muhammad's claim to apostleship was not, as many scholars assert, based on Muhammad's distortion of biblical thought and history. If we were to judge from the vast literature known as *Isrā'īliyyāt* (Israelite traditions) which entered Muslim tradition from Jewish converts, it would seem that the Bible was no more than a framework in which these traditions were presented. Muslims and Jews in Islamic lands have had far more in common in world view and general culture than most Jews or Muslims have been willing to admit. A more plausible reason for the Jewish rejection of Muhammad lies in the Jews' unwillingness to recognize a prophet either outside their own community or after the close of the biblical period of prophecy.

At least one important sect of Judaism, the 'Īsāwiyya, did recognize Muhammad, as well as Jesus, as prophets. This was the Jewish group closest to Islam. The sect appeared early in Muslim history and played a significant role in it.[11] The Qur'an in many places echoes the 'Īsāwiyya view by challenging the Jews to accept its message, and it praises those who do so. In a verse belonging to the middle Madīnan period, the Qur'an states, "There are some among the People of the Book who have faith in God and that which was sent down to them. They stand in awe of God and do not exchange God's revelations for a paltry price."[12]

Contrary to the general Islamic view, the Qur'an does not accuse Jews and Christians of altering the text of their scriptures, but rather of altering the truth which those scriptures contain. The people do this by concealing some of the sacred texts, by misapplying their precepts, or by "altering words from their right position."[13] However, this refers more to interpretation than to actual addition or deletion of words from the sacred books. The problem of alteration (*taḥrīf*) needs further study. The Qur'an states, "O People of the Book, our messenger has come to you to make clear for you much of what you used to conceal of the Book."[14] Here the Qur'an addresses first the Jews of the Prophet's day, and only by extension those of later generations. With perhaps a few exceptions, the Qur'an speaks in very definite historical and local terms when commending or criticizing the Jews. Historical references are used as examples or lessons for the Prophet's contemporaries, the same approach used to admonish the Meccans.[15]

The Qur'an views Judaism as an act of turning to God. Thus it sometimes uses the name in its verbal form. Moses, in articulating the repentant attitude of his people, declares, "We have returned (*hudnā*) to You."[16] Likewise, in one of the few instances where a verse occurs more than once in the Qur'an and in essentially the same words, we are told, "Those who have faith and those who have returned (*hādū*) . . . whoever has faith in God and the last day, no fear shall come upon them, nor will they grieve."[17] The Qur'an, however, generally uses the term "Jews" (*Yahūd*) for reproach and the phrase "Children of Israel" for approbation and praise.[18]

Before we discuss 'Uzayr, the ancient prophet of God to the Children of Israel, we must discuss two Qur'anic accusations which, like the accusation against the Jews of the sin of associating others with God, cannot be historically substantiated. The Qur'an calls on the people of faith to give alms to the poor: "Who shall lend God a goodly loan which He would repay in manifold measure?"[19] Some of the Jews of Madīna apparently heard the verse and mockingly remarked, "(So) God is poor and we are rich!" The Qur'an first warns that God has heard the words of those who have made such a statement and continues, "We shall record what they said . . . and We shall say (on the day of judgment), 'Taste the torment of burning!'"[20]

The other important verse which accuses the Jews of something not to be found in their scriptures or tradition is the assertion that "the Jews said, 'The hand of God is fettered.'"[21] In both cases, most likely the report is of what one or some of the Jews said when they heard the call to give God a goodly loan. It was the same person, according to some commentators (as will be seen later), who also said, "'Uzayr is the son of God."[22]

The purpose of the discussion so far has been to demonstrate that the Qur'anic attitude toward the Jews and Judaism was not one of consistent rejection or unquestioning acceptance; rather, it distinguishes between the Jews of the Prophet's society in Madīna and their ancient ancestors, the children of Israel. It judges both by the criteria of divine revelation and prophetic authority and the human response to them. The Qur'an leaves much room for discussion, because it first accuses the Jews of the all-too-human tendency to resist God's call to faith and obedience.

The Jews were the people of the Torah, "in which is the judgment (*ḥukm*) of God", and "according to which prophets must judge."[23] Human beings must, according to the Qur'an, receive knowledge before they can reject or accept faith. Knowledge must be transmitted. Hence the need for prophets. Prophets must, moreover, be granted miracles as proof of their mission. Among the one hundred and twenty-four thousand prophets, some were sent with major revelations of divine law for human society; the rest were reformers and preachers. In what follows, we will attempt to study the 'Uzayr of hagiographical piety whom God made "a sign for humankind." Having established 'Uzayr's claim to prophethood on the basis of a great miracle, we will discuss his mission as Muslim tradition saw it, and the response of the Jewish community to it.

'Uzayr, the Prophet of God

The Qur'an has been characterized by Muslim tradition as, among other things, a book of parables and stories.[24] In such stories and parables there are at times oblique references to prophets and other personages of bygone ages. Later tradition, wishing to identify these individuals, resorted to an eclectic technique by which the tale or explanation was used to explicate two or more verses. At other times, new tales or explanations were woven out of older narratives where the man identified becomes a composite personality made up of elements which figure in the picture of one or more biblical prophets. 'Uzayr, who is mentioned only once in the Qur'an without being in any way identified, was such an eclectic construct. If, as appears most probable, men like the famous rabbi Ka'b al-Aḥbār and the Yemenite Jewish savant Wahb b. Munabbih were responsible for such tales, then no doubt this process of hagiographical eclecticism came into Islamic tradition after a long period of Jewish development. As Muslim traditionists and later scholars knew more about biblical accounts and Jewish history in general, they began to cast doubt on such tales. Thus in an important way, both from the viewpoint of history and theology, Muslim tradition added its own contribution to the growth of Islamic prophetology.

'Uzayr, who appears to be Ezra the ancient scribe and priest who brought the exiles back to Jerusalem from Babylon, is identified by Muslim tradition as the one "who passed by a town in ruins and deserted."[25] He looked at the devastated town and exclaimed in astonishment, "How shall God revive this after its death?" God did not bring the town back to life in answer to 'Uzayr's challenge, but "caused him to die for a hundred years." God then revived him and asked challengingly, "How long have you remained dead?" 'Uzayr answered, "A day," but then seeing that the sun had not yet set, added, "Or part of a day." When 'Uzayr first came upon the town it must have been summer, the season of grapes and figs. Hence, he picked a basketful of figs and pressed a pitcher of grape juice or wine. He came riding on a donkey with a new rope around its neck. God continued in reply to 'Uzayr's challenge, "Look at your food and drink, how they have not aged, and look at your donkey! Look at the bones, how we set them up, then clothed them with flesh! We shall make you a sign for humankind."[26] Thus seeing God's great power, 'Uzayr finally exclaimed, "Now I know that God has power over all things!"

The verse just discussed follows the account of an unidentified man who disputed with Abraham about God's sovereignty and power to revive the dead. The man is later identified by tradition as Namrūd (Nimrod), a tyrannical king who arrogantly claimed to be God. The town of 'Uzayr, according to some traditions, was Jerusalem after it was destroyed by Bukhtnaṣṣar (Nebuchadnezzar), the Babylonian king. Tradition tells us that Nimrod was tormented by a fly that entered through his nostril into his skull and slowly ate up his brain until he died.[27] The same fate is also ascribed to Bukhtnaṣṣar, who was the instrument of divine punishment of the children of Israel for their wickedness. Yet he himself was punished in turn for being the tyrant whom God used for His vengeance.[28]

Commentators have widely differed on the identity of the man and the ruined town he passed. According to early authorities going back to Ibn 'Abbās, who in turn related it on the authority of Ka'b al-Aḥbār, the man was 'Uzayr (Ezra). According to Wahb b. Munabbih and the commentators who related this tradition on his authority, it was Jeremiah. According to other commentators, the man was Isaiah; and according to still others who based their sayings on the authority of Mujāhid, he was an unnamed man of the children of Israel. The town was either Jerusalem, a town in Persia, or Dayr Hiraql, a town on the banks of the Tigris River in Mesopotamia. In another verse of the Qur'an we read about people "who left their dwellings by the thousands in fear of death." God also caused these to die.[29] Here again the town is not identified. Thus it was quite natural for commentators and traditionists to identify these people and their dwellings with those discussed in verse 258 of the same sūra.[30]

It must be observed that even when early commentators disagreed on the identity of the man, their tales resembled each other to such an extent that a composite personality in every case emerged which includes characteristics of all the men on whom they are based. One example will illustrate:

God, according to Wahb b. Munabbih, sent the prophet Jeremiah to a pious king of the children of Israel to guide him and to be his prophet. Yet neither king nor prophet was able to restrain the people from committing acts of wickedness before God. God therefore ordered Jeremiah to convey to the people these words: "By my majesty do I swear that I shall bring upon them such trials as would cause a wise man to be distracted. I shall set over them a Persian tyrant, whom I shall clothe with awe and remove mercy from his heart. His troops will be so numerous that they will appear like a dark night." Jeremiah rent his garments and threw dust and ashes over his head. He begged God to spare the people or destroy him before he should witness such calamities. God assured him that He would not bring this about until Jeremiah himself wished for it. An angel came to the prophet in human form and by way of allegory made charges against the prophet's own near relatives. No matter how much he tried to show them kindness, they returned his kindness with hostility and ingratitude. After the angel had complained three times, Jeremiah prayed, "O Master of the heavens and earth, Lord of majesty and glory, if these people be in the right and are truthful, spare them. But if they are committing deeds which do not please you, destroy them." No sooner had he uttered these words than God sent a thunderbolt which consumed the Holy of Holies in the Temple and seven of its gates.

Jeremiah left the city and lived in the wilderness with the beasts. Bukhtnaṣṣar then came and destroyed the city, killed its inhabitants, and took captive 70,000 of its youths whom he divided among his chiefs. Among them were Daniel and Ezra ('Uzayr). After this, Jeremiah came on his donkey and, seeing the city empty and in ruins, exclaimed, "How shall God revive this after its death?"[31] God then caused him to die for a hundred years. Seventy years after his death, God ordered Yūshak (Cyrus), the king of Persia, to rebuild Jerusalem. He did so, and in thirty years the people increased and prospered. In the meantime, God sent a fly which entered through Bukhtnaṣṣar's nostrils into his skull and slowly gnawed at his brain until he died. Jeremiah was brought back to life, beginning with his eyes, then the rest of his body, as he looked on. He then heard a voice commanding the bones of his donkey to gather together, to be clothed with flesh, and finally to rise. Jeremiah returned to his people with black hair and found his children and their children old men and women.[32]

This is but one of a number of versions of the same essential saga (with different names applied to the main characters) that evolved to explain the verse under discussion. The biblical elements are clear. Hosea's anguish of love, Ezekiel's witness of the revival of dead bones, and the projection of Nebuchadnezzar into the Muslim tale of Nimrod are only some of the elements woven into the story of 'Uzayr. The same account also suggests that 'Uzayr was among the war captives of Nebuchadnezzar, along with Daniel and 70,000 Israelites. As the story continues, 'Uzayr escapes and comes upon a deserted town on the banks of the Tigris. He comes soon after the event, for the fruit orchards of the town are still untouched. Muslim jurists were anxious that a prophet of God not appear to drink wine. Thus the words "look at your food and drink" were made to refer to figs and water or juice pressed of the grapes belonging to the inhabitants of the ruined town.

Shī'ī tradition sought to embellish the story of 'Uzayr even further, adding to the confusion of the biblical and hagiographical accounts. Here, Nebuchadnezzar is made to avenge the blood of the beheaded John the Baptist (Yaḥyā). In the midst of this onslaught, God sent 'Uzayr as a prophet to the town whose people "left their dwellings in thousands in fear of death." God raised them up for 'Uzayr who loved them and found in their faith and piety great solace. 'Uzayr left the people for one day, but when he returned he found them all dead. He therefore exclaimed, "How shall God revive this after its death?" Thereupon God caused him to die for a hundred years, after which He raised him up along with the people. There were, tradition tells us, a hundred thousand fighters who had been exterminated by Nebuchadnezzar. We are not given the reason for this punishment.[33]

In another account, Nebuchadnezzar chose Daniel from the war captives as his viceroy over his entire realm. When Daniel died, his office passed to 'Uzayr. Then 'Uzayr left his home one day and came upon the town where he died for a hundred years. When he left, he was fifty years old and his wife was pregnant. He returned a hundred years later; he was still fifty but his son was a hundred years old.

One of the signs of an imām, according to Shī'ī traditions, is his unusual knowledge. Often we read about people coming to one or another of the imāms with strange questions about strange events. A man came to 'Alī and asked, "Has there been in the world a child older than his father?" "Yes," he answered, "it was the son of 'Uzayr." The tale makes clear the reason. This unusual phenomenon is cited in interpretation of the words, "And we shall surely make you a sign for mankind."[34]

Muslim tradition clearly regarded 'Uzayr as a mysterious personality and his experiences as a divine sign. It was therefore not wholly incredible for Jewish tradition to entertain the thought that he was the son of God.

According to one account, related on the authority of Ibn 'Abbās, when 'Uzayr returned to his people after his long absence, they did not recognize him. In his home he found an old woman who had lost her sight and the strength to walk. She had been a young maid in his house when 'Uzayr left. She demanded that he pray to God to restore her sight and strength so that she might recognize him, if indeed he was the prophet she knew and whose prayers were always answered. He prayed and laid his hands upon her, and she rose up healed and went with him to the assembled people, who still denied that he was their prophet who had disappeared a hundred years before and whom they thought to have been long dead. His son, then 118 years old, said that his father had a mole between his shoulders by which he would recognize him. The story implies that, like Muhammad, 'Uzayr had the mark of prophethood between his shoulders.[35] Thus, an ancient scribe whom Islam considered only a minor prophet was made to resemble the "seal of the prophets."

'Uzayr, the Son of God

The ninth sūra of the Qur'an, in which the assertion of 'Uzayr's divine sonship is recorded,[36] was one of the last sūras of the Qur'an to be revealed. It defined once and for all the relations between the firmly established community of Muslims and their non-Muslim subjects. Jurists have therefore taken the laws enunciated in this sūra to abrogate all previous injunctions. They took great pains to create a measure of uniformity in their characterization of Jews and Christians, and hence achieved a measure of uniformity in their legal treatment. The Qur'anic purpose may simply have been to condemn the sin of association or also possibly to provide some basis for such subsequent legal issues. The verse had, as we shall see, both juristic and theological ramifications for Muslim tradition.

The questions that occupied the attention of early commentators were who made such a claim for 'Uzayr, and why was it made? The first question arose from the early realization by Muslim traditionists and heresiographers that this claim had no basis in the Jewish scriptures or tradition. Al-Ṭabarī, therefore, relates that only one man, named Finḥas, said, "'Uzayr is the son of God" during the life of the Prophet. It was he who also said, "God is poor and we are rich."[37] Al-Ṭabarī relates further, as an occasion (*sabab*) of the revelation of this verse, that a group of Jews led by a man called Sallām b. Mishkam came to the Prophet and said, "How can we follow you when you have left our *qibla* (direction of prayer)[38] and do not accept the claim that 'Uzayr is the son of God?"[39]

The fact that either one or several Jewish people said that "'Uzayr is the son of God" did not deter commentators from relating traditions attributing this claim to the contemporaries of the ancient prophet himself. The question that concerned them was why the Jews had made such a claim. The reason was, of course, a special favor which God bestowed on His prophet which his people misconstrued, as did the Christians with regard to Jesus. In this way, Jews and Christians have committed the same heinous sin.

Al-Ṭabarī relates on the authority of Ibn 'Abbās that the children of Israel had the Torah and the Ark of the Covenant. But as they abandoned the Torah, God effaced it from their hearts and removed the Ark, which contained the tablets on which it was written. He moreover afflicted them with a painful stomach ailment which caused them to forget completely the Torah. 'Uzayr was a pious and learned man. He thus prayed that God would return the Torah to him. One day as he prayed, a light from God entered his body and the Torah returned to him. He taught the people the scriptures, and the Ark was also returned to them. When they compared what 'Uzayr taught of the Torah with the text contained in the Ark, they exclaimed, "'Uzayr was not so favored but that he be the son of God."[40]

In another account related on the authority of al-Suddī, the Torah was taken away by the Amalekites, who conquered the children of Israel and drove their rabbis out into the wilderness. The rabbis buried the sacred scrolls in the mountains. 'Uzayr was then a youth given to solitary worship in the hills around the city. He would only come down to the city on feast days. He wept continuously over the sad plight of the people until his eyelids fell off. One day as he was on his way back to his solitude, he saw a woman lamenting beside a grave and saying, "O you who used to feed and clothe me!" 'Uzayr said to her, "Alas for you, woman. Who was it that used to feed and clothe you?" She answered, "God." He said, "God is living and will never die!" The woman asked, "O 'Uzayr, who taught the scholars before the children of Israel?" He answered, "God!" She said, "Why do you then weep for them?" 'Uzayr knew that it was a parable to admonish him. The woman then told him to go to a river nearby, wash himself in it, and pray two *rak'a*s (units of prayer). After that, an old man would come to him, and 'Uzayr was to accept whatever the old man gave him. This he did, and the old man put in his mouth burning coals packed together like bottles. 'Uzayr went back to his people, having become thoroughly versed in the Torah. He tied pens to each of his ten fingers and wrote with each one separately until he wrote down the entire Torah. The scholars later returned and dug up copies of the Torah which they had buried. They compared 'Uzayr's version and their own and found it in complete agreement with them. They thus exclaimed, "God did not grant you such a favor except that you be His son!"[41]

The famous commentator al-Suyūṭī relates another version of the same tale in which the woman of the story tells 'Uzayr that she was not a woman but rather the world (*dunyā*) which appeared to him in the form of a woman. The woman tells 'Uzayr that a spring of water and a tree will appear in his prayer chamber. He should drink of the water and eat of the fruit of the tree. After that, two angels came to him with a vessel filled with light. He drank the light, whereupon God inspired the Torah in his heart. The people marvelled at this and said, "'Uzayr is the son of God."[42]

Commentators and traditionists differ on whether 'Uzayr was a prophet or not. The accounts just presented in which a man or men instead of angels inject knowledge into 'Uzayr's heart imply that he was not a prophet. It was not a miracle vouchsafed a prophet, but a favor (*karāma*) with which God favored him.[43] Qurṭubī perhaps comes closest to attributing prophetic revelation to the ancient scribe. He relates, without reference to any authority, that 'Uzayr was filled with grief for the sad condition of his people and left them to wander in the desert. Gabriel came to him and asked where he was going. 'Uzayr answered that he was seeking knowledge. The angel then taught him the Torah, which he in turn taught to his people. They marvelled at his knowledge and proclaimed him "the son of God."[44]

The tales with which we have been concerned not only provide an explanation for the verse, they also show the rich and often contradictory confluence of scriptural narrative and popular haggadic tale. Here again the Exile and Jeremiah's grief for the city and people provide the major motif. The woman, or the world in the form of a woman, is no doubt an element of popular Muslim folklore. The tree with fruit and the spring of water appearing in the prayer chamber of the prophet echo the story of Mary and her seclusion in the Temple, where she was miraculously provided summer fruits in winter and winter fruits in summer.[45] They also echo the lonely spot where Mary gave birth to Jesus and where both water and fruits were miraculously provided.[46] Isaiah's commission in the Temple through an angel touching his lips with the burning coals of the altar[47] is yet another element woven into the tale of 'Uzayr.

The Qur'anic assertion that the Jews claimed 'Uzayr to be the son of God created an exegetical problem for Muslim thinkers. The attitude they took in solving this problem has remained essentially the same throughout most of Muslim history. Commentators realized quite early that the Jews did not claim that 'Uzayr was the son of God. Al-Tha'ālibī relates the view of another well-known contemporary commentator who asserted that there were no longer any Jews who made such a claim. Still, he continued, "even if only one of their chiefs said it, the evil of this claim would apply to them all."[48]

The well-known traditionist and commentator Ibn Kathīr offers an unusual explanation, one that perhaps reflects more the long history of conflict between Muslims and western Christendom than a carefully conceived and argued position. He writes, "This is (reported) by way of enticement by God of the people of faith to fight the rejectors of faith of the Jews and Christians because of the ugly battles which they fought against the people of faith. It is also because of the lie which they (the Jews and Christians) invented about God. As for the Jews, it was their saying, ''Uzayr is the son of God.'" Yet Ibn Kathīr in the next sentence admits that not all their rabbis made such a claim, but only "some of the foolish among them."[49]

The famous theologian, philosopher, and commentator Fakhr al-Dīn al-Rāzī was so well known for his skepticism of any subject he discussed that he was called "the imām (leader) of the doubters." His treatment of this verse, however, was simply a polemical one. He begins by asserting that the *shirk* (association of other things with God) of the Jews and Christians by attributing a son to God is not different from that of the idol worshippers. This is because association means worshipping another being or thing, be it an idol or Jesus, along with God. Rāzī further asserts that God accepted the *jizya* (poll tax) from the Jews and Christians only because of their relationship to the great apostles Moses and Jesus and because their ancestors had true faith in God. Rāzī concludes, "The fact that the Jews deny such a belief proves nothing because God's report concerning them is more true (than their denial)."[50]

Shī'ī commentators treated the problem of 'Uzayr's divine sonship in essentially the same way. Abū Ja'far al-Ṭūsī, the juris-doctor (*shaykh*) of the Shī'ī community, was also concerned with the lack of evidence in Jewish tradition for the claim attributed to them in the Qur'an. He argues, "If it is objected, 'how could God relate about the Jews that they say 'Uzayr is the son of God while the Jews deny it,' it may be answered that God related this about them because some of them did make such a claim. The proof of this is that the Jews at the time when God sent down the Qur'an heard this verse and did not deny it."[51]

Shī'ī beliefs concerning the imāmate, God's justice, etc., are sufficiently different from those of Sunnī Islam that they established the necessity of argumentation (*iḥtijāj*) against their opponents on the basis of the Qur'an and *sunna*. A book entitled *Iḥtijāj* (disputation) has come down to us, in which the author reports such disputations between the Prophet and the rest of his family, the imāms, against their opponents in defense of various beliefs and claims. The disputation between the Prophet and the representatives of Judaism, Christianity, and Zoroastrianism as well as philosophers who asserted the eternity of the world (*dahriyyūn*) is reported. The dispute with the Jews concerned the claim that 'Uzayr was the son of God. The Jews are reported to have said, "We say, ''Uzayr is the son of God,' and we have come to you, Muhammad, to see what you say. If you follow us, we would have preceded you to the truth and thus could be better than you. If, on the other hand, you oppose us, we shall be able to defeat you." He asked the Jews, "What made you say that 'Uzayr is the son of God?" They answered, "Because he revived the Torah for the children of Israel after it had disappeared. He could not do this unless he was the son of God." The Prophet replied, "How could 'Uzayr be the son of God instead of Moses when the latter brought them the Torah and the miracles which were wrought at his hands are known to you. If, therefore, 'Uzayr deserves to be God's son because he revived the Torah, then Moses would deserve a much more exalted status." The Prophet then refuted the argument of even using this as an honorific, because that would make God subject to all human relations, which cannot be attributed to him.[52]

Shī'ī Muslims have incorporated all known prophets, be they major or minor, into their system of prophetic vicegerency (*wiṣāya*). Since, moreover, the twelfth imām is believed to be in occultation, it was argued that every prophet and imām before him had to experience a period of occultation (*ghayba).* 'Uzayr is therefore used to furnish the necessary evidence for the occultation of all prophets and imāms before the Mahdī, the twelfth imām of Imāmī Shī'ism.

After Moses and his immediate successors, the faithful among the children of Israel were tried with a long period of waiting for another prophet. At long last Daniel came, but he was imprisoned by Bukhtnaṣṣar (Nebuchadnezzar) in the lion's den, and that was his *ghayba.* Bukhtnaṣṣar slew or enslaved the children of Israel. This was also necessary from the point of view of Shī'ī imāmology, because suffering and trials were to be the tests of the faith and constancy of the aspiring faithful. The tyrannical king chose from the house of Judah five men, among whom were Daniel and 'Uzayr. Daniel, who was then the "proof (*ḥujja*) of God" (a term used for the imāms of the Shī'ī community), was a captive in the hands of Bukhtnaṣṣar for ninety years. When at last the king realized the status of Daniel with God and the people, and that they were all anticipating his "rising up" (*qiyām*) against oppression and wrongdoing, he had him imprisoned in a large well with a starving lion. God, however, sent a prophet to Daniel who brought him his daily food, and the lion did not touch him.

The story of Daniel is told in terms relevant to the fourth Islamic century, when the theology of occultation had fully crystallized. "Affliction grew harder still upon his followers (*shī'a*) and those who were waiting for him to appear. Many began to doubt religion because of the length of the period." Then, we are told, the tyrannical king saw in a dream angels coming down to greet Daniel and announce to him his imminent release. The king, filled with remorse, released Daniel. He also made him an overseer of his kingdom. The people who had hidden their faith, i.e., practiced *taqiyya*, came out and gathered around Daniel, certain of the final relief (*faraj*). Soon, however, Daniel died and 'Uzayr succeeded him. God then caused 'Uzayr to go into concealment (*ghayba*) for a hundred years. After that, He brought him back to life and he was succeeded by Yaḥyā (John the Baptist).[53]

A later Shī'ī author of a hagiographical work on the lives of the prophets carried the notion of 'Uzayr's occultation even further by suggesting two periods of *ghayba*. He thus established an even closer parallel with that of the twelfth imām. He tells us that when God destroyed Bukhtnaṣṣar and had mercy on the children of Israel, he revived those who had "left their dwellings by the thousands in fear of death." But when they were still under Bukhtnaṣṣar's oppressive rule,

"'Uzayr went into a spring of water in which he disappeared (i.e., went into occultation)."[54]

Shī'ī piety made of 'Uzayr a model of pious asceticism, not unlike that of Jesus, for Ṣūfi and Shī'ī tradition.[55] 'Uzayr is said to have prayed once, "My Lord, I have looked into all your commands and precepts, and have recognized your justice by my own reason. There remains, however, one matter which I do not know: You become wrathful with the people of trial (*balā'*) and you include them all, even the children." God then commanded him to go out into the wilderness on a hot day. There he slept in the shade of a tree. An ant came and bit him, but he rubbed his foot on the ground and crushed a multitude of ants. He thus knew that this was a parable for him. He was then told, "When people deserve my punishment, I decree that it come upon them at the end of the term of life of the children. The children die at their preordained time, but the others perish by my punishment." God counselled 'Uzayr, saying, "If you fall into transgression, look not at its insignificance, but consider who it is that you have disobeyed. If you receive sustenance from me, look not at its meager measure, but consider whose gift it was to you. If you are afflicted with trials, do not accuse me before my creatures, as I would not accuse you before my angels when your disgraceful deeds are brought before me."[56]

Modern commentators, both Shī'ī and Sunnī, in their treatment of 'Uzayr rely on biblical narrative as well as historical facts. They have not, however, succeeded any more than classical traditionists in solving the problem of the alleged Jewish claim that 'Uzayr is the son of God. The late Shī'ī jurist, philosopher, and theologian Sayyid Muḥammad Ḥusayn Ṭabaṭabā'ī (d. November 1980) bases his account on history and the Bible. After noting 'Uzayr's role in bringing his people out of the Babylonian Exile and collecting for them the books of the Torah after they had been destroyed, Ṭabaṭabā'ī continues:

> Because of the great services which he rendered to them, they exalted his status, greatly respected him and called him "son of God." We do not know whether this claim of sonship was meant in the same sense in which Christians used it when they call Christ the son of God. What is intended is that there was in him something of the divine substance, or that he was derived from it, or that he was synonymous with it.

Ṭabaṭabā'ī allows that the epithet may have been used as an honorific one. He relates this verse to the two others which cite the Jews as saying, "God is poor and we are rich" and "The hand of God is fettered." As for the problem of who made such a claim, Ṭabaṭabā'ī says, "In God's word it is attributed to all of them because some said it and the others consented to what they said. They were all of one opinion and general view."[57]

Ṭabaṭabā'ī quotes a *ḥadīth* of the Prophet which asserts that "God's wrath increased toward the Jews when they said ''Uzayr is the son of God.'

Likewise it increased toward the Christians when they said, 'Jesus is the son of God.'"[58] This *ḥadīth* provides clear evidence of the intention of Muslim traditionists and commentators. The verse, it seems fairly certain, referred to a small group of the Jews of Madīna. However, it gave Muslim polemicists a good prooftext for attributing to both Jews and Christians, their chief rivals, one major and unforgivable sin. As we shall see presently, other recent thinkers have used the verse to argue in support of a juristic, military, or theological status quo.

The well-known reformist Muḥammad Rashīd Riḍā (d. 1935), like Ṭabaṭabā'ī, bases his discussion on legitimate historical accounts, notably the 1903 *Jewish Encyclopedia* and biblical records. He says, "the Jews did and still do regard Ezra as a holy man so that some of them called him 'son of God.' We do not know if this was used as an honorific, as it was used for Israel, David, and others, or in the way that their philosopher Philo believed it. He was a philosopher whose philosophy was closest to that of India and which was the basis of the Christian belief."[59] Like classical commentators, Riḍā accepted the view that only some Jews of Madīna may have made such a claim. Yet he justifies its being a general accusation against the Jews because society, he argues, is an integral whole that must be held responsible for the views of its individual members. Elsewhere, however, he rejects this view; he argues that each individual is solely responsible before God for his or her own faith and ideas.[60]

Finally, Sayyid Quṭb (d. 1966), the well-known thinker of the Muslim Brothers, quotes at some length Riḍā's commentary on the verse in question. He then relates it to the wars and power struggles between Muslims and the People of the Book. He sees the verse as a justification for the *jizya* (poll tax law). He believes that only a small group of the Jews said, "''Uzayr is the son of God,' and thus their belief was a false one . . . according to which they could not be regarded as believers in God or as followers of the true religion. It was on this basic quality that the verdict to fight against them was based." The primary aim was, according to Sayyid Quṭb, not to compel them to accept Islam[61] but only to weaken their power.[62]

Among the heresiographers, only Ibn Ḥazm attempts briefly to assign this claim to a specific group later than the Prophet. He may have had the Qur'anic text in mind and intended his remarks as the confirmation of its claim. He writes: "The *ṣaddūqiyya*, named after a man called Ṣaddūq (Zadok), was the only sect of the Jews which claims that 'Uzayr is the son of God. They lived somewhere in Yemen."[63]

The phrase "The Jews said" (*qālat al-Yahūd*) in the verse with which we have been concerned need not, as Qurṭubī rightly observes, refer to all the Jews. Rather, "it is a statement which is meant to be specific."[64] Even though Muslim thinkers have generally agreed with this view, the temptation to use this verse as the basis for the legal, theological, and, above all, polemical relations with the Jews and Judaism, was too great to allow them to see the verse in the light of their own view. By insisting on attributing this claim to the Jewish people in general, they were not vindicating the truth of the Qur'an, but their own juristic and theological ideas. In fact, this assertion, in whatever form it has been made and argued for, flies in the face of one of the most important Qur'anic principles: "No soul shall be made to bear the burden of another soul."[65]

The Qur'anic challenge is, in the end, for all the People of the Book, including Muslims, to seek greater harmony and understanding among themselves. "Say, 'O People of the Book, come to a word of common agreement between us and you, that we worship no one other than God.'"[66] If the two communities accept this challenge, they will live and prosper. If they refuse, they may yet destroy one another in the name of the God who calls them both to serve and worship him.

NOTES

[1] J. S. Trimingham, *Christianity among the Arabs in Islamic Times* (London : Longman, 1979), 49-71.

[2] Tor Andrae, *Islamische Mystiker*, Helmhart Kanus-Crede, tr. (Stuttgart: Kohlhammer, 1960), esp. ch. 1.

[3] See S. D. Goitein, *Jews and Arabs: Their Contacts through the Ages* (New York: Schocken Books, Inc., 1964).

[4] Qur'an 7:157.

[5] For rules concerning the Qur'anic interpretation, see Abū Ja'far Muḥammad b. Jarīr al-Ṭabarī, *Jāmi' al-Bayān 'an Ta'wīl Āy al-Qur'ān*, Maḥmūd and Aḥmad Muḥammad Shākir, eds. (Cairo: Dār al-Ma'ārif, 1332/1954), 1:73-76.

[6] See Qur'an 2:47 and 2:122.

[7] See Qur'an 4:153-161 and 62:5.

[8] See Qur'an 2:51, 54, 55, 61, and 93; cf. M. Ayoub, *The Qur'an and its Interpreters* (New York: SUNY Press, 1983), 1:99-104, 113-15, 126, for commentaries on the above verses.

[9] Qur'an 7:168; see also Qur'an 7:163-68.

[10] Qur'an 7:159.

[11] Abū Muḥammad 'Alī ibn Ḥazm, *Al-Faṣl fī al-Milal wa'l-Ahwā' wa'l-Niḥal* (Baghdad: Maktabat al-Muthannā, n.d.), 1:99. See also in the margin, Abu al-Fatḥ 'Abd al-Karīm al-Shahrastānī, *Al-Milal wa'l-Nihal*, vol. 2:55-56.

[12] Qur'an 3:190.

[13] Qur'an 4:26 and 5:13 and 41; see also Qur'an 2:75.

[14] Qur'an 5:15.

[15] See Qur'an 4:153-55, 161.

[16] Qur'an 7:156.

[17] Qur'an 2:62. See also Qur'an 5:69.

[18] Qur'an 5:81.

[19] Qur'an 2:245.
[20] Qur'an 3:181.
[21] Qur'an 5:64.
[22] Qur'an 9:30.
[23] Qur'an 5:43-44.
[24] See al-Ṭabarī, *Jāmi' al-Bayān*, vol. 1:73-75.
[25] Qur'an 2:259.
[26] Modified from Qur'an 2:259, cf. Ayoub, *The Qur'an and Its Interpreters*, pp. 259-64.
[27] 'Abd al-Raḥmān b. Muḥammad b. Makhlūf al-Tha'ālibī, *Tafsīr al-Tha'ālibī*, known as *Jawāhir al-Ḥisan fī Tafsīr al-Qur'ān* (Beirut: Mu'asassat al-A'lamī, n.d.), 1:206-207.
[28] See Ayoub, *The Qur'an and Its Interpreters*, pp. 259-64, for commentaries on Qur'an 2:259.
[29] 'Alā' al-Dīn 'Alī b. Muḥammad b. Ibrāhīm al-Baghdādī al-Ṣūfī, known as al-Khāzin, *Lubāb al-Ta'wīl fī Ma'ānī al-Tanzīl* (Beirut: Dār al-Ma'rifa, n.d.), 1:189.
[30] Qur'an 2:243.
[31] Abū 'Abdallāh Muḥammad b. Aḥmad al-Anṣārī al-Qurṭubī, *Al-Jāmi' li-Aḥkām al-Qur'ān* (Cairo: Dār al-Kātib al-'Arabī, 1387/1967), 2:289-90.
[32] Al-Khāzin, *Lubāb al-Ta'wīl*, vol. 2:189-90.
[33] Mulla Muḥsin, known as Fayḍ Kashānī, *Tafsīr al-Ṣāfī*, Ḥusayn al-A'lamī, ed. (Beirut: Mu'assasat al-A'lamī, 1379/1959), 1:269.
[34] *Ibid.*, pp. 268-70.
[35] Abū Isḥāq Aḥmad b. Muḥammad b. Ibrāhīm al-Nisābūrī al-Tha'labī, *Qiṣaṣ al-Anbiyā'*, known as *'Arā'is al-Majālis* (Beirut: al-Maktabah al-Thaqāfiyyah, n.d.), 308-09.
[36] Qur'an 9:30.
[37] See Qur'an 3:181; see also al-Ṭabarī, *Jāmi' al-Bayān*, vol. 14:201.
[38] *Ibid.*, p. 202.
[39] *Ibid.*, pp. 202-03.
[40] *Ibid.*
[41] *Ibid.*, pp. 203-04.
[42] Jalāl al-Dīn al-Suyūṭī, *Al-Durr al-Manthūr fī al-Tafsīr bi'l-Ma'thūr* (Beirut: Dār al-Ma'rifa, n.d.), 3:230.
[43] See al-Tha'ālibī, *Jawāhir*, vol. 2:125; Qurṭubī, *Al-Jāmi'*, vol. 17:117.
[44] *Ibid.*, vol. 7:117.
[45] *Ibid.*, vol. 4:69-72.
[46] See Qur'an 19:13-26.
[47] See Isaiah 6:7.
[48] Al-Tha'ālibī, *Tafsīr*, vol. 2:125; Qurṭubī, *Al-Jāmi'*, vol. 7:117.
[49] Abū al-Fidā' 'Imād al-Dīn Ismā'il ibn Kathīr, *Tafsīr al-Qur'ān al-'Aẓīm*, 2nd ed. (Beirut: Dār al-Fikr, 1389/1970), 3:384-85.
[50] Fakhr al-Dīn al-Rāzī, *Al-Tafsīr al-Kabīr*, (Cairo: Al-Maṭba'ah al-Bahiyyah, 1357/1938), 16:33.

[51] Abū Ja'far Muḥammad b. al-Ḥasan b. 'Alī b. al-Ḥasan al-Ṭūsī, *Al-Ṭibyān fī Tafsīr al-Qur'ān* Aḥmad Habīb Quṣayr al-'Āmilī, ed. (Najaf: Maktabat al-Amīn, 1385/1965), 5:203.

[52] Abū Ja'far Muḥammad b. 'Alī b. Abī Ṭālib al-Ṭabarsī, *Al-Iḥtijāj* (Najaf: Dār al-Nu'mān, 1386/1966), 1:15-18.

[53] Abū Ja'far Muḥammad b. 'Alī b. al-Ḥusayn b. Babawayh al-Qummī, known as al-Ṣadūq, *Ikmāl al-Dīn wa-Itmām al-Ni'mah fī Ithbāt al-Raj'ah* (Najaf: al-Maṭba'a al-Ḥaydariyya, 1389/1970), 156.

[54] Na'matallāh al-Jazā'irī, *Al-Nūr al-Mubīn fī Qiṣaṣ al-Anbiyā' wa'l-Mursalīn*, 8th ed. (Beirut: Mu'asassat al-A'lamī, 1389/1978), 481.

[55] For an image of Jesus in Shī'ī piety, see M. Ayoub, "Towards an Islamic Christology: An Image of Jesus in Early Shī'ī Muslim Literature," *The Muslim World* 66:3(1976): 163-88.

[56] Jazā'irī, *Al-Nūr*, pp. 483-84.

[57] Muḥammad Ḥusayn Ṭabaṭabā'ī, *Al-Mīzān fī Tafsīr al-Qur'ān*, 2nd ed. (Beirut: Mu'asassat al-A'lamī, 1391/1971), 9:243-44.

[58] *Ibid.*, vol. 9:254.

[59] Muḥammad Rashid Riḍā, *Tafsīr al-Manār*, 2nd ed. (Beirut: Dār al-Ma'rifa, n.d.), 10:326.

[60] *Ibid.*, vol. 5:431-37.

[61] See Qur'an 2:256.

[62] Sayyid Quṭb, *Fī Ẓilāl al-Qur'ān*, 7th ed. (Beirut: Dār Iḥyā' al-Turāth al-'Arabī, 1391/1971), 4:197.

[63] Ibn Ḥazm, *Al-Faṣl*, vol. 1:99.

[64] Qurṭubī, *Al-Jāmi'*, vol. 7:116.

[65] Qur'an 35:18.

[66] Qur'an 3:64.

The Drowned Son: Midrash and Midrash Making in the Qur'an and *Tafsīr*

Gordon D. Newby

In this paper I examine two large blocks of material related to the Noah story as found in the Qur'an. The first body of material is associated with the story of Noah's antediluvian "son" who refused to repent, did not board the Ark, and was thus drowned in the Flood. The other body of material deals with the claim Noah makes that he is not an angel, that he does not know the secrets of the unseen, and that he is not the guardian of the treasures of Allah. Both of these groups of material are related in two ways. The Qur'anic story itself forms a unified whole, even when the individual elements of the story in the various sūras are examined. In addition, when I am able to find extra- and pre-Qur'anic parallels to aspects of the Qur'anic Noah story, the sources all relate to a particular body of pseudepigraphic literature.

Of all the portions of the Noah story in the Qur'an that have caused commentators difficulty, few have proved more vexing than the passage in Sūra 11:42-43:

> It [the ark] was running with them among the waves which were like mountains, and Noah called to his son, while he was standing apart, "O my son, ride with us and do not be among the ungrateful." He said, "I will take refuge on a mountain which will protect me from the water." He [Noah] said, "There is no protector today from the decree of Allah except for him upon whom is mercy." And the wave came between the two of them, and he was among the drowned.

On these two verses, Abū-Qāsim Maḥmūd b. 'Umar al-Zamakhsharī (538/1144) reports a conversation between Qatāda b. Di'āma (118/736) and al-Ḥasan al-Baṣrī (110/728), which along with other traditions illustrates some of the problems that arose with this passage in the early centuries of Islam:

> [Al-Zamakhsharī said:] It is said that the name of his (Noah's) son was Kana'an, and it is said that it was Yām, and 'Alī, may Allah be gracious unto him, read it as "her son" (*ibnahā*) with the pronoun referring to his wife, and Muḥammad b. 'Alī [Zayn al-'Ābidīn b. al-Ḥusayn Abū Ja'far al-Bāqīr, 114/732] and 'Urwa b. al-Zubayr (93/712) read it *ibnaha*, with a short "a" vowel on the letter "*hā'*," intending it to be "her son," and the two of them did not require the *alif*, and thereby the view of al-Ḥasan

> al-Baṣrī was supported. Qatāda said, "I asked him and he [al-Ḥasan al-Baṣrī] said, 'By Allah, it was not his son.' I said, 'But Allah quotes from him: My son is from my family, and you are saying that he was not his son, while the People of the Book do not disagree in the fact that he is his son.' He said, 'And who takes his religion from the People of the Book?!' He took his conclusion from his words, 'from my family,' and he did not say 'from me.' He can be related to the mother in two ways: one of them is that he can be a stepson just as 'Umar b. Abū Salama was for the Messenger of Allah, may the prayers and the peace of Allah be upon him, or he could have been an illegitimate child, but this would have been a blemish from which the prophets would have kept themselves pure.[1]

In this short passage from the Noah story, we see some examples of issues that confronted Muslims in the first Islamic centuries. One of the necessities was to determine the "text" of the Qur'an, how it was to be read, and how it was to be understood grammatically. Sometimes this was a matter of determining the best source of transmission, but most often that understanding was dependent on notions of the sense of the passage, as in the example above of the attempts to interpret or reinterpret the third masculine singular pronoun—the "his" on "his son"—to a third feminine singular—the "her" on "her son." The more fundamental questions depended on which methodologies and sources were regarded as acceptable. A central issue in the earliest periods of the development of *tafsīr* is summarized in the question posed by al-Ḥasan al-Baṣrī: "And who takes his religion from the People of the Book?!"

The circulation of non-Islamic materials for use as the basis for Qur'an commentary was present during Muhammad's lifetime and saw a considerable increase in the two generations after his death. The Companion, Abū Hurayra, although illiterate, had extensive knowledge of the Torah, as did 'Alī, Salmān al-Farisī, and, of course, the "Ocean of Tafsīr," or Ibn 'Abbās, who is often called the "*ḥibr al-umma*", or "Rabbi of the (Muslim) Community" because of his extensive knowledge of Judeo-Christian as well as Muslim scripture and commentary.[2] Muhammad, Abū Bakr, and 'Umar are reported to have made several trips to the *Bet Midrash* in Madīna; and Muhammad's amanuensis, Zayd b. Thābit, who was so central in Qur'anic matters, is reported to have gone so far as to learn *al-Yahūdiyya* in a *Bet Midrash* at Muhammad's behest in order to read Jewish material.[3] More to the point, converted Jews like Ubayy b. Ka'b (21/642) and Ka'b al-Aḥbār (or, sometimes, Ḥibr, the probable paradigm for Ibn 'Abbās' appellation), who converted to Islam under Abū Bakr, transmitted much information originally derived from rabbinic tradition.[4] Some of this material can be found in the Talmud and the Midrashim, but some of it is preserved only in Islamic versions.

Much credit has to be given, however, to three individuals whose participation in the nascent activities of history writing and Qur'an commentary lent respectability and sanction to the introduction of scriptural and parascriptural material derived from the People of the Book: Abū Hurayra; 'Abdullāh b. 'Amr b. al-'Āṣ, who read Syriac, engaged in theological discussions with converts, and had extensive knowledge of the Talmud; and Ibn 'Abbās.[5] Their names are featured over and over again in the *isnād*s and, even if some of what is attributed to them can be regarded as spurious, the point still remains that their names were the touchstones of proper conduct in this field. The generation of the Followers saw many who followed the paradigm of the Companions and actively pursued knowledge from Jews and Christians. Abū Jald of Baṣra, for example, was accustomed to reading both the Torah and the Qur'an in his daily devotionals, claiming that Divine Mercy derived from reading either one or both of them.[6] Wahb b. Munabbih was another source in this generation for the introduction of Judaeo-Christian material into the Islamic mainstream, and much that was known among the early Muslims of the Talmud and the Midrashim comes through traditions ascribed to him and whose *isnād*s go back no earlier than him, making him the authority for the introduction of this material.[7]

Many of the individuals involved in the transmission of interpretive traditions that derived ultimately from the People of the Book were *mawālī*, whose family background and place of origin could have given them special knowledge of Jewish, Christian, and Zoroastrian sources. Both al-Ḥasan al-Baṣrī, who was the son of a Persian slave and who rose to preeminence in Islam as one of the greatest teachers, dogmatists, preachers, and transmitters of Qur'anic interpretation; and Qatāda b. Di'āma, who was also from the city of Baṣra and rivaled al-Ḥasan al-Baṣrī in Qur'anic knowledge, were *mawālī* who capitalized on their wide range of knowledge of outside sources for their interpretation of the Qur'an. Both were regarded in their time as reliable interpreters of the Qur'an; and, from the point of view of modern investigation, they show a remarkable reliability in faithfully transmitting traditions from Judaism and Christianity when commenting on figures in the Qur'an that also appear in the Bible and other texts. They had access to knowledge of the Bible and its commentaries through a flood of translations distributed by stationers and booksellers. Works of doubtful origin were sometimes translated, copied, and marketed under the guise that they were part of the Seventy Scriptures which had been revealed to mankind.[8] One should remember the claim of Wahb b. Munabbih that he had read a large portion of the Seventy Scriptures which had been revealed in the seventy languages of mankind.[9] In fact, these often prove to be popular haggadic and midrashic works. Most of the major metropolitan centers had market streets selling such books. These streets were named after aspects of the profession, being called, for example, *Sūq al-Warraqīn* and *Sūq al-Kutub*. Further, prominent members of Islamic society kept libraries for friends and scholars.[10]

Assuming for the moment in our examination of the Noah account that there was normal and ready access to material from outside Islamic circles, it is somewhat surprising to see Qatāda take the position he does when he asserts that the People of the Book do not disagree that the son referred to in Sūra

11:42 is Noah's son. The usual Jewish and Christian sources indicate that both Judaism and Christianity do not hold that Noah had more than three antediluvian sons, namely Shem, Ham, and Japheth. And those same usual Jewish and Christian sources are in agreement that the three sons survived the flood by riding on the Ark with their father Noah. An additional problem comes when one tries to determine the name of the drowned son. In the Islamic traditions under consideration for this paper, two names are given, Canaan and Yām. Canaan is mentioned in the Bible as the fourth son of Ham, Noah's grandson, but Yām is nowhere mentioned in the Bible in connection with the Noah story.

Several questions about the narrative of Noah suggest themselves: 1) How is the Qur'anic text to be understood? 2) What are the sources of Qatāda's and other commentators' glosses on the Qur'anic texts? 3) What historical relationship does this kind of *tafsīr* have to the Qur'anic text? and 4) How, if at all, do the glosses help us understand the Qur'anic text? I start with the second of the four questions and try to discover what the possible analogs for the glosses we find in the *tafsīr* might be. One of my goals will be to try to find texts that are parallel and antecedent to the texts in both the Qur'an and *tafsīr*. I will then try to see what use the glosses are in making a "reading" of the Qur'anic narrative. This is the methodology which my colleague David Halperin and I employed in a recent article in which we were able to reconstruct a "lost" midrash by means of Islamic sources.[11] One of our goals was to try, insofar as possible, to understand the nature of Arabian Judaism around the time of the rise of Islam. This is not only important in itself, but can also be useful for understanding the background for the early development of Islam. One of the final questions I will pose about the Noah material concerns the psychological character of the story as it is told in the Qur'an.

When one examines the texts that comment on the biblical Noah story for clues to the identity of Canaan as an extra son, one finds that the narrative of Ham, Canaan, and the great transgression mentioned in Genesis 9:20-27 is most appropriate:

> And Noah the husbandman began and planted a vineyard. And he drank of the wine and was drunken; and he was uncovered within his tent. And Ham, the father of Canaan, saw the nakedness of his father and told his brothers without. And Shem and Japheth took a garment and laid it upon their shoulders and went backward and covered the nakedness of their father, and their faces were backward, and they saw not their father's nakedness. And Noah awoke from his wine and knew what his youngest son had done unto him. And he said, "Cursed be Canaan. . . . "

For the Rabbis, and later for the Church Fathers, this passage presents several problems. What did Ham do that is implied in the verb "saw"? It is more than just a glance, they reason, because the consequences are so great.

Further, why is Canaan cursed rather than Ham? Does he have a part in the crime, or might he be the real culprit and not his father, Ham?[12]

The usual opinion is that Ham could not have been cursed, no matter what he might have done, because God blessed him along with all the party of the Ark upon disembarking: "And God blessed Noah and his sons, and said unto them: 'Be fruitful, and multiply, and replenish the earth.'"[13] For the Rabbis, this verse not only establishes protection for Ham, but it also sets the context for the understanding of the interpretation. The blessing involves sexual activity and procreation. After all, that was the greatest need at the time, and so acts that would be cursed would be acts that would limit or inhibit fruitful procreation. It comes as no surprise, then, to find the following solution to the problem in the Talmud:

> [With respect to the last verse] Rab and Samuel differ, one maintaining that he castrated him whilst the other says that he [Ham] sexually abused him. He who maintains that he castrated him [reasons] thus: Since he cursed him by his fourth son, he must have injured him with respect to a fourth son. But he who says that he sexually abused him draws an analogy between "and he saw" written twice. Here it is written, and Ham the father of Canaan saw the nakedness of his father, whilst elsewhere it is written, And when Shechem the son of Hamor saw her [he took her and lay with her and defiled her]. How, on the view that he emasculated him, it is right that he cursed him by his fourth son; but on the view that he abused him, why did he curse his fourth son; he should have cursed him himself?—Both indignities were perpetrated.[14]

Following from this line of reasoning, it was then maintained that Canaan was alone and was also involved in the crime. Late Jewish sources, reflecting attitudes expressed among some of the Church Fathers, hold that it was, in reality, Canaan and not Ham who committed the major abuse of Noah, thus fully earning the curse.[15]

Another text of some interest in this matter is a passage in the Ethiopic version of the Book of Jubilees:[16] "And Noah awoke from his sleep and knew all that his younger son had done unto him, and he cursed his son and said: 'Cursed be Canaan. . . .'" The Ethiopic reads: "*wa-ragamo la-waldu wa-yebe Kana'an* . . ." The noted scholar of this text, J. C. VanderKam, dates this material about a century before our era, with the Ethiopic text redacted about a century before the time of Muhammad and the Qur'an. A literal reading of this text gives Noah a son named Canaan, whom he curses. We can make several observations about the possibility of a connection between this tradition and the Islamic material. One line of possible connection is to assume that the Ethiopic text reflects a tradition of interpretation that preserves material not found in extant "rabbinic" material. That this is the case with other material has been amply demonstrated by L. Ginzberg in his *Legends of the Jews*, particularly the material concerning the figure of Enoch, which I will discuss in more detail shortly. Another possible connection is through the South Arabian Jewish communities, from which transmitters like Wahb b. Munabbih draw so heavily. And, while a certain nexus cannot be made at this point, the parallelism is striking.

The other name given for the "son" of Noah is Yām. This name is more of a puzzle.[17] Al-Ṭabarī mentions one instance of the name Yām associated with a Himyaritic inscription, but without further explanation, and that instance appears not to be associated with the Yām of the *tafsīr*.[18] More likely we see a reflex of the widespread name in the Northwest Semitic dialects for the sea, Yam(m), in a *scriptum plenum* normal for foreign names. In the usual versions of the cycle of legends involving Yam, he represents the forces of evil against the good sky deity Baal, who is also a water deity, the god of rain. Rain is thought to be good and life-giving, while its opposite, the sea, is characterized as evil, destructive and ultimately desirous of overwhelming the dry land.[19]

A comparison of the typologies, then, between the coming together of Baal and Yam, the two deities of water, and the account of the Flood is attractive. Subterranean waters rising (for the land is viewed as being above the waters below, of which the sea is a part) as well as rain descending render the earth as it had been before the creation of dry land. We see in the Qur'anic description: "Then We opened the gates of heaven with pouring water, and We caused the earth to gush forth with springs, and the water met according to a predetermined command."[20] Noah and his fellow voyagers become the basis for the new creation after a journey that takes them, in the Jewish traditions, into another level of existence from which they start and where they end.

In Genesis, the placement of the lights in the heavens, that is, the sun, moon, and stars, comes after the division of the waters. With the view in mind that the coming together of the waters from above and the waters from below took the universe back to a time before there were lights, we read in Genesis Rabbah that the planets did not function during the entire twelve months that Noah was in the Ark, the sun and the moon not giving their usual illumination.[21] To maintain worship, however, illumination was provided that distinguished night from day, for we read: "R. Phinehas said in R. Levi's name: During the whole twelve months that Noah was in the Ark he did not require the light of the sun by day or the light of the moon by night, but he had a polished gem [Heb. *zohar*] which he hung up: when it was dim he knew that it was day, and when it shone he knew that it was night."[22] These *midrashim* pick up on what we find in T.B. Sanhedrin 108b, where it is said that Noah was instructed to "Set therein precious stones and jewels, so that they may give thee light, bright as the noon." These are often understood to be the same light-giving jewels that will illuminate Jerusalem in the Messianic year when the sun, moon, and the rest of the heavenly bodies will not function in their usual manner.[23] Islamic commentators also share this story, for al-Kisā'ī tells us:

> The people in the Ark could not tell day from night except by means of a white bead: when its light diminished they knew it was day, and when its light increased they knew it was night. The cock also crew at dawn, by which they knew it to be the break of day.
> Wahb ibn Munabbih said: Whenever the cock crew it would say "Praise be to the Blessed King. Praise be to Him who hath taken night away and brought the day of a new creation. To prayer, O Noah! God will have mercy upon thee."[24]

Of course, there is no explicit mention of the illuminating jewel in the Qur'an but rather a concentration on the marks of the impending inundation: the rain and the boiling of the oven.

The waters that come from beneath the earth are said to come up through an oven, *tannur* in Arabic, Hebrew, and Aramaic. This oven is mentioned twice in the Qur'an,[25] and commentators on these passages seem to have some difficulty in reconciling an oven that gives water instead of heat and bread. Some say that the word for oven means the face of the earth. Others say that it is the highest point of the earth, while still others say that it is an oven in which one bakes bread. Some locate it in India, saying that it was Adam's oven until it was given to Noah, and others place it in Kufa, to the right of the mosque. Al-Kisā'ī places it in Mecca, from which Noah took it after performing the rites of the pilgrimage before the Flood.[26] The location of the oven at the highest portion of the earth would place it in Jerusalem for both Islamic and Jewish cosmology, since Jerusalem as the center of the earth was also its highest point. It should be noted here that when motifs usually applied to Jerusalem are transferred to Mecca, Mecca gains pride of place as the highest geographical feature on the earth. Further, Jewish tradition places God's oven in Jerusalem, for we see in Isaiah 31:9 "a declaration of God whose fire is in Zion and His furnace (*tannur*) is in Jerusalem."[27] In the *faḍā'il al-Quds* traditions reported by Ibn al-Firkāḥ, Allah is reported as saying to Moses, "Go to Jerusalem, for in it are my light, and my fire, and my *tannur*, meaning the oven which boils."[28] It would seem from this that the oven was thought to remain awaiting the final day in readiness for the rejoining of the waters.

The association of the waters of the deep beneath the earth and Jerusalem involves the cycle of legends that develops around the foundation of the Temple and the stone that was supposed to be at the center of the Holy of Holies, the *Even Shetiyyah*. This is the stone upon which God was supposed to have stood when He first started Creation, and his footprint is reported to still be in the stone. Christian and Islamic legends adopt this feature and make the footprint that of Jesus from the Ascension and Muhammad from the Night Journey respectively. The Stone was supposed to contain the "Ineffable Name" of God which had the power to stem the flow of the waters so that the earth would not be flooded.[29] It is possible to trace the origins of these legends to other locations, even when one restricts the geography to that of the cycle of Jewish legends. However, the tendency is to make Jerusalem the locus for all supernatural and eschatological activity, as, for example, the ultimate, albeit late, identification of Jacob's Pillow with the *Even Shetiyyah*.[30]

Another aspect of the Noah account that I would like to examine is the passage in Sūra 11:31: "I do not say to you 'I have the treasures of Allah,' and I do not know the unseen, and I do not say 'Indeed, I am an angel,' and I do not say concerning those whom your eyes hold in little regard that Allah will not give them reward, [for] Allah knows best what is in their hearts." It would seem from this passage that the generation of the flood expected Noah to be an angelic messenger and are disappointed when they find him nothing "but a man like us."[31] How reasonable is their expectation? That is, to rephrase the question within our scholarly framework, can we find a text or complex of texts antecedent to the Qur'an in which Noah is thought to be an angel and/or is there a heavenly messenger that can be thought to be either human or angelic?

A fragment of the so-called Book of Noah found in the Ethiopic Book of Enoch reports that strange things happened at the birth of Noah:

> And after some days my son Methuselah took a wife for his son Lamech and she became pregnant by him and bore a son. And his body was white as snow and red as the blooming of a rose, and the hair of his head and his long locks were white as wool, and his eyes were beautiful. And when he opened his eyes, he lighted up the whole house like the sun, and the whole house was very bright. And thereupon he arose in the hands of the midwife, opened his mouth, and conversed with the Lord of righteousness. And his father Lamech was afraid of him and fled, and came to his father Methuselah. And he said unto him: "I have begotten a strange son, diverse from and unlike man, and resembling the sons of the God of heaven; and his nature is different and he is not like us, and his eyes are as the rays of the sun, and his countenance is glorious. And it seems to me that he is not sprung from me but from the angels, and I fear that in his days a wonder may be wrought on the earth. And now, my father, I am here to petition thee and implore thee that thou mayest go to Enoch, our father, and learn from him the truth, for his dwelling place is among the angels."[32]

Methuselah, when he heard the petition of his son, went to Enoch, the narrator in our text, and placed his question about the paternity of Noah to him. He was told that Noah was indeed the son of Lamech but, because angels had come to earth during Enoch's generation and had united with human women, thereby defiling themselves, there would be a great flood which would destroy everything except Noah and those with him.[33]

It would appear easy enough for others to assume that Noah was an angel when we see his own father uncertain of his nature and origin. But there is more to this than just the confusion of Noah with an angel. Noah also tells us that he does not claim to be the guardian of the treasures of Allah, nor does he claim that he knows the unseen. The creature that fulfills all the qualifications—being an angel, guarding the treasures of Allah, and knowing the unseen—is the angel Metatron, who started life as Noah's great-grandfather Enoch. Enoch was of the generation of the Flood, of those who transgressed. For the Rabbis, Enoch was nothing but a man, subject to the same failings as other men. In Genesis Rabbah, the Rabbis assert that it is the "sectarians," i.e., Christians and Jewish Christians, who subscribe to the view that Enoch was spared death.[34] In the popular books of Enoch, he was taken to heaven so that he would not be destroyed when God abandoned the earth and, as a sign of God's mercy, that one pious man would be saved. When translated into heaven, he was stripped of his humanity and transformed into the powerful angel Metatron, who was taught by God all the secrets, more than any other creature, and was given guardianship over the treasures of God. In 3 Enoch we read:

> (1) Aleph I made him [Enoch] strong, I took him, I appointed him: (namely) Metatron, my servant, who is one (unique) among all the children of heaven. I made him strong in the generation of the first Adam. But when I beheld the men of the generation of the flood, that they were corrupt, then I went and removed my Shekhina from among them. And I lifted it up on high with the sound of a trumpet and with a shout, as it is written (Ps. 47:6): "God is gone up with a shout, the Lord with the sound of a trumpet."
> (2) "And I took him": (that is) Enoch, the son of Jared, from among them. And I lifted him up with the sound of a trumpet and with a *teru'a* (shout) to the high heavens, to be my witness together with the Chayyoth by the Merkaba in the world to come.
> (3) I appointed him over all the treasuries and stores that I have in every heaven. And I committed into his hand the keys of every several one.
> (4) I made (of) him the prince over all the princes and a minister of the Throne of Glory (and) the Halls of 'Araboth: to open their doors to me, and of the Throne of Glory, to exalt and arrange it; (and I appointed him over) the Holy Chayyoth to wreathe crowns upon their heads; the majestic Ophanim, to crown them with strength and glory; the honored Kerubim, to clothe them in majesty; over the radiant sparks to make them shine with splendor and brilliance; over the flaming Seraphim, to cover them with highness; the *ḥashmallim* of light, to make

> them radiant with light and to prepare the seat for me every morning as I sit upon the Throne of Glory. And to extol and magnify my glory in the height of my power; (and I have committed unto him) the secrets of above and the secrets of below (heavenly secrets and earthly secrets).[35]

Apparently, then, the expectation was that Noah was Enoch returned to do as God had commanded: "And I appointed him to reveal secrets and to teach judgment and justice."[36]

It is particularly interesting to find this material in 3 Enoch because, as David Halperin has pointed out, we can deduce that the inhabitants of the Ḥijāz during Muhammad's time knew portions, at least, of 3 Enoch in association with the Jews.[37] For not only do we have this parallel, but we find another parallel from this same text. In Sūra 5:64, we read, "The Jews say: Allah's hand is fettered (Arabic *maghlūla,* "tied, shackled, fettered")." In chapter 48 of 3 Enoch, Rabbi Ishmael says that the right hand of God is fixed behind His back because of the destruction of the Temple and will reappear only at the eschaton with the rebuilding of the Temple:

> Metatron said to me: (1) Come, and I will show thee the Right Hand of MAQOM, laid behind (Him) because of the destruction of the Holy Temple.[38]

This follows chapter 44:7-10, which I quote in part:

> (7) And I saw the spirits of the Patriarchs, Abraham, Isaac, and Jacob and the rest of the righteous whom they have brought up out of their graves and who have ascended to the Heaven (*Raqīa'*). And they were praying before the Holy one, blessed be He, saying in their prayer: "Lord of the Universe! How long wilt thou sit upon (thy) Throne like a mourner in the days of his mourning with thy right hand behind thee and not deliver thy children and reveal thy Kingdom in the world? And for how long wilt thou have no pity upon thy children who are made slaves among the nations of the world? Nor upon thy right hand that is behind thee wherewith thou didst stretch out the heavens and the earth and the heavens of heavens? When wilt thou have compassion?"
> (8) Then the Holy One, blessed be He, answered every one of them, saying: "Since these wicked do sin so and so, and transgress with such and such transgressions against me, how could I deliver my great Right Hand in the downfall by their hands (caused by them)."[39]

Before returning to the Qur'anic narrative of the Noah account, I would note that the tendency in the development of *tafsīr* is similar to that of early Islamic scholarship in general. We find that detail and specificity increases during the period of the growth of the commentary. Thus we see added stories included in the collections which have no Qur'anic basis but are parallel to stories found in Jewish and Christian sources and reported to have come from the "People of the Book." Some of these stories are both amusing and etiological, such as the story of the origin of the pig. There were, apparently, no antediluvian pigs, but when the inhabitants of the Ark were bothered by the animal waste, God brought forth pigs from the tail of the elephant, and they consumed the waste matter. This not only accounts for the prohibition against eating pork, but also speaks to some early notions of animal taxonomy. Similarly, there were no cats among the animals of the Ark until they were brought forth from the nostrils of the lion, who sneezed them out so that they could eat the mice who had violated the proscription against procreation on the Ark.[40] As I have shown elsewhere, this tendency was curtailed around the middle of the second Islamic century as a reaction to *Tafsīr Isrā'īliyyāt* set in, and commentators on the Qur'an began to pursue modes of understanding the text that were thought to be more properly Islamic.[41] The *Isrā'īliyyāt* material was preserved, however, both for its antiquarian value and for its excellent and entertaining narrative.

When we return to the Qur'anic narrative of the Noah story in the eleventh chapter, we see that the parallels with rabbinic materials do not entirely explain the text before us; nor, I feel, should we expect that to be the case. Using the Qur'an to attempt to discover what texts might have been known and used by the Arabian Jewish community, as we did above with the Enoch material, is only one aspect of what can be read from the Qur'an, and a minor one at that. In a similar vein, *Tafsīr Isrā'īliyyāt* offers explication of the Qur'anic material that served as a genuine historical antecedent to the Qur'anic text. This was the assumption that most expositors of the Qur'an held during the first Islamic century. But our attempts and those of the early exegetes expound only one side of the text. Another side, in the example of Noah, portrays Noah in a manner different from what we know to be part of the extant Jewish views of him. Noah is represented as the concerned, compassionate paterfamilias, and he is severely distressed that his "son" might not heed his message and be lost. He cries to Allah, "O my Lord, my son is of my household! Certainly your promise is the Truth and you are the most just of judges." Allah has to chastise him and tell him that his son, because of his evil conduct, was not one of his household and should not have been saved. We see here a Noah of both passion and compassion, a Noah who is willing to argue with God for the salvation of one individual. In a very few words, the Qur'an shows us a Noah unlike that Noah of the rabbinic exegetes. Insofar as we can understand the story of Noah as an account parallel to that of Muhammad, and I would argue that we can, the compassion of Noah tells us of Muhammad's concern for those who would not heed his message.

On the whole, a careful examination of the early *Isrā'īliyyāt* traditions can yield interesting and useful information about the environment in which early Islam developed. In spite of the numerous historiographic problems, the early traditions and the Qur'an can be used to help reconstruct a little knowledge of the Arabian Jewish community. In this paper I have shown how we can include the text of 3 Enoch among the corpus of texts known in Arabian Jewish circles. I hope I have also shown that the Qur'anic narrative has, despite the analogs and parallels, a message unique to itself.

NOTES

[1] Abū Qāsim Maḥmūd b. 'Umar b. Muḥammad b. Aḥmad al-Khawarizmī al-Zamakhsharī, *Al-Kashshāf 'an Ḥaqā'iq al-Tanzīl wa-'Uyūn al-Aqāwīl fī Wujūh al-Ta'wīl* (Cairo: Muṣṭafā al-Ḥalabī and Sons, 1385/1966), 2:270. The *isnād* is incomplete in this account, and it is not possible to tell how this reached al-Zamakhsharī, although it is a reasonable assumption that he received the information through literary as well as oral sources.

[2] Nabia Abbott, *Studies in Arabic Literary Papyri* (Chicago: University of Chicago Press, 1967), 2:9.

[3] G. D. Newby, "Observations about an Early Judaeo-Arabic," *Jewish Quarterly Review* 61(1971): 220.

[4] The term "*Ḥibr*" is often translated as "Rabbi."

[5] Abbott, *Studies,* vol. 2:9.

[6] *Ibid.*

[7] One of the usual *isnād*s found in the material collected by Ibn Isḥāq and reported by al-Ṭabarī is from Ibn Ḥumayd from Salama from Ibn Isḥāq from the Ahl al-Yaman from Wahb b. Munabbih. Wahb is credited with writing a *Qiṣaṣ al-Anbiyā'* and a *K. al-Mubtada'*, both likely collections of Jewish stories and commentaries. At this point, it is not possible to identify the Ahl al-Yaman quoted by Wahb, but from the content of the quotations it is likely that he was in touch with a group of Yemenite Jews from whom he was obtaining this material. I hope to treat this problem in a forthcoming volume on the history of the Jews of Arabia.

[8] Abbott, *Studies,* vol. 1:87ff., describes the extensive literary activity of the early Islamic period. Much work needs to be done to determine the exact nature of the early works from which the Muslim exegetes like Ibn Isḥāq were drawing so much detail for their own works.

[9] Khayr al-Dīn al-Ziriklī, *Al-A'lām* (Cairo: al-Maṭba'a al-'Arabiyya, 1928), 10:150.

[10] Abbott, *Studies,* vol. 1:24.

[11] David J. Halperin and G. D. Newby, "Two Castrated Bulls: A Study in the Haggadah of Ka'b al-'Aḥbār," *Journal of the American Oriental Society* 102:4 (1982): 631-38.

[12] Genesis Rabbah 36:7, translated by H. Freedman, in H. Freedman and M. Simon, eds., *Midrash Rabbah* (New York: The Soncino Press, 1977), 1:293.

[13] Genesis 9:1.

[14] T. B. Sanhedrin 70a. The translation is that of the Soncino edition.

[15] *Pirke de Rabbi Eliezer*, G. Friedlander, ed. and tr. (New York: Hermon Press, 1965), 171; cf. Origen on Gen. 9:25.

[16] Jubilees 7:10. This text was provided to me by my colleague, Dr. J. C. VanderKam.

[17] Stephen Gero has written about the existence of a fourth son of Noah who was called Yonton: "The Legend of the Fourth Son of Noah," *Harvard Theological Review* 73(1980): 321-329. This son is, however, postdiluvian and is tied to the tradition of Nimrod and astronomy/astrology. Gero cites the same discussion mentioned above between Rav and Samuel and argues for the possibility that the tradition may reflect a variety of Judaism supportive of cosmological speculation. This would seem to fit some of the strains of Judaism found in Arabia (see, for example, Halperin and Newby, "Two Castrated Bulls," pp. 621-38). Gero rejects the view of Ginzberg that the castration story was used as part of a polemic against Christians. It is also possible that we have a story created for similar motives as the castration mentioned by Rav and Samuel and out of a similar rabbinic context, but not enough of the background material has survived for us to do more than speculate at this point. At any rate, there are considerable difficulties in the phonetic equation of the names Yām and Yonton.

[18] Abū Ja'far Muḥammad b. Jarīr al-Ṭabarī, *Ta'rīkh al-Rusul wa'l-Mulūk*, M. J. de Goeje, ed. (Leiden: E. J. Brill, repr. 1964), 3: 2487.

[19] The Baal/Anat cycle is to found in C. H. Gordon, *Ugaritic Textbook* (Rome: Pontifical Biblical Institute Press, 1965), texts 49, 51, and 68, and in numerous translations and studies, e.g., J. B. Pritchard, *The Ancient Near East: An Anthology of Texts and Pictures* (Princeton: Princeton University Press, 1958), 96ff.

[20] Qur'an 54:11-12.

[21] Genesis Rabbah 31:11, in H. Freedman and M. Simon, eds., *Midrash Rabbah*, vol. 1:244.

[22] Ibid.

[23] For various references, see L. Ginzberg, *The Legends of the Jews,* 7 vols. (Philadelphia: Jewish Publication Society, 1968), under "illuminating stones."

[24] Al-Kisā'ī, *The Tales of the Prophets*, W. M. Thackston, Jr. tr. (Boston: Twayne Publishers, 1978), 102-03.

[25] Qur'an 11:40 and 23:27.

[26] Al-Kisā'ī, *Tales,* p. 100.

[27] Note the use of *tannur* in several places in the Bible indicating either God's punishment or His presence: Gen. 15:17; Ps. 21:10; Ne. 3:11, 12:38.

28 Charles D. Matthews, *Palestine—Mohammedan Holy Land* (New Haven: Yale University Press, 1949), 29.

29 Ginzberg, *Legends of the Jews,* vol. 5:15.

30 G. Friedlander, ed. and tr., *Pirke de Rabbi Eliezer,* p. 265-67.

31 Qur'an 31:27.

32 R. H. Charles, *The Apocrypha and Pseudepigrapha of the Old Testament in English* (Oxford: Oxford University Press, 1977), 2:278-81. Charles has supposed the existence of a Book of Noah, but no extant volume exists. For a summary of the relevant arguments about the existence of such a book, see J. VanderKam, *Enoch and the Growth of an Apocalyptic Tradition* (Washington: Catholic Biblical Association of America, 1984), 174ff.

33 *Ibid.*

34 Genesis Rabbah 25:1, in H. Freedman and M. Simon, eds., *Midrash Rabbah,* p. 205.

35 *3 Enoch or the Hebrew Book of Enoch,* Hugo Odeberg, ed. and tr. (Cambridge: Cambridge University Press, 1928), 164-68.

36 *Ibid.*

37 This will soon appear in print in a book by David Halperin dealing with the Enoch material.

38 Odeberg, ed. and tr., *3 Enoch,* pp. 154 ff.

39 *Ibid.*

40 Abū Ja'far Muḥammad b. Jarīr al-Ṭabarī, *Tafsīr* (Cairo: Dār al-Ma'ārif, 1954), on Qur'an 11:40.

41 G. D. Newby, "Tafsīr Isrā'īliyyāt," *Journal of the American Academy of Religion* 47(1979): 685-97.

Sa'adya Gaon and Genesis 22: Aspects of Jewish-Muslim Interaction and Polemic

Andrew Rippin

The amount of work done on the person and opus of Sa'adya al-Fayyūmī is substantial and, in some aspects, overwhelming. Sometimes it seems as if there is very little left to discuss, given the number of studies produced in the nineteenth and early twentieth centuries by some of the finest scholars of the European tradition.[1] In recent decades, however, knowledge concerning the Islamic context in which Sa'adya was working—especially regarding the conception of scripture and its interpretation—has increased dramatically, and this renders desirable new studies of Sa'adya's works in light of contemporary Islamic research.

Sa'adya's Bible translations, especially of the Pentateuch, may particularly benefit from new insights and developments.[2] Sa'adya's life and scholarly activity focused on the Bible; his studies in grammar, lexicography, and theology, for example, were all undertaken for the benefit of understanding the Hebrew biblical text. Just why he found it necessary and desirable to occupy himself with the translation of the Bible into Arabic, however, is not totally clear; many explanations have been given. Various apologetic functions for his translation work have been proposed.[3] It has been suggested, for example, that he wished to make the Bible rationally acceptable to the intellectuals of his community; by rendering it into Arabic it was possible for him to accomplish that end. This understanding would fit well with the accepted motive behind his *Kitāb al-Amānāt wa'l-I'tiqādāt* (*The Book of Beliefs and Opinions*),[4] his major theological opus. It has also been suggested that Sa'adya wished to counter Karaite anti-oral law interpretation through clear presentation of the Bible; the Karaite use of Arabic as its main vehicle of expression would have necessitated Sa'adya's countering activity in the same language. Interreligious apologetic is also considered a possibility: Sa'adya may have wished to display to the non-Jewish world the perfection of Jewish scripture. That argument depends to some extent upon the notion that Sa'adya used the Arabic rather than the Hebrew script in his original translation, the only evidence for which is a statement by Abraham ibn Ezra several centuries after the fact;[5] the matter continues to be debated by scholars.[6] Finally, a rationale provided by Sa'adya himself in his brief introduction to his Torah translation is that his work was necessary for a Jewish audience who no longer had access to the Hebrew original. This, of course, is a simple enough explanation and is reasonable (perhaps in combination with the other reasons) in light of the motivation behind the earlier Aramaic translations. The targums arose, according to the Talmud, out of the need for people to hear the weekly recitation of the Bible in Aramaic because they had lost the ability to understand the Hebrew original.[7] The Aramaic translation would be recited after the Hebrew, and this practice continued in the synagogue even after the Jews lost their understanding of Aramaic, that is, in the wake of the Arab takeover and the adoption of Arabic as the lingua franca of the community. There can be no doubt of the impact of this linguistic transition on the Jewish community, and Blau's work has documented and explained the changeover in a most convincing manner.[8] But the emergence of an Arabic Torah cannot be traced historically with any certainty, nor can its function in liturgy, for example, be totally ascertained. The issue is simply open to speculation. It is likely that oral renderings in Arabic arose first; in the ninth century, for example, the Gaonate insisted upon use of the Aramaic targums in worship but also allowed each community to appoint an additional person to "interpret [Scripture] for them in their language."[9] Sa'adya's work on the translation may well have been an attempt to bring some uniformity into the Arabic versions; all the evidence points to his success in this regard. In the Yemen, for example, Sa'adya's version was not only always employed but also totally supplanted the targums in the liturgy.

Therefore, in producing his translation Sa'adya may well have been responding to his own community's need but, by employing Arabic as the vehicle of discourse, it was inevitable that his translation would be influenced by the Muslim community around him. From beginning to end, Sa'adya's work raises questions about the Islamic influence upon him and the general influence upon Judaism of the transformation of scripture from Hebrew to Arabic.

Sa'adya appears to have entitled his translation *Tafsīr Basīṭ Naṣṣ al-Torāh* (the simple [or small] *tafsīr* of the text of the Torah).[10] The use of the word *tafsīr* here has generally been accepted as simple employment of the Arabic word for "commentary," with the word *sharḥ* reserved for the actual exegesis of the Bible itself.[11] This unquestioned interpretation of such a basic matter must, however, be viewed in light of Sa'adya's Islamic context and in consideration of the time when he lived. Sa'adya died in 942, less than twenty years after the Muslim exegete al-Ṭabarī, who died in 923, and two years before the death of the Islamic theologian al-Māturīdī. The role of these two latter figures in establishing a fixed terminology in Muslim exegesis cannot be underestimated. Note that al-Ṭabarī's so-called *tafsīr* is actually entitled *Jāmi' al-Bayān 'an Ta'wīl Āy al-Qur'ān* and that al-Māturīdī entitled his work *Ta'wīlāt Ahl al-Sunna*;[12] clearly, *tafsīr* was not the generic term for works of commentary at the time of Sa'adya. Before this time, *ma'ānī* seems to have been the most popular term employed in titles of works of interpretation. While the word *tafsīr* was certainly used in the technical sense of "interpretation (of scripture)" even before al-Ṭabarī, as, for example, in various places in the work of al-Farrā', who died in 822[13] (and whose text is entitled, note, *Ma'ānī al-Qur'ān*), its primary early use has been demonstrated by Wansbrough to have been in the context of profane rhetoric.[14] The shift of the term *tafsīr* to the scriptural context has been argued by Wansbrough to be part of a dispute centered in the conflict *tafsīr* versus *ta'wīl*: "It seems clear that the *tafsīr: ta'wīl* dichotomy symbolized a dispute rather more fundamental than one merely of method or terminology, namely the exegetical relationship between canonical and noncanonical material in the witness to revelation preserved and transmitted by the Muslim community."[15] The question involved the ways in which traditional material could be employed to provide exegetical data. *Ta'wīl*, in some people's understanding of it, was interpretation that dispensed with tradition and was founded upon reason, personal opinion, individual research, or expertise. The point was certainly never clear, however, because other proposed differentiations between *ta'wīl* and *tafsīr* glossed the simple edges. Muqātil ibn Sulaymān, who died in 767, for example, implied a split between *tafsīr* as that known on the human level and *ta'wīl* as that known to God alone;[16] that point is continued in the suggestion that the Qur'an is divisable into two parts—the clear verses, *muḥkamāt*, and the ambiguous verses, *mutashābihāt*, the latter being known only to God. Similar perhaps is the notion that *tafsīr* applies to passages with one interpretation, *ta'wīl* to those with multiple aspects, *wujūh*. And of course the very title of al-Ṭabarī's text, using *ta'wīl* in a work which is tradition-oriented, in basic form at least, reveals a further complication. Wansbrough's argument[17] that sectarian differentiation through terminology is related to *muḥkamāt* versus *mutashābihāt* may well be worth pursuing.

Sa'adya seems to be taking a position in this debate, most likely vis-à-vis his dispute with the Karaites.[18] *Ta'wīl* as a term is used in his *Kitāb al-Amānāt wa'l-I'tiqādāt*, for example, to refer to interpretation that goes beyond the so-called literal sense of the text; *tafsīr* is then limited to the simple explanation of the text. Sa'adya enumerates four instances in which the literal sense of the text must be departed from: (1) where the observation of the senses is contradicted by the text; (2) where reason negates the text; (3) where two texts contradict each other; and (4) where authentic tradition contradicts the text.[19] The last of these is significant since it indicates that for Sa'adya the difference between *tafsīr* and *ta'wīl* is certainly not a simple matter of tradition versus opinion or reason. The key may well lie in the concept of the literal meaning, *ẓāhir* (sometimes contrasted to *majāz* in Sa'adya's works), which would seem to underlie the differentiation of *ta'wīl* and *tafsīr*; this term, too, is a great teaser in Muslim exegesis, as is the very concept of "literal meaning" in any context. For Sa'adya, the *ẓāhir* meaning was to be approached on the basis of a proper understanding of the Hebrew text, a factor that dictated his interest and his work in grammar. But grammar, of course, is no more an objective notion than the concept of the literal meaning, and no profitable excursus will result from investigations into that field. As Wansbrough has expressed it,[20] *ẓāhir* is an emotive term, one to which appeal is made in order to justify a given meaning which is, in fact, accepted by the community at large. The literal meaning is no more and no less than the authoritative meaning at a given time and place.[21] In Sa'adya's case, examples in the following analysis of Genesis 22 will reveal that his concept of the *ẓāhir* is firmly entrenched in the targumic tradition that established the authoritative meaning.

It would seem likely, therefore, that Sa'adya's use of *tafsīr* for the title of his translation is related to his concept of the literal meaning and its connection to the authoritative meaning accepted by the community, the latter as an implicit rejection of the Karaite repudiation of the tradition of rabbinic interpretation. But the point still remains why Sa'adya used the term *tafsīr* rather than, for example, *tarjama*, a cognate of the Aramaic *targum*.[22] Is something being suggested here about the relationship between the Hebrew original and its Arabic representation in the sense that the translation is not the text itself but an explication of it? In other words, do we have here in Sa'adya a similar attitude toward the literary character of the Hebrew Bible as found in the Muslim doctrine of *i'jāz*?[23] Halkin argues that Jews under Islam continued to write poetry in Hebrew because "their pride in their own language and in their own Bible not only restrained them from displaying the beauties of Arabic and its masterwork [i.e., the Qur'an], but also impelled them to do for Hebrew as their neighbors did for their tongue."[24] The Jewish attitude toward Hebrew may have been molded in reaction to the Muslim notion of *i'jāz*. Baron also suggests that Judaism, unlike Islam, never had to *debate* the literary merits of the Bible, since that was a given fact; since Hebrew was a dead language by Sa'adya's time, the linguistic status of the text *had* to be true, since all properties of the language were inherent in the text itself.[25] The use of the word *tafsīr* in Sa'adya's title to his translation would therefore seem multifaceted. Reflected in it are Sa'adya's views on the meaning of the term itself, his anti-Karaite stance, and his apologetic stance vis-à-vis Islam and its scripture.[26]

Just as Sa'adya was obviously aware of the subtleties involved in his use of the word *tafsīr*, so in his use of the Arabic language as a whole are reflected attitudes—some of them perhaps surprising—to his religious environment. Some previous studies of Sa'adya's translation have emphasized his obvious debt to the Aramaic *Vorlage* of Targum Onkelos. Others have isolated his relationship to the Hebrew original. No doubt both these elements represent a facet of Sa'adya's process of translation; he clearly enjoys playing with language and will stretch matters quite a distance in order to use cognate expressions or to follow the original syntax, for example. But, at the same time, his use of Arabic can be shown to employ the finer points of grammar and syntax available to him in Arabic (for example, in his use of particles) and even to avoid using cognates in certain instances, in order to achieve a more "literal" sense of the text. Another significant aspect of his use of Arabic is his acceptance of terms that would seem full of connotations in the Islamic theological context. Some of the following observations may seem trivial and even obvious, yet the sum of the evidence would seem to point in the direction of Sa'adya's pivotal role in integrating Judaism into its Islamic context.

To illustrate Sa'adya's translation process and his use of Arabic and how this reflects Muslim-Jewish interaction, Genesis 22:1-19 has been selected for analysis. This is, of course, the famous story of Abraham's test in being asked to sacrifice his son Isaac.

The first thing one notices in reading Sa'adya's Arabic translation is the nature of the language used and its Muslim religious context. Regardless whether *Elohim* or *Yahweh/Adonai* is used in the Hebrew, the word *Allāh* is used in Arabic.[27] *Allāh* is also used by Arabic-speaking Christians when referring to God, so the Jewish use is not distinctive, yet its prime referent is, of course, the Muslim concept of divinity. From the Muslim perspective, *Allāh* may well be *Elohim/Adonai*, but the apparently easy adoption of the word by Jews and Christians could raise some eyebrows.

Another such instance arises with the frequent response in the Bible of anyone who is addressed by God directly; they say *hinneni*, "Here I am." Sa'adya translates this as *labbayka*, an idiomatic expression usually translated identically as "here I am."[28] The word, however, has important Islamic ritual employment during the pilgrimage to Mecca in which the phrase *labbayka allāhumma*, "here I am, Oh God," is repeated constantly during the prescribed ritual preparations for the journey.[29]

Likewise, Sa'adya maintains traditional Arabic spellings of the names of the characters in the story, Abraham and Isaac, rather than attempting to represent the Hebrew originals more closely; thus *Ibrāhīm* appears rather than **Abrāhām* and *Isḥāq* rather than **Yiḍḥak* (?).[30] This fact has interesting consequences when the translation deals with an etiological narrative, one example of which will be discussed later in this paper. It should be noted in passing that the only other instance of the use of a proper name in Genesis 22 is "Moriyah" in verse 2. Sa'adya translates this as "the land of worship," *'ibāda*, once again showing the extent to which he will go to provide his Arabic reader an intelligible text. The translation itself has a long background in the Aramaic targums, with the same meaning being given in Onkelos, for example, as in Sa'adya.[31] Here then, too, is a clear example of Sa'adya's debt to his predecessors and of his conception of the *ẓāhir* or "literal" meaning of text as related to the "authoritative" rendering. All these instances suggest that Sa'adya is interested in using the common expressions of Arabic, regardless of their wider religious connotations and their implications of a relationship of Judaism to Islam, rather than inventing his own words or manner of representation of the original.

The extent to which the Jews adopted Arabic as their language and the ease with which they did so has already been mentioned. In Sa'adya's translation it is worthy to note the extent to which Arabic is used in all its subtleties as compared to the lack of expression of the text in the original Hebrew. Sa'adya's desire in his translations is to display the inner connections between the verses of the Bible and thereby create an overall narrative effect. Sa'adya uses Arabic to argue this point in cases where Hebrew does not have the same subtleties available to it. One area where this may readily be appreciated is in his use of conjunctions. The Hebrew text starts most of the verses with *ve*, "and," leaving the precise connection between verses subject to determination by context. Arabic, however allows for closer definition, and Sa'adya finds occasions to replace *ve* by *fa*, *thumma*, and *ḥattā*, along with *wa*, the latter used primarily in what are interpreted as circumstantial clauses.[32] The isolated instance of the use of *ḥattā* provides an interesting example, occurring in verse 9. The Hebrew text says literally "and the two of them went on together *and* came to the place of which God had spoken"; Sa'adya renders this "*until* they come to the place," the more technically correct conjunction in a literary-narrative sense. It should also be noted that Sa'adya leaves out conjunctions where Arabic does not demand them, most prominently in cases of direct speech where the Hebrew will connect the statements with *va-yomer*, "and he said," whereas Arabic will simply say *qāla*, "he said," and string them all together without a conjunction.[33] Once again, Sa'adya is not slavishly literal in the sense of being concerned to represent every Hebrew word; rather, he seems concerned to create a proper and understandable Arabic text for the advantage of his readers. This seems to display Sa'adya's attitude toward the culture and language around him, an attitude that encourages full integration.

Arabic and Hebrew both being Semitic languages, the use of cognates between the two reveals another aspect of the attitude taken in Sa'adya's translation. In certain instances Sa'adya would seem to opt for the most literal rendering possible, as opposed to using a possible cognate where the connotations may not prove totally accurate. In verse 2, Abraham is ordered to sacrifice his son with the words "*ve-ha'alehu sham le'olah,*" literally rendered as "there you will send him up as a going-up," the verb *'alah*, "to go up," being used in the sense of "to sacrifice." This verb is also used in the Bible in the context of the Exodus, the "going up" from Egypt to Canaan. Arabic has the cognate verb *'alā*, meaning "to go up," "to climb (a mountain)," and so forth. But it also has the verb *ṣa'ida*, meaning "to rise," "to go up," "to go upstream," "to travel to Upper Egypt." It is this verb which Sa'adya uses to translate *'alah* of the Hebrew, thereby maintaining a number of the semantic connotations of the verb, most especially the "traveling up"; this would have been lost had the common Arabic *'alā* been used. However, for the word *'olah*, "a going up" or "a sacrifice," Sa'adya could use neither the cognate nor a derivation from *ṣa'ida*, for neither has the correct sense. He therefore uses the word *qurbān*, a term borrowed into Arabic from Aramaic or Syriac and the word used in the Qur'an for "sacrifice;" it should be noted, however, that neither use of the word in the Qur'an refers to Abraham—in Sūra 3:179,[34] the reference is to general Jewish temple sacrifice and in Sūra 5:30, to Cain and Abel.

In another instance of the Hebrew use of *'alah/'olah*, in verse 13 where the ram is sacrificed, Sa'adya changes his vocabulary and uses *qurbān* plus the denominative verb *qarraba*. For reasons not totally evident, *ṣa'ida* is *not* used here although it may well relate to the desire to distinguish through choice of vocabulary a legitimate animal sacrifice (*qarraba*) and the potential human sacrifice of Isaac (*ṣa'ida*); since this latter could also be taken to mean "rising up," there could be additional implications here in the context of Sa'adya's understanding of the person of Isaac, a matter that will be raised later in this paper.

Another aspect of this matter, but a far more complex one which cannot be fully elucidated here, relates to the etiological narrative connected to *Elohim yir'eh lo* in verse 8. Sa'adya may well have read this *Elohim yar'eh lo*, for he translates the word as *yuẓhiru*, "will make appear," instead of using the cognate. He seems to desire to make his understanding of the verse clear. But this translation defeats the point of verse 14, where it is clear that the narrative is trying to explain why the mountain is called *Adonai yir'eh*, "the Lord will provide." Producing even more confusion here is the fact that in verse 14 Sa'adya changes his translation by translating *Adonai yir'eh* as *Allāh yatajallā*, "God is revealed," a rendering that reflects the latter half of verse 14 of the text and *its* attempt to explain itself with the gloss *Adonai yera'eh*, meaning, perhaps, "the Lord was seen."[35]

All these aspects of the use of the Arabic language on the part of Sa'adya indicate the degree of his willingness and desire to interact with his surroundings. But it would appear that certain defensive and apologetic concerns do have their overall effect on Sa'adya's works. One rather interesting example may be present in verse 17, which states that Abraham's descendants will inherit the cities of their enemies. The verb for inherit here in the Hebrew is *yirash*, cognate to the Arabic *waritha*, with the same meaning in Muslim religious parlance. But Sa'adya renders the word not with the cognate but with *ḥāza*, "to possess or gain in battle"; in the same vein, in verse 18 Abraham's descendants will inherit the cities, according to the Hebrew, simply because Abraham obeyed, while Sa'adya renders this "as a reward for his obedience." The Jewish possession of Israel, Sa'adya may be trying to suggest, had legitimacy not simply as a matter of inheritance but because of rightfully won battles in which God aided the Jews. It may also refer to the future when the Messianic *battles* will restore Israel. There does seem to be here, in my opinion, a touch of political defensiveness or apology, in the sense that Sa'adya is not denying Israel's *right* to the land, but is suggesting that only through God-aided Jewish activism will Israel return to the Jews. Note that supposed metaphorical resolution can take place for apologetic reasons as well as the more common rationalist premise.

Matters of apologetics are far clearer, however, in interpretations tinged by Sa'adya's rationalism. A simple case appears in verse 17 again. God tells Abraham that his descendants will inherit, literally, "all the gates of his enemies." *Sha'ar*, "gates," is used here as a synecdoche and means "the cities," just as Sa'adya renders it. Resolution of metaphor is an important aspect of keeping scripture rational and thereby preventing attack upon it or objection to it.

Sa'adya is also deeply concerned with anthropomorphism—another type of metaphor—and this is revealed in his treatment of verse 12. The angel of the Lord says in the Hebrew, "Now I know that you are a God-fearing man." What? Did God (and thus his angel) not know *before* that Abraham was a God-fearing man? Was God ignorant of that fact? Sa'adya renders the verse, "Indeed, I have now *informed the people* that you are a God-fearing man," a small change, albeit the most substantial one in this chapter, but any offense to God is removed and the text of the Bible remains free from the possibility of attack. It should be noted that anthropomorphism in the Bible was a frequent target of Muslim polemicists.[36]

Moving further into the field of polemic is Sa'adya's rendering of verse 12, which reads in the Hebrew, "You have not withheld from me your son." Sa'adya turns the emphasis of the verse from Abraham to Isaac by translating it as "You [Abraham] have not hindered [or alienated] your son from me." This clearly implies that Isaac was willing to go along with sacrifice and was not discouraged by Abraham from his resolution. This interpretation, emphasizing the willing self-sacrifice of Isaac, has a long history in both Judaism and Christianity and is also reflected in the Qur'anic account (Sūra 37:102); the debate still rages over whether or not the Jewish interpretation predates Christianity or is an apologetic-polemical reaction to Christian notions of Jesus and the search for "Old Testament" prefigurements. We do not need to rehearse these scholarly arguments and debates here.[37] That Sa'adya clearly stands in the Jewish line in this regard, elevating Isaac to the peak of Jewish faith, indicates both his interreligious concern and his position within the mainstream of rabbinic interpretation.

Another aspect of polemic to the Genesis 22 story is, in fact, the main reason for isolating this specific chapter for analysis, over and above its intrinsic merits as a story. This relates to arguments between Jews and Muslims over *naskh*, "abrogation," and Sa'adya's position in the debate and his relationship to Muslim thinkers on the topic. The basic problem seems to have been framed in the following way: did God change his mind by first ordering Abraham to sacrifice his son, then countermanding that order? Is this to be taken as an example of abrogation within the text of biblical scripture and therefore not only proof that the Muslim doctrine of abrogation in the text of the Qur'an was valid—that in fact was a very minor point in these arguments—but also proof that Islam had superseded Judaism (and Christianity), because even Jewish scripture, as the Muslims argued it, witnessed the possibility of God implementing abrogation? Because of the implications of this stance—ones that undermined the entire status of Judaism—Sa'adya was compelled to argue against it. He does so in his *Kitāb al-Amānāt wa'l-I'tiqādāt* in the following words:

> The fifth [perplexity] is [caused by] the injunction of God, exalted be He, to Abraham in regard to Isaac: *And offer him there for a burnt-offering* (Gen. 22:2) and His injunction to him later on, *Lay not thy hand upon the lad, neither do thou anything unto him* (Gen. 22:12). But this, too, did not constitute an abrogation either from our point of view or from that of the proponents of the doctrine of abrogation. For he who holds that abrogation is possible would not believe it to be so unless the law to be abrogated has been carried out at least once, lest it be thought that it had been ordained in vain. What God had really ordered Abraham to do was merely to reserve his son as a sacrifice. When, therefore, this reservation had been completed by him, as evidenced by his display of the fire and the wood and his taking in hand of the knife, God said to Abraham, "Enough for thee! I do not want any more from thee than this."[38]

While Sa'adya makes an appeal here to the notion of the impossibility of frivolous action (*'abath*) on the part of God,[39] his defense is really no more than a terminological sleight of hand. Reservation, *badhl*, implies that the commandment was contingent on God's future plan, which was not to require sacrifice regardless. This then is not abrogation, because the ruling was not intended to be implemented in the first place.[40]

The Muslim counterpart to Sa'adya's argument arises in a number of ways and a number of contexts,[41] most interestingly in the form of discussion of *naskh* in the Qur'an. After all, a similar problem, but without the necessary polemical tinge, arose in any discussion of the Qur'an: was God's command in Sūra 37:102, abrogated by verse 105? Discussion of this could easily lead to discussion of interreligious abrogation also, and in fact the latter may well have preceded the former.

Al-Naḥḥās (d. 950 CE) presents three possible answers to the question of this being an instance of abrogation in the Qur'an.[42] The position which argues for *naskh* in this case is the counter-assertion to Sa'adya's position, that is, that abrogation of something before it has been acted upon is indeed possible. Support for this is found in the notion that Muhammad had fifty prayers imposed upon him in the night journey and this was changed *(naqala)* to five. An intra-Qur'anic example is cited with the case of Sūra 58:13, where the notion of private consultation with Muhammad being preceded by charity is annulled by the statement in verse 14 that if that has not been done, God forgives and urges prayer instead. Another example is claimed in Sūra 8:66-67, with the changing of the ratio of Muslims to non-Muslims demanded in a battle. The story of Abraham provides the other instance.[43]

Such proofs would seem to be lacking in substance because, as al-Naḥḥās himself argues, there is no evidence that the initial law was not enacted. In fact, the only way this could be substantiated is by introducing narrative material in order to impose a framework of sequential events on the verses; within this narrative material it would then be possible to include "evidence" of nonenactment of the given legal statement. It would seem likely that, in fact, there is far more to this argument than simple Qur'anic exegesis; it seems likely that this position arises from interreligious polemic. The notion of abrogation of previous dispensations depended upon the possibility of God changing his will. Any evidence of that possibility of change added more substance to the overall argument. Cases of abrogation before enactment within the previous dispensations provided some of that ammunition. To find instances of the same within the Qur'anic context alone served to substantiate the Muslim position, at least within their own community.

But other Muslim thinkers, agreeing with Sa'adya, saw grave theological problems with such a position because of its implications of frivolous action on the part of God. From the Muslim point of view it had to be true, however, that all abrogation did not imply this, and therefore the notion of contingent versus noncontingent parts of religious dispensations provided a convenient hermeneutical tool. Since the law was always aiming at its final stance even in earlier provisions, any instance of abrogation *within* the text of the Qur'an could be declared a part of the contingent element of revelation without pushing that concept to the point of God's pointless activity. This is, in fact, Sa'adya's ultimate response, but he refuses to accept the Muslim terminology of the matter because of its consequent implications regarding the status of Judaism.[44]

It is hardly surprising, therefore, that al-Naḥḥās is able to cite two arguments against considering the story of Abraham and the sacrifice as abrogation. One of these depends on the distinction between *naskh* and *badā'*, and that the latter, from the Sunnī point of view at least, is not ascribable to God.[45] The argument seems to be that if this story intends to say that Abraham was commanded to sacrifice and then not to sacrifice, this is a contradiction, *badā'*, not *naskh*, which is defined by al-Naḥḥās as "cessation," *izāla*, or "transfer," *naql*.[46] Self-contradiction, al-Naḥḥās asserts, cannot be ascribed to

God. However, al-Naḥḥās does not explore just how the story of Abraham is to be explained from this point of view.

Sa'adya agrees with the third opinion provided by al-Naḥḥās. Abraham did as much as he could to fulfill God's command; being prevented from its ultimate completion was not his own action; therefore God's command to Abraham was not contradicted. The famous story of the knife turning away from the act of sacrifice, following *its* own command from God, becomes the crucial *haggada* around which this explanation turns.[47] One command of God is interfered with by another command of God, but both actors fulfill their own order as best they can.

For Sa'adya, of course, the most important thing to do was to find a response that would preserve the integrity of Judaism while at the same time allowing for hermeneutical flexibility. The rational character of the law for Sa'adya[48] necessitates its continual validity and its noncontingent nature (in Muslim terms), and likewise God's rational law cannot contain contradiction. Sa'adya, it would seem, depends upon an essentially apologetic answer, responding to the claim of abrogation with a simple negative by redefinition. Lying behind that fact, perhaps, is the easiest explanation of why the translation of the Torah does not seem to reveal any aspect of response to the polemic issue. In the crucial passage, verse 2, Sa'adya's rendering, *wa-aṣ'idhu thamma qurbānan*, "so make him ascend there as an offering," would not seem to blunt this particular polemical edge.[49] For the common person in need of an Arabic Torah, an issue such as abrogation would not be of such great concern. But *The Book of Beliefs and Opinions*, being a theological defense of Judaism, required that these sorts of issues be taken into account.

In sum, then, the intention of this paper has been to demonstrate at least the potential for future studies in the area of Sa'adya and his relationship to Islam. Most of the issues raised are complex ones and none of them has been treated here as fully as may be wished or indeed needed. The evidence of Sa'adya's interaction with the Islamic world is evident, most especially through his use of language. His response to polemical issues is present in isolated instances such as deanthropomorphism and abrogation but is also implicitly present throughout his translation of the Bible: the accusation was often made by Muslims that the Jews no longer had a true understanding of the Bible, that the tradition of interpretation was not an unbroken chain from Moses.[50] To this Sa'adya responds by putting the entire Bible into Arabic so that those who wished could respond to the Muslim controversalists appropriately.

NOTES

1 Basic biographical information on Sa'adya and bibliographical details are available in H. Malter, *Saadia Gaon, His Life and Works* (Philadelphia: Jewish

Publication Society, 1921); supplementary bibliography is available in Aron Freimann, "Saadia Bibliography: 1920-1942," in *Saadia Anniversary Volume* (New York: American Academy for Jewish Research, 1943), 327-39.

2 Reference in this paper is to *Version arabe du Pentateuque de R. Saadia Ben Josef al-Fayyoûmī*, J. Derenbourg, ed., in *Ouevres complètes de R. Saadia Ben Josef al-Fayyoûmī*, (Paris: Ernest Leroux, 1893), vol. 1; this is supplemented by reference to Josef Mieses, "Textkritische Bemerkungen zu R. Saadja Gaons arabischer Pentateuchübersetzung, Derenbourg, ed., Paris, 1893," *Monatsschrift für die Geschichte und Wissenschaft des Judentums* 63(1919): 269-90. The best treatment of Sa'adya in his Islamic environment, and concerned specifically with his exegesis, is found in A. S. Halkin, "Saadia's Exegesis and Polemics," in Louis Finkelstein, ed., *Rab Saadia Gaon: Studies in His Honour* (reprint New York: Arno Press, 1980), 117-41.

3 See A. S. Halkin, "Judeo-Arabic Literature," in Louis Finkelstein, ed., *The Jews: Their History, Culture and Religion* (New York: Harper, 1960), 2: 1124.

4 Ed. Y. Kafiḥ (Jerusalem: Sura Institute, 1970); tr. Samuel Rosenblat, (New Haven: Yale U. P., 1948).

5 See Malter, *Saadia Gaon*, pp. 142-43 and nn. 305, 306.

6 See, for example, J. Blau, *The Emergence and Linguistic Background of Judaeo-Arabic: A Study of the Origins of Middle Arabic*, 2nd ed. (Jerusalem: Ben-Zvi Institute, 1981), 39-44, 226; also, on the opposite side, Leon Nemoy, "The Factor of Script in the Textual Criticism of Judeo-Arabic Manuscripts," *Jewish Quarterly Review* 66 (1975-76): 148-59, and Blau's response, "R. Nissim's Book of Comfort and the Problem of Script in Judaeo-Arabic Manuscripts," *Jewish Quarterly Review* 67(1976-77): 185-94.

7 See S. W. Baron, *A Social and Religious History of the Jews* (New York: Columbia U. P., 1958), 6:262.

8 J. Blau, "Judaeo-Arabic in Its Linguistic Setting," *Proceedings of the American Academy for Jewish Research* 36(1968): 1-12, one of many of Blau's statements on this point.

9 Baron, *Social and Religious History*, vol. 6:264.

10 See the Introduction to the Pentateuch translation, p. 4, line 17.

11 See, e.g., Malter, *Saadia Gaon*, pp. 143-44.

12 On al-Māturīdī and *ta'wīl/tafsīr* see M. Götz, "Māturīdī und sein Kitāb Ta'wīlāt al-Qur'ān," *Der Islam* 41(1965): 27-70.

13 Yaḥyā ibn Ziyād al-Farrā', *Ma'ānī al-Qur'ān* (Cairo: al-Dār al-Miṣriyya li'l-Ta'līf wa'l-Tarjama, 1972), e.g., 3:248. Among other early figures in Muslim exegesis Ibn Qutayba (d. 889) would probably prove to be the most profitable for a full study in the employment and development of exegetical terminology. See further below, n. 22.

14 J. Wansbrough, "Arabic Rhetoric and Qur'anic Exegesis," *Bulletin of the School for Oriental and African Studies* 31(1968): 469-85, on the development of the figure *laff wa-nashr* from that termed at an earlier time *tafsīr* due to the appropriation/adaptation of the latter to scriptural exegesis; also see his reformulation in *Quranic Studies: Sources and Methods of Scriptural Interpretation* (Oxford: Oxford U. P., 1977), 233-35, and his statement: "That

'*tafsīr*' was as much the product of concern for rhetoric as for 'interpretation' in general seems certain" (235).

[15] *Ibid.*, p. 156

[16] *Ibid.*

[17] *Ibid.*, p. 157.

[18] This aspect is ignored in P. R. Weis, "The Anti-Karaite Tendency of R. Saadya Gaon's Arabic Version of the Pentateuch," in E. I. J. Rosenthal (ed.), *Saadya Studies* (Manchester: Manchester University Press, 1943), 227-44.

[19] *Kitāb al-Amānāt*, pp. 219-20, trans. pp. 265-67; the passage ends with the statement: "There exists, then, only these four possible reasons for a non-literal interpretation of the verses of the Sacred Writ, there being no fifth." These principles of interpretation were most certainly not invented by Sa'adya but in fact have a long history in Judaism, finding support, for example, in the Talmud. They are, as well, closely aligned to the Mu'tazilī approach to scripture as enunciated by al-Zamakhsharī, for example. The employment of these principles will account for a number of the phenomena noted below in the analysis of Genesis 22.

[20] Wansbrough, *Quranic Studies*, p. 187.

[21] See on this topic of the relationship between the term literal and the authoritative meaning Raphael Loewe, "The 'Plain' Meaning of Scripture in Early Jewish Exegesis," in J. G. Weiss (ed.), *Papers of the Institute of Jewish Studies, London* (Jerusalem: Magnes Press, 1964), 1:140-85. Also useful in this matter is James Barr, *The Typology of Literalism in Ancient Biblical Translations* (Göttingen:Vandenhoeck & Ruprecht, 1979). How to analyze and conceptualize translation as a whole is also extremely relevant; see, e.g., E. A. Nida, *Toward a Science of Translating* (Leiden: E. J. Brill, 1964).

[22] The word *tarjama*, like *tafsīr*, has a complex history of employment in early exegetical works, but it is clear that prior to Sa'adya the noun and its verbal formation were used in the sense of "translation." One clear example arises in Ibn Qutayba (d. 889), *Ta'wīl Mushkil al-Qur'ān* (Cairo: Dār al-Turāth, 1974), 21, where in reference to translations of other scriptures he defines the word as "*naqala ilā shay' min al-alsina*." This would also seem to occur in al-Ṭabarī although Shākir, the editor of the text, argues against that interpretation of the word. In *Jāmi' al-Bayān* (Cairo: Dār al-Ma'ārif, 1953), 1:70, al-Ṭabarī makes reference to the revelation of scriptures, all being in one language to begin with but then being changed (*ḥuwwila*) into the appropriate language; "*kāna dhālika lahu tarjama wa tafsīr*" is his conclusion. Also see my "Ibn 'Abbās's al-Lughāt fī'l-Qur'ān," *Bulletin of the School for Oriental and African Studies* 44(1981): 15-25 and the follow-up note "Ibn 'Abbās's Gharīb al-Qur'ān," *Bulletin of the School for Oriental and African Studies* 46(1983): 332-33, also Wansbrough, *Quranic Studies*, p. 218.

[23] See R. Paret, "Al-Ḳur'ān: 9. Translation of the Ḳur'ān," *Encyclopedia of Islam*, 2nd ed. (Leiden: E. J. Brill, 1981), 5:429-30 and bibliography there.

[24] A. S. Halkin, "The Medieval Jewish Attitude toward Hebrew," in A. Altmann, ed., *Biblical and Other Studies* (Cambridge, MA: Harvard U. P., 1963), 234.

[25] Baron, *Social and Religious History*, vol. 6:291.

26 On the relation of *pesher* to *tafsīr* and *ta'wīl* see Wansbrough, *Quranic Studies*, p. 246.
27 *Elohim*: verses 1, 3, 8, 9, 12; *Adonai*: verses 11, 14 (twice), 15, 16.
28 Verses 1, 7, 11.
29 For details and background to *labbayka allāhumma* see M. J. Kister, "Labbayka, Allāhumma, Labbayka. . .: On a Monotheistic Aspect of a Jāhiliyya Practice," *Jerusalem Studies in Arabic and Islam* 2(1980): 33-57.
30 *Ibrāhīm*: verses 1 (twice), 3, 4, 5, 6, 7, 8, 9, 10, 11 (twice), 13, 14, 15, 19. *Isḥāq*: verses 2, 3, 6, 7, 9. On the likely Syriac origin or influence on the form of these Arabic words see A. Jeffery, *The Foreign Vocabulary of the Qur'ān* (Baroda: Oriental Institute, 1938), 44-46, 60.
31 *The Bible in Aramaic: I, Targum Onkelos*, A. Sperber, ed. (Leiden: Brill, 1959), 31: *pulḥanā*, "service, worship."
32 The Hebrew verses which start with *ve* or *va* are all but 4 and 17. Sa'adya renders these *wa*: verses 3, 4, 7, 10, 14, 16, 18; *fa*: verses 1, 5, 6, 11, 12; *ḥattā*: verse 9; *thumma*: verses 13, 15, 19.
33 This happens, for example, at the beginning of verses 2 and 3.
34 Verse numbering and text of the Qur'an are according to the Flügel edition.
35 Interpretations of this part of the narrative vary as do interpretations of the biblical attempt to explain itself; see, for example, the New English Bible with its rendering "In the mountain of the Lord it was provided." For a good summary of the various points of view and some new insights see J. van Seters, *Abraham in History and Tradition* (New Haven: Yale University Press, 1975), 227-40. On etiological narratives in the Bible see B. O. Long, *The Problem of the Etiological Narrative in the Old Testament* (Berlin: Topelmann, 1968), esp. p. 28 and J. Fichtner, "Die etymologische Ätiologie in den Namengebungen der geschichtlichen Bücher des Alten Testaments," *Vetus Testamentum* 6(1965): 372-96.
36 See S. Rawidowicz, "Saadya's Purification of the Idea of God," in Rosenthal, *Saadya Studies*, pp. 139-65.
37 See, for example, Robert Hayward, "The Present State of Research into the Targumic Account of the Sacrifice of Isaac," *Journal of Jewish Studies* 32 (1981): 127-50 which contains references of all the basic bibliography. On the Qur'anic data on Isaac see J. A. Naude, "Isaac Typology in the Koran," in I. H. Eybers et al. (eds.), *De Fructu Oris Sui: Essays in Honour of Adrianus von Selms* (Leiden: Brill, 1971), 121-29. Also see W. M. Watt, "Isḥāk," *Encyclopedia of Islam*, 2nd ed., vol. 4:109-10.
38 Translation, p. 169, text, p. 140.
39 See also in Maimonides, *Guide of the Perplexed* 2:39, 3: 25, S. Pines, tr., *The Guide of the Perplexed* (Chicago: University of Chicago Press, 1963), 378-81, 502-06.
40 See J. Wansbrough, *The Sectarian Milieu: Content and Composition of Islamic Salvation History* (Oxford: Oxford U. P., 1978), 112-14.
41 See *ibid*., pp. 110-12 for a discussion of the verse by al-Naẓẓām.
42 Abū Ja'far al-Naḥḥās, *Kitāb al-Nāsikh wa'l-Mansūkh* (Cairo: Zakī Mujāhid, 1938), 210-12.

[43] These same examples are cited in proof of precisely the same point in Makkī al-Qaysī (d. 1045), *Al-Īḍāḥ li-Nāsikh al-Qur'ān wa'l-Mans ūkhihi* (Riyāḍ: Kulliyyat al-Sharī'a, 1976), 339. Also see 'Abd al-Qāhir al-Baghdādī (d. 1037), *Kitāb al-Nāsikh wa'l-Mansūkh*, manuscript, Istanbul Beyazit 445, ff. 45b-46a, where he discusses Qur'an 58:13-14 and concludes: "In this abrogating verse [i.e., verse 13] is proof of the soundness of the statement of he who permits abrogation of a legal verse of the Qur'an prior to the arrival of the time of its application."

[44] See Wansbrough, *Sectarian Milieu*, pp.110-14.

[45] See I. Goldziher, "Badā'," *Encyclopedia of Islam,* 1st ed., vol. 1:550-52; al-Naḥḥās, *Kitāb al- Nāsikh*, pp.10-11.

[46] Al-Naḥḥās, *ibid.*, p. 8.

[47] See, e.g., al-Kisā'ī, *Qiṣaṣ al-Anbiyā'* (Leiden: E. J. Brill, 1922), 150-51; al-Naḥḥās, *Kitāb al-Nāsikh*, p. 211; the vocabulary of these passages is well worth comparing to that of Sa'adya's translation of Genesis itself.

[48] See A. Altmann, "Saadya's Conception of the Law," *Bulletin of the John Rylands Library* 28(1944): 3-24.

[49] Whether *qurbān* can be suggested to have lost some of its "sacrificed" meaning and perhaps be intended more in the (New Testament?) sense of "dedicated" may be worth further investigation.

[50] This is probably to be connected to the charge of *taḥrīf* also; in general see Ibn Kammūna, *Tanqīḥ al-Abḥāth li'l-Milal al-Thal āth* (Berkeley: University of California Press, 1967): 27-33, tr. by M. Perlmann, pp. 47-54.

New Approaches to "Biblical" Materials in the Qur'an

Marilyn Robinson Waldman[1]

When scholars investigate the apparent transmission of material from one monotheistic scripture to another, they tend to assume that earlier materials are normative and later ones derivative. This tendency, if unmitigated, makes it difficult to appreciate either earlier or later materials in and of themselves; and it affects scholars' attitudes to the whole of the Judeo-Christian-Islamic tradition and each of its various parts. Often the recipient of the "transmitted" materials is assigned a relationship to the transmitter not unlike the one established in a certain Mulla Naṣruddīn story: Naṣruddīn had waited in vain all day in a *qāḍī*'s court for a gold coin of reparation to be brought back by a man whom the *qāḍī* had fined for slapping him across the face in a public market. Finally, exasperated, he went up to the *qāḍī* and slapped him hard across the face, saying, "Here's the slap. When he gets back, you get the gold coin."

A promising complement to influence and transmission studies is to be found in the analysis of narrative, or narratology. A narratological approach can elucidate "biblical" material in the Qur'an so as to clarify not only the relationship of Bible to Qur'an, but the art of Qur'anic narrative itself.[2] The Sūrat Yūsuf, the twelfth Qur'anic chapter, will serve as a specific example which has wider implications for the fields of history of religion and literary history as well.

When non-Muslims look at this sūra or any other Qur'anic chapter containing a story that appears in another scripture, they naturally tend to place it in a dependency relationship, to see it as a "version," as something passed on in altered, if not debased, form. Consider, for example, the conclusion reached by one biblical scholar of Genesis 39, after reading the Qur'anic Joseph narrative. A reader of the Qur'an would have to be familiar with the biblical version to be able to understand the Qur'anic version fully.

> Both the OT and Qur'an make special claims for the narratives contained within their pages. Each insists that the reader accept the stories given there as the "original version" in the deepest sense. Stories which include this claim to authority must be interpreted differently from texts which make no such claim. The situation presented by the Qur'anic and OT Joseph stories is especially complex, because both stories assume that the reader will accept their authority as given and final. Nevertheless, the situation is not "balanced," for only the Qur'an recognizes the existence of other "versions" of its stories, and self-consciously takes a polemical stance toward those versions. That is, the Qur'an is admittedly "dependent" on the OT, even if the

> dependence is only for the purpose of replacing the chronologically older stories with what it claims are the true stories.
> Therefore, the Qur'an itself leads the interpreter to view the relation between the OT and itself as a case of one-sided dependence. This means that the interpreter of the biblical Joseph story, for example, does not need to know the Qur'anic story in order to fully understand the biblical narrative, while the interpreter of Sura 12 must refer to the biblical Joseph to fully understand the Qur'anic Joseph.[3]

This particular author, however, does not limit himself to using the Bible to understand the Qur'an. Rather, he also appreciates the value of comparison in identifying the uniqueness of the biblical version:

> Understanding of the biblical story can of course [also] be facilitated by comparing the OT narrative with other stories which are based on it, or which have been viewed as "similar" to it in some respect. Such comparison can make the interpreter more aware of the unique traits of the biblical story, by recognizing its differences from other "versions."[4]

By extension, he is implying that comparison points to the uniqueness of each telling, a uniqueness that can be accounted for only through an internal analysis of each. Furthermore, he is implicitly calling for an approach to groups of seemingly related stories that focuses not just on the relationship of version to original/ancestor, but also on the strategies and constraints of each telling in its own larger context(s).

The components of such an approach might be assembled from the work of folklorists, narratologists, and speech-act theorists. Especially germane is a series of points make by Barbara Herrnstein Smith, a particularly articulate and effective spokesperson for new approaches to narrative.[5] Smith conceptualizes the relationship among versions or perhaps better, variants, not as the relationship of simulations to gem but more as the relationship of a string to the necklace of gems it holds together.[6] In Smith's rather radical view, no telling of a story is more basic than any other(s), and originals really do not exist. Drawing on research about various tellings of "the Cinderella story," she argues that

> 1. For any particular narrative, there is no singly *basically* basic story subsisting beneath it but, rather, an unlimited number of other narratives that can be *constructed in response* to it or *perceived as related to it*.

> 2. Among the narratives that can be constructed in response to a given narrative are not only those that we commonly refer to as "versions" of it (for example, translations, adaptations, abridgements, and paraphrases) but also those retellings that we call "plot summaries," "interpretations," and, sometimes, "basic stories." None of these retellings, however, is more absolutely basic than any of the others.
> 3. For any given narrative, there are always *multiple* basic stories that can be constructed in response to it because basic-ness is always arrived at by the exercise of some set of operations, in accord with some set of principles, that reflect some set of interests, all of which are, by nature, variable and thus multiple. . . .
> 4. The form and features of any "version" of a narrative will be a function of, among other things, the particular motives that elicited it and the particular interests and functions it was designed to serve. . . .
> 5. Among any array of narratives—tales or tellings—in the universe, there is an unlimited number of potentially perceptible *relations*. These relations may be of many different kinds and orders, including formal and thematic, synchronic and diachronic, and causal and non-causal. Whenever these potentially perceptible relations become actually perceived, it is by virtue of some set of interests on the part of the perceiver. . . . Since new sets of interests can emerge at any time and do emerge continuously, there can be no ultimately basic set of relations among narratives, and thus also no "natural" genres of "essential" types, and thus also no limit to the number or nature of narratives that may sometime be seen as versions or variants of each other.[7]

The implications of these positions for reading and making sense of the Joseph story in the Qur'an are far-reaching. If applied, they could correct the imbalance that usually informs Qur'an-Bible comparisons. For Smith is saying that no story is permanently "part" of a single diachronic series or synchronic set of stories with which it has a fixed objective affinity. There is never a single context in which a story can be heard or read or told. Stories always have plural contexts, even for a single hearer or reader. The perception of an affinity with other stories on the part of an individual or community arises out of their interests, as does their choice of criteria by which to determine affinity. Therefore, any given story can be at once part of many affinal groups, perceived as such by different individuals or groups or even by various individuals within the same group. Furthermore, when a story is perceived as "belonging" to a group of stories, it can affect the understanding of other stories in the group.

The Appendix to this article is a fine example of the importance of context and the fallacy of the idea of *ur*-stories. In that Appendix both the biblical and the Qur'anic Joseph stories are "told," but this time in terms of nineteen action-advancing steps or stages determined by the prose and shape of the Qur'anic telling.[8] Both tellings, constructed for the special needs of this essay (especially to highlight similarities and differences), are coherent; neither is more basic than the other; and the biblical variant proves to be tellable at approximately the same pace as the Qur'anic, even though its original is three times as long.

So, even if we could establish a possible line of transmission from Torah to Qur'an, say through orally carried midrash, we would still not exhaust the Qur'anic telling, either in its own contemporary contexts or in any historically accumulated ones. We must assume that there were many ways in which the Joseph story or something like it could be told in Muhammad's time (just as the biblical version is not the original Near Eastern one), and many disparate pieces which could be fitted together or excluded. No matter where else we might find those pieces, their use in a given telling is our primary focus. Smith would argue that for any given listener or reader from the seventh century on, the Qur'anic Joseph story's possible affinities cannot be limited to other Joseph stories and especially not to specific, say biblical or midrashic tellings, of a recognizable Joseph story.

To view the Qur'anic Joseph story as a version of the biblical one is itself a cultural decision and an essentially literary-historical one at that. Other motifs—for example, rags-to-riches, sibling rivalry, divinely guided friend of God—multiply the affinities almost infinitely. And the inclusion of this story in such a group, or the perception of it *as belonging* to those groups, could then also begin to affect future tellings of stories in that group. Thus did some later Qur'an commentators, presumably those concerned to explain how certain revelations expressed God's relationship with Muhammad, identify the Joseph story as something God told Muhammad to cheer and entertain him during a bad period in his career, full as the story is of sex and intrigue as well as triumph for the friends of God. For other writers, Joseph became *the* symbol of beauty, or Joseph and Zulaykha quintessential lovers and foci for eroticism, or Zulaykha a lesson in the human tendency to yield to baser temptations.[9]

Although Smith does help us to understand the nature of affinity once established, she seems to evade the question of what constitutes that affinity if the stories perceived as related are not to be viewed as versions of an original or basic telling. Implicitly, however, she seems to suggest that when one perceives stories as part of the same group, one is thinking in terms of similarities among certain minimal, often formal characteristics, for example, titles, names, and characters; overall plot; and order of occurrences or episodes. In putting the Qur'anic and biblical Joseph stories in the same set, we are relying on our perception of such affinities; yet I will argue, after comparing the two, that despite the extensive presence of numerous such formal affinities, the two do not tell the same story in thematic, theological, or moral terms. In fact, they are probably just as much like other stories as they are like each other.[10]

Since Smith emphasizes the need to set the context in which a given telling is told, let me begin with some general observations about the larger texts within which the individual stories appear. The two scriptures in question differ in a number of obvious and fundamental ways. Whatever the oral qualities and dimensions of the Hebrew Bible, it has come down to us as a written composition. The Qur'an, despite its having a written form, presents itself as essentially an oral composition. Many of the readily apparent divergences between the two books, overall or in renderings of a given story, are traceable primarily to the natural and predictable consequences of oral as opposed to written composition.

The Torah is, moreover, a continuous, extended historical account. The Qur'an contains very little narrated history (in fact, very little narration at all) and, in the standard order of the sūras, is a disjunctive and discontinuous book of lessons, warnings, instructions, and exhortations. The Torah is written in expository prose; the Qur'an in compact, often elliptical, quasi-poetic style. The Qur'anic story, like much of the narrative in the book to which it belongs, is less detailed and faster paced, one-third the length of the biblical story. The biblical story, approximately three times as long as the Qur'anic, is, like its container, very detailed and frequently interrupted by narrative digressions and genealogical materials. Qur'anic language presents itself as God's speech, verbatim; the Torah is not constructed throughout as God's quoted speech but rather as reliable third-person narration of divine action.

When one looks at the place of each story within its entire work, the differences are just as striking. In the Qur'an, Joseph is the subject of one of many teaching stories, albeit one of the longest, most detailed, and most colorful. Without it, however, the Qur'an would still make sense. And without the Qur'an, the "Sūra of Joseph" could still be read on its own, decontextualized as it is. For the Bible, however, the story of Joseph is essential; it accounts for twenty-eight per cent of the Book of Genesis and constitutes a key moment in the history of the Hebrew people. Within the overall purposes of the Qur'an, the Joseph story serves, like most other narrative therein, as a didactic vehicle, in this case to show how God sends signs and constantly guides and rewards the God-fearing. In the Bible, the telling of the Joseph story is an indispensable step in the unfolding of God's divine plan and manipulation of history to ensure the future of the Hebrews. Consequently, the figure of God seems somewhat more distant in the biblical story, less concentrated on a relationship with Joseph and more involved with the lives of all the many characters, whereas in the Qur'an God interferes with and guides His messenger constantly, the other characters remaining more shadowy and less clearly defined.

In addition to its not being part of a larger historical narrative, the Qur'anic story is strongly decontextualized in another way. Other than Joseph, no Qur'anic character is named directly ('Azīz, the "name" of Joseph's master, could be construed as a title). This anonymity of other characters has the effect of making the Qur'anic story even more the story of Joseph, Messenger of God, and less of "his people." It also emphasizes the universal meaning of the story and minimizes the need to compare it with any other telling. In fact, there is little indication that the contemporary listener would have to have heard a similar story previously in order to make at least some sense of the Qur'anic telling.

The two tellings can also be compared in other ways. Their shapes are different: the biblical story flows from one stage in Joseph's life to another; the Qur'anic story is self-contained—enclosed by the prediction of the initial dream's meaning and its fulfillment. In both cases the narrative is interrupted, but differently. The Qur'anic story is essentially a single tale, interrupted by shorter or longer homiletic editorializing, as it were, by God or a character. The biblical story is a composite, and the narrator(s) is (are) not nearly so strong a presence. The main story about Joseph in Egypt is interrupted by another significant related one (Judah's marriage to Shua and Tamar and the Sin of Onan) and by repetitions of the whole story to a given point thrice, which Robert Alter sees as part of the Bible's way of searching for multi-faceted truth.[11]

Jacob's roles differ, too. In the Qur'an, Jacob is an aid and mentor for Joseph, whose humanness and manipulability are stressed as marks of his dependence on God. Through his existence and ability to read God's signs, others learn to understand God's signs as well. The biblical Jacob is not a messenger of God or an insightful mentor for Joseph; rather, he seems more a victim of circumstances, and more psychologically and emotionally expressive of that condition.

One final type of comparison is suggested by Robert Alter's approach to biblical narrative. Although four of his major concerns—type-scenes, artful repetition, juxtaposition of versions (his composite artistry), and reticence in characterization[12]—seem not to apply to the Qur'an, his fifth major focus—preference for direct speech, particularly dialogue—does. According to Alter, although biblical authors sometimes restate in third-person voice what has been said in dialogue, they avoid indirect speech. By strongly preferring direct speech, they bring the speech-act into the foreground; make the reader more conscious of the speaker and his/her use of language; and produce complicating ambiguity for the interpreter of speech because the narrators, by not stating it in third-person, do not give it their stamp of authority.[13] He goes on to say that "when an actual process of contemplating specific possibilities, sorting out feelings, weighing alternatives, making resolutions, is a moment in the narrative event, it is reported as direct discourse."[14]

It is in his exploration of the reasons for the biblical preference for direct speech that we begin to have insights into the Qur'an as well, one of whose most fundamental theological points is shared with the Bible: the intimate relationships among speech (divine and human), creation, and revelation. Alter begins his discussion of the biblical preference for direct speech by surmising that the biblical authors may have reported thought as speech because they "did not distinguish sharply between the two in their assumptions about how the mind relates to reality. Perhaps with their strong sense of the primacy of language in the created order of things, they tended to feel that thought was not fully itself until it was articulated into speech."[15]

As Alter then penetrates more deeply the theological issues that promote the biblical narrators' preference for direct speech, he reaches conclusions that can also be applied to the Qur'anic treatment of Joseph:

> . . . what is important to him [the biblical writer] is human will confronted with alternatives which it may choose on its own or submit to divine determination. Articulated language provides the indispensable model for defining this rhythm of political or historical alternatives, question and response, creaturely uncertainty over against the Creator's intermittently revealed design, because in the biblical view words underlie reality. With words God called the world into being; the capacity for using language from the start set man apart from the other creatures; in words each person reveals his distinctive nature, his willingness to enter into binding compacts with men and God, his ability to control others, to deceive them, to feel for them, and to respond to them. Spoken language is the substratum of everything human and divine that transpires in the Bible.[16]

And again,

> Every human agent must be allowed the freedom to struggle with his destiny through his own works and acts. Formally, this means that the writer must permit each character to manifest or reveal himself or herself chiefly through dialogue but of course also significantly through action, without the imposition of an obtrusive apparatus of authorial interpretation and judgment. The Hebrew narrator does not openly meddle with the personages he presents, just as God creates in each human personality a fierce tangle of intentions, emotions, and calculations caught in a translucent net of language, which is left for the individual himself to sort out in the evanescence of a single lifetime.[17]

However, despite what appears to be a similar understanding of language itself, the Qur'an's narrative situation is still different from that of the Bible. Biblical narrators depend on God for their "omniscience" or reliability, and display it, according to Alter, in rather indirect ways in their reliable third-person narrative. The Qur'anic narrator *is* the omniscient God, speaking orally and committed to a high degree of explicitness—to giving clear guidance—but without being *so* explicit that the message does not capture the attention of the listener and draw him or her in. Even when direct speech appears in the Qur'an, it is being quoted by God. As we will see, the theological effects achieved by biblical authors by their use of direct speech are achieved by the Qur'an in the way in which the story is told and oriented. Also, since the Qur'an is organized as a cumulative oral revelation, the degree to which it is internally coherent and consistent increases to the extent that individual parts reinforce each other and its overall moral and spiritual vision.

The art of Qur'anic narrative, which often deals with particular well-known historical stories, is to get those small stories to tell themselves and bear a larger cosmic message at the same time.[18] Qur'anic characters are portrayed with an emblematic quality that one finds also in the aniconism of Islamic art. Figures whom the Bible characterizes thoroughly are minimally portrayed in the Qur'an. Because they thereby discourage the listener from becoming psychologically entrapped, they are freer to be instruments of a broader message.

All these differences between the two tellings, as well as the similarities, are largely consistent with their different purposes, natures, and settings, and cannot be explained adequately by an exclusively literary-historical approach. Most important, the Joseph the Qur'an portrays has to be recognizable as a messenger of God in terms of the composite definition of messengership that emerges from all the Qur'an's many references to such figures, whereas the Bible does not present Joseph as a messenger at all. The Qur'anic story of Joseph could in fact be said to focus on Joseph as a representative of instrumental messengership and as a measure of its nature and effect. It is quite possible to construct a general Qur'anic image of the prophetic role and to recognize Joseph according to it. The Qur'an's presentation of Joseph can in fact be seen to be governed by the role according to which he must be recognized, if one makes two assumptions not only about the Qur'an as a book but others as well: (1) The parts should always be readable in terms of a vision and reading the whole; and (2) when examples of particular types of characters are presented, their representation both reflects a larger idea of their type and also contributes to its formation.

A simple collating and analysis of all generic or proper mentions of messengers in the Qur'an produces a fairly clear and oft-repeated set of salient characteristics. But because the set has been constructed from mentions of both those called (*nabī*) and those sent (*rasūl*), not all characteristics apply equally to all figures.[19]

1. Each is to be seen as part of a large set of individuals—each of whom has a degree of individuality and an appropriate skill but who is like all others in fundamental ways.

2. Each is guided by God, but guidance is parceled out as needed.

3. They are chosen by God, usually from among their own people, without seeking to be chosen. Connected with this, their mortality is constantly stressed; in the terminology of the modern religionist, they are instrumental messengers. In particular the Qur'an takes pains to distinguish them from angels, who are presented as some kind of medial heavenly figure—not God but also recognizable as not man. Their humanity and instrumentality in turn emphasize God's power.

4. They polarize their audiences—being opposed by some and believed by others. Those who oppose them may physically harm them or expel them, but more often call them liars; such belying (*takdhīb*) is closely associated in

Qur'anic semantics with *kufr* (ingratitude). They oppose ancestral custom to *tawḥīd* (declaring God's oneness) and are in turn opposed by Satan.

5. They have two major functions—to bring good tidings and to warn—both of which involve explaining God's clear signs.

6. They have a constellation of exemplary personal characteristics: patience, unswerving devotion, compassion, trust in God, pure faith absolutely opposed to associating (*shirk*) anything with God.

7. Obeying them is not separate from the need to obey God and believe in His Book, the Angels, and the Last Day.

The Qur'anic story of Joseph is structured to emphasize his fit with these characteristics, which are in turn related to other key elements in the Qur'anic worldview. The story has a circular shape—its opening is echoed in its closing; in each an explicit motive is given for its telling—it is a sign of God's intentions for humanity and a lesson (*'ibra*). Because of this familiar Qur'anic motive for story-telling, the opening event (1) functions in a different way from the way it functions in the Bible. There the dream prefigures and advances the action, by the father's warning Joseph that it would make his brothers jealous, among other things. In the Qur'an it functions not primarily as an action-advancer but as a sign, like the entire story of which it is a part, that God's will shall be fulfilled no matter what. The father gives it that meaning explicitly.

The clearest evidence of the Qur'an's totally different orientation is the role the subplot of the master's wife plays in the story as a whole and what it reveals of Joseph's character as a messenger. This episode also marks the widest divergence from the biblical telling and demonstrates how the Qur'an is making different use of available materials, no matter what their sources. As a result of what emerges from the Qur'an's use of this subplot, Joseph appears more dependent for his every move on God *Himself*, rather than on His plan, and less *invested* with the ability to carry out God's will on his own (7-10). In fact, this episode in the Qur'an has Joseph save another person, the wife, before saving himself, and thereby has him show himself even more to be the instrument of God (10).

A detailed exploration of the Qur'an's handling of this incident will help expand the argument. In the Bible, Joseph's attractiveness to his father contributes to his brother's resentment (1). His handsomeness and attractiveness to Potiphar's wife serve, through her lies, to get him into prison (even though out of his innate strength of character he yields not at all to her advances) so that he can be brought out of prison to prosper and "redeem" his family (6-7, 11). After he is imprisoned, the wife does not figure in again, having served her purposes in the narrative.

In the Qur'an, the story of the wife is more inconclusive, oriented toward exploring and explaining Joseph's sexual attractiveness in very human terms, less clear about how or whether the encounter leads to his imprisonment (7-8). More specifically, in the Qur'an, the wife is the wife of Joseph's buyer, "'Azīz," who has her install Joseph in their house, perhaps even to be adopted by them (6). His stay there is used to teach him the dream interpretation he will need, although it is kept secret for the time being (6). According to the Qur'an, the wife solicits Joseph, closing him into her room with her. According to the

Qur'an, he would have taken her had he not seen God's signs not to do so (7). Forewarned against his all too human tendency to succumb, he runs to the door; as the wife grabs him, she tears his shirt from behind. At the door he meets his master, his seducer's husband, who refuses to believe his own wife's lie that Joseph seduced her (because one of his kin witnesses to the contrary and because the shirt is torn from behind), urging her instead to ask God's forgiveness for the sin she has committed by accusing someone falsely of adultery (7).

For the Qur'an, the story does not stop there. Certain of the women of the city blame the wife in their gossip, but the wife contrives to show them how tempting Joseph really is (7). She invites them to her house, presumably to eat, because when each has a knife in her hand, it has been arranged for them to glimpse this handsome youth (whom they mistake for an angel), whereupon they lose control of themselves enough to cut their hands with the knives.[20] Having made them empathize with her lust, she admits that she has solicited him but vows to have him imprisoned if she cannot have him. Joseph prays to God to turn him away from their guile but is imprisoned anyway, again for an unexplained reason (8). Often in the Qur'an, not everything has to be explained.[21]

When, two steps later in the narrative, Joseph receives a summons from the king which can release him from prison, he refuses to leave until he is finally cleared with the women—she who seduced him as well as those whom she corrupted (10). His former master's wife confesses, attributing no responsibility to God for her actions and all credit to Him for allowing her to correct her more evil human tendencies. Joseph then leaves prison to rise in the king's service (11).

This incident, which is treated very differently in the two tellings, is located at the center of the Qur'anic story. Its significance is also central to Qur'anic theology as a whole, illustrative of the intimate and constant relationship between the "instrumental" messenger and his God; the problematic struggle between human and/or Satanic action and Divine will, which is one of the Qur'an's most productive tensions or paradoxes; the twin human potential for understanding of God's will and for profound ignorance of it; and the process of revelation itself.

Throughout, the story emphasizes these key elements in the Qur'anic worldview. It is said to be related explicitly as a sign to all those who are able to understand (1). When Joseph relates his initial dream while tending his flocks, his father (who has a shrewd serenity unlike his frail and anxious biblical counterpart) warns him not to tell it to his brothers, lest Satan cause them to injure him (2). His father knows God's plan well enough to be able to explain to him that God will someday choose Joseph and give him the art of dream interpretation so that he can bring blessing to his family (the House of Jacob) just as God has helped Abraham and Isaac to do before (2). This is, by the way, the only allusion to genealogy in the story, but one which singles out certain figures as forming a chain of God's servants.

God is ever-present in the narrative, His cosmic omnipresence thus underscored. As the brothers put Joseph into the pit, God reveals to him that someday he will tell them what they have done (4). Even the brothers' jealousy is viewed as a sign (3). When the brothers bring back falsified evidence of what they have done, the father is suspicious and puts his trust in God, telling them that they have been tempted by "spirits." The travelers who find Joseph try to hide him, but the Qur'an reminds us that God knows what they are doing. After Joseph is established in the buyer's house, God reminds the listener again that He has established Joseph and is about to make him prosper according to His purposes. His linking His reward to Joseph with the reward He gives to *all* good-doers is yet another indication of the Qur'anic impulse to generalize its stories. The hiddenness of God's plan from most human beings is thereby transformed from a sign of His protectiveness over Israel to a sign of the willful ignorance of humankind. Joseph's spurning of the wife is taken as an indication of his being one of God's devoted servants, one who can be turned away from his natural but disreputable human proclivities. About to be imprisoned, perhaps (but not necessarily) because of the women's guile, Joseph tells God that he sees the prison of walls as preferable to the prison of wrong-doing, wishing not to be one of the ignorant. God supports him in his good intention and confirms it.[22]

On this level, the story gives a masterful account of the Qur'an's psychologically subtle understanding of the relationship between human will and God's power, a subtlety lost on many later theologians. When Joseph interprets the dreams of two youths imprisoned with him, he does so because they ask, associating his special abilities with his being a recognizable good-doer. A small but interesting difference from the biblical account occurs at this point: in the Bible, the butler who was to remember Joseph after prison just forgets; his youthful counterpart in the Qur'an, whose occupation is characteristically unspecified, is made to forget by Satan (9).

When Joseph is about to do the interpretation, he uses the forthcoming demonstration of his God-given ability as an occasion to sermonize about *tawḥīd* and *shirk*, as well as to link the worship of the one God with the tradition of his ancestors—Abraham, Isaac, and Jacob. Once again, when the brothers return home from seeing Joseph the first time, having been instructed by him to bring back a certain, unnamed brother, the father is suspicious until he sees a sign from Joseph. He, too, uses this as an occasion to sermonize on God's power, urging his sons to put their trust in Him and underscoring his own similarity to Joseph (13). Jacob then tells them how to enter Joseph's house. Although his intention in so doing is left unclear, we are again reminded that the knowledge behind his request has been given to him by God.

When Joseph's brothers have returned to Egypt and he has revealed himself to them and had them bring father *and* mother (not just father as in the Torah), the circle of the story's structure is closed (prematurely for the Bible) by Joseph's summary of the key points of God's involvement in his life and his father's: God's giving him the initial dream, bringing him out of prison, and bringing his father out of the desert. Any troubles Joseph has had in his life, he attributes not to God but to Satan (18).

The Qur'an does not continue the story beyond this point, as does the Bible, to chronicle the rest of Joseph's life. It ends, rather, with a longish homily about the way in which such tales are signs of God's power and judgment as well as vehicles for revelation, just as are the messengers who bring (or live) them (19). The Qur'an is interested mainly in Joseph's role as exemplary God-fearing man and Messenger.

There, in Sūra 12:110ff., we are reminded by allusion that a salient feature in the lives of all messengers (especially Muhammad) was also exemplified in Joseph:

> Till, when the Messengers despaired, deeming they were counted liars, Our help came to them and whosoever We willed was delivered. Our might will never be turned back from the people of the sinners. In their stories is surely a lesson to men possessed of minds; it is not a tale forged, but a confirmation of what is before it, and a distinguishing of everything, and a guidance, and a mercy to a people who believe.[23]

At this point, the way in which the wife's story has been structured takes on a new dimension. Messengers who are clearly telling the truth, even according to some witnesses, can still suffer from being given the lie by the ignorant, a key point in the Qur'anic understanding of the challenge of messengership and the nature of faithlessness (*kufr*), and of the constant opposition of *taṣdīq* and *takdhīb* in the making of a messenger.

Thus does the story of Joseph show itself to be a vision rather than a version. And thus does it come to illustrate a number of truths, not just about messengers, but about all human beings in their relationship with God. Except for what God gives Joseph, and his own will to serve God, Joseph is not extraordinary. He even could be said to appear a bit wide-eyed and ingenuous, with the same natural human failings and God-given ability to correct them that even the errant wife and her cohort possess. Even his illustrious ancestry and genealogy are set into a universal context.

It is now possible to restate and answer the questions raised in the beginning: Is it helpful to think of the Qur'anic Joseph as a version of the biblical one? Not if it precludes us from also approaching both as equally "basic" variants of the same story whose real form logically can never exist apart from a given telling.

Is it necessary to be aware of the biblical story, or forms of it that might have been current in Muhammad's milieu, in order to understand the Qur'anic one? Not unless we are prepared to compare the two scriptures in order to discover the integrity of each. An affinity between the two exists only to an extent; formal similarities do not necessarily mean they tell the same story in a thematic, moral, or theological sense.

It is ironic that retrieving the integrity of the Qur'anic story seems to have required suspending the claim of each scripture to be telling the "real" Joseph story. Yet the concomitant awareness that each is equally "basic" may prepare the way for mutually sympathetic understanding.

Concerning exegesis, the sociologist Edward Shils has recently written,

> In the field of religious knowledge, the revisions of the understanding of the sacred text are not understood as innovations; they are byproducts of the quest for better understanding. The truth is already present in the sacred text and it is the task of the student to elicit it by interpretation. An innovation in interpretation does not imply an innovation in the sacred text; it is a better disclosure of what was already there.[24]

One of the remarkable characteristics of sacred texts (and one that they share with a very small body of secular literary compositions) is that, read either in a community of faith or in another admiring respectful context, they can prompt the reader to seek almost endlessly what Shils calls "a better disclosure of what was already there." But it is difficult to disclose what was already there if one concentrates on what was not.

Appendix

Steps in the Qur'anic and Biblical Joseph Narratives
Sūrat Yūsuf (Sūra 12) and Genesis 37-46

1. *Purpose for relating story explained—as a sign to be understood by those who can.*
Joseph, age seventeen, feeding flocks brings bad report of brothers to father, Jacob, who loves him best and makes him a special coat, leading to brothers' resentment; Joseph explains first dream to brothers, leading to further resentment.
2. *Joseph explains dream* [which parallels second biblical dream] *to father, who warns him not to relate it to brothers, lest Satan cause them to injure him; father explains that God will choose Joseph and give him the art of dream interpretation so he can bring blessing to his family, just as God had helped Abraham and Isaac to do before.*
Joseph explains second dream to brothers and father; sent to Shechem to check on brothers; follows them on to Dothan.
3. *Attention called to signs present in brothers' jealousy of Joseph and another brother and in their decision to kill him so as to concentrate father's attention on them.*
On seeing Joseph, brothers conspire to kill him.
4. *One brother mitigates punishment, suggesting that he will be picked up by traveller if left in pit instead of killed; brothers know father does not trust them with Joseph, but convince him to let Joseph go with them; brothers put Joseph in pit, where God reveals to him that someday he will make his brothers aware of what they have done.*
Joseph put into pit; Reuben mitigates punishment; Joseph sold to Ishmaelites' passing caravan.
5. *Brothers tell father that wolf has eaten Joseph, but he is suspicious of them.*
Jacob convinced by sons that Joseph has been eaten by a wild animal.
6. *Travellers find Joseph and take him, under God's watchful eye, selling him for a small price; buyer has his wife install Joseph in their house, perhaps to be adopted; God establishes Joseph and teaches him dream interpretation as a reward for his loyalty, keeping his purpose hidden from most.*
Joseph sold to Potiphar; long interpolation on Judah's marriages to Shua and Tamar; sin of Onan described; Joseph shown prospering through God, becoming Potiphar's overseer; described as very handsome.
7. *Wife of buyer solicits Joseph, closing him into her room with her; Joseph is inclined to yield to her until he sees God's signs not to; as he runs to the door, wife tears his shirt; her husband meets both of them at the door, disbelieving wife because Joseph's shirt is torn from behind, not in front; urges wife to ask God forgiveness for her lies; women of the city blame the wife in their gossip, but the wife contrives to show them how tempting Joseph's beauty really is; admits she solicited him but vows to have him imprisoned if she cannot have him; Joseph prays to God to save him from their guile.*

Joseph propositioned repeatedly by Potiphar's wife; his garment is left in her hand when he flees, she lies to her husband.

8. *Joseph imprisoned anyway, for unexplained reason.*

Joseph imprisoned, becoming overseer of prison through God.

9. *Joseph interprets dreams of one of two youths in prison as symbolizing the need to attest the unity of God, as Joseph's forefathers had done, delivering short sermon on the point; predicts two different fates for the two youths; asks the one who is to survive to remember him to the king, but Satan makes the youth forget.*

Butler and baker of Pharoah imprisoned under Joseph's overseership; Joseph interprets their dreams, saying "interpretations belong to God"; predicts their different fortunes and has his predictions fulfilled; butler, who survives, forgets Joseph.

10. *King tells dream which counsellors cannot interpret; telling jogs youth's memory of Joseph; asks Joseph's interpretation and carries it back to king; king summons Joseph, who sends king's messenger back with a request first to have king clear him with the women; wife confesses and attributes no responsibility for her actions to God.*

After two years, Pharoah dreams a disturbing dream, which jogs butler's memory of Joseph.

11. *Joseph brought to king and attached to him; God then establishes Joseph's success in the land.*

Joseph brought out of prison to interpret Pharoah's dream; Pharoah repeats dream, which Joseph interprets; Pharoah sees the spirit of God in Joseph's ability to do so; Joseph appointed prime minister, given a wife; at age thirty, he makes Egypt prosperous.

12. *Joseph's brothers come to Egypt asking for "merchandise" of some sort; Joseph asks them to bring "a certain brother" of his or he will not do what they want, but he puts the merchandise in their bags anyway.*

Jacob, seeing that there is food in Egypt, sends all his sons but Benjamin to Egypt, where they are recognized by Joseph and accused of being spies; Joseph asks them to leave Simeon and bring Benjamin; the brothers begin to connect their misfortune with their evil treatment of Joseph earlier; brothers are sent back with their own money in their sacks, which causes them to question God's intentions for them.

13. *On their return home, their father is suspicious again and afraid to entrust the "certain brother" to them, but convinced to do so when the merchandise is found in their bags; father sermonizes on God's power and gives instructions to the brothers how to enter Joseph's house when they return to it.*

Brothers repeat the whole story to Jacob, who refuses to send Benjamin back to Egypt; but when the famine worsens, he asks them to go back to Egypt; out of fear of Joseph, they refuse to return to Egypt unless they can bring Benjamin with them.

14. *As soon as the brothers arrive at Joseph's house, he reveals himself to the "certain brother."*

When Joseph sees all of his brothers, he orders them to dine with him; meanwhile, the brothers repeat their story to Joseph's steward, who reassures them; they are reunited with Simeon and return the money to Joseph, who asks after their family, giving Benjamin a much larger portion of food.

15. *Joseph gives brothers what they want, putting his goblet into the "certain brother's" bag; brothers accused of robbery by Joseph's servants; brothers promise whoever has the goblet will be the recompense; goblet found in the "certain brother's" bag; God has contrived all this for Joseph's sake; Joseph threatens brothers, who beg him to keep someone else; eldest son convinces his brothers to go home* [this return not made in the biblical version], *where their father insists they go back to seek news of Joseph.*

Joseph commands their sacks filled and their money returned again, putting his own goblet in Benjamin's sack; orders them followed and brought back; brothers repeat their whole story to captors; Joseph decides to send them back and keep Benjamin with him; Judah intervenes, repeating whole story from beginning to Joseph, letting him in on what Jacob has said.

16. *Brothers return to Joseph, who reveals himself to them; they admit sin but Joseph says God will forgive them.*

Joseph, overcome with emotion, sends out all except brothers, to whom he reveals himself, saying that God, not they, has sent him to Egypt for a larger purpose; it becomes known at court that his brothers have returned.

17. *Joseph sends them back for his father, bearing his shirt as proof; as father begins journey, he picks up Joseph's scent from the shirt and attests God's mercy.*

Pharoah has Joseph send for his father and all his people.

18. *Joseph embraces father and mother, raises them up, gives them security, saying this had been a fulfillment of the original dream he told his father; attests God's power over his life.*

Jacob agrees to return; journeys, reassured by conversations with God along the way; settled by Pharoah in Goshen.

19. *Story closes with reminder that it brings "tidings of the unseen," how one must never associate anything with God, how God always helps his messengers even when others turn away from them, explaining that such stories are a true guidance to those who believe.*

Story continues through Jacob's sojourn and death and through Joseph's death, with much genealogical material to maintain continuity with the overall biblical narrative.

NOTES

[1] This paper was originally printed in a slightly different form in *The Muslim World* 75:1 (1985): 1-16.

[2] It is only Genesis 37-46 that parallels the Qur'anic Joseph story. The Bible contains much more about Joseph than does the Qur'an, which concerns itself only with Joseph in Egypt.
[3] Stuart Lasine, "The Functions of Genesis 39 in the Joseph Narrative," unpublished paper (1982), 11-12.
[4] *Ibid.*, p. 12.
[5] Barbara Herrnstein Smith, "Narrative Versions, Narrative Theories," *Critical Inquiry* 7 (1980): 213-36.
[6] I am indebted to Jean Blacker-Knight of Kenyon College for this metaphor.
[7] Smith, "Narrative Versions," 221-22. Compare Robert Alter, *The Art of Biblical Narrative* (New York: Basic Books, 1981), 50.
[8] Parenthetical references are made to these numbers from p. 55 below on.
[9] Concerning the story as prophetic morale booster, oral communication from Mahmoud Ayoub, April 18, 1983; concerning Joseph's beauty, see Cornell Hugh Fleischer, "Gelibolulu Mustafa Ali Efendi, 1541-1600: A Study in Ottoman Historical Consciousness" (Ph.D. dissertation, Princeton University, 1982), 27; concerning Joseph and Zulaykha as lovers, see Robert Dankoff "The Lyric in the Romance: The Use of Ghazals in Persian and Turkish Masnavis," *Journal of Near Eastern Studies* 43:1 (1984): 18; and W. M. Thackston, Jr. tr., *The Tales of the Prophets of al-Kisa'i* (Library of Classical Arabic Literature, vol. 2; Boston: Twayne Publishers, 1978), 167-80; and concerning Zulaykha as symbol of human failings, see Jane I. Smith and Yvonne Y. Haddad, *The Islamic Understanding of Death and Resurrection* (Albany: State University of New York Press, 1981), 16. Joseph's "almost" yielding to the wife took on a different meaning as the concept of the prophets' being *ma'ṣūm* (protected from sin) crystallized.
[10] Alter, *The Art*, pp. 3-10, referring to Gen. 38.
[11] *Ibid.*, pp. 138, 140, and 153-54.
[12] *Ibid.*, p. 65.
[13] *Ibid.*, p. 67.
[14] *Ibid.*, p. 68.
[15] *Ibid.*,
[16] *Ibid.*, pp. 69-70.
[17] *Ibid.*, p. 87.
[18] Alter sees type-scenes as providing this ability to biblical authors.
[19] For a discussion of the usage of *nabī* and *rasūl* in the Qur'an, see Willem A. Bijlefeld, "A Prophet and More Than a Prophet?" *The Muslim World* 59 (1969): 9-28.
[20] See Lasine, "The Functions," pp. 9-10, for another discussion of these differences.
[21] The inclusion of details known to have existed in other Joseph stories without explaining them thoroughly has a number of possible explanations, among which is the idea that the listener did not require explanation or was so familiar with various possible details of the story that they could be used without explanation. It could also be argued that the failure to explain and name reinforces the Qur'an's claim to be telling the "real" story, stripped of its particularistic associations.

[22] In the Qur'an as a whole, being hidden and being ungrateful and being unfaithful are semantically linked. See Marilyn Robinson Waldman, "The Concept of *Kufr* in the Qur'an," *Journal of the American Oriental Society* 88 (1965): 442-55.

[23] Qur'an 12:110ff. Arthur J. Arberry, tr., *The Koran Interpreted* (London: Oxford University Press, 1964), 238.

[24] Edward Shils, *Tradition* (Chicago: The University of Chicago Press, 1981), 8.

Part Two:

Religion and Law

An Islamic Decalogue

William M. Brinner

Within the context of what is usually called Judaeo-Christian civilization, it is almost a commonplace expectation that any religious tradition possesses, or should possess, a basic set of moral principles similar to the Ten Commandments, or Decalogue, of the Hebrew scriptures. In his book *The Religions of Man*, Huston Smith says: "It is through the Ten Commandments that Hebraic morality has made its greatest impact upon the world. Taken over by Christianity and Islam, the Ten Commandments constitute the moral foundation of half the world's present population."[1] While we assume that Smith's statement is true regarding Christianity, at least part of the second sentence quoted above raises questions, the responses to which can lead to some interesting ideas about the development of Islamic religious history. We are actually asking two rather distinct, but perhaps connected, questions in response to Smith's assumption that the biblical Ten Commandments were "taken over" by Islam:

1) Are the Ten Commandments of the Bible actually known in Islam? If we grant that they were "taken over" by Christianity, was this also the case with Islam? Did Islam borrow, appropriate, or otherwise "take over" the Ten Commandments? If so, how and where are they presented?

2) Does Islam have its own indigenous equivalent of the Ten Commandments? If so, in what context does it appear, and where does it resemble the biblical version or differ from it?

To begin with, it is important to avoid the rather obvious pitfall (often met when comparing religious traditions, but especially when dealing with Islam) of ascribing origins or finding borrowings. It is important to raise this point because Islam—unlike Christianity, which has always avowed its Jewish origins—does not acknowledge a debt to the Jewish tradition, whatever the tempting similarities may be. If anything, these similarities are often not so much an actual borrowing from the Jewish tradition as a response to it and to the long Jewish presence in Arabia. Islam certainly acknowledges the fact of this presence, beginning with the Qur'an, a considerable portion of which consists of exhortations and condemnations addressed directly to the Children of Israel.[2] But this acknowledgment is evidenced most strongly in the many traditions which are preserved about the prophets of the Hebrew Bible or—to put it better—those figures in Jewish sacred history who are called prophets or messengers in the Qur'an.[3]

Among these, no doubt the two most prominently mentioned and of greatest significance to the prophetic mission of Muhammad are Abraham and Moses. Abraham has been taken over—in a sense—by Islam; that is, he is portrayed neither as Jew nor Christian but as one submissive (i.e., *muslim*) to Allah, whose religious teachings Islam is renewing. Moses, on the other hand, is presented as the true messenger and prophet of the religion which Judaism should have become, and would have become had it not been for the deviations and falsifications introduced into his teaching by the Rabbis[4]—just as Christianity is a deviation from the teachings of another prophet, the Word of Allah, Jesus.

While Jesus remains a rather shadowy figure in the Qur'an and in later Islamic literature (attention being centered on his birth, identity, and death), Moses and his life experiences play an important role. Here is a figure whose career as a messenger of God, a lawgiver, and a leader of his community most closely parallels and foreshadows that of Muhammad. This context must be kept in mind when we examine the first question posed above, whether Islam knows the Ten Commandments of the Bible.

The response to this question begins with a reference to the divine source of Islam, the Qur'an, and specifically to Sūra 7, *al-A'rāf* (The Heights), where Allah speaks to Moses on Mount Sinai and says:

> O Moses! I have preferred you above mankind by My messages and by My speaking (to you). So hold that which I have given you, and be among the thankful. And We wrote for him, upon the tablets, the lesson, to be drawn from all things, then (commanded him): Hold it fast, and command your people (saying): Take the better (course) therein. I shall show you the abode of the evil-livers.[5]

Although the tablets are mentioned here, there is no account of the lesson or explanation written upon them. In Sūra 17, known either as *Banū Isrā'īl* (Children of Israel) or as *al-Isrā'* (The Night Journey), there is another rather veiled statement:

> And We gave to Moses nine tokens (*āyāt*), clear proofs (of Allah's sovereignty). Do not ask the Children of Israel how he came to them, then Pharaoh said to him: I consider you are bewitched, O Moses.[6]

Although the latter passage seems to point to the ten (here nine) plagues rather than the Ten Commandments, especially within the context of this sūra, commentators have confused the two passages. A *ḥadīth* relates that when a Jew came to the Prophet Muhammad and asked him about the nine clear signs or wonders which appeared by the hand of Moses, he said:

> Do not associate anything with Allah.[7]
> Do not steal.[8]
> Do not commit fornication.[9]
> Do not kill anyone without a just cause whom Allah has declared inviolate.[10]
> Do not bring an innocent person before a ruler in order that he may put him to death.[11]
> Do not use magic.[12]
> Do not devour usury.[13]
> Do not slander a chaste woman.[14]

> Do not turn in flight on the day the army marches.[15]
> And a matter which affects you Jews particularly, do not break the Sabbath.[16]

'Abd al-Ḥaqq remarks concerning this tradition that whereas the Jew asked about the nine tokens or signs of Egypt, the Prophet recited to him the Ten Commandments.[17]

The Qur'anic passages cited previously, as well as this commentary, make it clear that Islam has no definite concept of the Ten Commandments, although five of the above are more or less faithful to the biblical version. Another important Muslim source in which the Ten Commandments are treated—given in full, in fact—is the semipopular genre of religious literature known as *Qiṣaṣ al-Anbiyā'* or Tales of the Prophets.[18] The collection of such tales by al-Tha'labī contains an entire chapter, which is translated here, devoted to the Ten Words or Decalogue:

> Chapter concerning the text of the Ten Words which Allah wrote for His Prophet and His Sincere Friend on the tablets, which is the main portion of the Torah on which all divine law centers.
> It consists of:
> In the name of Allah the Compassionate, the Merciful. This is a book from Allah, the all-powerful King, the Mighty, the Subduer, to his servant and Messenger Moses b. Amram. May I be Praised and Sanctified, there is no God but I.
> 1) Worship Me and associate nothing with Me and be grateful to Me and to your parents. Destiny is Mine and I shall make you live a good life.[19]
> 2) Do not kill the soul that Allah has forbidden you or I will make strait for you Heaven and its environs as well as the Earth and its expanses.[20]
> 3) Do not swear falsely by My name, for I shall not purify or exculpate whoever does not glorify My name.[21]
> 4) Do not bear witness by what your hearing does not perceive, nor your eyes see, nor your heart instruct you, for I shall call the attention of those who bear witness to their witnessing on the Day of Resurrection and I shall ask them about it.[22]
> 5) Do not envy people because of My graciousness and sustenance which reaches them, for the envier is an enemy to My favor, is displeased with My allotment.[23]
> 6) Do not fornicate.[24]
> 7) Do not steal, for I shall veil My face from you and lock the gates of Heaven against your prayers.[25]

> 8) Do not sacrifice to any but Me, for the sacrifice of mankind shall ascend to Me only if My name is mentioned over it.[26]
> 9) Do not commit adultery with your neighbor's wife for that is most abominable to Me.[27]
> 10) Love for people what you love for yourself and dislike for them what you dislike for yourself.[28]
> This is the text of the Ten Words.

As in the previous instance quoted from the *Ḥadīth*, there are obvious parallels with the text of the biblical Ten Commandments, but there are significant deviations as well. To begin with, each version contains nine negative commandments and only one positive one. The actual textual deviations are of interest as well, for example, the linking of worship of God alone and gratitude to Him and to one's parents. The version in the *Ḥadīth* contains four commandments regarding magic, interest, false accusation of adultery, and fleeing from battle, which are all found in the Bible but which are not part of the Hebrew Decalogue. The version from al-Tha'labī's *Qiṣaṣ al-Anbiyā'* parallels the biblical commandments more closely than does the one from the *ḥadīth*, but lacks two of the central positive ones regarding honoring one's parents (except for the passing reference noted above) and observing the Sabbath.

The answer to the first question posed above must therefore be that, while Islam knows of the Ten Commandments and has presented versions of the same in earlier and later traditions, it does not know the Ten Commandments as found in the biblical texts in Exodus and Deuteronomy, and has certainly not "taken them over."

The second question is a more problematic one, for the texts that will be brought as evidence have heretofore been treated quite differently by Muslim and Christian interpreters of Islam. In response to the query whether Islam has its own equivalent of the Decalogue, one may respond positively and point to two different but somewhat similar texts within the Qur'an. The reference is to verses in Sūra 17, *al-Isrā'* (The Night Journey) and Sūra 6, *al-An'ām* (Cattle), which will be quoted and discussed below. On the whole, Muslim scholars have paid no special attention to these passages aside from pointing to the moral principles involved and at times to their superiority to those found in Judaism and Christianity.[29] At least two Christian commentators have, however, taken these Qur'anic passages actually to represent versions of the biblical commandments.

Thomas P. Hughes, in his *Dictionary of Islam* (published in 1885), refers to these two texts and says:

> A comparison of the Ten Commandments given by the great Jewish law-giver with those recorded in the above tradition[s] . . . will show how imperfectly the Arabian Prophet was acquainted with the Old Testament Scriptures.[30]

This belittling comparison may be attributed to what are today fashionably known as "Orientalist" attitudes, especially given the period in which it was written. However, a more recent work, *Qur'an and Bible* by M. S. Seale (published in 1978), says:

> Scholars have not sufficiently taken note of the fact that the Qur'an provides a version of the Ten Commandments, even though an incomplete one. The principal omission is the commandment to observe the Sabbath as a day of rest, but, as this was meant for the Jews alone, the omission is hardly surprising. Another understandable omission is the biblical introduction to the Commandments: "I am the Lord your God who brought you out of Egypt, out of the land of slavery." Indeed, there is little emphasis in the Qur'an on the deliverance of the Hebrews from Egyptian bondage, an event given great prominence in the Bible. Nor do the Qur'anic commandments include the prohibition to take the Lord's name in vain or, in the words of the new English Bible, make "wrong use of the name of the Lord your God." To this day in the Middle East, the name of Allah is on every lip, in contexts sacred and profane.[31]

He then presents in tabular form the passage in Sūra 17 in Dawood's translation, listing nine commandments, and gives parallels from Exodus as well as an additional four parallel passages for the remaining commandments from various portions of Deuteronomy and Numbers.[32]

It seems more likely, however, that what we have in the two versions in the Qur'an is an *Islamic* decalogue, intended not as a representation of the biblical text but rather as a revelation of Allah to Muhammad within the context of Arabian society. This assertion is especially important when we see the references to the slaying of one's children (repeated elsewhere in the Qur'an), or the special form in which the prohibition of killing is made—both very specifically products of the Arabian society to which at least part of the Qur'an is directed.

It is tempting, however, to go beyond this simple assertion (which will be discussed in greater detail) and place the Islamic decalogue in a special relationship with events in the prophetic career of Muhammad the Messenger of Allah—events that clarify his relationship with previous prophets, especially with Moses. As we have seen, the career of Moses serves, together with Abraham's, as the biblical model closest to that of Muhammad, while both foreshadow aspects of Muhammad's life and thought. Throughout the Qur'an and the later traditions the ambivalent attitude of Islam toward Jews and Judaism becomes very apparent. In the Muslim accounts of Moses we find this ambivalence expressed quite clearly: great respect for this prophet and for his message, but a simultaneous condemnation of his community for its abandonment of his teachings. More than that, there is a triumphant note that proclaims: Moses was a great prophet, but Muhammad was greater; the community of Moses may have received its revelation earlier, but by falsifying and rejecting it they lost pride of place and primacy to the community of Muhammad.[33]

Nowhere is this polemical theme more forcefully expressed than in the comparison between the central events in the lives of the two prophets: their respective meetings with God. Indeed, in the Islamic account of the spiritual experience of Moses, his meeting with God and his speaking with Him *are* central; whereas in the Jewish tradition, although this experience is without any doubt important and valued, what becomes central is a tangible product of his meeting rather than the meeting itself. That is to say, the Ten Commandments, or Decalogue, which Moses brought down from Mount Sinai, symbolically become the great contribution of Moses to his people, just as a plastic representation of the two tablets on which the Decalogue is written becomes one of the major symbols of Judaism. This is in spite of the fact that in Exodus these ten statements are only the beginning of a long series of laws and statutes revealed by God to Israel. The account of Moses's ascent of Mount Sinai and his desire to see God face to face is recorded in Exodus 33:18-23, where Moses prays:

> "Oh, let me behold Your presence!" And He answered, "I will make all My goodness pass before you as I proclaim the name of the Lord before you; I will be gracious to whom I will be gracious, and show compassion to whom I will show compassion. But," He said, "you cannot see My face, for man may not see Me and live." And the Lord said, "See, there is a place near Me. Station yourself on the rock and, as My presence passes by, I will put you in a cleft of the rock and shield you with My hand until I have passed by. Then I will take My hand away and you will see My back; but My face must not be seen."

In the Qur'an we find this account in a somewhat different form in Sūra 7, *al-A'rāf* (The Heights):143-44:

> And when Moses came to Our appointed tryst and his Lord had spoken unto him, he said: My Lord! Show me Yourself, that I may gaze upon You. He said: You will not see Me, but gaze upon the mountain! If it stand still in its place, then you will see Me. And when his Lord revealed His glory to the mountain, He sent it crashing down. And Moses fell down senseless. And when he woke he said: Glory to You! I turn to You repentant, and I am the first of the believers.
> He said: O Moses! I have preferred you above mankind by My messages and by My speaking to you.

> So hold what I have given you, and be among the thankful.

While the biblical account continues here with the carving of the second set of tablets of the Law bearing the Decalogue, the Qur'an continues thus (as quoted previously):

> And We wrote for him upon the tablets the lesson to be drawn from all things, then said: Hold it fast, and command your people: Take the better course therein. I will show you the abode of evil-livers.
> I shall turn away from My revelations those who magnify themselves wrongfully in the Earth . . .

Here no mention of an explicit kind is made of the Ten Commandments, only the general statement that what the tablets contain is "the lesson to be drawn from all things," whereas in the biblical account, after God passes by Moses, God commands him to make two tablets upon which He writes "the words which were in the first tablets, which you broke." Then God appears with Moses on the mountain in the midst of a cloud, passing before him and proclaiming what are known in Judaism as the Thirteen Attributes. A new covenant is made, confirming and expanding the one made centuries earlier with Abraham.

If we look for an Islamic equivalent of this experience, for a case in which Muhammad meets with God (one might almost say) face to face, we find only hints and allusions in the Qur'an. In the *Sīra*, or biography of the prophet, and in the *tafsīr* (the literature of Qur'anic commentary), these hints and allusions are expanded and amplified into accounts which some—though not all—of the later commentators link to a single continuous experience. We are speaking, of course, of the *isrā'* or night journey, and the *mi'rāj* or ascension. Examples can be found in *Sīrat Rasūl Allāh* by Ibn Isḥāq[34] (704-767), as well as in later compilations, such as the one by al-Baghawī (d. 1117).[35]

Let us first of all examine the story of the *mi'rāj*, the ascension of Muhammad to Heaven, with its Qur'anic basis in Sūra 53, *al-Najm* (The Star) and its much greater expansion in the *sīra* and *tafsīr* literature. In the Qur'anic verses, after mentioning the first revelation on Mt. Ḥirā' when Muhammad saw the Angel Gabriel, we read:

> And verily we saw him yet another time
> By the *sidra*-tree of the utmost boundary
> Near which is the Garden of Abode
> When that which enshrouds did enshroud the *sidra*-tree
> The eye turned not aside nor yet was overbold
> Verily he saw one of the greater revelations of his Lord.[36]

In some of the traditional accounts which expand on this theme and give further details of the ascension, Muhammad is guided by Gabriel through the seven heavens, in each of which he is greeted by one of the major biblical prophets. In the sixth heaven he is greeted by Moses. Unlike the accounts regarding the other prophets, which relate that they greet Muhammad as a son (in the case of Adam and Abraham) or as a brother, in the case of Moses we are given additional detail and are told, in the aforementioned triumphant tone, that "When I (i.e., Muhammad) passed on he wept, and one asked him why he wept. 'I weep,' said he, 'because of a youth (i.e., Muhammad) who has been sent after me, more of whose community will enter Paradise than my community.'"[37]

Beyond the seven heavens Muhammad goes on alone, entering the realm mentioned in the Qur'an in the passages cited above. There, in the presence of Allah's majesty, the religious duty of performing fifty prayer services daily is laid upon Muhammad and his community. It is significant again that Moses alone, of all the prophets, intervenes and sends Muhammad back time and again to have the number reduced—ultimately to the five prayers, which have been incumbent upon Muslims ever since. In addition, the concluding verses of Sūra 2, *al-Baqara* (The Cow) are revealed to Muhammad here, as is the assurance of pardon for anyone of his community who refrains from ascribing a partner to Allah. Each time Moses, basing his statement on his experience with his own people, says: "Prayer is a weighty matter and your people are weak, so go back to your Lord and ask Him to reduce the number for you and your community."

When God finally agrees to the five daily prayers (which, when performed in faith and trust and proper intention, would have the reward of fifty prayers), it is clearly one of the special acts of grace which God bestows upon Islam in lightening for believers those burdens which had been placed upon the Children of Israel. We also see this in regard to the laws of food, of the Sabbath, and the like.[38]

In the accretion of tales surrounding this event, Muhammad is taken into the very presence of Allah's majesty, where even Gabriel cannot accompany him. By transferring his sight from his eyes to his heart, he can look upon God's majesty without becoming blind. When Muhammad is able to speak to Allah to make a request of Him, he says (according to al-Suyūṭī): "O Lord, You took Abraham as a friend, You spoke with Moses face to face, You raised Enoch (Idrīs) to a high place, You gave Solomon a kingdom such as none after him might attain, and gave to David a psalter. What then is there for me, O Lord?"[39]

Allah answers him by saying: "O Muhammad, I take you as a friend just as I took Abraham, I am speaking to you just as I spoke to Moses face to face." But then Allah continues by mentioning these other special favors: (1) the sūra *al-Fātiḥa* (the opening of the Qur'an) and the closing verses of *al-Baqara* (The Cow)—both of which are of the treasuries of His throne; (2) a mission to the white, red, and black folk of the Earth, to jinn and to men—such as was given to no prophet before him; (3) the dry land and the seas—the entire Earth—appointed for Muhammad and his community as a place for purification and worship; (4) the right to booty, given to no other previous community; (5) aid in conquest by means of such terrors as will make enemies flee while (the Muslims) are still a month away; (6) the master of all the books and their guardian, the Qur'an; and finally (7) the exaltation of Muhammad's name exalted so that none of the regulations of God's religion will ever be mentioned without Muhammad's name being joined with Allah's.[40]

However, one aspect of comparison between the experience of Muhammad and that of Moses seems to be missing—not only an explicit reference to the Mosaic Decalogue, as indicated above, but to an Islamic equivalent, an actual brief summation of the essential moral and ethical commands that would be a guide to the faithful. Or is it missing?

While studying the seventeenth sūra which, as we have seen, is variously known as the Children of Israel or the Night Journey, the miraculous event mentioned in the sūra's first verse, it became apparent that here we do indeed have a close Islamic parallel that seems to have gone unnoticed. The very context is special—the journey by night from the sacred place of worship to the far-distant place of worship, understood by most later Muslim commentators to refer to Mecca and Jerusalem respectively. As noted previously, though not explicitly mentioned here, the *mi'rāj* or ascension through the heavens is connected with this event by most commentators.

After the somewhat enigmatic opening verse referring to the night journey, there follow twenty verses, beginning (significantly, we would say, since they seem to tie this experience to precisely what we have been describing) with the words: "We gave unto Moses the Scripture, and We appointed it a guidance for the Children of Israel, saying: Choose no guardian beside Me."

This reference to what might be interpreted as the beginning of the Mosaic Decalogue is followed by a definition of the Children of Israel as "The seed of those whom We carried along with Noah. Lo, he was a grateful worshipper."

A summation of the events in early Jewish history is then given in verses 4-8, ending with a reference to the punishment which the Israelites suffered for not hearkening to the commandments:

> We sent against you Our servants to ravage you, and to enter the Temple even as they entered it the first time, and to lay waste all that they conquered with an utter wasting. It may be that your Lord will have mercy on you, but if you repeat (the crime), We shall repeat (the punishment), and We have appointed Hell a dungeon for the disbelievers.[41]

Attention turns now to the role of the Qur'an as guidance and tidings to all mankind, admonishing them to heed its words, to believe in the hereafter, and to know that each man's account will be brought forth on the Day of Resurrection. The process of divine punishment is outlined:

> No laden soul can bear another's load, We never punish until We have sent a messenger. And when We would destroy a township, We send commandments to its folk who live at ease, and afterward they commit abomination therein, and so the Word of

> Doom has effect for it, and We annihilate it completely.[42]

This section ends with verses 19-21, which make it clear that Allah prefers mankind to choose the hereafter rather than the punishment of hell. There then follow verses 22-39, containing material that can be seen as equivalent to a Muslim decalogue, commandments of a moral and ethical nature parallel in many cases either to the biblical Decalogue or to the commands that follow almost immediately thereafter in chapters 21 and 22 of Exodus. In no case do they simply imitate the Bible. The wording and tenor of the Qur'anic commandments present a uniquely Muslim set of universal values.

Below are the following sixteen verses of *Sūrat al-Isrā'* in the form of a decalogue, showing parallels where they exist. Whether there are, indeed, ten or only eight significant commandments is not the issue here. It is, we believe, significant that this essence of Islamic ethics is repeated (just as the Decalogue of Exodus is repeated in Deuteronomy), albeit in a shorter form, in Sūra 6, *al-An'ām* (Cattle).[43] This is presented with considerable trepidation since it is clear that this is a personal interpretation of a sacred text which Muslims have not understood in the same way.[44] However, there seems to be some merit in this exercise in terms both of a study of the development of Islam and of presenting the teaching of Islam to non-Muslims.

I. Verse 22:

> Set not up with Allah another god, or you will sit condemned and forsaken.[45]

This would be the equivalent of what is counted as the third commandment in Jewish tradition, beginning with Exodus 20:4:

> You shall not make for yourself a sculptured image, or any likeness of what is in the heavens above, or on the Earth below, or in the waters under the Earth. You shall not bow down to them or serve them. For I the Lord your God am an impassioned God, visiting the guilt of the fathers upon the children, upon the third and upon the fourth generations of those who reject Me, but showing kindness to the thousandth generation of those who love Me and keep My commandments.

II. Verse 23 begins with what is clearly a continuation of the previous commandment:

> The Lord has decreed you shall not serve any but Him.

These words echo the second commandment in the Bible, Exodus 20:3:

> You shall have no other god beside Me.

These Qur'anic words are followed immediately by a second commandment—so abruptly that most Muslim commentators insert here some connecting words.

> And (that you) show kindness to parents, whether one or both of them attains old age with you; say not to them "Fie," neither chide them, but speak unto them words respectful, and lower to them the wing of humbleness out of mercy and say, "My Lord, have mercy upon them as they raised me up when I was little." Your Lord knows very well what is in your hearts if you are righteous, for He is All-forgiving to those who are penitent (23-25).

For all the difference in tone and rationalization, this commandment parallels the fifth biblical command, verse 12:

> Honor your father and your mother, that you may long endure on the land which the Lord your God is giving you.

III. Verses 26-30:

> And give the kinsman his due, and the needy, and the traveler; and never squander; the squanderers are the brothers of Satan, and Satan is ungrateful to his Lord. But if you turn from them, seeking mercy from your Lord that you hope for, then speak to them gentle words. And keep not your hand chained to your neck, nor open it completely, or you will sit reproached and denuded. Surely your Lord outspreads and straitens His provision to whom He will; surely He is aware of and sees His servants.

The form and content of this command seem to arise from the Arabian reality of Muhammad's time, where the ideal of *muruwwa*, or manliness, might involve ostentatious generosity that could lead to the giver's impoverishment. While there is no exact biblical parallel to these commands regarding the kinsman, the needy, and the traveler with its motif of being neither a miser nor a spendthrift, the idea of the correct treatment of others is found in Exodus 22:20-26:

> You shall not wrong a stranger nor oppress him, for you were strangers in the land of Egypt, You shall not mistreat any widow or orphan. If you do mistreat them, I will hear their outcry as soon as they cry out to Me, and My anger shall blast forth and I will put you to the sword and your wives shall become widows and your children orphans. If you lend money to My people, to the poor who is in your

> power, do not act towards him as a creditor; exact no interest from him. If you take your neighbor's garment in pledge, you must return it to him before the sun sets; it is his only clothing, the sole covering for his skin. In what else shall he sleep? Therefore, if he cries out to Me, I will pay heed, for I am compassionate.

Perhaps a closer parallel is found after the repetition of the Decalogue in Deuteronomy 15:7-11, in discussing the remission of debts in the seventh year.

> If, however, there is a needy person among you, one of your kinsmen in any of your settlements in the land that the Lord your God is giving you, do not harden your heart and shut your hand against your needy kinsman. Rather, you must open your hand and lend him sufficient for whatever he needs. . . . For there will never cease to be needy ones in your land, which is why I command you: Open your hand to the poor and needy kinsman in your land.

IV. Verse 31:

> And slay not your children for fear of poverty; We will provide for you and for them; surely the slaying of them is a grievous sin.

Again there is no parallel to this Arabian situation in the biblical text except in the entirely different context of the prohibition of sacrificing one's chidlren to Molech, the Canaanite deity whose cult involved such offerings. In Leviticus 18:21 we find:

> Do not allow any of your offspring to be offered up to Molech, and do not profane the name of your God; I am the Lord.

This is, rather, connected with the prohibition to be found in Sūra 6, *al-An'ām*, verse 151 (to which we will return later), which says:

> . . . and that you slay not your children because of poverty; we will provide for you and them.

Both occurrences are usually connected with the pre-Islamic practice of female infanticide in Arabia.[46]

V. Verse 32:

> And approach not fornication; surely it is an indecency, and evil as a way.

The biblical injunction, the seventh commandment, is very brief and deals with a specific form of fornication, adultery:[47]

> You shall not commit adultery.

VI. Verse 33:

> And slay not the soul Allah has forbidden, except by right. Whosoever is slain unjustly, We have appointed to his next-of-kin authority; but let him not exceed in slaying; he shall be helped.

The biblical injunction—the sixth commandment—is unequivocal:

> You shall not commit murder.

However, there are laws throughout the text which impose the death penalty for certain sins and crimes. Clearly this is the type of situation involved here, together with the ancient conception of blood vengeance by relatives for those killed unjustly—a concept not unknown in the Hebrew Bible as well. An injunction close to the Qur'anic one is found in Exodus 23:7:

> Do not bring death upon the innocent and righteous, for I will not acquit the wrongdoer.

VII. Verse 34:

> And do not approach the property of the orphan save in the fairest manner, until he is of age. And fulfill the covenant; surely the covenant shall be questioned of.

We have already quoted in a different context Exodus 22:21:

> You shall not mistreat any widow or orphan . . .

Although there are many other such statements throughout the Bible, little more specific is said in any of them.

VIII. Verse 35:

> And fill up the measure when you measure, and weigh with the straight balance; that is better and fairer in the outcome.

The biblical equivalent is found in a list of commandments in the Holiness Code of Leviticus 19:35:

> You shall not falsify measures of length, weight, or capacity. You shall have an honest balance, honest weights, an honest *ephah*, and honest *hin*.

IX. Verse 36:

> And do not pursue what you have no knowledge of; the hearing, the sight, the heart—all of these shall be questioned of.

Although the ninth commandment in the Bible, "You shall not bear false witness against your neighbor," condemns speaking falsely, that is clearly not what is meant here and thus it has no real parallel.

X. Verses 37-38:

> And walk not in the Earth exultantly; certainly you will never tear the Earth open, nor attain the mountains in height. All of that—the wickedness of it is hateful in the sight of thy Lord.

This may parallel Deuteronomy 8:14: "Do not become proud and forget the Lord your God."[48] The prayer of Hannah in I Samuel 2:3, however, puts the biblical attitude beautifully:

> Talk no more with lofty pride, let no arrogance cross your lips! For the Lord is an all-knowing God; by Him actions are measured.

It is also reminiscent of the summation of God's moral commandments in Micah 6:8:

> It has been told you, O man, what is good, and what the Lord requries of you. Only to do justly, to have mercy, and to walk humbly with your God.

This section of Sūra 17 ends with the following in verse 39:

> That is of the wisdom your Lord has revealed to thee; set up not with God another god, or you will be cast into Hell, reproached and rejected.

The remainder of this remarkable sūra—from verse 40 to the final verse 111, with the possible exception of verses 76-82, which many Qur'an commentators date to a later, Madīnan period—consists of a direct confrontation with the unbelievers of Mecca to whom this revelation was first preached, refuting the charges and arguments made against Muhammad and the message which he brought. Verse 60[49] is interpreted as a reference to the ascension, and indicates that those who first heard of this event refused to accept the truth of it. This sūra mentions not only opposition to Muhammad by his fellow townspeople, but also their efforts at tempting him to compromise his beliefs and modify his message to accept at least part of their pagan ideas. Muhammad is encouraged to remain steadfast and strong in resisting their blandishments and in proclaiming the miracle of the Qur'an.

A shorter form of these basic commandments of Islam is to be found in Sūra 6, *al-An'ām*, verses 152-54. It may be noted that the order followed here is the same as the order in the longer version just quoted.

> Say: Come, I will recite to you that which your Lord has made a sacred duty for you: (1) that you ascribe no thing as a partner to Him and (2) that you do good to parents, and (3) that you slay not your children

> because of poverty—we provide for you and for them—and (4) that you do not draw nigh to lewd things whether open or concealed. And (5) that you slay not the life that Allah has forbidden, except by right. That then he has charged you with; perhaps you will understand. And (6) that you not approach the property of the orphan, except in the fairer manner, until he is of age. And (7) fill up the measure and the balance with justice. We charge not any soul save to its capacity. (8) And when you speak, be just, even if it should be to a near kinsman. (9) And fulfill God's covenant. That then He has charged you with; perhaps you will remember. (10) And: This is my straight path, so follow it. Follow not other ways, lest you be parted from His way. This has He ordained for you, that you may ward off (evil).[50]

This version, shorter in verses and words but seeming to contain ten injunctions, is then followed by the very important statements in verses 155-56:

> Again, We gave the Scripture unto Moses, complete for him who would do good, an explanation of all things, a guidance and a mercy, that they might believe in the meeting with their Lord. And this is a blessed Scripture which we have revealed. So follow it and ward off (evil), that you may find mercy.

Once again the revelation to Moses and the one to Muhammad are placed in juxtaposition. Given all the great differences that the almost 2,000 years between these two figures has brought into the religious experience of mankind, it is striking to witness the similarity of the basic moral and ethical code.

What makes this even more striking is the juxtaposition of the experience of Moses with that of Muhammad while providing a context for the act of revelation of the code. As has been noted before, the many varying interpretations by Muslim scholars of the *isrā'* and of the *mi'rāj* make it all but impossible to tie these events in the prophet's life directly to the moral codes which have been discussed—especially to the earlier version discussed in *Sūrat al-Isrā'*. What I have attempted is to draw attention to the existence of this code within the framework of the sūra as a whole, and in the context of the rivalry for precedence between Moses and Muhammad. Here there is a dual conclusion: that there is an Islamic moral code similar to the biblical Decalogue but differing in significant details, and that just as the revelation of the Ten Commandments falls within the framework of the meeting between Moses and God, so the Qur'anic "decalogue" is placed within the context of the ascension of Muhammad and in close connection with it.

NOTES

1 Huston Smith, *The Religions of Man* (New York: Harper and Row, 1958), 239.
2 See, for example, Sūra 2 with its repetition of "O Children of Israel . . .," followed by such exhortations, e.g., verse 40 ff., 47 ff., 122 ff., or the same sūra with other references to the Israelites, e.g. v. 83 ff., 211, 246 ff.
3 The reference here is to the type of tradition known as *Isrā'īliyyāt*, or "of Israelite origin," primarily found in the tales of biblical figures encountered in the Qur'an and in later Muslim tradition. See the article "Isrā'īliyyāt" in the *Encyclopedia of Islam*, new ed. (Leiden: E. J. Brill, 1960), 4:211-12 (henceforth cited as *EI*).
4 See, for example, a modern reverberation of this idea in the contrast between Mosaic religion and Judaism in the book *The Isrā'īliyyāt in the Intellectual Struggle* by the Egyptian writer 'Ā'isha 'Abd al-Raḥman (pseud. Bint al-Shāṭi'), quoted in W. M. Brinner, "An Egyptian Anti-Orientalist," in G. R. Warburg and U. M. Kupferschmidt, eds., *Islam, Nationalism, and Radicalism in Egypt and the Sudan* (New York: Praeger, 1983), 243-44.
5 Qur'an 7:144-45. Qur'anic citations are taken from M. M. Pickthall, *The Meaning of the Glorious Koran* (London: Allen & Unwin, 1930), occasionally altered slightly.
6 Qur'an 17:101.
7 The biblical Decalogue has: "You shall have no other gods beside Me," Ex. 20:3; Deut. 5:7, traditionally taken as the second commandment by Jews. Cf. *Encyclopedia Judaica*, 16 vols. (Jerusalem: Keter Press, 1971), 5:1442 (henceforth cited as *EJ*).
8 The eighth commandment in the Bible, Ex. 20:2; Deut. 5:17.
9 Cf. Ex. 20:13; Deut. 5:17. Although the Muslim version uses the verb *znh*, "to fornicate," the Bible has the Hebrew verb *n'f*, which refers specifically to adultery, i.e., fornication with a woman married to another.
10 Ex. 20:13; Deut. 5:17. Cf. with the Muslim limitations "without a just cause," as here, or "the soul that Allah has forbidden you" in the version cited below.
11 Possibly related to the concept of prohibiting false witness, as in Ex. 20:13; Deut. 5:17. But see also Ex. 23:1, which has the general injunction, "You shall not utter a false report: put not your hand with the wicked to be an unrighteous witness."
12 Not in the Bible, but see Deut. 18:10-11 prohibiting one "that uses divination, a soothsayer, or an enchanter, or a sorcerer, or a charmer, or one that consults a ghost or a familiar spirit, or a necromancer." Cf. also Ex. 22:17, "You shall not let a sorceress live." See *EJ* 11:703.
13 Not found in the biblical Decalogue but prohibited in Ex. 22:24; Lev. 25: 36-37; Deut. 20-21.

[14] The closest biblical parallel is Deut. 22:13-19, which specifically prohibits the unjust slander of a virgin and prescribes the punishment. See also note 11 above.

[15] There is no specific biblical commandment to this effect. Deut. 20:1-9, however, after urging the people not to be afraid and to put their trust in God, provides the possibility of leaving the front for those who have a valid reason not to risk death in battle (one who has built a new house but has not yet lived in it; has planted a new vineyard but has not eaten of its fruit; has betrothed a woman but has not yet cohabited with her). Verse 8 says, "And the officers shall speak further to the people, and they shall say: What man is fearful and faint-hearted? Let him go and return unto his house . . ."

[16] The fourth commandment, cf. Ex. 20:8-11; Deut. 5:12-15. This version is found in al-Khaṭīb al-Tibrīzī (d. 1342), *Mishkāt al-Maṣābīḥ*, 2 vols. (n.c.: n.p., 1961), 1:62, translated in J. Robson, *Mishkat al-Masabih* , 4 vols (Lahore: Muhammad Ashraf, 1960), 1:18. According to this, when the Jew heard this he testified that Muhammad was a prophet, but would not do so publicly for fear that the Jews would kill him, *ibid.*, p. 19. This is followed by a version of ten sayings attributed to Muhammad on the authority of Mu'ādh, which include some of the Muslim ideas of the Ten Commandments and contain wide deviations as well.

[17] Cf. Thomas P. Hughes, *A Dictionary of Islam* (London: W. H. Allen & Co., 1885), p. 58.

[18] The two major collections of this type of tale are by the otherwise unknown al-Kisā'ī and the better-known al-Tha'labī (d. 1030). For the former see W. M. Thackston, Jr., *The Tales of the Prophets* (Boston: Twayne Publ., 1978). See the article "Ḳiṣaṣ al-Anbiyā'" in *EI* 5: 180-81.

[19] Equivalent to the second and fifth biblical commandments; see text below, p. 70.

[20] Cf. n. 10 above.

[21] Cf. n. 11 above.

[22] Cf. n. 11 above.

[23] The last two commandments of the biblical Decalogue deal with envy, or coveting what belongs to one's neighbor, cf. Ex. 20:14; Deut. 5:18.

[24] See the comments in n. 9 above and cf. n. 27 which indicates that a different sexual practice is intended here.

[25] Cf. n. 8 above.

[26] See the second biblical commandment; Ex. 20:5; Deut. 5:9, ". . . you shall not bow down to them or serve them," speaking of graven images of any god, or of any thing that is in heaven or on the Earth.

[27] Cf. nn. 9, 24 above.

[28] Not found in the biblical commandments, but echoes both the biblical injunction, "You shall love your neighbor as yourself," Lev. 19:18, as well as the famous saying of Hillel, "What is hateful to you, do not unto your neighbor," cf. *EJ*, 8:484. The text quoted here is from al-Tha'labī, *Qiṣaṣ al-Anbiyā' al-Musammā 'Arā'is al-Majālis* (Beirut: al-Maktaba al-Thaqafīya, n.d.), 180-81.

[29] See, for example, the modern Qur'an commentary by A. Yusuf Ali, *The Holy Qur'ān: Text, Translation, Commentary* (Lahore: Muhammad Ashraf, 1946), pp. 699-705.

[30] Hughes, *Dictionary of Islam*, p. 59.

[31] M. S. Seale, *Qur'an and Bible: Studies in Interpretation and Dialogue* (London: Croon Helm, 1978), 74.

[32] *Ibid.*, p. 75.

[33] See below, for example, p. 74, n. 37.

[34] *The Life of Muhammad,* a translation of Isḥāq's *Sīrat Rasūl Allāh*, with an introduction and notes by A. Guillaume (London: Oxford University Press, 1955).

[35] Al-Baghawī (d. 1117), *Maṣābīḥ al-Sunna, 2 vols.* (Cairo: Khairiya ed., 1900).

[36] Qur'an 53:13-18.

[37] Al-Baghawī, *Maṣābīḥ*, vol. 2:170.

[38] See Qur'an 6:146-47, where the food laws of Islam are compared with those of Judaism, the Jews being punished for their rebellion. Cf. also Qur'an 16:114-18. The institution of the Sabbath for the Jews is mentioned in the same sūra, 16:124.

[39] Al-Suyūṭī (d. 1505), *Al-La'ālī al-Maṣnū'a* (Cairo: n.p., 1899), 1:39.

[40] *Ibid.*

[41] Qur'an 17:7-8.

[42] Qur'an 7:15-16.

[43] This statement about repetition is based on the assumption made by most scholars that Sūra 17 is a middle Meccan sūra, while 6 is a late Meccan sūra. So in the Egyptian official text (17 is 50 and 6 is 55), Nöldeke (67 and 89 or 91), Grimme (82 and 89), but not Muir (87 and 81); cf. W. M. Watt, *Bell's Introduction to the Qur'an* (Edinburgh: University of Edinburgh Press, 1970), 206-07.

[44] The great Indian Muslim reformer Abu 'l-A'lā Maudūdī saw in these verses the basis of the "Islamic Order." For an elaboration of this idea see H. Enayat, *Modern Islamic Political Thought* (Austin: University of Texas Press, 1982), 105-07.

[45] Cf. n. 26 above.

[46] See also Qur'an 81:8-9.

[47] Cf. nn. 9, 24 above.

[48] Compare this with the biblical injunction (Num. 15:39), "That ye go not about after your own heart and your own eyes, after which ye used to go astray."

[49] "We appointed the vision which we showed thee as an ordeal for mankind."

[50] This final commandment seems to parallel and even explain verses 37-38 of Sūra 17. Compare with Num. 15:39-40: "And that you go not about after your own heart and your own eyes, after which ye use to go astray; that you may remember and do all My commandments and be holy unto your God." Cf. n. 48 above.

Supererogation in Jewish *Halakhah* and Islamic *Sharī'a*

Joshua Halberstam

"Jerusalem was destroyed because its inhabitants based their judgments on the Torah but did not act beyond the measure of the law."[1] Rabbi Joḥanan's pronouncement forcefully underscores the importance of acting beyond the letter of the law in suggesting that failure to do so can invite the most dire consequences.

Supererogatory acts, acts performed beyond the call of duty, are characterized as being both meritorious and optional. However, as evidenced by the above Talmudic dictum, the extent to which these acts are genuinely optional is problematic. Indeed, the status of this class of actions will be a problem for any system whose rules extend, at least in principle, to all spheres of human behavior. Jewish *Halakhah* and Islamic *Sharī'a* are examples *par excellence* of such total systems, for within them all actions—religious, political, social, and personal—can be judged as enjoined or discouraged by the divine source from which these rules are said to emanate. The problem can be posed as a dilemma: (1) either we recognize a realm of actions that is permitted but praiseworthy, in which case we seem to countenance value judgments which are arrived at independently of the legal code and thus must draw limits to the range of that code, or (2) we explicate the merit of these acts as subsumed by or derivative of explicit legal obligations in which case the distinction between duty and beyond duty is blurred. The first horn of this dilemma directs us to recognize an extralegal sphere of moral judgment, while the second rejects *sui generis* values outside the law.

An investigation of supererogatory acts reaches to the very foundations of such legal structures, as it must include consideration of the parameters of individual autonomy within the law, the relationship between law and morality, and the respective limits of each domain. Not surprisingly, the analysis of supererogation by Jewish and Islamic scholars provides a critical locus from which we can extrapolate their views on the larger matter of the nature of the divine law itself. And perhaps even less surprisingly, the variety in approaches these thinkers have pursued, both within and across these two traditions, reflects the complexities to which the question of supererogation gives rise.

We can explore the notion of supererogation from one of two routes, either as a problem arising from, but embedded within, some particular moral or legal schema or as a prior, distinct conceptual issue. In fact, a comprehensive investigation should pursue both approaches; accordingly, I will first examine the nature of supererogation as an independent moral issue and as reflected in current philosophical discussions. I then consider the treatment of supererogation in Jewish and Islamic law and note how each of these systems (re)defines the notion in its own terms. Finally, I draw some larger conclusions concerning the range and limits of these respective legal systems.

Supererogation and Morality

The Latin etymology of the term "supererogation" refers to paying out more than what is required, but the term has been employed primarily in religious and moral contexts, where it stands for doing more than is mandated by moral imperatives or religious legislation. The word appears once in the Vulgate with regard to the story of the Good Samaritan and has since been associated with saintly acts, acts of benificence, charity, and heroism. As we shall see, what sort of acts can correctly be identified as supererogatory turns on a more precise explication of the notion.

We speak of actions as being supererogatory but rarely of persons or their character traits, and then only derivatively. Therefore, the concept will have greater import in those moral theories in which duties are the primary units of the moral rules as compared with axiological theories, in which values rather than actions are central. In such axiological systems as that of Aristotle's in which virtue and not obligation is the fundamental moral feature, the notion of acts "beyond the call of duty" has no ready meaning and, indeed, the term does not appear in his ethical writings.

It is with regard to the two dominant contemporary moral theories, Kantian and utilitarian ethics, that supererogation has engaged increased philosophical attention. While consequentialist and deontological theories differ with respect to the role of motive and results in the formation of moral judgments, both theories emphasize actions as the basis of morality. In the classical statement of either theory, actions are understood to be obligatory, forbidden, or morally neutral. However, as J. O. Urmson points out in his seminal article "Saints and Heroes," any such threefold classification is inadequate, for it disregards a significant aspect of our moral life, i.e., acts which though nonobligatory are nonetheless praiseworthy.[2] These supererogatory acts, Urmson suggests, are typified by the behavior of saints and heroes, and though we may all aspire to their level we do not ordinarily blame anyone for failing to achieve this status.

Neither Kantian nor utilitarian morality can easily accommodate this class of actions, though for different, indeed, converse reasons. For Kant, an act attains its moral worth only if performed from a moral motive, that is, in order to fulfill one's duty. If supererogatory acts are beyond the class of duty but not duty proper, they cannot possess moral worth. For utilitarians, an act will be deemed obligatory only if it results (or tends to result, in the view of rule utilitarians) in greater positive utility, e.g., greater happiness than any alternative act one might do in the circumstance which obtains (including "acts of omission"). Inasmuch as supererogatory acts do have positive utility they should be obligatory for all and not "beyond" the call of duty. Thus for Kantian-like deontological theories, if supererogatory acts are nonobligatory, they cannot be morally meritorious, while for utilitarian-like consequentialist theories, if such acts are meritorious, they cannot be nonobligatory. Nevertheless, there does seem to be a straightforward rationale for judging someone who jumps on a live grenade in order to save the lives of others as having acted in an especially praiseworthy manner while at the same time not blaming others who did not do so.

Another way to formulate the issue is to stress the reasons for performing a supererogatory act: if an act is morally praiseworthy, then the reason for doing it must outweigh the reasons for not doing it; since, on balance, there exists a conclusive reason (or reasons) for committing the act, then one ought to do it, and if one fails to do what one ought to do, he is blameworthy. Therefore, there cannot be any morally good optional actions.[3]

Three different responses emerge to meet this challenge. Antisupererogationists or reductionists conclude that the notion of supererogation is indeed incompatible with their (favored) moral system and insist that a reification of such a class of actions is illegitimate. For example, in reaction to the Catholic practice of indulgences, which was based on the idea that the supererogatory merit of Jesus and the Saints was bequeathed to the Church for dispersal to sinners, Luther railed against the very idea of religious supererogation, arguing that man can be saved by the Grace of God alone and that even the sacrifices of the saints were not beyond the call of duty and were insufficient at that.[4] Similarly, some recent utilitarians and neo-Kantians have concluded that in fact there is no genuine distinct class of supererogatory acts.

Qualified supererogation is marked by the attempt to deny that supererogatory acts can be positioned outside the realm of obligatory acts, while allowing that these acts have morally relevant features which distinguish them from other explicit duties. So while supererogatory acts are interpreted as obligatory in some broader sense, the failure to perform them is construed as excusable and thus not blameworthy; given the inherent limitations of most of us, we cannot be expected always to act in the appropriate manner as the more saintly or heroic are prone to do. Both reductionists or antisupererogationists and qualified supererogationists wish to preserve an entailment between good and ought, but where the antisupererogationist concludes that no action can be both good and optional, the qualified view disagrees insofar as psychological or moral conditions prevent or limit our blaming their omission.

In the third view, unqualified supererogation, the claim that "*x* is good" is to be understood as entailing only that *x* is a good state-of-affairs and that *x* ought to be brought about, but not that any particular individual has some particular obligation to bring about this state-of-affairs; genuine obligations, on the other hand, do require that a specific duty obtain for a specific agent because of some specific relationship between the agent and the act in question.[5] In cases of supererogation, this relationship is absent and the "ought" here should be interpreted as being commendatory but not prescriptive.

Which view one espouses depends in part on how one defines supererogation. Because Jewish and Islamic legalists interpret supererogation in different ways, it will be helpful to spell out more carefully the constitutent features of this class of action as a background against which the Jewish and Islamic positions can be compared.

In its most encompassing definition an act is considered supererogatory if and only if[6] (1) it is neither obligatory nor forbidden; (2) its omission is not wrong and does not deserve moral condemnation; (3) it is morally good (insofar as it is performed with the intention of bringing about positive results and is beyond the call of duty); and (4) it is performed voluntarily for the sake of others.

Some brief comment about these stipulations is necessary. It will be noticed that the second condition is broader than the first and entails it. Indeed, some moral theorists reject (2) as too strong and submit that it is sufficient to regard an act as supererogatory if it is a "nonobligatory well-doing" and even if its omission does incur some degree of moral criticism. The third condition emphasizes that supererogatory acts are not morally neutral but possess positive moral worth. On a more inclusive reading, this moral goodness stems from two factors: the motive for its commission is the desire to bring about beneficial results; in being beyond the call of duty, it is connected to duty and has intrinsic value. Less inclusive formulations run the gamut: for some, one but not the other factor is necessary, or one but not the other is sufficient; in other formulations either is necessary, and in still others either is sufficient. The fourth condition stresses two salient characteristics of supererogation. First, unlike other duties, which can sometimes be discharged unknowingly or even against one's will—this is particularly true of some legal and religious duties—supererogatory acts are always performed voluntarily. Second, supererogatory acts are never self-serving but always other-regarding.

An interesting and relevant controversial matter is whether or not supererogation has a symmetrical class of actions on the negative side—acts which, while not forbidden, are nonetheless blameworthy. Roderick Chisholm labels these acts as "offensive." But to preserve this symmetry one must deny, as he does, the second condition in which optionality entails the absence of blameworthiness, and one must also somehow explain how some morally untoward behavior can, nonetheless, be genuinely permitted.[7]

What sort of behavior typifies supererogatory actions will depend on whether or not we accept all of the above conditions. For example, inasmuch as supererogatory acts must be beyond the call of duty, the mere manifestation of extraordinary courage or concern will not be enough to qualify as supererogatory. The doctor who tends to the plague-ridden within the domain of his assigned responsibility may exhibit unusual conscientiousness and courage but will, nonetheless, be merely fulfilling his duty. In contrast, the doctor who administers his care to the plague-ridden denizens of a town outside his sphere of responsibility is acting supererogatorily. Paradoxically, such small favors as providing a match to someone who requested one are acts beyond the call of duty and, on this ground, supererogatory—after all, we do not have a duty to perform favors, else they would not be deemed favors. Alternatively, we might deny that minor favors of this sort are genuinely supererogative, inasmuch as we do criticize those who rarely perform such acts (condition 2), because they do not involve any appreciable sacrifice (as some require for supererogation), or because we regard such minor actions as part of our binding social obligations. However, a number of less controversial acts do clearly meet the conditions postulated above; such acts include forgiveness, charity, volunteering, and perhaps mercy.

Whether supererogation forms a distinct category of moral action whose characteristics can be independently ascertained, whether it can successfully be absorbed into the various moral theories, its role and significance in our moral and social life are complex issues widely discussed in contemporary moral philosophy. While the brief overview of the matter presented above hardly reflects the intricacies involved, it does suggest some of the essential features of supererogation, whose analysis in Jewish and Islamic law we turn to now.

Supererogation in *Halakhah*

Jewish law clearly recognizes that mere overt fulfillment of the commandments does not exhaust the truly religious outlook. The manner in which the precepts are satisfied—the motive, intention, and attention that promote and accompany their performance, and the care taken not to violate them—all figure in the proper exercise of duty. This cluster of attitudinal factors, *hiddur mitzvah*, *kavvanah*, and being *maḥmir*, all attend proper compliance of explicit duties. But *Halakhah* also recognizes a class of actions that is not an accompaniment of some specific duty but is beyond the confines of the law; these supererogatory acts are designated as *lifnim mi-shurat ha-din*. However, no precise single definition of the notion or clear statement of the degree to which these acts are "beyond the call of duty" is readily forthcoming. Though the term appears with some frequency in the Talmud, it is employed in a variety of contexts, and later commentators offer a number of different expositions of the term. In order to gain some overview of these different rabbinical accounts, we can, as in our earlier discussion, distinguish broadly between reductionist views, which deny any genuinely extralegal status to supererogatory acts, and nonreductionist views, which do preserve an independent status for this category of behavior.

Reductionist Approaches

In this view, *lifnim mi-shurat ha-din* is considered a genuine obligation, albeit lacking the specific content of other determinate precepts. And since all obligations can be traced to a divine source, so too the prescriptive nature of *lifnim mi-shurat ha-din* is grounded in scripture. Thus, one primary rabbinic source is that submitted by Rabbi Eleazar of Modi'in, who expounds the biblical verse "And thou shalt show them the way wherein they must walk and the work they must do" as follows: "and the work" refers to *din*, law proper, "and they shall do" refers to *lifnim mi-shurat ha-din*, works beyond the call of duty.[8] Other commentators trace the obligation to act *lifnim mi-shurat ha-din* to other scriptural sources. Thus, Nahmanides says that if one restricts himself to fulfilling only the letter of the law he could be "a scoundrel with Torah license." In fact, one is obligated to transcend the *din* itself, and Nahmanides finds support for this in the biblical injunctions "And thou shalt do the right and the good," and "Ye shall be holy." The former obliges us to act *lifnim mi-shurat ha-din* with regard to interpersonal matters and the latter in personal affairs; both exhortations, he notes, are stated as broad-based principles of action, and neither is stated in the optative or indicative.[9]

The view that one has a genuine obligation to act beyond the measure of the law is manifested in a number of Talmudic discussions. The following exchange is often alluded to in support of this contention:

> Certain porters employed by Rabbah bar bar Ḥana broke one of his wine barrels, and in compensation he seized their cloaks. They complained to Rav, who in turn told Rabbah bar bar Ḥana to return the cloaks to their owners. "Is this the law" he asked? "Yes," replied Rav, as it is written, "That thou mayest walk in the way of good men." He then returned the clothes, whereupon they said to him, "We are poor and have labored all day, and now we are hungry and left with nothing." So Rav said (to Rabbah bar bar Ḥana), "Go and pay the wages." "Is this the law?" he asked. "Yes," he answered, (as it is written) "And keep the path of the righteous."[10]

From the strictly legal point of view, Rabbah bar bar Ḥana had acted within the law but was ordered to do otherwise—on the basis of the scriptural maxims to act in a manner consonant with higher degrees of probity and righteousness. Indeed, some later scholars as the Tosafist Rabbi Isaac of Corbeil, go so far as to include the obligation to perform supererogatory acts as one of the 613 biblical commandments.[11] And while other reductionists do not equate the obligation to perform acts *lifnim mi-shurat ha-din* on par with such other commandments as the duty to eat *matzah* or wear *tefillin* they nonetheless view these acts as part of the corpus of *Halakhah* and not extraneous to it, as integral to Jewish observance.

A somewhat different interpretation of *lifnim mi-shurat ha-din*, reductionist in orientation as well, pertains not to actions but to character development. In this view it is the inner life, which motivates outward performance, which is or should be the central concern of the law-abiding Jew. The tenth-century ethicist Baḥya ibn Paquda insists that proper intention must accompany all religious performances if they are to have genuine worth. All our actions, including the seemingly more prosaic ones, can be judged as proceeding or not proceeding from a motive of godliness.[12] Thus for Baḥya there do not seem to be any purely neutral voluntary actions. Moreover, the development of a higher state of religious consciousness is obligatory, and is, indeed, the fundamental obligation of observance; this idea is reflected in the title of his magnum opus, *The Duties of the Heart*. In the view espoused by Baḥya and adopted by a number of later Jewish ethicists, the individual is obligated to perfect his religious understanding and commitment. This orientation provides the meritoriousness of overt fulfillment of all duties. There is, therefore, no caesura between the dutiful and that which is beyond the dutiful. If, according to the reductionist view, supererogatory acts, acts *lifnim mi-shurat ha-din*, are obligatory, are they also actionable? Reductionists differ on this score, but support for mandating a legal sanction can be found in the Talmudic injunction *kofin 'al middot Sedom.*[13] Because offensive behavior, extreme exhibitions of obnoxious inconsiderateness in the "manner of Sodom," are anathema to the spirit of the law, *Halakhah* allows legal action to overturn such tendencies forcibly. Thus the realm of juridical sanction is not coextensive with the legal category of explicitly proscribed behavior.

If *lifnim mi-shurat ha-din* is a genuine obligation, how can it be construed as being "beyond the measure of the law?" If compulsory, how can this class of actions be distinguished from *din*, the law, proper?

One way to mark this distinction is to focus on the circumstances that attend the duty to act *lifnim mi-shurat ha-din.* Here we find, generally, greater flexibility in the means of executing aims, and, in addition, the specific features of the situation have greater weight in the determination of the proper response. A good example of this is the Talmudic report that in one instance Rav Nahman did not compel the finder of a lost object whose owner had despaired of recovery to return the object; legally, one is allowed to keep the object, but as a rule, Rav Nahman dictated its return on the grounds of *lifnim mi-shurat ha-din.* The Talmud explains the omission of such an order by noting the exceptional nature of the case, namely, that (perhaps) the finder was poor, while the object's owner was rich.[14] This sort of consideration clearly has no place in straightforward administration of law but is relevant in determining the compulsory nature of supererogation; *lifnim mi-shurat ha-din* is derived from more abstract biblical exhortations calling for elevated standards of behavior. *Din* proper is more contextually based in this way. Because the obligation to perform acts *lifnim mi-shurat ha-din* is derived from more abstract biblical exhortations calling for higher standards of behavior, its fulfillment, unlike some other non-supererogatory commands, must always be intentional.

The reductionist position distinguishes, finally, between *lifnim mi-shurat ha-din* and *din* proper; it nevertheless insists on its obligatory character. For this view recognizes no supralegal standard of merit but only that mandated by the *Halakhah.*

Nonreductionist Views

The dichotomy between reductionist and nonreductionist explications of supererogation is not nearly as sharp in Jewish legal theory as it is in moral theory. For even those who reject the need to posit a specific halakhic duty to each and every meritorious act maintain, nonetheless, that *Halakhah*, properly construed, provides the guiding principles and criteria for the determination of appropriate conduct. In fact, it would be nearer to the truth to characterize the halakhic realm as one of the qualified reductive theories rather than one of the nonreductive theories.

A clear line is drawn, however, between actions committed *lifnim mi-shurat ha-din* and *din* proper—the latter are enforceable and the former ideal. R. Simon b. Eliakim appeals to the necessity of this division in his response to R. Eleazar's decision that daughters be given maintenance for the moveable property of the deceased father's estate: "Master," he said, "I understand that thou are not acting according to the strict letter of the law but in accordance with the principle of compassion, but the danger exists that your students will note your ruling and consider it legally binding in future cases as well."[15] Compassion, like other virtues, is a moral necessity but is beyond the reach of legal implementation.

Maimonides adopts the nonreductionist interpretation of *lifnim mi-shurat ha-din.* Although he employs the notion in a number of places he does not offer a uniform definition of the term, and in some instances his applications of the concept seem at variance with one another. However, his general approach can be discerned, particularly if approached from within the broader framework of Maimonides' philosophy of law.

There are two essential presumptions in this framework, both of which inform his analysis of *lifnim mi-shurat ha-din.* The first is the intellectualist-rationalist interpretation of the *mitzvot*, i.e., although the rationale for the commandments may not be readily accessible to the multitude, "There is not even one command which has not a reason and a cause, remote or immediate."[16] The second pivotal assumption is the teleological explanation of *Halakhah*; the laws have an educative utility, and adherence to them inculcates true belief and moral virtue.[17]

Underlying both these presumptions is the guiding aim of the Torah, *imitatio dei*, the quest for perfection. This pursuit cannot be achieved by mere compliance with the letter of explicitly prescribed law, for, as Twersky describes the Maimonidean view, "there is rather a continuum from clearly prescribed legislation to open-ended supererogatory performances, for the goals of the Torah is the maximum satisfaction of life."[18]

Nothwithstanding Maimonides' placing supererogation along a continuum with prescribed duties, he sees the need for a two-tiered level of standards, one that applies to the masses and another, more refined, that applies to those who have achieved a higher degree of spiritual and intellectual development. While in our earlier discussion of the morality of supererogation we noted that supererogatory acts will typically be performed by saints and heroes—that one becomes a saint or hero by performing such acts—in Maimonides' view supererogatory behavior is a duty of the saintly. Being learned, saintly, or in a position of authority brings with it additional responsibility and higher expectations: "Although one is not bound, still it is not right for a pious man."[19]

For Maimonides, these higher expectations and duties refer not only to overt actions but to the development of character as well. Thus, while we all ought to train our character and avoid the extremes of asceticism on the one hand and incontinence on the other, the pious man is expected to lean away from the direct mean on the side of greater humility and forbearance.[20]

This emphasis on character development illuminates as well Maimonides' discussion of internal struggle. Who is the greater saint or hero—he who shares the desires and fears of ordinary men but exercises an unusual power of will in order to overcome these inclinations, or he whose character is so finely developed that the fears and desires of the common man have been expunged? The Rabbinic tradition favors the former, while the Greek philosophical tradition the latter.[21] Maimonides strikes a compromise: with regard to those commandments whose rationale is obscure, the more meritorious individual is he who successfully battles his desires; but in responding to those duties whose rationale is apparent, it is he who fulfills his obligation naturally as a matter of course.[22] Inasmuch as supererogatory acts are intentional and must be undertaken with the express desire to assist others, the saintly and pious are distinguished by the naturalness with which they perform these acts.

The nonreductionist postulates a double standard: laws prescribed for those of ordinary religious/social consciousness; and the standard of supererogation, *lifnim mi-shurat ha-din*, for those who have transcended the level of the commonplace. This additional set of requirements is more rarefied and more refined, and flow from the more profound principles of piety and holiness. Nonetheless, the nonreductionist too considers *lifnim mi-shurat ha-din* as a halakhic requirement, albeit one without universal application. He need not be understood as advocating an extralegal criterion of goodness, as rejecting what A. J. Heschel called "pan-halakhism." For the nonreductionist and certainly the reductionist defines *lifnim mi-shurat ha-din* in legal terms and determines its scope and application in halakhic terms alone.

One general feature of *lifnim mi-shurat ha-din* that should be noted is that the term is applied almost exclusively to interpersonal affairs, dealings *ben adam le-adam*. Supererogatory acts serve to strengthen communal bonds and counter a tendency to withdraw into isolation, a personal boundary protected by the technicalities of the law. This encouragement of concern for others is manifested both in terms of character and action. Discussions of supererogation in contemporary moral theory are almost wholly relegated to actions, as we have seen, traditional Jewish law employs the concept both with regard to performance and the development of virtuous character.

Supererogation in *Sharī'a*

Islam like Judaism is a religion of laws—it is the legal code, not a theology, which establishes the criteria of right and wrong, proper and improper behavior.[23] Like *Halakhah*, *Sharī'a* is believed to be ordained by God and its scope to be total, ranging from the loftiest ideals to the minutiae of daily life.

Fiqh scholars early on recognized that any system that purported to be truly encompassing could not restrict itself to the three categories of obligation, permission, and the forbidden, and ignore, as later moral theories seem to ignore, the optional but value-laden. Instead, the *Sharī'a* recognizes an exhaustive fivefold classification that covers any and all actions: (1) *wājib* - obligatory acts, duties prescribed by God, neglect of which is punishable; (2) *mandūb* - recommended acts (*masnūn*), not obligatory, fulfillment of which is rewarded, omission not punishable; (3) *jā'iz* - indifferent, permitted (*mubāḥ*), actions that may or may not be done; neither punished nor rewarded; (4) *makrūh* - disapproved, discouraged but not forbidden, the not doing of which is rewarded but commission of which not punishable; and (5) *maḥẓūr* - prohibited (*ḥarām*), forbidden by God and punishable.

The reductionist/nonreductionist distinction suggested earlier has no ready parallel in this schema. "Recommended acts" that correspond to supererogatory acts are distinguished here as a distinct class of actions; their performance is specifically designated as desirable but not independent or beyond the framework of the legal structure. Islamic legalists differ with regard to the precise formulation of these categories and to the specific acts which qualify as members of the respective classes of actions.

The category of prohibited acts refers to those acts that are forbidden by an explicit *naṣṣ* (Qur'anic or *sunna*). The "orthodox" (e.g., Ash'arite) position views the evilness of an act as inhering in its being forbidden by God, while those who reject the divine command theory of good and bad (e.g, the Mu'tazilites) see the rightness or wrongness of an act as a quality of the act itself independent of its being a divine imperative or prohibition. But all agree that divine revelation is an infallible guide to the rules of conduct. To prohibit that which is *ḥalāl*, permitted, is to defy God's own determination. Such inversions gainsay the spirit of commandments given in the Qur'an, which teaches, "The wish of Allah is your ease not your distress,"[24] and instructs further, "Eat of that which in God's name has been mentioned, if you believe in His signs. How is it with you, that you do not eat of that which God's name has been mentioned, seeing that He has distinguished for you that He has forbidden you, unless you are constrained to it?"[25] Thus 'Abdallāh ibn Ma'sūd warns: "He who forbids that which is permitted is to be judged as he who declares the forbidden permissable."[26] The general operative legal principle is that when in doubt whether some act act is forbidden or permissable, proceed under the assumption that it is permitted.[27]

Due to their disagreement over the use of the various hermeneutic techniques, the four recognized schools of Islamic jurisprudence do not always agree on which acts are genuinely optional and neutral in value. For some, but not all, such Qur'anic imperatives as "take into marriage" two to four wives is transformed into the optative (or weaker in modernist readings), while others insist that it be understood as a command and not a concession. Mālik and his followers consider the eating of predators as permitted but disapproved (*makrūh*), others consider it forbidden, still others permitted and neutral. The Shāfi'ites deem the *zakāt al-fitr*, the alms distributed at the end of Ramadan as "*farḍ*," a strict obligation; the Ḥanafites as *wājib*, obligatory but less stringently; while the Mālikites view it as as *sunna*, customary but not obligatory. Differences over particular content nothwithstanding, there is general agreement among the orthodox views with regard to the formal structure of the fivefold classification of actions.[28]

Important differences do emerge, however, in the interpretation and definition of optional actions that have value. The Mu'tazilites reject entirely the category of permitted but disapproved actions. In the traditional schema, the hierarchy of acts is established by the presence or absence of punishment. For the Mu'tazilites, however, in particular as their position is articulated by 'Abd al-Jabbār, the criterion of judgment is desert (*istiḥqāq*) and undesert; that which is inherently evil is blameworthy. Whether punishment is due at the hands of God or man is a matter of law, not ethics. Value judgments, in this view, are not a subjectivist-theistic (voluntarist) affair but objective, independent, and integral to the act itself. ʻAbd al-Jabbār distinguishes, therefore, between the imposition of an obligation (*taklīf*) and the duty itself (*wujūb*). Allah employs the language of command when he only recommends, he notes, as when Allah says to the people of paradise, "Eat and drink merrily."[29]

The absence of evil is a necessary but not sufficient condition for the positive moral worth of an act. ʻAbd al-Jabbār distinguishes between two sorts of recommended actions, those, *nabdh*, which do not benefit others, such as extra fasting and extra prayers; and gracious, supererogatory acts, *tafaḍḍul*, which are undertaken for the sake of others. Since in the Muʻtazilite view, none of God's actions are obligatory (with the exception of the punishment of sinners), all His acts must be deemed as *tafaḍḍul*, acts of grace, supererogatory; the theological ramifications of this conclusion are, of course, not insignificant.[30]

The orthodox classification of optional behavior is also challenged by the mystical wing of Islamic tradition. Al-Ghazālī, for example, like Baḥya, insists that *fiqh* must be related to one's inner spiritual life; its function is the discipline of the agent, the purification of his soul and the means of preparing oneself for enlightenment. In this emphasis on intention and character, elaborated in the Ṣūfī tradition, the *Sharīʻa* becomes an outward manifestation of an inner religious consciousness. There is a continuum between the disapproved, recommended, and obligatory; and the separation between them is blurred: one has travelled more or less further on the path toward union with God.[31] Supererogation, in this antinomian tradition, is relatively unimportant.

With regard to the development of the virtues in general, we can note that while Islamic ethical treatises are often devoted to the "correction of dispositions" and the attainment of purer moral sensitivity, and, in addition, warn of the greater expectations attending such attainment, they do not suggest, as does Jewish law in some instances, a double standard of legal obligation—one for the middling multitude and another for those in a higher moral/religious state. The *Sharīʻa* is, finally, a code of behavior that applies to all in the same way and in equal measure. All of one's obligations and prohibitions are clearly adumbrated, but so too are those actions which are recommended—they are not "beyond the law" but part of it.

Supererogation and the Law

We began this discussion by asking how total legal systems such as *Halakhah* and *Sharīʻa* can countenance a sphere of optative behavior and allow, moreover, that some optional acts have positive moral worth. Both *Halakhah* and *Sharīʻa* directly address this challenge and designate a special category for supererogatory actions. These recommended praiseworthy performances are not external to the legal network but, like other commands, derive their merit from God's mandate, albeit broadly construed.

Why then the need to mark off a special domain of the supererogatory? The need to restrict the reach of legal sanctions, to establish a realm of the optional, is, in fact, especially important in such comprehensive legal systems as those under consideration here. That is, even in an ideal world composed of ideal observers, there remains a need to demarcate the required from the supererogatory. This is due to two features of supererogation, one social, the other personal.

Contemporary Western law stipulates a clear division between acts of commission and acts of omission. The central legal notion is the "harm principle," which prohibits illegitimate interference in and abridgment of another's rights. With few qualified exceptions, the law does not require that one prevent harm or help those being harmed, nor are sanctions instituted for those who fail to do so. Such beneficent acts are considered matters of morality, outside the proper domain of the law.

Halakhah and *Sharīʿa*, on the other hand, recognize no such legal distinction between committed and omitted acts, for such a distinction recognizes no such split between the individual and society. No one can claim unrestricted isolation and independence from his community: salvation is shared as a matter of mutual concern. Society itself, as well as the nation itself, are perceived as religious entities that fall within the compass of the law. The individual has obligations to others in his community and to the community itself; he must give charity, care for the needy, instruct, and be instructed. Notwithstanding this comprehensive framework, however, a realm of the optional is preserved where omissions invite no legal recrimination. Such legal limits are essential for the preservation of the sense of privacy and liberty which, in turn, are necessary for social stability. Were supererogation eliminated, one would be legally required always to act in an optimum manner and fear legal punishment for failing to act accordingly. As a result, the vast majority would always be legally guilty. Inasmuch as the "optimum" course is often obscure, even those inclined to what is best would be in fear of having chosen or acted incorrectly and thereby be legally liable as well. Moreover, in making no distinction between minimum requirements and superior conduct, the very notion of exemplary behavior toward which others ought to aspire would be undercut; the saintly and heroic would be no more than "mere" compliance with the laws.

There is, in addition, a positive value in supererogation which relates to personal autonomy. To be sure, the value of autonomy in these systems is understood in a manner quite different from the notion of autonomy in contemporary moral theory. No one is awarded the prerogative of inventing his own moral code nor encouraged to do so—morality is determined only by reference to God's will. Nevertheless, the development and manifestation of autonomy are genuinely valued as operative in the realm of the supererogatory. Here we are given the freedom to do more than the minimum stipulatio, and to act to the limits of our capacity. In establishing a domain of actions beyond the call of duty, recommended acts that are nonetheless tethered to the law, *Halakhah* and *Sharīʿa* provide a flexible but sturdy guide for those who aspire to do better, who wish to exercise their personal values consonant with the law. In addition, supererogation provides room for religious and moral creativity. Just how much room should be so allocated is an internal legal question, but one that reflects the tensions that are part of the history of Judaism and Islam.[32]

NOTES

[1] T. B. Bava Meṣia 30b.

[2] J. O. Urmson, "Saints and Heroes," in A. I. Melden, ed., *Essays in Moral Philosophy* (Seattle: University of Washington Press, 1958).

[3] This approach is adopted by J. Raz, "Permission and Supererogation," *American Philosophical Quarterly* 12(1975): 161-68.

[4] Aquinas argues for the importance of supererogation in the *Summa Theologica* I, II, Q. 108, Art. 4, and in *Summa Contra Gentiles*, Bk. III, Pt. II. Luther's criticism is part of his Thesis, 58.

[5] Supererogation is sometimes confused with the notion of imperfect duty. An "imperfect duty" is one that applies to a specific person because of a specific relationship, e.g., a doctor to his patient or parent to a child, in contrast to "perfect duties," such as the universal duty to come to the aid of a dying man. Both perfect and imperfect duties are genuine duties and are not beyond the call of duty, as are supererogatory performances.

[6] This formulation is derived from David Heyd, *Supererogation: Its Status in Ethical Theory* (Cambridge: Cambridge University Press, 1982).

[7] R. M. Chisholm, "Supererogation and Offence: A Conceptual Schema for Ethics," *Ratio* 5(1963): 1-14.

[8] Mekhilta, Yithro, Massekhta d'Amalek.

[9] Nahmanides, *Commentary*, on Lev. 19:2 and Deut. 6:18.

[10] T. B. Bava Meṣia 83a. Note, however, that the account of this exchange in the Yerushalmi omits the affirmation that this is the law.

[11] *Sefer Mitzvot Qaṭan* (Semak) 49.

[12] Baḥya ibn Paquda, *Duties of the Heart* (*Ḥovot ha-Levavot*), especially chapter 1. In passing, we might note that the term *mitzvah*, which has such wide employment in Jewish tradition, ranging from specific commandments to minor elective favors, also connotes the element of duty and command. For a helpful review of the sources dealing with the concept of *mitzvah*, see Ephraim E. Urbach, *The Sages: Their Concepts and Beliefs* (Jerusalem: Magnes Press, 1975), 1:337-42.

[13] The Mordecai on Bava Meṣia, Sec. 327, argues that *lifnim mi-shurat ha-din* can be compelled and cites the Ravin and Ravya in support of his view. The "Rosh" explicitly denies such coercion, Pesaḥim, Bava Meṣia, 2:7. The connection between *lifnim mi-shurat ha-din* and *kofin 'al middot Sedom* is developed in Aharon Lichtenstein, "An Ethic Independent of Halakha?" in Menachem M. Kellner, ed., *Contemporary Jewish Ethics* (New York: Sanhedrin Press, 1978). A related analysis is presented in Shubert Spero in *Morality, Halakha and the Jewish Tradition* (New York: Ktav Publishing House/Yeshiva University Press, 1983), ch. 5.

[14] T. B. Bava Meṣia 24b.

[15] T. B. Ketubbot 50b.

[16] Maimonides, *Sefer ha-Mitzvot*; see also *Guide of the Perplexed* (*Moreh Nevukhim*) 3:21, in *The Guide of the Perplexed*, S. Pines, tr. (Chicago: University of Chicago Press, 1963), 484-85.

[17] *Guide* 2:31 and 3:27, in Pines, tr., *Guide*, pp. 359-60, 510-12

[18] Isadore Twersky, *Introduction to the Code of Maimonides* (New Haven: Yale University Press, 1980), 427.

[19] Maimonides, *Mishneh Torah*, "Hilkhot Ṣiṣit" 3:12, "Yesodei ha-Torah" 5:11; "Hilkhot De'ot" 5:13.

[20] *Mishneh Torah*, "Hilkhot De'ot" 1:4. In the *Shemonah Perakim*, Maimonides seems to consider acting within the mean as always ideal. For a particularly clear overview of the Maimonidean view of character-traits, see Lenn E. Goodman, *Rambam: Readings in the Philosophy of Moses Maimonides* (New York: Shocken Books, 1977), Pt. III.

[21] Aristotle is a good representative of the Greek view in this regard. The rabbinic position is reflected in the dictum that one ought not say he is refraining from eating unkosher meat because he dislikes it but because he is commanded to refrain from eating it.

[22] *Shemonah Perakim*, Ch. 6.

[23] Joseph Schacht, "Theology and Law in Islam," in G. E. von Grunebaum, ed., *Theology and Law in Islam* (Wiesbaden: Harrassowitz, 1971), provides a concise discussion of the central importance of law in Islam.

[24] Qur'an 2:180.

[25] Qur'an 6:15-55.

[26] Quoted in Ignaz Goldziher, *Introduction to Islamic Theology and Law*, Andras and Ruth Hamori, trs. (Princeton: Princeton University Press, 1981), 56.

[27] *Ibid.*, pp. 50-81. Compare this with the halakhic juridical rule that when in doubt whether some act is forbidden or permitted according to scripture (*safek d'araita*), one should proceed as if it were forbidden.

[28] The distinction between minimum requirements and supererogation is attributed directly to Muhammad. In one *ḥadīth*, someone asks the Prophet to tell him about Islam. He is told to performs the five ṣalāt daily. "No more?" he asks. "No," he is told, "more is supererogatory." He is told to fast on Ramaḍān. "No more than that?" he asks. "More than that is supererogatory," is the response. The man left, saying, "By Allah, I shall add nothing nor omit anything." Then Muhammad said, "He is saved if he keeps his promise." From Muslim, *Al-Jāmi' al-Ṣaḥīḥ*, "Bab al-Imān" 8, cited in A. J. Wensinck, *The Muslim Creed* (London: Frank Cass and Co., 1965).

[29] Qur'an 17:115.

[30] 'Abd al-Jabbār, *Mughnī*. George F. Hourani provides a detailed analysis of the structure and significance of 'Abd al-Jabbār's ethics in *Islamic Rationalism: The Ethics of 'Abd al-Jabbar* (Oxford: Clarendon Press, 1971).

[31] A helpful discussion of al-Ghazālī's theory of law that touches on our present concern can be found in Fazlur Rahman, "Functional Interdependence of Law and Theology," in G. von Grunebaum, ed., *Theology and Law in Islam*.

[32] My thanks to Lenn E. Goodman and David Greenwald for their helpful suggestions.

Tajdīd al-Dīn: A Reconsideration of Its Meaning, Roots, and Influence in Islam[1]

Hava Lazarus-Yafeh

Modern research and the media have emphasized, perhaps excessively, the concept of periodic Islamic "renewal," thereby enhancing the status and importance of the term. A study of its characteristics and origins clearly shows that the concept has never struck solid roots in Islam, unlike millenarian ideas in Western Christendom. In fact, it seems that it was used in medieval Islam only as a way to pay tribute to those who were concerned with the study of Islamic tradition and its dissemination. Only in the modern era, particularly at the periphery of the Islamic world (in both the geographical and the ideological sense), were the concepts of "renewal" and periodic purification of Islam emphasized by some authors and the idea of a millenarian revolution advanced. Still, it never became a central theme in the writings of contemporary Arab Radicals.

In speaking of "renewal" in Islam, I am referring to such expressions as *iḥyā' al-sunna*, *iḥyā' al-dīn*, *tajdīd al-Islām*, and *iqāmat al-dīn*, but not to more recent terms such as *iṣlāḥ* and *thawra*, nor to the eschatological concept of Mahdī, although some scholars and Muslim authors relate the latter also to the idea of *tajdīd*.[2] Originally, all these expressions referred to the dissemination of true knowledge or to the study and strengthening of the existing tradition. In this sense, these terms refer to the restoration of tradition to its pristine splendor, just as it was in the beginning, without any renewal, change, or "reform." Indeed, as recently as a generation ago the use of the term *tajdīd dīnī*, in the sense of change, was explicitly rejected as foreign to the spirit of Islam and more appropriate to that of Christian Protestantism, by certain sages of al-Azhar.[3]

It appears that in both Judaism and Islam the study of the law, in its broadest sense, is the focus of both history and eschatology. Any religious "renewal" can be understood only in terms of spreading true religious knowledge. All other social, ethical, or political achievements depend on this and should be considered only as direct results of it.

In this context, *tajdīd al-dīn* seems to have appeared initially in Islam under the influence of Jewish sources, but the term gradually became consolidated there in a more formalistic way, as has been the case with some other Jewish terms and ideas that found their way into Islam.[4] However, its appearance in Arabic literature never became very frequent, and it is questionable whether it has ever served in classical Islam as the stimulus for a movement or a concrete action.

Until the end of the fourth century A.H. (10th century C.E.), the expression *iḥyā' al-sunna* was apparently mainly reserved for instances of revival of some religious customs that had traditionally been neglected, whereas the expression *tajdīd al-dīn*—which was subsequently to become a supplementary and parallel term—was probably not used at all. Goldziher gives several examples of *iḥyā' al-sunna*, the opposite of which is a "sunna that was killed" (i.e., forgotten) or a *bid'a,* which usually refers to a new (and therefore forbidden) custom that has no support in tradition. But his examples are all very specific (e.g., the revivial of the previously abolished *li'ān* ceremony in the mosque; the conduct of war at specific hours, like those of the Prophet, etc.) and lack a general context.[5] The famous *ḥadīth* on the "renewal of religion" was apparently not prevalent in Arabic literature until that period, and even afterwards it appears so rarely that it is hardly possible to derive from it some general, basic information about Islam's view of itself.

The *ḥadīth* appears, as is well known, for the first time only in the third century A.H. in the *Sunan* of of Abū Da'ūd[6] in an eschatological context, and some scholars regard it therefore as an expression of the attempt to soften, moderate, and even delay, as it were, the awe of the Day of Judgment.[7] The usual version is *inna Allāh yab'athu li-hādhihi 'l-umma 'alā ra's kull mi'a sana man yujaddidu lahā dīnahā,* "Allah shall send to this nation at the beginning of every period of one hundred years a man who shall renew their religion for them"; but we find the same *ḥadīth* again in a different version in later literature, ascribed to Aḥmad ibn Ḥanbal, and the changes are interesting: *man yuṣaḥḥiḥu li-hādhihi 'l-umma dīnahā* (i.e., who shall mend what has been impaired in religion), and even *man yu'allimuhum al-sunan wa-yanfī 'an rasūl Allāh al-kidhb* (i.e., who shall teach them the [right] *sunan* and remove the falsehood from the Messenger of Allah).[8] It seems probable that even in a later period no version of the *ḥadīth* was generally accepted as an agreed upon principle, and that it was rather conceived of as a general expression of praise for whoever disseminates true religious knowledge and mends what had been distorted. This doubtless also explains why al-Ghazālī could later easily introduce an additional linguistic change in the *ḥadīth,* thereby making the confusion even greater (see below).

There is also a third term of the same type, to which so far no attention has been paid, and which probably also was of a very general nature, but not widespread and not a matter of principle. This is the term *tajdīd al-īmān*," the renewal of faith, which appears in the *Musnad* of Ibn Ḥanbal: "The Messenger of Allah, Allah's prayer and blessing of peace be upon him, said: 'Renew your faith' (*jaddidū īmānakum*). It was said: Oh, Messenger of Allah, how shall we renew our faith? He answered: Say often: 'There is no God but Allah.'"[9]

This tradition was transmitted by Abū Hurayra, who is known for his unreliability and for the many quotations from Jewish sources that are usually ascribed to him. The above saying is indeed presented in a Jewish midrashic context, for in the preceding *ḥadīth* cited from the same source, Allah promises the Prophet: "If my children will listen to Me, I shall give them rain at night and sun at day and shall not let them hear the voice of thunder"—a motif that appears several times in Jewish midrashim.[10]

The expression "renewal" in relation to faith appears frequently in Jewish sources, both in the Bible and in rabbinic literature, usually in an eschatological context, but without any attempts to delay or moderate the awe of the Day of Judgment. Thus, for instance, we read in Psalm 51:10: "Create in me a clean heart, O God, and put a new and right spirit within me," or in Ezekiel 36:26: "A new heart I will give you, and a new spirit I will put within you." Compare also Song of Songs Rabbah: "In the third year of the seven, at the end of which the Son of David will come . . . the Torah will be forgotten by Israel, . . . and in the fifth year the Torah shall be renewed for Israel."[11]

In the Bible the verb "to renew" is also used in relation with the kingdom[12] and the building of the altar[13] or the House of God.[14] In the last mentioned verse the parallel is "to strengthen the House of the Lord," and the term "renewal" in these contexts does not mean return to pristine splendour, but repair, restoration, and similar terms. The well-known text from the last chapter of Lamentations, "Restore us to thyself, O Lord, that we may be restored! Renew our days as of old!" which has become part of Jewish prayers, is perhaps an additional proof of this. Sa'adya Gaon translated this verse in the tenth century as follows: "*wa-jaddid ayyāmanā ka'l-qadīma.*"

As we shall presently see, the Hebrew verb *ḥiddesh* is in this context found not only in the Jewish sources, but also had "practical" applications among the Jews in exactly the same sense, whereas the Arab verb *jaddada* is not found in the Qur'an at all (unlike the adjective *jadīd*), and in the *Ḥadīth* it seems to appear only in the two traditions we quoted above, of which one is clearly of Jewish provenance. It seems, therefore, that we may assume that the term and concept came to Islam at a later stage and from Jewish sources. But in Islam its formulation became more formalistic—in the famous *ḥadīth* which led to the fixation of a "time table" (every hundred years) for renewal and later to the search for the renewing "key persons" in this scheme. Even this cyclic view has a precedent in a famous Talmudic saying (see below).

In the eleventh century C.E. the term *tajdīd* appears more often in both Jewish and Muslim writings. In the mid-eleventh century the expression "religious renewal" seems to have been in practical use in Jewish circles, as is shown by two letters from the Cairo Geniza, relating to Rav Nissim of Qayrawān (d. 1062). The letter, from the Leningrad collection (published by S. D. Goitein in *Tarbiẓ*), was written about one year before Rav Nissim's death and deals with the copying of one of the latter's writings and with his sickness. The writer of the letter expresses his great admiration for Rav Nissim and his work and writes, among other things: *li'anna ḥayātahu ṭulū' al-madhhab wa-iqāmat al-Torah wa-tajdīd al-dīn* (in Goitein's translation: "For his life was dedicated to raising the banner of the nation, reinstating the Torah (*iqāmat al-Tawrāt*) and renewing religion (*tajdīd al-dīn*))."[15] All these expressions apparently intend to emphasize his teaching and dissemination of forgotten knowledge, an assumption vindicated by an additional document from the Geniza. From this document we learn that one of Rav Nissim's disciples brought about a "revival of the Torah" (*tajdīd al-Torah*) in Egypt by bringing the books and teachings of Nissim and of other teachers from Qayrawān, North Africa, to Egypt after the decline of the Jewish center of learning at Qayrawān. The establishment of a new Jewish center of learning in Egypt was thus obviously regarded as a "revival of the Torah."[16]

At first glance it may seem that the expression "religious revival" is a foreign, perhaps Muslim, notion that was adopted by the Jewish world, like so many other Muslim religious expressions.[17] But at second glance the opposite seems to be the case, particularly in view of all we have said thus far about the frequent occurrence of the term in Judaism and its almost total absence in the world of Islam, especially if we consider the expression *iqāmat al-Tawrāt* which accompanies it and about which we shall say more presently when relating the story of Ezra-'Uzayr. Before doing so, it is important to note that Rav Nissim was a contemporary of the Spanish Muslim author Ibn Ḥazm (d. 1064) and, like him, lived in the western part of the Islamic world and was well versed in Arabic-Muslim thought and literature. He was a relative of Samuel ha-Nagid (through the marriage of their children), with whom Ibn Ḥazm apparently had a strongly worded theological dispute about the reliability of the text of the Torah.[18] In fact, in the works of Rav Nissim we may discern echoes of this dispute, which may have paved the way toward modern European Bible criticism initiated by Spinoza. In this dispute Ezra the scribe plays a very special role,[19] but we shall restrict our discussion to the Muslim terminology used to describe his work. The story of Ezra-'Uzayr is complex and highly interesting. 'Uzayr is mentioned only once in the Qur'an,[20] in Sūra 9:30, where the Jews are accused of worshipping him just as the Christians worship Jesus: "The Jews claim that 'Uzayr is the son of God and the Christians claim that the Messiah is the son of God. Such utterings from their mouth resemble the words of the earlier unbelievers. Be they cursed by Allah! How they do lie!" The classical Islamic commentators wondered much about the meaning of this unusual verse, just as modern scholars do, and brought forward many different explanations of it. One rather common interpretation is that the Jews revered Ezra excessively because he performed for them the greatest miracle of all by giving them back the Torah, which had been lost or forgotten. Various versions of this story appear in Muslim historiographic literature, from al-Ṭabarī (d. 923)[21] on and in a particularly detailed form in the *Qiṣaṣ al-Anbiyā'* by al-Tha'labī, who lived in the eleventh century. The story contains Jewish motifs about Ezra from the Bible and rabbinic sources and in particular from the early Jewish book the Vision of Ezra (the Fourth Book of Ezra),[22] the Coptic version of which was later translated several times into Arabic in Christian circles.[23]

The work of Ezra, who was given a miraculous portion by an angel of God which enabled him to remember and dictate again to the Children of Israel their lost or burnt Torah with all its details and laws, is called by al-Ṭabarī *iqāmat al-Tawrāt*, a term we also encountered in the letter about Rav Nissim.[24] But it is only in the work of al-Tha'labī that we find the expressions *iḥyā' al-Tawrāt wa'l-sunna* and *tajdīd al-Torah* in the context of the story of Ezra-'Uzayr: *wa-aḥyā lahum al-Tawrāh wa'l-sunna . . . wa-ba'atha Allāh lahum 'Uzayran li-yujaddida lahum al-Tawrāh.*[25] The story is transmitted there by Ibn 'Abbās, who we know often presented material from Jewish sources. The central motif in all the versions of this story (al-Tha'labī in particular repeats it several times) is that the Torah which Ezra remembered in a miraculous way and which he dictated with all his fingers (in the ancient Vision of Ezra he dictates it to five men simultaneously) was amazingly accurate, and the Children of Israel acknowledged it as the true Torah that had been lost. In one version of the story, the Holy Ark (*Tābūt*) is returned to the Children of Israel on acount of Ezra after God had taken it away from them as punishment for their wicked deeds (*wa-ansāhum al-Tawrāh wa-nassakhaha min ṣudūrihim*).[26] When they compared what was written in it [*sic*] with the words of Ezra they found that they were identical. Another version tells that they took the Torah from the place where it was hidden or buried, compared it with Ezra's dictation, and found that not one verse, not even one letter, was missing.[27] This was what probably caused them to revere Ezra-'Uzayr so excessively that they even regarded him as the son of God, as the Qur'anic verse has it.

I believe that this story stems from Jewish sources in which Ezra's role is considerable.[28] According to the sages of the Talmud, "Ezra was worthy of the Torah being given to him."[29] Ten important renewals are ascribed to him, among them the change of the Hebrew script. Moreover, the expression *iqāmat al-Tawrāt* seems to me the only possible translation of the Hebrew term *yissud ha-Torah*, which the Talmud ascribes to a recurring cycle of persons (as in the famous *ḥadīth*) such as Ezra, Hillel, and others: "When the Torah was forgotten by Israel, Ezra came from Babylon and reestablished it (*yissedah*)."[30] Yet, what is most important is the fact that the term *iqāmat al-Tawrāt* again appears here—in the eleventh-century Arabic literature in an explicitly Jewish context—and that its meaning is the study of the Torah and dissemination of knowledge that had been forgotten.

There is also an additional late eleventh-century source for the history of the expression we have been discussing: the writings of the famous al-Ghazālī (d. 1111). In the last chapter of his autobiography, al-Ghazālī provides a paraphrase of the famous *ḥadīth* mentioned above, but in a different version, which may have strengthened the link between the terms *iḥyā' al-sunna* and *tajdīd al-dīn*. Al-Ghazālī speaks of Allah's promise to renew his religion at the beginning of every period of one hundred years (*wa-qad wa'ada Allāhu subḥānahu bi-'iḥyā' dīnihi 'alā ra's kull mi'at sana*).[31] Bauer has already shown that there is a connection between this deliberate choice of a different version of the famous *ḥadīth* and the title of al-Ghazālī's well-known work *Iḥyā' 'Ulūm al-Dīn*.[32] In any case, there seems to be no doubt that al-Ghazālī understood these terms in an educational sense and thought of religious renewal in terms of the dissemination of religious knowledge.[33] Moreover, although al-Ghazālī considered himself destined to be a messenger of religious renewal, and therefore wrote this book, there is no indication that he believed that this was the special task of a specific person at the end of every century—a conviction that was subsequently consolidated in Islam. Bauer holds that the very general formulation of the *ḥadīth* (*man*) hints at the possibility of this task being fulfilled by different persons, or even by a group of persons. In fact, al-Ghazālī certainly did not yet know that this mission would later be ascribed to people he mentions in his book, such as 'Umar ibn 'Abd al-'Azīz, or al-Shāfi'ī, al-Ash'arī, or al-Bāqillānī, and that they would be connected with the famous *ḥadīth* he quoted.

In fact, Islam apparently never accepted a uniform list of persons who were regarded as the "renewers" (*mujaddidūn*). Although certain names do recur in this context (mostly Shāfi'ites), varying names are also mentioned for each century.[34] In general, in the vast biographical literature of Islam the title *Mujaddid* is a late and rare phenomenon. In the eleventh century, for example, it was not yet applied to 'Umar II, who seems later to be regarded as the first

Mujaddid.[35] Only in the second half of the twelfth century is it found in some of his biographies in a different version of the famous *ḥadīth*. Al-Shāfi'ī is also mentioned there in the same context.[36] Later, al-Suyūṭī (d. 1505) used the word as a term of praise for himself and others, and in this sense it has been used up to the present day.[37] There seems never and nowhere, in the course of the centuries, to have existed a generally acknowledged and updated list of *Mujaddidūn*, although there is apparently some consensus for the first few centuries A.H.

This matter, of course, requires a thorough study of the biographies of the people who are mentioned as *mujaddidūn*, but modern writers and scholars have generally accepted the list of 'Abd al-Qādir al-'Aydarūs (d. 1628) as quoted in his *Ta'rīf al-Aḥyā' bi-Faḍā'il al-Iḥyā'*. Since this book was printed on the margin of al-Murtaḍā al-Zabīdī's (d. 1791) introduction to his commentary on al-Ghazālī's *Iḥyā'*, the list is often quoted in his name as well.[38] While paying tribute to al-Ghazālī, al-'Aydarūs says: "A group from among the *'Ulamā'*—Allah's peace be upon them—and among them the learned Imām Ibn 'Asākir,[39] said with regard to the *ḥadīth* of the Prophet—Allah's prayer and blessing of peace be upon him—that Allah shall send (printed *yujaddidu*, "shall renew," which should be *yab'athu* "shall send") to his people a man who shall renew their religion at the beginning of every century. At the beginning of the first century,[40] there was 'Umar ibn 'Abd al-'Azīz—may Allah give him peace—and at the beginning of the second century was al-Shāfi'ī—Allah's peace be upon him—and at the beginning of the third century was Abū al-Ḥasan al-Ash'arī—Allah's peace upon him—and at the beginning of the fourth century Abū Bakr al-Bāqillānī, and at the beginning of the fifth century Abū Ḥāmid al-Ghazālī." Al-'Aydarūs adds that the names of the first two were transmitted by Ibn Ḥanbal, but he does not bother to explain why the list does not continue up to his own time (where several people are missing). In fact, very few attempts were made to update this casual list,[41] which contains mainly words of praise for a few individuals, but no real "doctrine" of Islamic renewal.

Al-Zabīdī also discusses the *ḥadīth* at length and, following earlier authors, explains that in every century several *mujaddidūn* may appear—one among the *fuqahā'*-Jurists, one among the theologians, the transmitters of tradition, the Ṣūfīs, the rulers, the preachers, the reciters of the Qur'an. He mentions several names for each century, some of them highly unusual, such as the 'Abbāsid Caliph al-Ma'mūn for the second century.[42] This was at the end of the eighteenth century and—with respect to this list, to the *ḥadīth*, and to the terms of renewal—little has changed since. Only recent political events, and perhaps especially their coverage by the media, seem to have invested the *Mudjaddid* idea with new importance.

NOTES

[1] An earlier version of this paper was first read at a colloquium on the ideas of Renewal, Reform, and Revolution in Islam, held by the Center for the Study of Islamic Civilization, The Hebrew University, Jerusalem, in June 1984, and will be published in Hebrew with the other papers of this colloquium, in a special edition of *Ha-Mizraḥ he-Ḥadash*. A shorter English version was read at the Fourth Annual Conference of the Institute for Islamic-Judaic Studies in May 1985.

[2] See, for example, Abu 'l-A'lā al-Maudūdī, *A Short History of the Revivalist Movement in Islam*, al-Ash'arī, tr. (Lahore: Islamic Publications, 1963). See also Shams al-Dīn al-Sukhawī (d. 1496), *Al-Maqāṣid al-Ḥasana fī Bayān Kathīr min al-Aḥadīth al-Mushtahara* (Cairo: Maktabat al-Khānjī, 1956/1375), 122, who, after updating the list of "Revivers" up to his times, hopes for the Mahdī (or al-Masīḥ) to be the next and last one.

[3] See my *Some Religious Aspects of Islam* (Leiden: Brill, 1981), 101 and 160, n. 60, on the rejection of the term *tajdīd.*

[4] See the example of *niyya* (*kavvana*) in S. D. Goitein, *Jews and Arabs: Their Contacts through the Ages* (New York: Schocken Books, 1955), 178-79.

[5] See I. Goldziher, *Muslim Studies*, Barber and Stern, trs. (London: Allen and Unwin, 1971), 2:32-37. See also al-Tirmidhī, "Kitāb al-'Ilm," Bāb 16, in *Sunan* (Cairo: Al-Azhar, 1934/1353), 9:147-48, and Ibn Māja, "Muqaddima," Bāb 15, in *Sunan* (Cairo: Dār Iḥyā' al-Kutub al-'Arabiyya, 1952/1372), 9:76.

[6] Abū Da'ūd, "Kitāb al-Malāḥim," in *Sunan* (Cairo: Maṭba'at Muṣṭafā Maḥmūd, 1950/1353AH), 4:159 (this *ḥadīth* may, of course, be much older). Cf. also Muḥammad Shams al-Ḥaqq al-'Aẓīmābādī's *Sharḥ Abī Da'ūd* (al-Madīna: al-Maktaba al-Salafiyya, 1969), 11: 385-96, especially his explanation of the term on p. 391. Late *ḥadīth* compilations usually quote Abū Da'ūd's version.

[7] See Y. Friedmann, *Shaykh Aḥmad Sirhindī* (Montreal: McGill University Press, 1971), 13-14. It seems that in India the concept of *mujaddid* was especially widespread. Although Maudūdī's books, among others, deeply influenced contemporary Arab writers, this term was nevertheless hardly adopted by them.

[8] See Ibn al-Jawzī, *Sīrat 'Umar ibn 'Abd al-'Azīz* (Cairo: Maṭba'at al-Mu'ayyid, 1331 A.H.), 60. Cf. also al-Suyūṭī's (d. 1505) version, quoted by I. Goldziher in "Zur Charakteristik Gelāl ud-Dīn us-Suyutis und seiner literarischen Thätigkeit," in *Gesammelte Schriften*, J. Desomogyi, ed. (Hildesheim: Georg Olms Verlag, 1967), 1:53ff. (translated as "Ignaz Goldziher on al-Suyūṭī" by Michael Barry, with additional notes by J. O. Hunwick, in *The Muslim World* 68[1978]: 81ff). This version adds that the renewer must be one of the Prophet's family (*min ahli baytī*), but al-Suyūṭī explains that this holds only for the first centuries.

9 Ibn Ḥanbal, *Musnad* (Beirut: Al-Maktab al-Islām, 1978/1398), 2:359.

10 See Sifrei Deuteronomy, Parashat 'Eqev 38, or Rashi's commentary to Deuteronomy 11:4 ("That I will give you the rain of your land in his due season"—at night, so as not to bother you, or on Friday evenings when everybody is at his home!).

11 Song of Songs Rabbah 2:29.

12 1 Sam. 11:14.

13 2 Chron. 15:8.

14 2 Chron. 24:4, 12.

15 S. D. Goitein, "A Letter by Labrat b. Moses b. Sigmar," *Tarbiẓ* 36(1967): 65, ll. 16-17 (tr. p. 69).

16 S. D. Goitein, "New Sources Concerning the Nagids of Qayrawan and R. Nissim," *Zion* 27(1962): 21.

17 See H. Lazarus-Yafeh, *Some Religious Aspects of Islam*, pp. 81-82.

18 See also the article by D. Powers, "Reading/Misreading One Another's Scriptures: Ibn Ḥazm's Refutation of Ibn Nagrella al-Yahūdī," in this volume, pp. 109-21.

19 See my forthcoming studies "Ezra-'Uzayr," in *Tarbiẓ*, and "Medieval Muslim Polemics and the Beginnings of Modern Bible Criticism." See also the article by M. Ayoub, "'Uzayr in the Qur'an and Muslim Tradition," in this volume, pp. 3-18.

20 Some commentators also connect Ezra-'Uzayr with Qur'an 2:259. See also al-Damīrī, *Kitāb al-Ḥayawān* (Cairo: Muḥammad 'Alī Ṣubayḥ 1284 A.H.), 1:301-05, and cf. Bernard Heller, "Éléments, Parallèles, et Origine de la Légende des Septs Dormants," in *Revue des Études Juives* 49(1904): 190-218.

21 See al-Ṭabarī, *Ta'rīkh al-Rusul wa'l-Mulūk*, M. de Goeje, ed. (Leiden: Brill, 1879), 1:669-71. Ibn al-Athīr repeats this story verbatim in his *Ta'rīkh* (Beirut: Dār al-Ṣādir—Dār Beirut, 1965/1385), 1:270-71.

22 See especially the seventh vision (4 Ezra 14:1-48) and cf. also the fourth (4 Ezra 9:26-10:59).

23 G. Graf, *Geschichte der christlichen arabischen Literatur* (Città del Vaticano: Biblioteca apostolica vaticana, 1944), 1: 219-221, and cf. the Arabic editions of V. Ewald (1863), J. Gildemeister (1877), and B. Violet (1910).

24 Al-Ṭabarī, *Ta'rīkh*, p. 670, last line. See also line 14, where the contents of the Torah are described in plain Qur'anic terms (*ḥalāl wa- ḥarām, sunan wa-farā'iḍ, ḥudūd*).

25 Al-Tha'labī, *Qiṣaṣ al-Anbiyā'* (n.c.: Dār Iḥyā' al-Kutub al-'Arabiyya, n.d.), 310 (following the story of Daniel!). These expressions are very unusual with al-Tha'labī. Ibn Kathīr, in the fourteenth century, states explicitly with regard to Ezra, in his *Al-Bidāya wa'l-Nihāya* (Cairo: Maṭba'at al-Sa'āda, 1932/1351), 2:45, "*fa-jaddada lahum al-Tawrāt.*"

26 Cf. Qur'an 2:106.

27 Al-Tha'labī, *Qiṣaṣ*, pp. 309-10 (this sounds very much like the story of the Septuagint, which was known to Muslim authors, cf. al-Mas'ūdī, *Prairies d'Or* (Paris: Imprimerie Nationale, 1917), 9:369-72 (note 32 by De Sacy).

[28] It may well be that the high esteem in which Ezra was held in Jewish (and later Muslim) circles should be considered already as a reaction to early accusations that he falsified the Torah. Cf. note 19 above.

[29] T. B. Sanhedrin 21b.

[30] T. B. Sukkah 20a.

[31] See his *Al-Munqidh min al-Ḍalāl*, fifth ed., Jamīl Ṣalība and Kāmil Iyād, eds. (Damascus: Maṭba'at al-Jāmi'a al-Sūriyya, 1956/1376 A.H.), 115, and W. M. Watt's translation (in his *Faith and Practice of al-Ghazālī* [London: Allen and Unwin, 1953], 1: 75). The book was in fact composed in the early twelfth century (501-02 A.H.); see M. Bonyges, *Essai de chronologie des ouevres d'Al-Gazālī* (Beirut: Imprimerie Catholique Beyrouth, 1959), 71, but the events described there apparently took place just before the beginning of the sixth century.

[32] Hans Bauer, "Zum Titel und zur Abfassung von Al-Gazālīs Iḥyā," *Der Islam* 4(1913): 159-60.

[33] Later Ṣūfīs, in particular, like the terms *iḥyā' al-. . .*, but the combination *iḥyā' al-Islām* is already found before al-Ghazālī, e.g., in al-Dārimī's *Sunan*, 'Abdallāh Hāshim Yamānī, ed. (Al-Madīna: Sharikat al-Ṭibā'a al-Fanniya al-Muttaḥida, 1966/1386), 1:84-85, "Muqaddima," Bāb 32, 360 (*li-yuḥiya al-Islām*).

[34] See, e.g., 'Alī ibn 'Asākir, *Tabyīn Kidhb al-Muftarī fīmā Nusiba ilā 'l-Imām al-Ash'arī* (Damascus: Maṭba'at al-Tawfīq, 1374 A.H.), 51ff. (Ibn 'Asākir, who died in 1176, is the famous author of *Ta'rīkh Madīnat Dimashq*), or al-Maudūdī, *A Short History*, p. 49. The Shī'ites have their own lists. See also al-'Aẓimābādī, *Sharḥ*, p. 395.

[35] Abū Nu'aym al-Iṣfahānī, for example, calls 'Umar II *Siddiq, Nabiyy* (!)," or *Mahdī* in his *Ḥilyat al-Awliyā'* (Cairo: Maktabat al-Khānjī wa-Maṭba'at al-Sa'āda, 1935/1354), 5: 340, 345-46, but does not use the term *Mujaddid*. Yet an echo of the famous *ḥadīth* appears in his book in the following interesting version: *kāna Allāh yata'āhadu al-nās bi-nabī ba'da nabī wa-inna Allāh ta'āhada al-nās bi-'Umar b. 'Abd al-'Azīz.*

[36] Cf. Ibn al-Jawzī, *Sīrat 'Umar*, p. 60.

[37] See Goldziher, "Zur Charakteristik," and cf. Amīn al-Khūlī, *Al-Mujaddidūn fī al-Islām* (Cairo: Dār al-Ma'rifa, 1965), which is based on the books by al-Suyūṭī and al-Marāghī al-Jurjāwī that deal with this subject. See also al-Sakhawī, *Al-Maqāṣid*, p. 121 ff.

[38] See Murtaḍā al-Zabīdī, *Itḥāf al-Sāda al-Muttaqīn* (n.c.: n.p., n.d.), 1:29. On the margin, al-'Aydarūs is given as quoted here. His book is also reprinted at the end of the last volume of the Cairo edition of *Iḥyā' Imlā'* (Cairo: Lajnat al-Thaqāfa al-Islāmiyya, 1356-57 A.H.), 16.

[39] See footnote 34 above. Al-'Aydarūs does not mention Ibn 'Asākir's discussion of various names for the fifth century (e.g., the 29th 'Abbāsid caliph al-Mustarshid bi-Allāh!) before he decided on al-Ghazālī.

[40] Meaning the beginning of the first century after the Prophet's death, that is, the second century of the Hijra. See, for a different explanation, al-Aẓīmābādī, *Sharḥ*, pp. 386 ff.

[41] See, e.g., *ibid.*, p. 395.

[42] Al-Zabīdī, *Itḥāf*, p. 42, *faṣl* 18. His introduction is reprinted in ʻAbd al-Karīm ʻUthmān's *Sīrat al-Ghazālī wa-Aqwāl al-Mutaqaddimīn Fīhi* (Damascus: Dār al-Fikr, n.d.), 185-87.

Reading/Misreading One Another's Scriptures: Ibn Ḥazm's Refutation of Ibn Nagrella al-Yahūdī

David S. Powers

Islamic tradition teaches that the Torah, New Testament, and the Qur'an are all derived from the same heavenly source, but that the Jews and Christians have, over the course of time, distorted the texts of their respective scriptures, whereas the Muslims have in their possession the pure, unadulterated text. The doctrine of scriptural distortion, known in Arabic as *taḥrīf*,[1] has contributed to the tendency of Muslims and Jews to disregard and ignore one another's scriptures. Although Muslims are certainly familiar with the biblical narratives, as related in the Qur'an and later developed and amplified in the genre of literature known as the *Isrā'īliyyāt,* as a rule they have relied on what others say about the Bible, rather than read the text itself.[2] If the Jewish version of scripture has been distorted and, further, if the Qur'an contains the undistorted version of the biblical narratives, why bother to read the Jewish version? The fact that the Jewish scriptures are written in Hebrew, a language with which very few Muslims were familiar, contributed further to the Muslim disregard for the Old Testament.[3] And while the Jews, as speakers of Judaeo-Arabic, did have access to the Qur'an, they apparently felt little or no compulsion to study that text which, in their opinion, does not represent the word of God. As a rule, the Jews adhered to the Muslim injunction forbidding non-Muslims to teach the Qur'an to their children.[4] In short, neither group deemed the other's scripture worthy of serious consideration.

But there does exist at least one significant exception to the general tendency of Jews and Muslims to neglect one another's scriptures. In the eleventh century A.D., a certain Jew wrote a treatise in which he pointed out contradictions in the Qur'an. Although this treatise has not survived, portions of it may be preserved in a refutation composed by the famous Muslim savant, Abū Muḥammad 'Alī b. Ḥazm (d. 1064).[5] Although Ibn Ḥazm does not identify his Jewish adversary—except to refer to him as, for example, "that shameless ignoramus"—most scholars have concluded, on the basis of allusions in the text, that the Jew whose treatise prompted the refutation was Samuel b. Nagrella ha-Nagid (b. 993).[6] Ibn Ḥazm's *Refutation* satisfies our search for an instance in which Jews and Muslims read one another's scripture, for the Muslim scholar not only refutes the arguments of his Jewish adversary—whoever he may have been—but also proceeds to advance his own analysis of the deficiencies of the Torah. Before examining this text, it will be appropriate to consider the respective careers of Samuel b. Nagrella and Ibn Ḥazm.

Samuel b. Nagrella was born in Córdoba, in the year A.D. 993, to a prominent Jewish family which came, originally, from Merida. He received an excellent Jewish and general education, including training in Arabic and, possibly, the Qur'an, and studied Jewish law with a leading Spanish scholar, Ḥanokh b. Moses. In 1013 Samuel fled from Córdoba in the wake of the Berber conquest and made his way to Malaga, where he opened a spice shop. He worked as a scribe, and the beautiful Arabic style of his letters so impressed Ibn al-'Arīf, the secretary *(kātib)* to the vizier of Granada, that the latter advised the Berber king, Habūs, to appoint Samuel to his staff. Samuel advanced rapidly from tax collector to secretary (after the death of Ibn al-'Arīf), to assistant to the vizier, Abu al-'Abbās, in the year 1020. Soon thereafter he himself became vizier, a post he occupied until his death in 1055 or 1056. When Habūs died in 1038, Samuel became the leading influence on his successor, Bādis. It is significant that, unlike many Jews who rose to positions of power in Muslim society, Samuel never renounced his Judaism; indeed, in 1027 Hai Gaon of Babylonia conferred upon him the title of *Nagid,* or "head of the Jews."[7]

Samuel led a many-faceted career as a politician, military commander, poet, and scholar. In his capacity as vizier, he led the army of Granada that, from 1038 to 1056, knew only two years of respite from fighting. He was also an accomplished poet who wrote on a variety of subjects, including war, love and wine, friendship, mourning and holiness, morality, and meditation. His scholarly output included a major compilation and explanation of Jewish law, the *Sefer Hilkheta Gavrata,* which was based on a wide variety of sources. In his capacity as leader of Spanish Jewry, Samuel corresponded with leading scholars in North Africa, while maintaining good relations with the Babylonian geonim.[8]

Although the Jews had written theological essays and polemics defending Judaism against the attacks of Muslim theologians, they had previously taken care not to denigrate the Qur'an. But Samuel, perhaps emboldened by his position as vizier, had the audacity to compose a treatise in which he pointed out contradictions and errors in the Muslim sacred scripture. The treatise, probably written in Judaeo-Arabic, was intended to circulate exclusively within the Jewish community; but due perhaps to the efforts of a Jewish informant or a Jewish convert to Islam, the treatise made its way into the hands of an unknown Muslim theologian, who wrote a refutation of it. It was this refutation which served as the basis for Ibn Ḥazm's own *Radd 'alā Ibn Nagrilla al-Yahūdī.*

The career of Ibn Ḥazm provides some interesting parallels and contrasts to that of Samuel b. Nagrella. Virtual contemporaries (Samuel was a year older), both men came from prominent families (Ibn Ḥazm's father served as vizier to al-Manṣūr and his son, al-Muẓaffar, in Madīnat al-Zahrā); both received an excellent education; both were politically ambitious; and both were forced into exile as a result of the political upheavals that plagued Spain at the turn of the eleventh century A.D. But unlike Samuel, whose political career spanned a period of three decades, Ibn Ḥazm's political ambitions were repeatedly frustrated. As a convinced supporter of the Umayyad caliphate, he made enemies easily. Although he was appointed to the office of vizier several times, his tenure of office was short-lived, and he ended up in prison at least twice. Eventually, he was forced to retire to the family estate at Manta Lisham.[9]

Ibn Ḥazm had met Samuel b. Nagrella many years before the latter wrote his attack on the Qur'an. In the year 1013, when the two men were both refugees, they had met in Almeria, where they engaged in a heated debate during the course of which Ibn Ḥazm attempted to demonstrate the corrupt nature of the Torah by pointing out instances in which it is either unethical (Abraham marries his sister, Sarah), or false (God promised that "the scepter shall not depart from Judah").[10] So we can perhaps imagine Ibn Ḥazm's anger when, many years later, he heard that his Jewish adversary—who, in the meantime, had risen to a high political office—had written a treatise attacking the Qur'an. Although unable to obtain a copy of the treatise itself, Ibn Ḥazm acquired a copy of a refutation by another, unnamed Muslim theologian, which he used to compose his own *Refutation.*[11]

The Structure of the *Refutation*

The *Refutation* is composed of an introduction, eight "chapters," an epilogue, and a conclusion. In the introduction, which opens with a scathing attack on the Andalusian party-kings *(mulūk al-ṭawā'if),* Ibn Ḥazm explains the circumstances which led to the composition of the treatise. Then, in the eight chapters which follow, he refutes eight different contradictions that Ibn Nagrella had found in the Qur'an. Each individual refutation is structured in the same manner: first, Ibn Ḥazm restates his adversary's argument; then he demonstrates that the contradictions are only apparent, not real, and result from Ibn Nagrella's ignorance or perfidy; finally, Ibn Ḥazm turns his attention to the Torah and shows that it contains passages that are more damning than the Qur'an passages to which Ibn Nagrella had objected. This completes the *Refutation,* properly speaking. In the Epilogue, which is approximately as long as the refutation itself, Ibn Ḥazm moves from a specific attack on Ibn Nagrella to a general attack on Judaism, listing numerous "abominations," "oddities," and "lies" found in the Torah, Psalms, Talmud, and other sacred writings of the Jews. By demonstrating that the Jewish sacred writings portray God and His Prophets in a way that is, to his mind, absurd, Ibn Ḥazm reaffirms his contention that the Jews have corrupted and distorted their scriptures. In the Conclusion, Ibn Ḥazm reiterates his reasons for writing the treatise. In the following discussion, I will focus primarily on the eight chapters in which the two men critique one another's scripture.

Synopsis of the *Refutation*

1. The first contradiction noticed by Ibn Nagrella relates to the problem of good and evil. In Q. 4:78 the Divinity states, in response to an attempt by those who reject faith to blame Muhammad for the evil things that happen to them, "Say: 'Everything is from God.'" But in the very next verse the Divinity says, "Whatever good visits thee, it is of God; whatever evil visits thee is of thyself."[12] Ibn Ḥazm quotes Ibn Nagrella as saying, "So He goes back [on himself] . . . contradicting what was said in the previous verse."[13]

Ibn Ḥazm explains that there is no contradiction between these two statements. The evildoer is responsible for his deeds ("of thyself"), while God is the source of the punishment. Man's neglect of his obligations causes God to punish the evildoers.[14]

Satisfied with his refutation of Ibn Nagrella, Ibn Ḥazm turns his attention to the Torah, which, in his opinion, contains real contradictions, not apparent ones. He moves, by way of association, from the general subject raised by Ibn Nagrella to a similar subject in the Torah. As a counterpoint to the Jew's discussion of divine punishment, Ibn Ḥazm notes the failure of the Torah to mention reward and punishment in the next life (a standard point in Jewish-Muslim polemics). Further, the Torah openly contradicts itself with regard to punishment in this life, for it says, in one place, that the Lord "visits the sin of the father upon the son up to the third and fourth generation,"[15] but elsewhere we read that God punished Cain "to the seventh [generation] of his sons."[16] To add insult to injury, Deut. 24:16 states, "Do not kill fathers on account of the sons, nor the sons on account of the fathers. . . ."[17] If only Ibn Nagrella had reflected on these matters, Ibn Ḥazm concludes, he would not have dared to cast doubt on the speech of God, which is the clear and only truth.[18]

2. From good and evil Ibn Nagrella moves on to the creation of the world. Q. 79:27-32 indicates that God created the heavens first and then the earth, while Q. 2:29 suggests the opposite, i.e., "It is He who created for you all that is in the earth, then He lifted Himself to heaven and levelled them seven heavens." The two verses, according to Ibn Nagrella, contradict one another.[19]

Ibn Ḥazm again appeals to the literal meaning of the text in order to dispose of the apparent discrepancy. God did in fact create the heavens first and then the earth, as is immediately apparent from Q. 79:27-32. But he did not divide the heavens into seven spheres until after he created the earth, as Q. 2:29 makes clear: "It is He who created for you all that is in the earth, then He lifted Himself to heaven and levelled them seven heavens." The levelling of the heavens here refers not to their creation, which had taken place earlier, but to their subsequent modification.[20]

Ibn Ḥazm levels his own attack on the Jewish version of creation. The story of Adam and Eve in the Garden of Eden suggests to him that the status of Divinity can be acquired by consuming certain fruits; for if Adam, after eating from the Tree of Good and Evil, had gone on to eat from the Tree of Life, "he would attain immortality and he would be exactly like Us," he quotes God as saying, "leaving Us no superiority over him." Further, Ibn Ḥazm states that a certain unnamed Jewish sect believes that God is merely a mortal who ate from both the trees in the Garden.[21]

3. Ibn Nagrella's third objection also has to do with the creation of the world. According to Q. 41:9-12, it took God two days to create the earth, and four days to "ordain therein its diverse sustenances"—this makes six days—and two more days to "determine" the heavens as seven. In other words, the creation of the world seems to have taken place in eight days. But in Q. 50:38 God says, "We created the heavens and the earth, and what between them is, in six days."[22]

Ibn Ḥazm retorts that the apparent discrepancy in the number of days it took to create the world results from the Jew's lack of understanding, blindness, and ignorance. God did in fact create the world in six days, as stated in Q. 50:38, and He spelled out the exact sequence of creation in Q. 41:9-12: first, He created [the heavens and the] earth in two days; and He "ordained the diverse sustenance in the earth" on days three through six.[23] But the two days on which God "determined them as seven heavens"[24] are not two *additional* days of creation, but rather the last two days of the four on which God "ordained the diverse sustenances of the earth." That is to say, on the fifth and sixth days of creation, God (a) continued the work of ordaining the diverse sustenance in the earth and, (b) levelled the heavens (which had been created on days one and two) as seven. This should be clear, Ibn Ḥazm concludes, to anyone who adopts a proper attitude toward the text and seeks to understand it; for the Qur'an makes a clear distinction between "creating," which means to bring forth something from nonexistence to existence; and "ordaining," which means to arrange and consolidate things after creating them.[25]

Ibn Nagrella's confusion over the number of days it took to create the world suggests to Ibn Ḥazm another problem with the Jewish creation story, namely, the way in which it attributes human characteristics to the Divinity. (This is one of Ibn Ḥazm's favorite criticisms of the Jewish scripture.) Gen. 2:2 states that God "rested on the seventh day." But why should God, who is all-powerful, have any need for rest, Ibn Ḥazm asks? If only Ibn Nagrella had considered this, he would have renounced Judaism and converted to Islam.[26]

4. From the creation of the world Ibn Nagrella moves to the Day of Judgment. Q. 77:35-36 says, referring to the "Day of Decision" *(yawm al-faṣl),* "This is the day they shall not speak neither be given leave, and excuse themselves." But Q. 16:111 refers to the day of Judgment as "the day that every soul shall come disputing in its own behalf." "This," according to Ibn Nagrella, "is an enormous contradiction."[27]

In his refutation, Ibn Ḥazm gives two separate answers, the first derived from earlier scholars who resolved the discrepancy by resorting to *ta'wīl* (i.e., interpretation), the second his own, based on an (alleged) literal reading of the text. The unnamed earlier scholars harmonized the apparent contradiction between the two verses by drawing a distinction between several stages of the Day of Resurrection; during one of these stages, i.e., on the day the unbelievers are put into the Fire, no speech is permitted; but during a subsequent stage, the Day of Reckoning itself, every soul will dispute on its own behalf.[28]

Ibn Ḥazm prefers to resolve the apparent discrepancy on the basis of the literal sense of the text, without resorting to *ta'wīl*. He harmonizes the two verses by drawing a distinction between man's disobeying God, on the one hand, and the claims that people have against one another for injustices they suffered, on the other. Rejection of faith *(kufr)* is inexcusable, and for this reason the rejecters are forbidden to speak—to God—on the Day of Resurrection. The "disputing" mentioned in Q. 16:111 refers to the people who dispute with one another. This conclusion is corroborated, according to Ibn Ḥazm, by a linguistic consideration, for the verb *jādala* ("to dispute or contend") refers to an action performed (mutually) by two agents, and God does not contend with anyone.[29]

While on the subject of the Day of Resurrection, Ibn Ḥazm reiterates one of his harshest criticisms of Judaism, namely that neither in the Torah nor in the Prophets does one find any mention of reward or punishment after death.

For good measure, he throws in a further, unrelated, jab at the Hebrew scriptures, quoting Prov. 8:22ff., "I was with God when He created the earth and the heavens." The subject of this statement, according to Ibn Ḥazm, is Solomon! Ibn Nagrella would spend his time more productively, Ibn Ḥazm concludes, if he were to ponder such lies, rather than pretend to understand what he has no understanding of, i.e., the Qur'an.[30]

5. Ibn Nagrella noticed a second contradiction in the Qur'anic description of the Day of Judgment. According to Q. 55:39, "On that day none shall be questioned about his sin, neither man nor jinn." But in Q. 7:6 God states, "So We shall question those unto whom a message was sent, and We shall question the envoys." Again, Ibn Nagrella sees a problem.[31]

Ibn Ḥazm harmonizes the two verses by drawing a distinction (is this not *ta'wīl*?) between the day on which believers, such as Ibn Nagrella, will be brought to Hell, and the Day of Resurrection itself. "Surely," Ibn Ḥazm declares with mock humor, Ibn Nagrella will end up in Hell, "and there is no doubt that when he is seized by his forelocks and his feet so that he may be dropped into the fire . . . he will not be asked about his religion." But on the Day of Resurrection itself, when those who reject faith take their stand before God—on that day they shall be questioned.[32]

Having already pointed out the deficiencies of the Torah on the subject of reward and punishment in the next world, Ibn Ḥazm brings up an unrelated subject, namely, the manner in which the Torah anthropomorphizes the Divinity, attributing to Him caprice or weakness of mind, movement in space, corporeality, etc. In Ex. 32:9f., for example, God states His intention to destroy the Children of Israel because they are a stiff-necked people, but fails to carry out His stated intention due to the intervention of Moses, who apparently persuaded the Divinity to change His mind. Further, in Ex. 33, when God orders the Children of Israel to enter Canaan, He says, "I will not go down with you, because you are a stiff-necked people, lest you be destroyed on the way." Again, Moses intervenes—he actually speaks to God "face-to-face"—and persuades the Divinity to change his mind. There is no way, Ibn Ḥazm concludes, for the Jews to escape the blatant anthropomorphisms contained in such stories.[33]

6. Ibn Nagrella also claimed to have identified a passage which suggests that Muhammad was not convinced of the validity of what God had revealed to him. In Q. 10:94 God says to Muhammad, "So, if thou art in doubt regarding what We have sent down to thee, ask those who recited the Book before thee...." Ibn Nagrella comments, "So Muhammad was in doubt about what God had revealed to him."[34]

Ibn Ḥazm disposes of the Jew's contention by exposing his faulty understanding of Arabic. Ibn Nagrella attributes doubt to Muhammad only because he is not sufficiently proficient in the Arabic language. The phrase in question reads, *fa-in kunta fī shakk*. Although the particle *in* usually denotes a condition, i.e., "if," it is frequently used in the Qur'an in the sense of a negation, i.e., "not"—as evidenced by a series of Qur'anic verses cited by Ibn Ḥazm.[35] Thus, the phrase *fa-in kunta fī shakk* means not "if you are in doubt," but rather "you are *not* in doubt about that which we revealed to you" (nor are the people to whom the Book was revealed before you in doubt).[36]

If anyone was in doubt about the message revealed to him by God, it was Moses, not Muhammad, for Ex. 3:11 portrays Moses as lacking confidence in himself when God wants to send him to Pharaoh. "Who am I," he is quoted as saying, "that I should go to Pharaoh?"[37]

At this point Ibn Ḥazm passes to a seemingly unrelated subject, to wit, Jacob's wrestling with God, as narrated in Gen. 32:23ff. How is it possible, he asks, that a man would actually wrestle with the Divinity and, further, overpower Him? And let not any Jew contend that Jacob wrestled with an angel, for the Hebrew word used in the text is *Elohim,* which can only mean "God."[38]

7. Ibn Nagrella also objects to a statement in Q. 16:69, referring to honey—"wherein is healing for men"—apparently on the grounds that honey is harmful to people with certain illnesses.[39]

Ibn Ḥazm counters by declaring that the Jew understands neither the Arabic language nor the science of medicine. Ibn Nagrella seems to have misunderstood Q. 16:69, he argues, for God did not say, "honey is a remedy for every disease"; rather, He merely stated that honey contains "healing for men," i.e., healing for some men and some diseases. The truth of this statement should be apparent to anyone familiar with medicine, for honey is used in the preparation of most potions and electuaries; indeed, every potion mentioned by Galen and Hippocrates contains honey as an ingredient.[40]

Again Ibn Ḥazm suggests that his adversary would not have raised such an objection if he had considered the text of his own scriptures with greater care. The Torah mentions a prophet who cured a gangrenous sore with ground figs, and "if figs are a remedy for some diseases, how can this knave deny the numerous remedial effects of honey?" Further, God describes the Holy Land as "flowing with milk and honey," thereby indicating that honey is a beneficial substance, not a harmful one.[41]

8. Finally, Ibn Nagrella objects to the use of the adjective "blessed" *(mubārak)* to refer to water. "How can it be blessed," he is reported to have said, "when it destroys buildings and kills many animals?"[42]

Ibn Ḥazm refutes this statement with relative ease. Doesn't Ibn Nagrella know that without water there could be no life, that human beings and animals would die, that nothing would grow, and that civilization, as we know it, could not exist. Furthermore, God speaks highly of water in the Torah, where He refers to it as a blessing, not a curse.[43]

Discussion

Clearly, it was a desire to undermine the authority of the Torah that led Ibn Ḥazm to the study of the Jewish sacred writings. In order to confirm the Muslim contention, mentioned already in the Qur'an, that the Jews had distorted the text of the Torah (a phenomenon known in Arabic as *taḥrīf),* the Ẓāhirī jurist examined the Torah with an eye to finding in it contradictions, errors, inconsistencies, and anthropomorphisms. It is important to note that Ibn Ḥazm does not deny that God revealed the Torah to Moses on Mount Sinai. Rather, he contends that the Jews did not faithfully preserve the original text *(al-*

Tawrā al-Ṣaḥīḥa),[44] for if they had, it would not contain all the—to his mind—offensive material.

Ibn Nagrella's reading of the Qur'an was also motivated by polemical considerations, but of a slightly different nature. In an effort to counter the Muslim claim that the Qur'an had come to abrogate *(naskh)* or replace the Torah, he sought to find in the text of the Qur'an statements that are so blatantly contradictory that no Jew could possibly accept it as the word of God.[45]

Ibn Ḥazm deals with the doctrine of *taḥrīf*, or distortion of scripture, in greater detail in the Epilogue, where he cites, for example, God's promise to the Jews that they would inherit the Holy Land and inhabit it forever. It is not difficult for Ibn Ḥazm to demonstrate that the Jews lived in *Eretz Israel* for only a short duration of eternity, and that it is the Muslims who now inhabit the land. He concludes from this discrepancy between Scripture and History not that God lied—heaven forbid—but that He never made the statement in question, i.e., the Jews mistakenly attribute such a statement to God. This is *taḥrīf*.[46] Similarly, Ibn Ḥazm cannot reconcile the story of Aaron (whom Muslims revere as a prophet) and the golden calf with the Muslim conception of prophecy. Again, he finds in this episode evidence that someone distorted *(baddala)* the original, authentic, Torah by adding this account to it in an effort, he suggests, to discredit the office of prophecy.[47]

The distortion of the authentic Torah can be explained, according to Ibn Ḥazm, by the defective manner of its transmission from generation to generation. Unlike the Qur'an, which was passed down from one generation to the next along multiple lines of transmission, thereby assuring its authenticity, the Torah, according to Ibn Ḥazm, was the exclusive possession of the *Kohanim* or priestly class, who passed it down from father to son for over 1200 years. This, he asserts, is a virtual guarantee of change, corruption, alteration, addition, and subtraction. Indeed, the Jews themselves admit that the real Torah was altered or destroyed between the seventh and fifth centuries B.C. For they supposedly acknowledge that Jehoahaz b. Josiah, king of Judah (609 B.C.) removed the names of God from the Torah, replacing them with the names of idols, and that his successor, Jehoiakim b. Josiah, burned the Torah. And the Jews admit, further, that at the time of the restoration in the fifth century B.C., the Torah had been forgotten, so that Ezra the Scribe had to reconstruct it, to the best of his ability, from memory.[48]

Both Ibn Ḥazm and Ibn Nagrella are religious polemicists, not disinterested scholars, and even a cursory examination of their arguments reveals the application of a double standard; what is acceptable within one's own religious tradition is not acceptable within another. For example, Ibn Ḥazm objects to the manner in which the Torah portrays Moses as lacking self-confidence. But the same can be said of Muhammad who, according to Islamic tradition, lacked confidence in himself when the angel Gabriel first appeared to him and told him to "recite." Further, the Qur'an itself contains anthropomorphisms which Ibn Ḥazm can only dismiss with the statement "*bi-lā kayf*," i.e., "we do not ask how this is possible." At the same time he seems not to be aware of the fact that the Jews understand the anthropomorphisms in the Torah as metaphors for the Divinity.

It is, perhaps, the deceptive similarities between Judaism and Islam, and the many elements shared in common by the two religions, that explain many of the misunderstandings: monotheism, scripture supplemented by oral tradition, prophecy, and divine law are only some of the structural elements that Judaism and Islam share in common. But each religion has its own set of assumptions about what constitutes a valid scripture or a valid prophet, and these assumptions are not always identical. When Ibn Nagrella attempts to apply his assumptions about scripture to the Qur'an, or when Ibn Ḥazm tries to apply his assumptions about the Qur'an to the Bible, the result is, more often than not, a misreading, or misunderstanding of the other's scripture. For example, Islamic tradition recognizes all of the major heroes of the Bible, from Adam to Moses, as prophets who are considered to be *ma'ṣūm* or infallible. It is therefore difficult for Ibn Ḥazm to accept the fact that Aaron played a role in creation of the golden calf, that David had illicit sexual relations with Bathsheba, and that Solomon married non-Israelite women. But, according to the biblical conception, Aaron was a priest, and David and Solomon were kings, and it is their humanity, with their strengths and weaknesses, that Jewish tradition emphasizes.

As mentioned at the outset, I was initially attracted to the exchange between Ibn Ḥazm and Ibn Nagrella because it seemed to constitute one of those rare instances in which Jews and Muslims have read and responded to one another's scriptures. Having examined Ibn Ḥazm's *Refutation,* I must admit that my expectations have only been partially fulfilled. The more familiar I have become with their respective arguments, the less convinced I am that either one actually sat down and *read* the other's scripture. True, each had access to the other's scripture, either in the original or by means of a translation. But it is doubtful, to my mind, that Ibn Nagrella identified his contradictory passages in the Qur'an by sitting down and reading that text from beginning to end, for the issues he raises had been identified and explained by the earliest Muslim commentators. For example, in an appendix to the *Tafsīr al-Khamsmi'āt Āya* by Muqātil b. Sulaymān (d. 767), Ibn 'Abbās, a Companion to the Prophet (d. 688), introduces the topic of scriptural contradiction (*ikhtilāf al-qur'ān*), listing nine pairs of contradictory verses which he harmonizes by arguing that the opposing verses refer to different situations, or different aspects of the same situation.[49] Two of the nine pairs mentioned here are similar to those cited by Ibn Nagrella three centuries later, viz., Q. 79:27-30 vs. 41:9-11 (Did God create the heavens or the earth first?), and Q. 55:39 vs. 15:92-93 (Will those being tried on the Day of Judgment be asked about their misdeeds?). It is not unreasonable to assume that discussions such as these would have made their way into Jewish circles, in the context of polemics between Muslims and Jews, and that the problematic passages would have been familiar to interested Jewish scholars, such as Ibn Nagrella.

Similarly, earlier generations of Jews, Jewish sectarians, and Christians had prepared the ground for Ibn Ḥazm's attack on the Torah. For example, the question of why God punishes the children for the sins of the parents had been raised in Talmudic times, if not earlier, by Jewish heretics. The Rabbis responded by arguing that God punishes the children only when they follow the course of their parents; according to Sa'adya, God repaid the children of Abraham for their sufferings.[50] The failure of the Bible to mention reward and punishment in the next world had been pointed out already by Josephus, Marcion, and the Manichaeans.[51] As for the problem of God *resting*, Philo and the Rabbis explained the words *va-yishbot* and *va-yanuaḥ* as causative verbs, i.e., God made the world rest.[52]

Closer to Ibn Ḥazm's own time, Ismā'īl al-Ukbarī, a ninth-century proto-Karaite, had asserted that "some things in the scripture were not [originally] as they are now written."[53] And Ḥiwī al-Balkhī (d. 893), a Jew with definite sectarian leanings, had formulated 200 questions aimed at demonstrating the shortcomings of the Bible from the standpoint of ethics and reason. Several of his objections, as reconstructed from the statements of his opponents, may be mentioned here: God changed His mind, which indicates that He is neither omniscient nor consistent; the Bible contains numerous anthropomorphisms, e.g., God rested; the Bible contains contradictions; and the Bible is unreasonable, e.g., it contains no mention of reward or punishment in the next world.[54] The resemblance to Ibn Ḥazm is striking. Although Ḥiwī lived in Khurāsān, it is not out of the question that Ibn Ḥazm could have been familiar with his writings, either directly or indirectly, for Ḥiwī is mentioned by several of Ibn Ḥazm's Spanish contemporaries and near contemporaries, such as Moses b. Ezra (1070-1139), Abraham b. Ezra (1092-1167), and Abraham b. Da'ud (1110-1180).[55]

Our examination of the interchange between Ibn Ḥazm and Ibn Nagrella provides us with an example of one way to read a sacred text, namely, with the intent of undermining the claim of the Hebrew Bible or the Qur'an to be a scripture. It is to be hoped, however, that today, when increasing numbers of Jews and Muslims have access to the other's scripture, either in the original language or in translation, and when the need for mutual understanding is so great, that the adherents of these two major religions will begin to read one another's sacred text from a nonpolemical perspective. The creation of an Institute for Jewish/Muslim studies that seeks to provide an academic forum for the study of the interaction between Jewish and Islamic civilizations certainly marks a step forward in this direction.

NOTES

1 H. A. R. Gibb and J. Kramers, eds., *The Shorter Encyclopedia of Islam* (Ithaca: Cornell University Press, 1953), s.v. "*Taḥrīf.*"

2 On the *Isrā'īliyyāt*, see *The Encyclopedia of Islam,* New ed. (Leiden: Brill, 1978), 4:211-12.

3 Certainly, converts to Islam, such as 'Alī al-Ṭabarī, a Christian turned Muslim at about the age of seventy (ca. 838-40), or Samau'al b. Yaḥyā al-

Maghribī (mid-twelfth century) had grown up with a truly firsthand knowledge of Scriptures. See S. Baron, *A Social and Religious History of the Jews* (New York: Columbia University Press, 1954), 5:85.

[4] But Professor Lenn Goodman informs me that he finds echoes of Qur'anic vocabulary in the works of the Jewish jurist and philosopher Sa'adya Gaon. For an English translation of the so-called "Pact of 'Umar," in which non-Muslims are prohibited from teaching the Qur'an to their children, see Norman Stillman, *The Jews of Arab Lands* (Philadelphia: Jewish Publication Society, 1979), 157.

[5] The refutation was published in part by E. Garcia Gomez, "Polemica religiosa entre Ibn Ḥazm e Ibn al-Nagrīla," *Al-Andalus* 4 (1936-39): 1-28; and again, in its entirety, by Iḥsan 'Abbās, ed., *Al-Radd 'alā Ibn al-Naghrīla al-Yahūdī wa-Rasā'il Ukhrā* (Cairo: al-Maṭba' al-Madanī, 1960), pp. 45-81. (All references in this paper are to the 1960 edition.)

[6] Moshe Perlmann, in his "Eleventh-Century Andalusian Authors on the Jews of Granada," *Proceedings of the American Academy of Jewish Research* 18 (1948-49): 269-90, accepts the attribution of such a polemic to Samuel. But Iḥsān 'Abbās, in his introduction to the *Radd,* argues that Samuel ha-Nagid was too clever to have written a polemic pointing out contradictions in the Qur'an, and that the probable author of the text was his son, Joseph. E. Ashtor responds to this argument in his *The Jews of Moslem Spain* (Philadelphia: Jewish Publication Society of America, 1979): 2:322, n. 116; although he does see some merit in the idea that Joseph was the author of the polemic, Ashtor rejects this opinion on the strength of Ibn Ḥazm's statement in which he refers to the Jew "as we knew him long ago" (Ibn Ḥazm, *Radd,* p. 47), in all likelihood a reference to the debate of A.D. 1013 (see below, pp. 110-11). Professor Brinner informs me that in a lecture delivered at the University of Chicago in May 1984, Dr. Sara Stroumsa referred to recent Israeli scholarship which revives the idea that Samuel could not have written the polemic. Thus, the issue is still moot, and until such time as it is finally resolved, I will continue to refer to Samuel as the author of the polemic. See also Moritz Steinschneider, *Die Arabische Literatur der Juden* (Frankfurt: Kauffmann, 1902), 129-30.

[7] *Encyclopedia Judaica,* 14:816, s.v. "Samuel ha-Nagid"; see also H. Schirmann, "Samuel Hannagid, the Man, the Soldier, the Politician," *Jewish Social Studies* 13 (1951): 99-126.

[8] *Ibid.*, pp. 816-17.

[9] For further details on the life and writings of Ibn Ḥazm, see *Encyclopedia of Islam,* 2nd ed., 3:79-99, s.v., "Ibn Ḥazm"; R. Arnaldez. *Grammaire et théologie chez Ibn Ḥazm de Cordoue* (Paris: J. Vrin, 1956); A. Chejne, *Ibn Ḥazm* (Chicago: Kazi Publications, 1982).

[10] Ibn Ḥazm states that the debate between himself and Samuel b. Nagrella took place in A.H. 404 (A.D. 1013). See his *Kitāb al-Fiṣal fi' l-Milal wa'l-Ahwā' wa'l-Niḥal* (Baghdad: Maktabat al-Muthanna, 1964): 1:152; for a summary of the debate, in English, see Ashtor, vol. 2, pp. 53-55.

[11] As he himself explains, Ibn Ḥazm, *Radd,* p. 47, par. 2; see also the comments by 'Abbās in his introduction, p. 18.

[12] All translations from the Qur'an are taken from A. J. Arberry, *The Koran Interpreted* (New York: Macmillan Publishing Co., 1955).

[13] Ibn Ḥazm, *Radd*, p. 47, par. 3.

[14] *Ibid.*, pp. 47-48.

[15] Num. 14:17-18.

[16] Gen. 4:15, 24.

[17] All biblical verses cited in this article are my translations of Ibn Ḥazm's Arabic citation in his *Radd*. By the eleventh century A.D., several attempts had been made to translate the Hebrew Bible into Arabic. An early translation by Aḥmad b. 'Abd Allāh b. Salām in the days of Hārūn al-Rashīd (r. 786-809) is mentioned by Ibn al-Nadīm in his *Fihrist*, Bayard Dodge, tr. (New York: Columbia University Press, 1970), 1:41-43. Ḥunayn b. Isḥāq (d. 873) is reported to have produced a translation of the Old Testament from the Septuagint (Baron, *Social and Religious History*, 6:264). Only the *names* of the earliest Jewish translators have been preserved (*Ibid.*, vol. 6, pp. 265-68; see also H. Malter, *Saadiah Gaon: His Life and Works* [New York: Jewish Publication Society of America, 1921], 141-42). But Ibn Ḥazm did not make exclusive use of Sa'adya's translation, for, according to 'Abbās, he had access to several Arabic translations of the Old Testament and did not rely on any single one of these. For more on Ibn Ḥazm's use of the Hebrew Bible see E. Algermissen, *Die Pentateuchzitate Ibn Ḥazms* (Münster Ph.D. Dissertation, 1933).

[18] Ibn Ḥazm, *Radd*, p. 50, par. 8.

[19] *Ibid.*, p. 51, par. 9.

[20] *Ibid.*, pp. 51-52, pars. 10-11.

[21] *Ibid.*, p. 52, par. 11.

[22] *Ibid.*, pp. 52-53, par. 12.

[23] Qur'an 41:10.

[24] Qur'an 41:12.

[25] Ibn Ḥazm, *Radd*, pp. 53-54, par. 13.

[26] *Ibid.*, p. 54, par. 14.

[27] *Ibid.*, p. 54, par. 15.

[28] *Ibid.*, pp. 55-56, par. 16.

[29] *Ibid.*, par. 17.

[30] *Ibid.*, p. 56, par. 18.

[31] *Ibid.*, par. 19.

[32] *Ibid.*, p. 57, par. 20.

[33] *Ibid.*, pp.57-59, pars. 21-23.

[34] *Ibid.*, p. 60, par. 26.

[35] Qur'an 7:188, 12:31, 14:11, 21:17.

[36] Ibn Ḥazm, *Radd*, pp. 60-61, par. 27.

[37] *Ibid.*, pp. 61-62, par. 28.

[38] *Ibid.*, p. 62, par. 28.

[39] *Ibid.*, par. 29.

[40] *Ibid.*, pp. 62-63, par. 30.

[41] *Ibid.*, p. 63, par. 31.

[42] *Ibid.*, par. 32.

[43] *Ibid.*, pp. 63-64, par. 33.

[44] *Ibid.*, p. 77, par. 60.

[45] On the doctrine of abrogation, as applied to the Hebrew Bible, see *Ibn Kammuna's Examination of the Three Faiths,* M. Perlmann, tr. (Berkeley: University of California Press, 1971), pp. 47, 70-71.

[46] Ibn Ḥazm, *Radd*, p. 68, par. 42.

[47] *Ibid.*, p. 71, pars. 48-49.

[48] *Ibid.*, p. 77, par. 60; cf. *Encyclopedia Judaica,* 9:1315, 1318.

[49] Muqātil b. Sulaymān, *Tafsīr al-Khamsmi'āt Āya,* I. Goldfeld, ed. (Shfaram: al-Mashriq Press, 1980), 281-82; cf. J. Wansbrough, *Quranic Studies* (London: Oxford University Press, 1977), 163-64.

[50] Judah Rosenthal, "Al-Balkhī: A Comparative Study," *Jewish Quarterly Review*, n.s. 38 (2948): 325.

[51] *Ibid.*, p. 329.

[52] *Ibid.*, p. 333.

[53] Baron, *Social and Religious History,* vol. 6:478-79.

[54] *Ibid.*, pp. 299-301; Rosenthal, "Ḥiwī," pp. 323-40.

[55] Baron, *Social and Religious History,* vol. 6:304.

Kinship Bars to Marriage in Jewish and Islamic Law

Stephen D. Ricks

Introduction

Marriage, with its resultant structures of kinship[1] and affinity,[2] is a characteristic feature of societal organization. Nearly as universal are bars to sexual relations and, *a fortiori*, to marriage on the basis of consanguinity or affinity.[3] Such kinship bars to marriage are reflected in the legislation of both Judaism and Islam. This study will focus on these impediments to marriage resulting from consanguinity and affinity (as well as fosterage in Islam) in the primary legal sources of Judaism (Bible and Talmud) and Islam (Qur'an and *Ḥadīth*, as well as the opinions of the jurists), discuss their historical development, and consider what relation, if any, they may have to each other.

Bars to Marriage in Judaism Based on Consanguinity and Affinity

The sources for our discussion of kinship bars to marriage in Jewish law derive, in the first place, from the Bible, where there are legal sanctions (especially in Leviticus and Deuteronomy) which outline incest prohibitions,[4] as well as historical passages which incidentally illustrate actual practices. These biblical passages provide the basis for subsequent talmudic discussions and expansions of prohibited degrees.

The marriage practices reflected in the patriarchal narratives, which often conflict with the injunctions in Leviticus and Deuteronomy, suggest a stage of development anterior to that revealed in the codes. The priestly injunctions at Leviticus 18:8, 11, forbid "uncovering the nakedness"[5] of a maternal or paternal sister, whereas paternal sisters were available for marriage during the patriarchal period. Thus Abraham, in justifying himself before Abimelech for having told him that Sarah was his sister but having failed to mention that she was also his wife, said: "And besides, she is in truth my sister, my father's daughter though not my mother's; and she became my wife."[6] A proposal of marriage between paternal siblings is made as late as David's reign. David's daughter Tamar, while rebuffing her paternal brother Amnon's advances, told him: "Don't, brother. Don't force me. Such things are not done in Israel! . . . Please, speak to the king; he will not refuse me to you."[7] There is no hint of blame on Tamar for having suggested such a marriage with her brother. However, it is notoriously difficult to generalize normative marriage practices based on the conduct of members of the royal family. In the case of incest in particular, what is forbidden to the general populace may be permitted to members of the royal family. Perhaps it would be most correct to say that the prohibition of marriage between paternal siblings was not universally observed until well into the period of the monarchy.

Marriage with two sisters simultaneously was also explicitly forbidden in Leviticus 18:18: "Do not marry a woman as a rival to her sister. . . ." In contrast to this prohibition, Jacob married Leah and Rachel,[8] although this was the result as much (or more) of Laban's cunning as Jacob's own designs (on the other hand, Laban seems not to have hesitated to offer Rachel to Jacob after his marriage to Leah, and Jacob also seems to have expressed no ethical or legal reservations to Laban's proposal). Further, where Leviticus prohibits intercourse between nephew and paternal aunt as incestuous,[9] the marriage of Moses' parents Amran and Jochabed represents just such a union.[10] Thus, our records of the patriarchal period suggest a freer pattern of marriages then than that reflected in the priestly and deuteronomic codes, with paternal sister, aunt, and two sisters simultaneously among the permissible conjugal partners.

Deuteronomy, whose redaction dates, according to the preponderance of scholarly opinion, to the latter period of the monarchy,[11] lists three incest prohibitions in a section that enumerates curses for violations of moral conduct:

> Cursed be he who lies with his father's wife, for he has removed his father's garment. —And all the people shall say, Amen.
> Cursed be he who lies with his sister, whether daughter of his father or of his mother. —And all the people shall say, Amen. Cursed be he who lies with his mother-in-law. —And all the people shall say, Amen.[12]

The compiler of these laws no doubt consciously chose these particular incestuous relationships to represent a far larger number of prohibitions. It strikes me as somewhat rash to suppose (as some commentators do) that these represent the only incest and marriage bars observed during this period (i.e., before the observance of the legislation in Leviticus).

Leviticus, which is generally accorded a redactional date after that of Deuteronomy,[13] includes at 18:6-18 and 20:12-14, 14, 17, 19-21 a much larger group of incest prohibitions: mother,[14] father's (other) wife/wives,[15] father's brother's wife,[16] maternal or paternal sister,[17] son's daughter or daughter's daughter,[18] father's sister,[19] mother's sister,[20] son's wife,[21] brother's wife,[22] wife's mother,[23] wife's son's daughter,[24] wife's daughter's daughter.[25] The most obvious lack in this list of incest prohibitions is the daughter. However, the explicit mention of the daughter's daughter among those who are within the forbidden degrees[26] makes it plausible that the daughter was inadvertently dropped from any list in Leviticus through scribal or editorial oversight.[27] In any event, the daughter is included in the Mishnah's list of prohibited degrees.[28]

The forbidden degrees in Leviticus may be schematized in the following manner according to consanguinity and affinity in the ascending, descending, and lateral lines:

I. In the ascending line, through the mother:
1. Mother (Lev. 18:7) and (laterally)

2. Mother's sister (Lev. 18:13, 20:19).

II. In the ascending line, through the father:
3. Father's wife (Lev. 18:8, 20:11; cf. Deut. 23:1, 27:20), and (laterally)
4. Father's sister (Lev. 18:12, 20:19), and
5. Father's sister-in-law, i.e., the wife of the father's brother (Lev. 18:14).

III. In the descending line, through the daughter:
6. Daughter (implicit in Lev. 18:10; cf. M. Yevamot 1:1) and
7. Daughter's daughter (Lev. 18:10).

IV. In the descending line, through the son:
8. Son's wife (Lev. 18:15, 20:12) and
9. Son's daughter (Lev. 18:10).

V. In the lateral line, through the sister:
10. Sister or half-sister (Lev. 18:9, 11, 20:17, cf. Deut. 27:22).

VI. In the lateral line, through the brother:
11. Brother's wife (Lev. 18:17, 20:21).

VII. In the line of affinity, through the wife:
12. Wife's mother (Lev. 20:14; cf. Deut. 27:23),
13. Wife's daughter (Lev. 18:17),
14. Wife's son's daughter (Lev. 18:17),
15. Wife's daughter's daughter (Lev. 18:17), and
16. Wife's sister (during the lifetime of the wife) (Lev. 18:18).[29]

In only one instance does the Bible indicate that the impediment to marriage resulting from affinity is removed through the death of the marriage partner or the dissolution of the marriage through divorce. At Leviticus 18:18, a man is forbidden to take the sister of his wife in marriage "in the other's lifetime," implying that after her death such a marriage would be permissible. In other cases rabbinic sources show that the bar to marriage resulting from affinity was understood to be permanent. Thus, a man is forbidden to have sexual relations with his father's wife or with his son's wife "both during his father's lifetime and after his death."[30]

J. R. Porter plausibly suggests that the incest prohibitions outlined in Leviticus and Deuteronomy reflect the limit of the extended family in ancient Israel, which included:

> The head of the family and his wife, his father and mother, step-mothers, sisters (and sometimes their husbands), sons and daughters and their spouses, grandsons and granddaughters (and sometimes their husbands), the father's brothers and their wives, and head's brothers and their wives, and his mother-in-law or mothers-in-law.[31]

These family members would have lived in the same domicile or in nearly contiguous domiciles. The biblical incest prohibitions were introduced, according to Porter, in order to prevent the role disruption that would otherwise inevitably occur.[32]

Before continuing to the list of rabbinically forbidden degrees, one addition should be made to the biblically prohibited bars: the wife's grandmother. This prohibition was not expressly stated in the biblical text, but was viewed by the rabbis as being clearly implied. Deuteronomy 27:23 mentions the prohibition of one's "mother-in-law," while Leviticus speaks of "a woman and her daugher" and Leviticus 20:14 of "a woman and her mother." In both of these latter cases, the prohibition is concluded by "it is *zimmah* (wickedness)." Thus, all three generations—mother, woman, and daughter—are included in the *zimmah* prohibition. In the rabbinic view, this *zimmah* prohibition would obtain no matter which of the generations the wife belonged to. A woman and her daughter or a woman and her granddaughter are both expressly forbidden to a man in Leviticus 18:17 but, according to the rabbis, the prohibition would also apply if the wife were the granddaughter. Hence, a woman and her grandmother also fell within the forbidden degrees.[33]

The inclusion of the wife's grandmother among the biblically sanctioned incest prohibitions is significant, since the biblical bars were viewed in a fundamentally different way than the rabbinically established bars. In the rabbinic view, marriages within the biblically forbidden degrees were void, with no divorce necessary; any offspring of that union were declared *mamzerim* (bastards).[34] The penalty for the act of incest itself was severe. Leviticus 20:14 demands death by burning for a man and his mother-in-law who have sexual relations. An unspecified form of capital punishment is required for those guilty of the incestuous relations listed in Leviticus 20:21, 12, 19, while *karet* (lit. "cutting off," a divine punishment, presumably death) is to be visited upon those who commit the incestuous acts named in Leviticus 20:17, 20, 21. In the Mishnah,[35] stoning is the punishment prescribed for those committing incest with mother, stepmother, and daughter-in-law, while those having incestuous relations with a stepdaughter, step-granddaughter, mother-in-law, grandmother-in-law, daughter, or granddaughter were to be executed by burning.[36] On the other hand, rabbinically forbidden marriages were viewed as "prohibited but valid," and the children of such unions were deemed legitimate. Because the marriage itself was prohibited, the dissolution of the marriage by divorce was required.[37] However, because the marriage was itself not viewed as criminally incestuous, no further penalties were attached.

The additional bars to marriage that were established by the rabbis, probably over a period of years, were not intended "to create additional criminal offenses, but as additional prohibitions of intercourse and impediments to marriage."[38] At T. B. Yevamot 21a, eight additional kinship bars to marriage are enumerated: "(a man's) mother, his father's mother, his father's father's wife, his mother's father's wife, the wife of his father's maternal brother, the wife of his mother's paternal brother, the daughter-in-law of his son and the daughter-in-law of his daughter."[39] Later in this same section of Yevamot, the wife of the mother's maternal brother is barred to marriage just as the wife of her paternal brother had been.[40]

There was some dispute about which of these prohibitions were terminable and which interminable. Based on the opinions of Rav and R. Ḥanina (students of R. Judah ha-Nasi), Ze'iri declared four of the prohibitions that are given in T. B. Yevamot 21a to be terminable: the wife of a mother's paternal brother, the wife of a father's maternal brother, the wife of the mother's father, and the daughter-in-law.[41] The other bars given there are thus interminable. Bar Kappara, another of R. Judah ha-Nasi's students, added two more prohibitions but made them terminable: mother's father's mother and father's father's mother.[42] The school of R. Ḥiyya added twelve more prohibitions: the four great-granddaughters, the four great-granddaughters of the wife, and the four great-grandmothers of the wife. There was some discussion about whether these were terminable or interminable, but no final decision is given in the Talmud.[43]

Following the schematization previously used, the biblical and rabbinic bars to marriage resulting from affinity or consanguinity may be illustrated in the following manner along ascending, descending, and lateral lines:

I. In the ascending line, through the mother, the Bible forbids marriage with the
1. Mother and (laterally)
2. Mother's sister.
The rabbis further prohibit marriage with the
a. Mother's mother,
b. Mother's mother's mother, *ad infinitum*,
c. Mother's father's wife,
d. Mother's father's mother,
e. Mother's paternal brother's wife, and
f. Mother's maternal brother's wife.

II. In the ascending line, through the father, the Bible prohibits marriage with the
3. Father's wife, and (laterally)
4. Father's sister, and
5. Father's paternal brother's wife.
The rabbis further forbid unions with the
a. Father's mother,
b. Father's mother's mother, *ad infinitum*,
c. Father's father's wife,
d. Father's father's father's wife, *ad infinitum*, and
e. Father's maternal brother's wife.

III. In the descending line, through the daughter, the Bible prohibits marriage with the
6. Daughter (by implication) and
7. Daughter's daughter.
The rabbis further forbid unions with the
a. Daughter's daughter's daughter,

b. Daughter's son's wife, and
c. Daughter's son's daughter.

IV. In the descending line, through the son, the Bible forbids marriage with the
8. Son's wife and
9. Son's daughter.
The rabbis forbid unions with the
a. Son's daughter's daughter,
b. Son's son's wife,
c. Son's son's daughter, and
d. Son's son's son's wife, *ad infinitum.*

V. In the lateral line, through the sister, the Bible forbids marriage with the
10. Sister or half-sister.
The rabbis add no further prohibitions.

VI. In the lateral line, through the wife, the Bible forbids marriage with the
11. Brother's wife.
The rabbis add no further prohibitions.

VII. In the line of affinity, through the wife, the Bible forbids marriage with the
12. Wife's mother,
13. Wife's daughter,
14. Wife's son's daughter,
15. Wife's daughter's daughter,
16. Wife's sister (during her lifetime),
17. Wife's mother's mother (by implication), and
18. Wife's father's mother (by implication).
The rabbis further prohibit marriage with
a. All four great-grandmothers of the wife and
b. All four great-granddaughters of the wife.

Bars to Marriage in Islam Based on Affinity and Consanguinity

Information concerning impediments to marriage in pre-Islamic Central Arabia can be determined only from passing references in Islamic sources that either treat explicitly the marriage customs current at that time or mention them incidentally in the course of a narrative. Unfortunately, even those few sources available may not be free from inaccuracy because of their author's or compiler's distance in time from the practices being described, because of the flawed sources from which their reports are drawn, or because of the writer's own tendentious purposes in composing the material. Muḥammad ibn Ḥabīb, for instance, notes in his *Kitāb al-Muḥabbar* that Arabs before the time of Muhammad did not marry mothers, daughters, sisters, or maternal and paternal aunts.[44] In a somewhat similar vein, the geographer Yaqūt says that the Meccans before Muhammad were unlike the uncultured bedouins and their allies in that they avoided marriages with mother, daughters, granddaughters, sisters, or sisters' daughters "because they disliked and shunned the Magian custom."[45] Yaqūt's statement in particular may have been inspired by the desire to portray the Meccans (from whom Muhammad was descended) in the most favorable light possible at the expense of the Arabs of the desert. In any event, the statements of Muḥammad ibn Ḥabīb and Yaqūt do not agree with each other nor with other notices of marriage practices in Mecca during the pre-Islamic period: for instance, it is recorded of 'Auf, the father of Muhammad's companion 'Abd al-Raḥmān and a Meccan, that he married his paternal sister al-Shafā.[46]

The Qur'an itself mentioned two marriage practices of the pre-Islamic era that were forbidden to the Muslim community. In Sūra 4:23, Muslim men are forbidden to marry "two sisters together, except what hath already happened (of that nature) in the past."[47] In the previous verse of Sūra 4, Muslim men are also prohibited from marrying "those women whom your father married, except what hath already happened (of that nature) in the past. Lo! It was ever lewdness and an abomination, and an evil way." This is probably connected with the more general pre-Islamic practice mentioned a few verses earlier of forcibly inheriting the women of a deceased kinsman.[48] According to al-Ṭabarī, during the *Jāhiliyya* it was the custom for the son, brother, or other legal heir of the deceased to inherit the wives of the dead man and either to marry them or at least prevent them from marrying.[49]

The prohibited degrees are outlined *in extenso* in Sūra 4:23:

> Forbidden unto you are your mothers, and your daughters, and your sisters, and your father's sisters, and your mother's sisters, and your brother's daughters, and your foster-sisters, and your mothers-in-law, and your step-daughters who are under your protection (born) of your women unto whom ye have gone in—but if you have not gone in unto them, then it is no sin for you to marry their daughters—and the wives of your sons who (spring) from your own loins. And it is forbidden unto you that ye should have two sisters together, except what hath already happened (of that nature) in the past.

On the authority of Ibn 'Abbās, al-Ṭabarī cites the tradition that seven groups of women are barred to marriage on the basis of *nasab* (consanguinity): mother, daughter, sister, maternal aunt, paternal aunt, brother's daughter, sister's daughter; similarly, seven groups of women are prohibited to marriage because of *ṣihr* (affinity): foster mother, foster sister, wife's mother, stepdaughter of a wife with whom one has consummated the marriage, daughter-in-law, woman already married, and father's wife.[50] The symmetry of these prohibitions is, however, more apparent than real, since (as we shall see in greater detail below), fosterage is generally treated in a category separate from that of affinity, with bars more closely approximating those of consanguinity than affinity.

These Qur'anically dictated prohibitions to marriage, cited in Sūra 4:22-23, may be schematized in the following manner according to consanguinity and affinity in ascending, descending, and lateral lines:

I. In the ascending line, through the mother:
1. Mother (4:23) and (laterally)
2. Mother's sister (4:23).

II. In the ascending line, through the father:
3. Father's wife (4:22) and (laterally)
4. Father's sister (4:23).

III. In the descending line, through the daughter:
5. Daughter (4:23).

IV. In the descending line, through the son:
6. Son's wife (4:23).

V. In the lateral line, through the sister:
7. Sister or half-sister (4:23) and
8. Sister's daughter (4:23).

VI. In the lateral line, through the brother:
9. Brother's daughter (4:23).

VII. In the line of affinity, through the wife:
10. Wife's mother (4:23),
11. Daughter of wife with whom the marriage has already been consummated, and
12. Wife's sister (4:23).

The forbidden degrees outlined in the Qur'an reveal striking similarities with Jewish bars to marriage: with the sole exception of the prohibition of uncle-niece marriages—as well as the consummation of the marriage with the mother acting as a bar to marriage with her daughter—every Qur'anic kinship bar based on affinity or consanguinity has its parallel in the biblical injunctions, a fact that has led some scholars to suggest the influence of the marriage ethics and practices of rabbinic Judaism or some related group.[51] On the other hand, the Qur'an makes no mention of prohibitions of the daughter's daughter, the son's daughter, the wife's granddaughter, and the brother's wife, all of which are included in the biblical lists.

The prohibition of uncle-niece marriages in Islam and their practice in rabbinic Judaism was the source of subsequent polemic between Jews and Muslims. Both the levirate and uncle-niece marriage (as well as accusations of father-daughter marriage) are the subject of an anecdote in al-Mas'ūdī's universal history *Murūj al-Dhahab*. According to al-Mas'ūdī, a Jewish physician happened to hear an argument in the presence of Ibn Ṭūlūn. The physician requested that he be permitted to respond to a Copt who was carrying on a disputation. The Copt asked the physician his religion. When the physician replied that he was Jewish, the Copt said that he was a Magian. Asked what he meant by his remark, the Copt replied that Jews considered marrying a daughter permissible under certain circumstances. According to the Copt, Jews permitted uncle-niece marriages and also observed the levirate, i.e., the custom of marrying the wife of one's brother in the event that the brother dies without issue. Thus, it might occur that a man might marry his daughter in order to observe the levirate, an act that in the Copt's estimation was no less despicable than what occurred among the Magians. In response, the Jewish physician said that he knew of nothing of the sort occurring among the Jews. Afterwards, however (al-Mas'ūdī continues), Ibn Ṭūlūn made inquiries and discovered that the Jewish physician had himself married his own daughter who had been the wife of his late brother.[52]

This was not the first time that the pharisaic-rabbinic practice of uncle-niece marriage had been the source of controversy and conflict. In the Damascus Rule, a document probably ultimately of Essene origin, members of the community are reminded that "each man marries the daughter of his brother or sister," an apparent reference to the pharisaic practice of uncle-niece marriages current during the beginning of the Common Era.[53] Similarly, the early Christians, Samaritans, Karaites, and Falashas all rejected uncle-niece marriages and sometimes mentioned these in their polemics with rabbinic Jews.[54]

The *ḥadīth* add no additional categories of degrees prohibited on account of consanguinity and only one additional category barring marriage because of affinity: a woman and her maternal or paternal aunt are forbidden to be married to the same man simultaneously. In a narration reported by Abū Hurayra, Muhammad said: "A woman and her paternal aunt cannot be joined (i.e., to the same man) nor a woman and her maternal aunt."[55] In another narration, Abū Hurayra reported that Muhammad forbade the marriage of a woman with her paternal aunt (i.e., to the same man) or an aunt to the daughter of her brother or of a woman with her maternal aunt or the maternal aunt with the sister's daughter.[56] The jurists subsequently developed and extended the prohibition so that two women who would have been prohibited to each other if one of them had been a man may not be married to the same man.[57] Thus, while only a marriage to a woman and her mother—as well as to a woman and her daughter in the event that the marriage to the woman has been consummated—was Qur'anically forbidden, now all the bars based on consanguinity and fosterage are applicable in determining the legitimacy of marrying two women simultaneously.

The jurists' contribution to the development of bars to marriage based on kinship consists primarily of extension along ascending, descending, and lateral lines of bars already in existence. Thus, where the Qur'anic directive prohibits the marriage of a man to his mother, the jurists forbid the union of a man and his mother or any of his female ascendants on either maternal or paternal side; where the Qur'an bars marriage between a man and his daughter, the jurists prohibit marriage between a man and any of his female descendants through either his son or his daughter. Similarly, where the Qur'an forbids the marriage of a man and his maternal or paternal aunt, the jurists forbid such a union between a man and his maternal or paternal aunt or the maternal or paternal aunt of any of his ascendants; the Qur'an forbids the marriage of a man to his niece, while the jurists prohibit marriage between a man and his niece or the niece of any of his descendants. The Qur'an forbids a conjugal relationship between a man and the wife of his father, whereas the jurists bar the marriage of a man and the wife of any of his ascendants; where the Qur'an forbids the marriage of a man to the wife of his son, the jurists prohibit such a union with the wife of any of the man's descendants. In the line of affinity, all female ascendants of the wife are disallowed for marriage by the jurists, whereas only the wife's mother is mentioned in the Qur'an. Descendants of the wife are also forbidden by the jurists on the same condition that is mentioned in the Qur'an: in the event that the man has already consummated the marriage with his wife, he is not allowed to marry her daughter or any of her descendants; otherwise, the man is permitted to be joined to them.[58]

Following the schematization previously given and taking into consideration the developments in the traditions and by the jurists, we thus have:

I. In the ascending line, through the mother, the Qur'an forbids marriage with the
1. Mother and (laterally)
2. Mother's sister.
The jurists further forbid marriage with the
a. Ancestresses of the mother, *ad infinitum*, and (laterally)
b. Paternal aunts of all ascendants.

II. In the ascending line, through the father, the Qur'an forbids marriage with the
3. Father's wife and (laterally)
4. Father's sister.
The jurists prohibit, in addition, marriage with the
a. Father's mother and all ancestresses of the mother, *ad infinitum*, and
b. Paternal aunts of all ascendants.

III. In the descending line, through the daughter, the Qur'an forbids marriage with the
5. Daughter.
The jurists further bar marriage with the
a. Daughter's daughter and all other female descendants of the daughter[59] or
b. Wife of any male descendants of the daughter.

IV. In the descending line, through the son, the Qur'an forbids marriage with the
6. Son's wife.
The jurists further forbide marriage with the
a. Female descendants of the son in the direct line of descent, *ad infinitum*, and
b. Wives of all male descendants of the son, *ad infinitum*.

V. In the lateral line, through the sister, the Qur'an forbids marriage with the
7. Sister or half-sister and
8. Sister's daughter.
The jurists further prohibit marriage with the
a. Sister's daughter or any of her female descendants.

VI. In the lateral line, through the brother, the Qur'an forbids marriage with the
9. Brother's daughter.
The jurists further forbid marriage with the
a. Brother's daughter or any of his female descendants.

VII. In the line of affinity, through the wife, the Qur'an forbids marriage with the
10. Wife's mother,
11. Daughters of wives with whom the marriage has already been consummated, and
12. Wife and her sister together.
The traditions further forbid marriage with a woman and her maternal or paternal aunt simultaneously.
The jurists further forbid a union between
a. A man and any of his wife's ancestresses or descendants and
b. A woman and anyone who would be forbidden because of consanguinity or fosterage if one of them (i.e., the woman whom the man wishes to marry) were a man.

Fosterage as a Bar to Marriage in Islam

As has been noted above, fosterage acted as a Qur'anically enjoined impediment to marriage: "Forbidden unto you are . . . your foster-mothers and your foster-sisters."[60] This prohibition reflects the long-standing Meccan custom of placing nursing children in the care of wetnurses (a practice which, incidentally, has persisted in Mecca until the present century). Muhammad was said to have been nursed by three different women, the first of whom was Thuwayba, a former slave of his uncle Abū Lahab, who had also suckled his uncle Ḥamza; the others were Ḥalīma and Umm Aymān. This custom of fosterage seems to have had its roots in the Meccan aversion to *ghīla* (sexual relations with a woman who is nursing), since Muhammad is reported to have said that the practice of *ghīla* would either result in the death of the child who was being suckled or would cause it to grow up in such a weakened condition that the child would not even be able to remain seated on a horse.[61] The Madīnans, on the other hand, did not share the Meccans' abhorrence of the practice of *ghīla*. Muhammad was finally persuaded from prohibiting *ghīla* by the resistance of the Madīnans as well as the example of the Greeks and Persians. In a *ḥadīth* narrated on the authority of Jumādā bint Wahb al-Asadiyya, Muhammad is reported to have said: "I intended to forbid *ghīla* until I considered that the Greeks and the Persians do it without any harm being caused to their children thereby."[62]

On the other hand, the practice of fosterage did persist. The Qur'anic prohibition against marriage with a foster mother or foster sister probably reflects a pre-Islamic Meccan custom. In the numerous *ḥadīth* dealing with fosterage, the circle of prohibited degrees resulting from fosterage was widened until it became coextensive with the prohibitions to marriage resulting from consanguinity. "What is unlawful by reason of consanguinity is unlawful by reason of fosterage" is a phrase found frequently at the end of traditions dealing with fosterage.[63] This must have represented a significant departure from the practice of the pre-Islamic period since, as the traditions show, there was considerable uncertainty in the early Muslim community about the extent of prohibited degrees based on fosterage. In a narration, 'Ā'isha reported that while she was with Muhammad, she heard a voice of a man asking permission to enter the dwelling of Ḥafṣa, one of Muhammad's wives. When she told Muhammad that a man was asking to enter his abode where Ḥafṣa was secluded, he said, "I think that it is So and So," naming the brother of the husband of Ḥafṣa's foster mother. To this 'Ā'isha replied, "If So and So were living (i.e., 'Ā'isha's own foster uncle) could he enter my presence?" The Prophet replied affirmatively, adding that those things which are unlawful through consanguinity are also unlawful through fosterage.[64] In another tradition of similar purport, 'Ā'isha reported that her foster uncle (*'amm*) came at one time and asked permission to enter the presence of 'Ā'isha, who was then in seclusion. She refused to allow him to enter until she had asked Muhammad for his advice. He told her, "He is your uncle. Give him permission to enter." When 'Ā'isha protested that she had been nursed by a woman and not a man, Muhammad reiterated his previous statement.[65] From 'Ā'isha's responses in these two narrations we may conclude that whereas 'Ā'isha fully expected her foster mother (and, by implication, the consanguineous relatives of her foster mother) to be within the prohibited degrees, it came as a surprise (probably because it was an innovation from the practice of pre-Islamic time) that the husband of her foster mother and his consanguineous relatives were similarly *maḥram* (barred from marriage).

On another occasion, 'Alī reported that he asked the Prophet if he wished to take the daughter of his uncle Ḥamza in marriage, since she was "the most beautiful of the young women of the Quraysh." Whereas under other circumstances a marriage between first cousins would have been not merely permissible, but even commendable, because both Ḥamza and Muhammad had been nursed by Thuwayba, they thereby became foster brothers, and Ḥamza's daughter became Muhammad's foster niece, and therefore within the prohibited degrees. As a result, Muhammad declined.[66]

Given the importance of fosterage in determining marriage and in influencing social relations, it is not surprising that numerous traditions deal with what conditions establish fosterage. The *ḥadīth* generally restricts suckling and, consequently, fosterage, to infancy. In a narration reported by 'Ā'isha, Muhammad came upon her when a man was sitting with her. Because Muhammad appeared to be angry, 'Ā'isha explained that he was her foster brother. To this Muhammad replied, "Be certain who are your foster brothers, since fosterage is established by hunger (*al-raḍā'a min al-majā'a*—i.e., when milk is the only food of the child)."[67] In a similar vein, Umm Salama reported that Muhammad said that suckling (and, consequently, the establishment of the foster relationship) must take place before weaning.[68] The period for suckling is generally reckoned by the jurists at two years, based on the Qur'anic directive: "Mothers shall suckle their children for two whole years; (that is) for those who wish to complete the suckling."[69] On the other hand, Abū Ḥanīfa and his school set the time for nursing at two and a half years.[70]

A set of traditions recorded by Muslim reveals an instance in which Muhammad approved of, if not actually promoted, the creation of a foster relationship with a youth. In a *ḥadīth* narrated by 'Ā'isha, she reported that Sahla bint Suhayl came to Muhammad and said that she had perceived signs of disgust on Abū Hudhayfa's face when his former slave Sālim entered her presence, since he was not within the prohibited degrees. Muhammad told her to suckle him. When Sahla asked in astonishment how she could suckle him when he had already reached puberty, Muhammad laughed and said, "I already know that he is a young man." Thereupon Sahla nursed him (or, perhaps more likely, she simply expressed some drops of milk and gave them to Sālim to drink) and Abū Hudhayfa ceased to be rankled by the situation.[71] But this case seems to have been exceptional rather than normative. In any event, the jurists do not appear to have treated it as normative.

Whereas there is general agreement that fosterage may be established only when the child is still in infancy, there is considerable divergence of opinion among the various schools concerning the minimum number of sucklings necessary to create the foster relationship. Umm al-Faḍl reported that a person from the Banū 'Āmir ibn Ṣa'ṣa'a came to Muhammad and asked if one suckling made marriage unlawful. To this query Muhammad replied negatively.[72] Similarly, 'Ā'isha reported that Muhammad said that one or two sucklings do not make a marriage unlawful.[73] 'Ā'isha is also reported to have said that "it was revealed in the Qur'an that ten discrete sucklings made the marriage unlawful, whereupon it was abrogated by five sucklings. The Messenger of God died and they (i.e., the directives concerning five discrete sucklings) were (still) among what was recited in the Qur'an."[74] On the basis of this tradition, the Shāfi'īs and the Ḥanbalīs require a minimum of five sucklings in order to establish a foster relationship. The Mālikīs and the Ḥanafīs, on the other hand, reject five as the required number of sucklings and demand only one suckling, of greater or lesser duration, in order to establish the foster relationship.[75]

A marriage within the prohibited degrees of fosterage—as also marriages within the prohibited degrees of consanguinity or affinity—could be voided. 'Aqba ibn Ḥārith reported: "I married a woman. Thereafter, a black woman came to us and said, 'I suckled both of you.' So I came to the Prophet and said, 'I married So and So. Then a black woman came to us and said to me, "I suckled both of you." But I think that she is a liar,' The Prophet turned his face away, and I moved to face him, and said, 'She is a liar,' The Prophet said, 'How can you keep her as your wife when that woman said that she suckled both of you? So abandon (i.e., divorce) her.' So I divorced her and she married another man."[76]

Claim of fosterage was also clearly susceptible of abuse. Umm al-Faḍl narrated that a bedouin came to Muhammad and told him that he had just married a second wife but that his first wife claimed that she had suckled her once or twice. His first wife's intention in saying this was apparently to create a bar in marriage to the second wife, thereby eliminating the second wife from competition for her husband's affections. Muhammad replied that one or two sucklings do not make a marriage unlawful, and therefore he was not barred from his marriage to his second wife.[77]

Conclusion

Muslim legislation dealing with marriages prohibited because of consanguinity and affinity, both in its original Qur'anic expression as well as in its subsequent development in the traditions and in the orthodox schools of jurisprudence, displays striking similarities to the biblical and rabbinic Jewish bars. In only two major respects did Muslim law differ significantly from that of rabbinic Jewish legislation: (1) in the marriage bars recognized on account of fosterage (which is lacking in rabbinic discussions), and (2) in its prohibition of uncle-niece marriages. So sharply was this latter difference felt by Muslims that it became a part of their polemics with the Jews—perhaps the only instance where an awareness of the marriage bars observed by the other group is explicitly indicated.

In the light of these similarities, it would not be unreasonable to conclude (as has been done[78]) that rabbinic Judaism (or a group closely akin to it in observances) influenced the shaping of Muslim legislation on marriage bars. However, in the absence of direct evidence of Jewish influence on Muslim bars to marriage, or of an awareness, even, of Jewish practices in this respect during the earliest period of Islam (the polemics concerning uncle-niece marriages deriving from a period centuries after the time of Muhammad), such a conclusion must necessarily remain tentative.

NOTES

1 Kinship has been described as the "social recognition of biological ties," Lucy Mair, *An Introduction to Social Anthropology*, 2nd ed. (Oxford: Clarendon Press, 1972), 69.

2 Affinity is relationship deriving from marriage. Properly speaking, affinity and kinship are separate categories of relation deriving from different sources (thus L. Mair, *ibid.*, p. 71). For the sake of simplicity, "kinship" will sometimes be used as a cover term for both consanguinity (i.e., relationship deriving from biological ties) and affinity.

3 Nearly all societies carefully regulate sexual relations or marriage between unmarried members of the same family. Special circumstances occasionally result in the elimination of this ban: thus, the Azande of Africa allow the high chief to marry his daughter, and Inca and some Hawaiian kings were permitted to enter brother-sister marriages; see George P. Murdock, *Social Structure* (New York: Macmillan Company, 1949), 266. On the other hand, J. S. Slotkin, "On

a Possible Lack of Incest Regulations in Old Iran," *American Anthropologist* 49(1947): 612-15, notes that incest may have been permitted in ancient Iran for the general population. According to J. Černy, "Consanguineous Marriages in Pharaonic Egypt," *Journal of Egyptian Archaeology* 40(1954): 22-29, and R. Middleton, "Brother-Sister and Father-Daughter Marriage in Ancient Egypt," *American Sociological Review* 27(1962): 603-11, brother-sister and father-daughter marriages were known among the general populace during the Greco-Roman era, while the evidence for such marriages in previous periods is scant. In any event, such marital configurations were not normative, certainly not for Jewish and Muslim societies. The reasons for the nearly universal incest taboos have been treated succinctly in Bernard I. Murstein, *Love, Sex, and Marriage through the Ages* (New York: Springer Publishing Company, 1974), 19-28. Robin Fox has also treated the subject in a highly readable fashion in *The Red Lamp of Incest* (London: Hutchinson, 1980).

[4] While the actual prohibitions in Leviticus and Deuteronomy are against incest, marriage would *a fortiori* be banned.

[5] "To uncover the nakedness of" someone is a euphemism meaning "to have sexual relations." The phrase is found in each of the verses from Leviticus 18:7-17 and serves as the element binding this pericope on prohibited degrees together.

[6] Gen. 20:12. All biblical citations are from the new Jewish Publication Society translation. That marriages were permitted between paternal but not uterine siblings suggests a vestige of matrilineality during the patriarchal era, which is parallelled (as we shall see below) by the customs observed in pre-Islamic Central Arabia.

[7] 2 Sam. 13:12-13.

[8] Gen. 29:21-30.

[9] Lev. 18:12.

[10] Ex. 6:20; Num. 26:59.

[11] According to Moshe Weinfeld, *Deuteronomy and the Deuteronomic School* (Oxford: Clarendon Press, 1972), 7, "The Book of Deuteronomy was composed in the latter half of the seventh century B.C." Similarly, Gerhard von Rad, *Deuteronomy* (Philadelphia: Westminster Press, 1966), 26, places the origin of Deuteronomy at one of the sanctuaries of Northern Israel (Shechem or Bethel) in the century before 621 B.C.E. Norbert Lohfink, "Deuteronomy," in Keith Crim, ed., *Interpreter's Dictionary of the Bible*, Supplementary Volume (Nashville: Abingdon Press, 1976), 229, thinks that the court of Hezekiah (715-687 BCE) is the most likely place of origin for Deuteronomy. It should be pointed out, however, that the materials from which Deuteronomy (and Leviticus) are composed date from a period earlier (and, in some instances, much earlier) than the later monarch (or, in the case of Leviticus, the exile).

[12] Deut. 27:20, 22-23. At Deut. 23:1, the prohibition of the father's (former) wife is also mentioned.

[13] According to Otto Eissfeldt, *The Old Testament, an Introduction,* tr. P. R. Ackroyd, tr. (New York: Harper and Row, 1965), 207, the priestly writings (including Leviticus) "came into existence in the exile, i.e., in the fifth or perhaps already in the sixth century."

[14] Lev. 18:7.
[15] Lev. 18:8, 20:11.
[16] Lev. 18:14.
[17] Lev. 18:9, 11, 20:17.
[18] Lev. 18:10.
[19] Lev. 18:12, 20:19.
[20] Lev. 18:13, 20:19.
[21] Lev. 18:16, 20:12.
[22] Lev. 18:17, 20:21. According to Deut. 25:3-10, if a man died without issue, it was the responsibility of his brother to take the deceased man's wife as a spouse or to follow a set procedure to relieve himself of this duty. However, later Jewish tradition understood *yibbum* (levirate) as being distinct from the prohibition against marrying a brother's wife in Leviticus 18:17, 10:21, since the injunction in Leviticus applied only where the deceased man already had sons; see Menachem Elon, "Levirate Marriage and Ḥaliẓah," in Menachem Elon, ed., *The Principles of Jewish Law* (Jerusalem: Keter Publishing House, 1975), 406.

In this, as in all other cases, the impediments to marriage are addressed to the man. This is because, in general, the Torah (as well as the Qur'an) "addresses itself to the man, especially in matters of marriage, for it is the man who marries the woman," Louis M. Epstein, *Marriage Laws in the Bible and the Talmud* (Cambridge, Mass.: Harvard University Press, 1942), 235.
[23] Lev. 20:14.
[24] Lev. 18:17.
[25] Lev. 18:17.
[26] Lev. 18:10.
[27] Thus Karl Elliger, "Das Gesetz Leviticus 18," *Zeitschrift für die alttestamentliche Wissenschaft* 67(1955): 2, 7. Other recent analyses of this passage in Leviticus 18 include F. J. Stendebach, "Überlegungen zum Ethos des alten Testaments," *Kairos* 18(1976): 273-80; Stephen F. Bigger, "The Family Laws of Leviticus 18 in Their Setting," *Journal of Biblical Literature* 98(1979): 187-203; Jörn Halbe, "Die Reihe der Inzestverbote Lev 18:7-18: Entstehung und Gestaltung," *Zeitschrift für die alttestamentliche Wissenschaft* 92(1980): 60-88.
[28] M. Yevamot 1:1; cf. T.B. Sanhedrin 76a. At this point, in fact, the Mishnah is dealing with those who exempt themselves, their co-wives, and their co-wives' co-wives, *ad infinitum*, from *yibbum* or *ḥaliṣah* (leviratic separation).
[29] This schematization follows that of Epstein, *Marriage Laws*, p. 234-35. I have found his discussion of incest and kinship bars to marriage (*ibid.*, 220-74) very illuminating and helpful, particularly for the Talmudic period.
[30] M. Sanhedrin 7:4.
[31] J. R. Porter, *The Extended Family in the Old Testament* (London: Edutext Publications, 1967), 21.
[32] *Ibid.*
[33] T. B. Sanhedrin 75a-b.
[34] T. B. Kiddushin 67b.
[35] M. Sanhedrin 7:4.

[36] M. Sanhedrin 9:1. According to Maimonides, *Mishneh Torah*, "Issurei Biah" 1:7, other incest offenses were to be punished by flogging or *karet*.
[37] Ben-Zion Schereschewsky, "Marriage, Prohibited," in Elon, ed., *The Principles of Jewish Law*, p. 360.
[38] Haim C. Cohn, "Incest," in *ibid*., p. 487.
[39] T. B. Yevamot 21a.
[40] T. B. Yevamot 21b. Thus, with the biblical prohibition of the wife of the father's paternal brother and the three rabbinic additions of the wife of the father's maternal brother, the wife of the mother's paternal brother, and the wife of the mother's maternal brother, the bars to the wives of the brother of father or mother are complete.
[41] T. B. Yevamot 21a; T. Y. Yevamot 2:4.
[42] T. Y. Yevamot 2:4.
[43] For a brief overview of the discussion in the codes of the terminability or interminability of marriage bars, see Epstein, *Marriage Laws*, 260-61.
[44] Abū Ja'far Muḥammad b. Ḥabīb, *Kitāb al-Muḥabbar* (Beirut: al-Maktab al-Tijārī li'l-Ṭibā'a wa'l-Nashr wa'l-Tawzī', n.d.), 325. This same passage concerning the marriage customs of the pre-Islamic Arabs is also found word for word—without attribution—in al-Shahrastānī, *Al-Milal wa'l-Niḥal*, W. Cureton, ed. (London: Society for the Publication of Oriental Texts, 1846), 440.
[45] Yaqūt b. 'Abd Allāh al-Ḥamawī, *Kitāb Mu'jam al-Buldān*, F. Wüstenfeld (Leipzig: F. A. Brockhaus, 1869), 4:620.
[46] W. Robertson Smith, *Kinship and Marriage in Early Arabia*, Stanley Cook, ed. (London: A. and C. Black, 1903), 192.
[47] There are solid grounds for supposing that Meccans during the pre-Islamic period were not forbidden to be married to two sisters at the same time. In a tradition reported in *Ṣaḥīḥ al-Bukhārī* (n.c.: Maṭābi' al-Sha'b, AH 1378), 7:12, by Umm Ḥabība, the daughter of the Meccan merchant Abū Sufyān and one of Muhammad's wives, she asked Muhammad to marry her sister. Muhammad refused, saying that marrying two sisters was unlawful. Had such a marriage been forbidden in pre-Islamic Mecca, it seems unlikely that Umm Ḥabība would have suggested it to Muhammad.

This and other citations from the Qur'an are from the version of Mohammed Marmaduke Pickthall, *The Meaning of the Glorious Koran* (New York: Mentor Books, n.d.)
[48] Qur'an 4:19.
[49] Abū Ja'far Muḥammad b. Jarīr al-Ṭabarī, *Jāmi' al-Bayān*, 40 vols. (Cairo: Muṣṭafā al-Bābī al-Ḥalabī, 1968), 4:318.
[50] *Ibid*., p. 320.
[51] Samuel Bialoblocki, *Materialien zum islamischen und jüdischen Eherecht* (Giessen: Verlag von Alfred Töpelmann, 1928), 38; S. D. Goitein, *Jews and Arabs: Their Contacts through the Ages*, 3rd ed. (New York: Schocken Books, 1974), 74.
[52] Abū Ḥasan 'Alī b. al-Ḥusayn al-Mas'ūdī, *Murūj al-Dhahab* (*Les prairies d'or)*, C. Barbière de Meynard and Pavet de Courteille, eds. and trs. (Paris: Imprimerie impériale, 1863), 2:388. In fact, M. Yevamot 1:1 already

makes provisions so that a father would never marry his daughter in order to observe the levirate. Similarly, in a polemical work against the Jews, cited in Moritz Steinschneider, *Polemische und apologetische Literatur in arabischer Sprache zwischen Muslimen, Christen, und Juden nebst Anhängen verwandeten Inhalts* (Hildesheim: Georg Old Verlagsbuchhandlung, 1966), 398, Aḥmad b. Tachtjar included the remark: "Among their (i.e., the Jews') abominations is their deeming it lawful that a man marry the daughter of his brother."

[53] Damascus Rule 5:7, in Geza Vermes, ed. and tr., *The Dead Sea Scrolls in English* (New York: Penquin Books, 1982), 101. The Essenes rejected the practice by analogy: if it were prohibited for a man to marry his maternal or paternal aunt, it would equally be forbidden for a woman to marry her uncle. In general, however, rabbinic Judaism rejected such extensions by analogy.

[54] Samuel Krauss, "Die Ehe zwischen Onkel und Nichte," *Studies in Jewish Literature Issued in Honor of Professor Kaufmann Kohler* (Berlin: Georg Reimer, 1913), 167-68.

[55] *Ṣaḥīḥ al-Bukhārī* 7:15.

[56] *Ibid.*

[57] M. b. 'Abd al-Wāḥid Ibn al-Humām, *Fatḥ al-Q ādir* (Cairo: Muṣṭafā al-Bābī al-Ḥalabī, 1970), 3:216-18, of the Ḥanafī school, presents this view. For a general discussion of the prohibition, see Tanzil-ur-Rahman, *A Code of Muslim Personal Law* (Karachi: Hamdard Academy, 1978), 1:142-47.

[58] Ibn al-Humām, *Fatḥ al-Qādir*, vol. 3:208-10 (Ḥanafī); Yaḥyā b. Sharīf al-Nawāwī, *Minhāj al-Ṭālibīn*, E. C. Howard, ed. and tr. (London: W. Thacker & Co., 1914), 291 (Shāfi'ī); Muwaffaq al-Din 'Abd Allāh Aḥmad b. Qudāma, *Kitāb 'Umdāt al-Fiqh 'alā Madhab al-Imām Aḥmad b. Ḥanbal*, Abū al-Samḥ 'Abd al-Ẓāhir and Ibrāhīm al-Shūrā, eds., (Cairo: Maṭba'at al-Manār, 1352/1934), 101-03 (Ḥanbalī). For a summary of the positions of the schools, see *Five Schools of Islamic Fiqha (Jurisprudence): Kitab un-Nikah Wa-Talaq* (Karachi: Peermahomed Ebrahim Trust, 1976), 3:23-27.

[59] There is, however, some divergence of opinion among the jurists about the permissibility of marrying illegitimate daughters. According to the Shāfi'ī school, sexual relations outside of marriage do not create in impediment to marriage. Thus al-Nawāwī, *Minhāj al-Ṭālibīn*, p. 291: "The prohibition (against marrying one's daughter) does not extend to children born of a criminal connection." The Ḥanafī and Ḥanbalī schools, on the other hand, make no such distinction between legitimate and illegitimate daughters; thus Ibn Qudāma, *Kitāb 'Umdāt al-Fiqh*, p. 101-03; Ibn al-Humām, *Fatḥ al-Qādir*, vol. 3:219-21.

[60] Qur'an 4:23.

[61] Aḥmad ibn Ḥanbal, *Musnad* (Cairo: Dār al-Ma'ārif, AH 1313) 453, cited in Gertrude Stern, *Marriage in Early Islam* (London: Royal Asiatic Society, 1937), 96-7. The outrageous audicity of Imru' al-Qays in "coming by night" to pregnant and nursing women *(al-Sab' al-Mu'allaqāt* 1:18-19) stands out in sharper relief in the light of the abhorrence of the Meccans to *ghīla*, a feeling that was doubtless shared by other inhabitants of the Arabian peninsula (though not by all, as we shall see below in the case of the Madīnans).

[62] Muslim, *Al-Jāmi' al-Ṣaḥīḥ*, 8 vols. (n.c.: n.p., n.d.), 4:162.

[63] There are, however, exceptions to this principle. Thus marriage with the following women is not barred on acount of fosterage: foster mother of the full sister, mother-in-law of the foster sister of a male not nursed at the mother-in-law's breast, other foster mothers of foster sister, foster mother of son by consanguinity, daughter or mother of foster mother of son by consanguinity; see Tanzil-ur-Rahman, *A Code*, vol. 1:138.

[64] *Ṣaḥīḥ al-Bukhārī*, vol. 7:11-12.

[65] *Ibid.*, p. 13.

[66] *Ibid.*, p. 12; Muslim, *Al-Jāmi' al-Ṣaḥīḥ*, vol. 4:164.

[67] *Ṣaḥīḥ al-Bukhārī*, vol. 7:12.

[68] *Sunan al-Tirmidhī*, 'Abd al-Wahhāb 'Abd al-Laṭīf and 'Abd al-Raḥmān Muḥammad 'Uthmān, eds., 5 vols. (Madīna al-Munawwara: al-Maktaba al-Salafiyya, 1966), 3:311.

[69] Qur'an 2:133.

[70] Ibn al-Humām, *Fatḥ al-Qādir*, vol. 2:441.

[71] Muslim, *Al-Jamī' al-Ṣaḥīḥ*, vol. 4:169.

[72] *Ibid.*, p. 167.

[73] *Ibid.*, p. 166.

[74] *Ibid.*, p. 165.

[75] Ibn al-Humām, *Fatḥ al-Qādir*, vol. 2:438-39. Joseph Shacht, "Raḍā'," in H. A. R. Gibb and J. H. Kramers, eds., *Shorter Encyclopedia of Islam* (Leiden: E. J. Brill, 1953), 464, considers the attribution to the Qur'an of the stipulation of five sucklings to be specious. See John Burton, *The Collection of the Qur'an* (Cambridge: Cambrige University Press, 1977), 87, 94-98, for further details of the controversy between the Shāfi'ī and Mālikī schools on this point, as well as for a discussion of its implications for the development of the Qur'anic canon.

[76] *Ṣaḥīḥ al-Bukhārī*, vol. 7:13.

[77] Muslim, *Al-Jāmi' al-Ṣaḥīḥ*, vol. 4:167.

[78] See footnote 54.

Adab al-Qāḍī and the Protection of Rights at Court

Farhat J. Ziadeh

Modern scholars interested in Islamic law, whether in the West or in Islamic countries, have concentrated their attention on matters of substantive law, particularly those pertaining to personal status, without paying much attention to questions of procedure, evidence, court organization, and court records, despite the importance of these latter subjects in protecting the rights of parties in a case at court. Perhaps this neglect is attributable to the fact that most modern Muslim states have adopted codes of procedure and evidence for Islamic jurisdictions that depart substantially from procedural and evidentiary matters in traditional Islamic practice. But we cannot understand the concern of traditional Islamic society in general, or of Islamic jurists in particular, for justice, equality before the law, and protection of the rights of parties to an issue without examining procedural and evidentiary matters developed by Islamic law.

Muslim jurists accorded these matters considerable attention. They incorporated their writings on the subject in a genre they called Adab al-Qāḍī ("The Discipline of the Judge"). In most cases this genre comprised a section in a general work on jurisprudence, but sometimes it consisted of independent works devoted to it. As in the case of other subjects of jurisprudence, these works were later commented upon and, still later, abridged by succeeding generations of jurists. *Kashf al-Ẓunūn* lists five original works on this subject by Ḥanafī jurists. One of these works—that by Aḥmad ibn 'Amr al-Khaṣṣāf—has nine separate commentaries devoted to it. Shāfi'ī jurists were no less prolific: they authored thirteen original works and one commentary on the same subject.[1]

Until recently hardly any of these works had received scholarly editions. Fortunately, this situation has been corrected during the past several years.[2] In the following pages I will content myself with an account of al-Khaṣṣāf's treatment of the subject of the assumption of court records by an incoming judge from a former judge, including ascertaining the rights to property and the verification of the status of persons imprisoned for nonpayment of debt. Al-Khaṣṣāf's opus is the earliest extensive work on the subject, and since al-Khaṣṣāf died in 261 A.H. (874 A.D.), his account reflects a very early treatment of the topic. Even the commentary on it, which we will have occasion to refer to, is clearly early, since the commentator, al-Jaṣṣāṣ, died in 370 A.H. (980 A.D.).

Scholars of Islamic institutions have been accustomed to say that offices in Islam are more personal than institutional in nature. Perhaps this is so because Islam insists on personal responsibility and shies away from situations where this responsibility is diffused and vitiated. Nowhere is this more evident than in the office of the *qāḍī*. It is not that the institution of the judiciary continues through time with its administrators, clerks, and records, as much as it is that one *qāḍī* in his personal capacity takes over from another *qāḍī* his records for which he was responsible. Apparently, even in the period of al-

Khaṣṣāf the *qāḍī* did not have a courthouse, but held court at the cathedral mosque (*al-masjid al-jāmi'*).[3]

Concerning the transfer of records al-Khaṣṣāf writes:

> When a *qāḍī* would want to take over the records (*dīwān*) of the previous *qāḍī* he should dispatch two of his trustworthy men to take delivery of it. They would find out what acknowledgments and testimonies of witnesses and records of court sessions (*maḥāḍir*) there were, and they would take delivery of the sealed boxes (*qamāṭir*) in which they are found. The judgment records (*sijillāt*) and deeds of debt (*ṣikāk*) owing by some people, as well as legal documents (*ḥujaj*) for others, they would write down one by one, as to say: One box contains a copy of a judgment in favor of So and So for such and such, and a copy of a judgment in favor of So and So for such and such, etc., until they would write down all the copies—that being in the presence of the former *qāḍī* or of two of his trustworthy men. Concerning deeds of debt this would be written: A box containing so many deeds of debt; one deed for such and such money owing by So and So to So and So, the orphan, etc., etc., until they would write down all the deeds in this fashion. They would write the particulars of that money, to whom and by whom it is owing; they would ask the *qāḍī* about those matters, one by one, and they would take delivery from him [with all things] explained by his words, which they would write down. Likewise, the matters of *waqf*s and their monies, and the number of *waqf* estates and their location, the names of the trustees of the former *qāḍī*: the names of each one of them together with the estates he controls and what their origins were and for what reason they came into his hands. If these estates be *waqf*, they would record for whose benefit they were constituted as *waqf*, and would explain all of that, item by item. If they are estates that the *qāḍī* has seized as a result of suits or disputes, they would record that accordingly, and they would record the names of those in charge of deposits and the names of their fathers, and what each one of them holds, and to whom the property belongs—all clearly explained.[4]

It is evident from the above that great care was to be taken by an incoming *qāḍī* in ascertaining and protecting the rights and properties of citizens. This care is often reiterated by a saying found throughout the book, that the *qāḍī* was appointed to enable those who have rights to attain them (*li-īṣāl dhawi al-ḥuqūq ilā ḥuqūqihim*). The author, enumerating the type of documents to be handed by one *qāḍī* to another, has carefully distinquished between evidentiary documents that lead to a judgment, but are not themselves executory documents, and judgments and debt deeds which are executory. The first category consists of acknowledgments, testimonies, and records of court sessions generally. Concerning an acknowledgment, the commentator al-Jaṣṣāṣ explains: It is when a person admits before the *qāḍī* the entitlement of another person to a right without the *qāḍī* passing judgment on the basis of it. As for a testimony, it is when two witnesses give testimony before the *qāḍī* in favor of a person and against another regarding a right, but the *qāḍī* does not give judgment on the strength of the testimony pending an investigation to ascertain whether they are trustworthy witnesses. Similarly, the record of the court session might include an ackowledgment or a testimony of a witness that might be crucial to the final determination of a case. All of these are to be handed to the incoming judge so as to protect the legal rights of the parties. Persons making ackowledgments or giving testimonies might die or become unavailable, so their statements are to be as well-secured as judgments and debt deeds. These latter need no further proceedings for their efficacy. They are usually in very concise formats. The judgment reads: I have ruled for So and So against So and So for such and such, and this judgment has accordingly been recorded. The deed of debt reads: So and So owes So and So such and such *dirhems*.[5]

The meticulous process by which records are conveyed from one judge to another protects not only the rights of citizens but the judges as well. The commentator al-Jaṣṣāṣ could think of two situations where this would be so. The former judge would be protected if the incoming judge should deny receiving from him a document or a thing belonging to a third person, for when he himself is present at the transfer of his *dīwān* he would not be suspect because he would always be able to establish through witnesses the transfer of the document or thing to the other. Likewise the incoming judge, if he should accept the transfer without the other being present, might become suspect for such a claim, although in fact he did not receive the item from the other.[6]

The care taken concerning *waqfs* and estates in the hands of the trustees of the former judge is for the purpose of ascertaining and safeguarding several matters. The names of the trustees, the estates constituted as *waqfs*, the locale of the estates, the purposes for which they were dedicated, and how their income was to be expended are all matters of primary concern for the new *qāḍī*. Besides, it is quite possible for a trustee to deny being in charge of an estate, in which case the new *qāḍī* can easily establish that fact through the accounting he had with the former *qāḍī*. Or, alternatively, it is quite possible that an estate be in the hands of a trustee not on account of a *waqf*, but on account of a dispute or a suit at court, or on deposit for an absent person, or property belonging to an orphan—all these matters are to be ascertained and recorded.[7]

Greater care is demanded in matters touching on human liberty and imprisonment, and here the statements of the former judge why persons are imprisoned are not enough. Al-Khaṣṣāf writes:

> Then he should write down the names of the prisoners in the Qāḍī's Jail and for what each person was imprisoned . . . and for whom. [The two trustees of the new *qāḍī*] should ask the former *qāḍī* about that. If it be mentioned in his *dīwān*, they should inform [the new *qāḍī*] of their names. He, then, should ask the prisoners about the reasons for their imprisonment and for whom they were imprisoned.[8]

In commenting on the last statement, al-Jaṣṣāṣ says that the prisoners are questioned because the statements of the former *qāḍī* alone cannot stand against the prisoners because, after removal from office, he is just like any other person whose mere statement cannot stand against another. He distinguishes this case from those of other records by saying that in those cases the new judge can only know what is in the *dīwān* through the former judge, but in this case he can ascertain the matter through the prisoners.

Al-Khaṣṣāf resumes the description of this procedure thus:

> If [the prisoners] should corroborate the statements of the former *qāḍī* and acknowledge the claim that necessitated their imprisonment, the new *qāḍī* should keep them in prison after he assiduously brings them face to face with their adversaries. If the adversaries demand their imprisonment, he should keep them in prison because the right for imprisoning them has been established in favor of the adversaries, and it is not permissible to set them free. If they should deny the cause for their imprisonment, the *qāḍī* should examine their cases one by one. He should then summon the adversary of each prisoner so that he would establish his right by evidence. If the prisoner should then acknowledge the right and the adversary still demands his [continued] imprisonment, the *qāḍī* should return him to prison. If he did not so acknowledge, and the adversary should establish his right by witnesses, the *qāḍī* [should follow the following procedure]: If he should know the witnesses to be trustworthy, he should return the prisoner to prison—if the adversary wanted that—but if he did not know the witnesses, then he should release the prisoner upon the production of a surety [for his return] until such time as he is able to investigate the trustworthiness of the witnesses. If

> they should be declared trustworthy, and the adversary should demand his imprisonment, then the *qāḍī* should return him to prison.[9]

It is to be noticed that the *qāḍī* should be as protective of the rights of the adversary as of the rights of the prisoner; that is why he can only release the prisoner upon the production of a surety. As al-Jaṣṣāṣ notes: "The order of the former *qāḍī* should be presumed to be correct and that the prisoners were imprisoned by right, and not unjustly; that is why the new judge should investigate their cases."[10] Another reason for care in releasing them is that they might have been imprisoned for some other adversaries who were absent, and who therefore would have lost their opportunity to vindicate their rights by the *qāḍī*'s action in releasing them without taking a surety. In such a case al-Khaṣṣāf says that if the prisoners should claim that they were imprisoned unjustly and that they had no adversaries, the *qāḍī* should order the court crier to call out for several days at the beginning of court sessions: He who has a claim against So and So, the prisoner, let him present himself so as to face his adversary! If no claimant should appear, the *qāḍī* should release him, but only after taking a surety from him.[11]

An interesting safeguard in cases of this nature is the ascertainment of the identity of the claimant or plaintiff in whose favor the prisoner was incarcerated. For it is entirely possible that a person should appear before the *qāḍī* and claim falsely that he is So and So, the plaintiff, for whom the prisoner was imprisoned, that he has already received payment for his claim, or that he wishes to release the prisoner without such payment. In such a situation the *qāḍī* must be certain of the identity of the claimant; otherwise he would have released the prisoner at the insistence of a stranger. He therefore should follow the procedure outlined above concerning the court crier, and should in any case release him only after taking a surety.[12]

So far we have been dealing with imprisonment for debt. It is possible, of course, for imprisonment to be in consequence of a crime, whether it be a *ḥadd*, where the punishment is specifically provided for in the law, or a *ta'zīr*, where the punishment is left to the discretion of the judge. Whether or not we agree with Professor Emile Tyan (with whom I tend to agree) that the *qāḍī* lost his criminal jurisdiction very early in Islamic history due to several factors, jurists continued to write as if the *qāḍī* persisted in exercising that jurisdiction.[13] Al-Khaṣṣāf and his commentator al-Jaṣṣāṣ are no exception to this statement: they specifically deal with the "theoretical" cases where a *qāḍī* finds, in prison, prisoners who have been convicted of crimes. One observes here the liberal spirit of the jurists in their efforts to avoid as far as possible the infliction of the heavy *ḥadd* punishments, at least as far as they pertain to God's rights, not those of an individual. Al-Khaṣṣāf says:

> If a prisoner should say: The [former] *qāḍī* imprisoned me for my quadruple admission of adultery so that he might inflict on me the punishment of *ḥadd*—I having been previously

> married (*muḥṣan*)—or: He imprisoned me to subject me to so many lashes of the whip as punishment for adultery; or if he should say: I admitted before that *qāḍī* that I had drunk wine and he imprisoned me to get around to inflicting the *ḥadd* punishment on me; the [new] *qāḍī* should reopen the case (*yastaqbil al-naẓar*), and should pay no attention to any admission he made before the former *qāḍī*, or to any testimony of witnesses given against him.[14]

The commentator al-Jaṣṣāṣ further elucidates this statement by noting that the new *qāḍī* should proceed as though the prisoner were a man he had seen for the first time and had admitted before him what was described above. If an adversary should show up, he would proceed with the case; otherwise, he would release him after taking a surety from him. In the case of adultery, if the prisoner admits the act four times, then the *qāḍī* should impose the punishment, which cannot be barred by prescription. As for drinking grape wine, or getting drunk on date wine, an admission concerning these cannot be effective, because the punishment for drunkenness is obligatory as long as the wine is still in the stomach of the accused or it shows on his breath, i.e., for a period of a day and a night since he drank it. Thus, an admission of adultery or drinking (both being violations of what is due God) must fail because the punishment for such violations must be avoided if there is even a semblance of doubt (*shubuhāt*). Such cases are to be carefully distinquished from cases where the rights of an individual are involved; in the latter, a previous admission or ackowledgment of indebtedness may be transferred from the former *qāḍī* to the new *qāḍī*. Likewise, a previous admission of a *ḥadd* involving individual rights can be accepted. Al-Khaṣṣāf says, "If the admission was of ascribing unchastity to a free Muslim adult (*qadhf*) or of stealing, the *qāḍī* would accept it." Al-Jaṣṣāṣ explains that these involve the rights of individuals, and such rights cannot fail by a semblance of doubt.

A matter of prime importance to human rights that has not been dealt with thus far is why a person ought to be imprisoned for nonpayment of a debt. Aside from the reported traditions of the Prophet that imprisonment was prescribed in certain cases,[15] al-Jaṣṣāṣ asserts that reflection (*naẓar*) necessitates such a course. Since the *qāḍī* is installed to enable people to attain their rights, if the defendant should refuse to pay what is owing to the plaintiff, the *qāḍī* has no recourse but to force the defendant to pay; and since it is generally agreed that he should not be thus forced by beating, it becomes necessary to force him to pay by imprisonment. Both al-Khaṣṣāf and his commentator advise the *qāḍī*, though, not to act with haste in imprisoning him and to persuade the plaintiff to forfeit his right to that imprisonment. If he should insist on his right, after a delay of some time, then the *qāḍī* should imprison the defendant and write in his *dīwān:* So and So was imprisoned in favor of So and So for such and such *dirhem*s on such and such day of such and such month of such and such year.[16] The date is important, of course, because the *qāḍī* usually imprisons the defendant for four months or so in an attempt to make him reveal his means for payment. If no such means or riches are revealed, the *qāḍī* should release him and, at his discretion, declare him bankrupt. Within the four-month period the defendant can always produce witnesses who might testify to his indigence, in which case the *qāḍī* would release him from prison and declare him bankrupt.[17]

Finally, a few remarks illustrating the humane treatment of prisoners under Islamic law would be in order. A special prison, known as the Qāḍī's Jail, was where debtors were to be held; it was different from the Robbers' Jail which, in the nature of things, must have had more security. Al-Khaṣṣāf specifies that a debtor was not to be placed in the Robbers' Jail unless the *qāḍī* had reason to fear that he might flee from the Qāḍī's Jail, but only if the *qāḍī* had reason to believe that he would not be hurt by the robbers. Al-Khaṣṣāf also prescribed that, should the prisoner become ill, and should he have no servant to take care of him in prison, then the *qāḍī* should release him. Even the sexual rights of the prisoner were to be safeguarded! Al-Khaṣṣāf quotes al-Shaybāni, the student of Abu Ḥanīfa, to the effect that a prisoner should be allowed to receive his concubine and to have sexual relations with her if there is a private place in prison for that. Al-Jaṣṣāṣ agrees and states further that imprisonment should not abridge the prisoner's right of having sexual relations with his wife in the same way that his right to food and drink should not be abridged.[18] One cannot help but muse that the question of conjugal right for prisoners, which is being seriously discussed by legislators nowadays and gingerly tried in certain localities as a humane measure, was advocated by jurists in ninth-century Baghdad!

NOTES

1 See Mulla Kātib Celebi, Kashf al-Ẓunūn, 2 vol. (Istanbul: Maarif Matbaası, 1941), 1:72-73.

2 Among these recent works are 'Alī ibn Muḥammad al-Māwardī, *Adab al-Qāḍī*, Muḥyī Hilāl al-Sarḥān, ed., 2 vol. (Baghdad: Ri'āsat Dīwān al-Awqāf, 1971-72), a Shāfi'ī work; Haytham ibn Sulaymān al-Qaysi, *Waraqāt fī Adab al-Qāḍī wa-al-Qaḍā'*, Farhat al-Dashrāwī, ed., (Tunis, 1970), a Ḥanafī work; Ibn Abī al-Dām, *Adab al-Qaḍā'*, Muḥammad Muṣṭafā al-Zuḥayli, ed., (Damascus: Majma' al-Lugha al-'Arabiyya bi-Dimashq, 1975); and Aḥmad ibn 'Amr al-Khaṣṣāf, *Adab al-Qāḍī*, with a commentary by Aḥmad ibn 'Ali al-Jaṣṣāṣ, Farhat J. Ziadeh, ed. (Cairo: Qism al-Nashr bi'l-Jāmi'a al-Amrikiyya, 1979), a Ḥanafī work.

3 *Ibid.*, pp. 84-86.

4 *Ibid.*, pp. 57-58.

5 *Ibid.*, pp. 58-59.

6 *Ibid.*, p. 60.

[7] *Ibid.*, p. 61.
[8] *Ibid.*, pp. 61-2.
[9] *Ibid.*, p. 63.
[10] *Ibid.*
[11] *Ibid.*, p. 64.
[12] *Ibid.*, pp. 64-66.
[13] See the chapter entitled "Judicial Organization" in M. Khadduri and H. J. Liebesny, *Law in the Middle-East* (Washington, D. C.: Middle East Institute, 1955), esp. p. 274.
[14] Al-Khaṣṣāf, *Adab al-Qāḍī*, p. 68.
[15] Al-Bukhārī, *Saḥīḥ*, Bāb Istiqrād 13.
[16] Al-Khaṣṣāf, *Adab al-Qāḍī*, p. 254.
[17] *Ibid.*, pp. 256, 260.
[18] *Ibid.*, pp. 264-65.

Part Three:

Philosophy and the Role of Maimonides

Maimonides and Islam

George F. Hourani[1]

In this paper, I offer an account of the views and attitudes of Moses Maimonides concerning Islam, Islamic theologians, and Muslim philosophers. Two of his works, the *Epistle to Yemen* [2] and the *Guide of the Perplexed*,[3] have already been examined from this perspective. Also relevant are his brief judgments on some of the Muslim philosophers in a letter to his contemporary, Samuel ibn Tibbon, the translator of the *Guide* from Arabic into Hebrew.[4]

In order to understand the different styles and contents of the two treatises we need to take note of the context in which each was written. The *Epistle to Yemen* was sent in response to an appeal from Rabbi Jacob b. Netan'el al-Fayyūmī, the head of the Jewish community in Yemen, for a letter of guidance and encouragement in the face of pressures on the community to accept conversion to Islam. This situation had been going on for some half dozen years (c. 1165-72).[5] Maimonides was highly qualified to respond to this appeal, not only because of his Judaic learning and his reputation based on it, but also because of his personal experience as a refugee who had gone through similar trials at the hands of the Almohad government in Andalusia and Morocco. But, if he was to do this effectively, he had to send a message which would reinforce belief in Judaism and combat the challenge of Islam, and he had to do this by public methods which would allow the message to be circulated within the Jewish community. Obviously, this was a difficult task for him personally because, if his action became known to Muslims in Egypt and especially to the newly established Ayyūbid dynasty of Saladin who had approved his appointment to a high medical post at the sultan's court, he might be forced to give up his position in disgrace for his unpardonable ingratitude in criticizing the religion of the ruler and most of his subjects.

There was a certain limited security in the fact that the *Epistle,* composed in Judeo-Arabic (following a short Hebrew introduction) so that it might be understood by the Jews of Yemen, was written in Hebrew script, which few if any Arabs could read. Still, if it were read aloud in Arabic in a synagogue or at a private gathering no one could guarantee that its contents combatting Islam would not be reported to some Muslims. Probably a surer security for Maimonides was provided by the remoteness of Yemen from Egypt.

After weighing the facts, Maimonides decided to respond positively to the request, on the ground that the public interest should take priority over his own safety. These considerations were presented by him in the final sentences of the *Epistle,* which are worth quoting in full:

> I beg you to send a copy of this missive to every community in the cities and hamlets, in order to strengthen the people in their faith and to put them on their feet. Read it at public gatherings and in private, and you will thus become a public

> benefactor. Take adequate precautions lest its contents be divulged to the Gentiles by an evil person and mishap overtake us (God spare us therefrom). When I began writing this letter I had some misgivings about it, but they were overruled by my conviction that the public welfare takes precedence over one's personal safety. Moreover, I am sending it to a personage such as you, "and the secret of the Lord may be entrusted to those who fear Him." Our sages, the successors of the prophets, assured us that persons engaged in a religious mission will meet with no disaster (Pesaḥim 8b). What more important religious mission is there than this. Peace be unto all Israel. Amen.[6]

What use did Maimonides make of the liberty he had allowed himself? Obviously he had to combat Islam, but how did he do it and how boldly? Being an excellent and experienced teacher, he put his primary emphasis on the positive aspects of the Law of Moses, the only authentic revealed Law and the best set of commandments to be found in the world. He urges all Jews to follow this Law steadily in the face of all pressures and temptations from other religious systems. Then he gives a short survey of the enemies of the Judaic Law in chronological order, classifying them according to the methods by which they attempted to destroy Judaism. The first class consisted of despotic rulers who relied on force, and he lists a few from Amalek to Hadrian. The second tried to demolish the Law by polemical arguments; these were "the most intelligent and educated among the nations, such as the Syrians, Persians and Greeks."[7] Both classes failed in their attempts. Then there arose a third class which combined force and controversy, and they were much more dangerous. The first example was Jesus of Nazareth, who claimed to be a prophet and then interpreted the Torah in such a way as to lead to the abolition of its commandments and the violation of its prohibitions. But the sages of Israel "having become aware of his plans before his reputation spread among our people, meted out fitting punishment to him."[8] A second person, who is hard to identify, is mentioned next, but he was not dangerous to Israel and so we shall not delay the account by discussing the problem of his identification. "After him arose a Madman," who aimed at "rule and submission, and he invented his well known religion."[9] His religion has some superficial resemblance to Judaism, but it misses the deeper meaning of the latter's commands and prohibitions.

> This event was predicted in the divinely inspired prophecy of Daniel, according to which, at some future time a person would appear with a religion similar to the true one, with a book of Scriptures and oral communications, who will arrogantly pretend that God had vouchsafed him a revelation, and that he held converse with Him, besides making other

> arrogant claims. Thus Daniel in his description of the rise of the Arabic kingdom after the fall of the Roman empire, alluded to the appearance of the Madman and his victories over the Roman, Persian and Byzantine empires in the vision concerning a horn which grew. . . .[10]

After this brief review of false religions, Maimonides again exhorts Jews to be steadfast under oppressors, all of whom will ultimately fail to suppress the true religion. But although he condemns these religions as false by assertions that appear to be excessively dogmatic and to beg the question of authenticity, he does at length reach the crucial point of finding the distinguishing feature of the Jewish religion. This feature is the experience of the Revelation on Mount Sinai, witnessed by the whole nation, a unique experience that was never granted to any other nation. Moses was the mediating figure between God and the Jews in that awesome drama, and this position assures the nation of the truth of his claim to be a prophet. Jews are exhorted to keep the Covenant made on Mount Sinai by observing all the commandments, major and minor, and even emigrating if they can from the land of an oppressor to another one where they can practice their religion.

Up to this point,[11] Maimonides has covered considerable ground in criticizing Islam without ever mentioning by name Islam, Muslims, the Qur'an, or Muhammad. But it is very clear to whom he is alluding as the Madman, who had no authentic claims to prophecy. These pages in themselves are bold in their attacks on the dominant religion. In the next two pages he abandons this minimum precaution and refers to the Muslims by name.[12] Perhaps the reason for this change was his discussion of the supposed prophecies in the Old Testament which mention a prophet named Aḥmad.[13] Maimonides is concerned to refute the existence of any such statements in the Bible. He goes over all the statements which were claimed to forecast an Arabian prophet and shows patiently how each one does nothing of the sort when understood accurately in its context. However, not much significance should be seen in this change to an open use of the names Muhammad, Islam, etc., since it had already become quite clear in the preceding pages that the main thrust of these criticisms was directed against Islam, the most formidable alternative to Judaism which might tempt Jews to conversion. On the whole, Maimonides was bold in the *Epistle,* saying in a direct manner what he felt had to be said to bolster the morale of the persecuted Jews of South Arabia.

The *Guide of the Perplexed* was written for a very different audience and with a very different purpose than the *Epistle to Yemen.* Here we are in a milieu of literate and well-educated Jews in the Arabic countries around the Mediterranean and in Iraq, and the book's primary concern is with the truths of biblical theology and the manner in which they must be established and understood by Jews qualified and motivated to undertake a profound study of their religion.[14] But since a large part of the rational proofs of these truths depends on premises learned in the natural sciences and philosophy, it is essential to the author's purpose to discuss this learning at length as it is presented by Aristotle and developed by Muslim philosophers. The few remarks about the religion of Islam, on the other hand, are incidental to his subject. The treatment of *kalām* falls somewhere in between, having been requested by Rabbi Joseph b. Judah to whom the work is addressed,[15] and dealt with there by Maimonides at considerable length, perhaps to destroy any temptation his readers might have to be impressed by these elaborate systems of Islamic theology. But regardless of his purpose, his views on all three spheres of Islamic thought are of interest to us today. I shall consider them in the chronological order of the topics: Islam, *kalām,* and then philosophy, which arose last in Islamic civilization.

The *Guide* never mentions by name the Qur'an or Muhammad and refers to "the Muslims" and "the community of Islam" only on four pages where he is discussing the *mutakallimūn.*[16] But there are a few places where he refers to the religion itself or its prophet in a veiled manner, and these passages are of great interest for what they reveal to us of his attitude to Islam.

Since he was critical of Islam while still the physician of Saladin's vizier in Cairo and in constant contact with Muslims, he had to be extremely careful of the way in which he stated his opinions. Therefore, he employed some of the devices of secret writing described by Leo Strauss in *Persecution and the Art of Writing.*[17] To begin with, the *Guide* is written in Judaeo-Arabic and was therefore inaccessible to most Muslims. There might, however, have been a few converts from Judaism who already knew the script and, of course, would also have known Arabic. As a further precaution, then, Maimonides uses vague references in criticizing Muhammad's claim to genuine prophecy. He does not mention him by name but refers to attributes that would be recognized by a discerning reader.

At the outset of his discussion of prophecy,[18] he sets forth three opinions that were held by those who believed in God concerning the qualifications and selection of prophets:

> 1. The first opinion—that of the multitude of those among the Pagans who considered prophecy as true and also believed by some of the common people professing our Law—is that God, may He be exalted, chooses whom He wishes from among men, turns him into a prophet, and sends him with a mission. According to them it makes no difference whether this individual is a man of knowledge or ignorant, aged or young. However, they also posit as a condition his having a certain goodness and sound morality. For up to now people have not gone so far as to say that God sometimes turns a wicked man into a prophet unless He has first, according to this opinion, turned him into a good man.[19]

The words used for "the Pagans" are *ahl al-Jāhiliyya,* which means in normal Arabic usage the pagan Arabs and others such as the ancient Greeks and Romans who lived in "the age of ignorance" without having received a revelation. But these people had no specific doctrine such as the one described about prophecy. On the other hand, the description fits exactly the traditional Muslim doctrine that God chose an illiterate man (taking this to be the meaning of *ummī* in the Qur'an)[20] of excellent character to deliver the divine message.

> 2. The second opinion is that of the Muslim philosophers, that a certain perfection of intellect and imagination is necessary and sufficient to make a man a prophet.
> 3. The third opinion is that of Judaism, that these qualifications are necessary for a prophet, but that an act of God's will is required to actually make someone a prophet.

Since, in this exhaustive classification of theories of prophecy, it would be surprising if that of the Muslims were not mentioned, I take it as certain that their theory is being referred to by the phrase "the multitude of those among the Pagans who considered prophecy as true."[21]

Guide 2:39 is devoted to showing that the Law given to Moses is superior to any other, being perfect in its balance of justice.

> For these are manners of worship in which there is no burden and excess—such as monastic life and pilgrimage and similar things—nor a deficiency necessarily leading to greed and being engrossed in the indulgence of appetites, so that in consequence the perfection of man is diminished with respect to his moral habits and to his speculation—this being the case with regard to all the other *nomoi* of the religious communities of the past.[22]

I think we can see in the example of monastic life a criticism of Christian monasteries, such as the Coptic ones in the desert not far from Cairo. Pilgrimage can be assigned to both Christian and Muslim practice (and Jewish, for that matter). Greed and self-indulgence are more likely to be mentioned as deficiencies characteristic of Muslims as, for instance, in the permitted practice of polygamy.

In the next chapter,[23] Maimonides attacks the claim of Muhammad to genuine prophecy. He has just mentioned genuine prophets as being lawgivers.[24] Then he mentions two classes of people of a lower status: secular rulers who adopt the divine Laws of a prophet and execute it, and

> Someone claiming to be a prophet who adopts the Law of the prophet [i.e., Moses]—either the whole of it or a portion. His adopting a portion and abandoning another portion may be due either to this being easier for him or to his wishing out of jealousy

> to make people fancy that those matters came to him through a prophetic revelation and that with regard to them he does not follow somebody else.[25]

Then Maimonides goes on to explain that just as there is plagiarism in poetry and science, so also there is plagiarism in prophecy. He gives an example from the Bible.

> And we find other people who laid a claim to prophecy and said things that God has indubitably said—I mean things that had come through a prophetic revelation, but a prophetic revelation addressed to other people; thus, for instance, Hananiah son of Azzur.[26]

The charge of partial adoption of the laws of another religion would apply to Islam in relation to Judaism, e.g., in the dietary prohibitions. The charge of "plagiarisms" would apply both to some laws and to the adaptations of Bible stories in the Qur'an.[27] The example of Ḥananiah b. Azzur is remote from contemporary life; the contemporary example can only be Muhammad, but Maimonides is unwilling to name him.

The best test of prophecy is the moral character of the claimant, especially his renunciation of bodily pleasures, in particular those of sex.[28] Here again he gives biblical examples, Zedekiah and Ahab, but his thought may well have been directed toward the polygamy practiced and permitted by the Prophet of Islam. However, there seems to be a contradiction here with what he has stated previously about the first opinion of "the Pagans," that they posit as a condition that a prophet must have "a certain goodness and sound morality."[29]

The last example concerns the relation of the Arabs to Abraham. Maimonides says that most of the earth's population agrees in glorifying him, "so that even those who do not belong to his progeny pretend to descend from him." The only exceptions are the remnants of "the Sabians" who worshipped the stars, such as "the Turks in the extreme north and the Hindus in the extreme south."[30] Here is a clear denial of the claim of the Qur'an that the Arabs are descended from Abraham through Ishmael.

In all these passages Maimonides is concerned to uphold Moses as the only genuine Prophet and his Law as the only true Law, and in doing so he contrasts him with other claimants to prophecy. His repudiation of the claims of Muhammad and the Qur'an are pointed and clear.

There is nothing abnormal in his critical attitude to Islam. In the medieval context this was the normal attitude of each of the three religions of the Mediterranean and the Near East to the others. We might even have expected from him a more bitter feeling in the light of his family's experiences of exile from their home in Córdoba to Morocco, resulting from the intolerance of the Almohads towards Jews and Christians. In view of this background we should rather take note of his remark:

> There is no doubt that there are things that are common to all three of us, I mean the Jews, the Christians, and the Moslems: namely, the affirmation of the temporal creation of the world, the validity of which entails the validity of miracles and other things of that kind.[31]

Kalām is criticized very severely and openly in the *Guide* 1:71-76. This was possible because *kalām* was not Islam itself, but several interpretations of it propounded by different schools of Islamic theologians. A little before the writing of the *Guide* in Cairo, Ibn Rushd in Córdoba, enjoying the protection of the Almohad rulers in Marrākish, had attacked the Ash'arite school in two public treatises, *Faṣl al-Maqāl* and *Kitāb al-Kashf 'an Manāhij al-Adilla.* Eventually, in 1195, these attacks were no doubt part of the reason for his trial and exile together with other philosophers and scientists. But Maimonides, writing for Jews in Hebrew script, in the more tolerant environment of Ayyubid Cairo, experienced no known opposition to his views on *kalām.*

The main thrust of his criticism is made very clear by him: that the *mutakallimūn* used an invalid method of argument, by moving backwards from their desired conclusions to the premises that would prove them.

> All the first *Mutakallimūn* from among the Greeks who had adopted Christianity and from among the Moslems did not conform in their premises to the appearance of that which exists, but considered how being ought to be in order that it should furnish a proof for the correctness of a particular opinion, or at least should not refute it.[32]

They merely asserted their premises without proofs, then made their deductions from them. For instance,

> Everything created is created by a living being,
> The word is created,
> Therefore it must have a living creator.
> (Proof of God's existence).

In order to arrive at their desired conclusions, they employ wild and arbitrary premises, such as their atomic theory, that run "counter to the nature of existence and . . . [violate] that which is perceived by the senses."[33]

In this manner the *mutakallimūn* undermined the possibility of the sciences, since the sciences rest on observation and inferences about permanent causal relations between the parts of nature. Ibn Rushd had recently made the same charge against Ash'arite theology in his *Tahāfut at-Tahāfut.*

Maimonides also mounted a historical attack against Islamic *kalām,* claiming that there was nothing original in it.

> Know also that all the statements that the men of Islam—both the Mu'tazila and the Ash'ariyya—have made concerning these notions are all of them opinions founded upon premises that are taken over from the books of the Greeks and the Syrians who wished to disagree with the opinions of the philosophers and to reject their statements.[34]

In particular, they borrowed from the writings of John Philoponus and Yaḥyā ibn 'Adī against the philosophers. (Here Maimonides makes a double error concerning Yaḥyā ibn 'Adī, an Aristotelian philosopher who lived in the tenth century A.D., long after the beginnings of *kalām*).

Maimonides' opinion is exaggerated, for the *mutakallimūn* of Islam developed elaborate theories going far beyond anything known from the Christian polemicists as, for instance, in their ethical controversy between voluntarism and objectivism and in their atomic theory of substance and accidents renewed by God as the only cause of existence at every moment of time. Yet his opinion has been taken as the starting point for the study of *kalām* by certain modern Western scholars, including Van den Bergh, Walzer, Wolfson, and others who became obsessed with the search for Greek sources for everything written by the *mutakallimūn,* sometimes even taking parallel statements made centuries apart as evidence of derivations, even though the lines of transmission cannot be traced at all. But more recently the discovery of 'Abd al-Jabbār's *Mughnī* has given a new impetus to the study of *kalām* in its own context and tradition.

How familiar was Maimonides with the books of the *mutakallimūn?* He says he had studied them "as far as I had the opportunity,"[35] although in the *Guide* he does not mention a single author or book by name. But he distinguished clearly between the Mu'tazilite and Ash'arite schools and in a general way represented their main doctrines accurately as a basis for his penetrating criticisms of them. Pines, in his introduction to the *Guide,* gives a fine review of Maimonides' relations with *kalām.*[36] He also discusses whether Maimonides knew the works of al-Ghazālī, who was not an ordinary *mutakallim* but whose theology was basically Ash'arite. Pines thinks that Maimonides could not have been ignorant of al-Ghazālī's *Tahāfut al-Falāsifa,* and that his opinions on several matters, e.g., the nature of God's will, may show Ghazālian influences. Perhaps after his sweeping condemnation of *kalām* he would have been embarrassed to acknowledge debts to its most distinguished exponent.

Turning now to the Muslim philosophers, we find that Maimonides was very familiar with the philosophic theories of the two most eminent of the earlier philosophers, al-Fārābī and Ibn Sīnā, as well as his Andalusian predecessor Ibn Bājja. He was strongly influenced by ideas from all three of them, more especially al-Fārābī and Ibn Bājja, both of whom he mentions by name several times. His debts to them have been thoroughly investigated by Pines in his introduction to the *Guide* and by L. V. Berman in an article.[37] It is both unnecessary and impossible to summarize here all that these scholars have to say about the extensive relations between the thought of these three philosophers. Two examples will suffice to illustrate the influence of the three Muslims on Maimonides.

Al-Fārābī, in his *Excellent City*, puts forward a peculiar theory of the prophetic imagination as a power of the prophet to project images from his mind into the external world and actually "see" them reflected there. Maimonides repeats this theory precisely.[38]

From Ibn Bājja he adopted the theory of the Unity of the Intellect, in its ultimate form after the dissolution of the soul-body complex.

> Now you know . . . that regarding the things separate from matter—I mean intellects—there can be no thought of multiplicity. . . . Consequently all are one in number, as Abū Bakr Ibn al-Ṣā'igh [Ibn Bājja] and others have made clear.[39]

He mentions elsewhere that he had read texts under the guidance of one of the (former) students of "the excellent philosopher Abū Bakr Ibn al-Ṣā'igh."[40]

Towards Ibn Sīnā, Maimonides was less sympathetic. Although he never mentions him by name in the *Guide*, there are clear signs of interactions, mentioned by Pines.[41] There is a possible allusion to Ibn Sīnā's personal habits in a passage where Maimonides is declaiming against the pleasures of the sense of touch, which includes eating, drinking, and sexual intercourse. Then he adds:

> We have been led to speak of things that are not to the purpose, but there was need for it. For most of the thoughts of those who are outstanding among the men of knowledge are preoccupied with the pleasures of this sense, are desirous of them. And then they wonder how it is that they do not become prophets, if prophecy is something natural.[42]

The reactions in the *Guide* toward these three philosophers correspond closely with the author's judgment of them in his letter to Samuel ibn Tibbon, his translator:

> I tell you: as for works on logic, one should only study the writings of Abū Naṣr al-Fārābī. All his writings are faultlessly excellent. One ought to study and understand them. For he is a great man.
> Though the works of Avicenna may give rise to objections and are not as [good] as those of Abū Naṣr, Abū Bakr al-Ṣā'igh [Ibn Bājja] was also a great philosopher, and all his writings are of a high standard.[43]

Now what about Ibn Rushd, his great contemporary, also a Córdoban? In the same letter he recommends his commentaries on Aristotle in the following words:

> The works of Aristotle are the roots and foundations of all works on the sciences. But they cannot be understood except with the help of commentaries, those of Alexander of Aphrodisias, those of Themistius, and those of Averroes.[44]

This is high praise, since Ibn Rushd is the sole Arabic commentator to be mentioned along with the two Greeks.[45] But there is no clear evidence that Maimonides had read any of Ibn Rushd's works at the time that he was writing the *Guide*. This fact makes all the more striking the independent parallels between their ideas on the relations of religion and philosophy, the restrictions to be placed on the teaching of philosophy, and the qualifications required for the student of philosophy to be able to profit from it. These similar views must spring from their common heritage in the Andalusian scientific tradition, with strong Farabian influences on both of them.

There is a notable contrast between Maimonides' manner of referring to the *mutakallimūn*, on the one hand, and the Muslim philosophers on the other. He calls the former specifically the *Muslim* theologians, as indeed he must do since their particular theologies were all derived from the Qur'an. He even speaks of Christian and Jewish *mutakallimūn*, so the word comes to mean simply theologians. When speaking of the Muslim philosophers, on the other hand, he never refers to them by their religious denomination. That is because he regards them as first and foremost philosophers, the heirs of Aristotle and developers of a long philosophical tradition. Since their work depended entirely on reason and natural evidence, their religious background was irrelevant to their teaching and accidental to their being philosophers. He respects them more than the Muslim theologians, because of their scientific and philosophical methods.

Yet, ultimately, although Maimonides shares deeply with them in his education in the heritage of Aristotle, he is always his own man, with views of his own on everything. Hence he does not call himself a philosopher. As Leo Strauss pointed out in his part of the introduction to Pines' translation, the *Guide* is "a book written by a Jew for Jews."[46] This is perhaps most clearly illustrated at a crucial point in the *Guide* 2:16. After stating that neither the *mutakallimūn* could prove the creation of the world nor the philosophers its everlastingness, he concludes:

> Inasmuch as this question—I mean to say that of the eternity of the world or its creation in time—becomes an open question, it [the world's creation] should in my opinion be accepted without proof because of prophecy, which explains things to which it is not in the power of speculation to accede.[47]

This had been the view of al-Ghazālī who, one century before, had attempted in his *Tahāfut al-Falāsifa* to undermine the claimed proofs of the philosophers and to go back to the Qur'an as the only sure guide to the truth on this question.

NOTES

[1] Prof. Hourani died on Sept. 19, 1984. He had submitted this paper in 1983 but was too ill to attend the meeting at which it was read for him.
[2] *Epistle to Yemen,* Arabic and Hebrew versions, A. S. Halkin, ed.; English tr. by Boaz Cohen (New York: American Academy for Jewish Research, 1952). The quotations in this paper are from Cohen's translation, with references to the page numbers of the English translation.
[3] *Le guide des égarés*, Arabic with French tr. by S. Munk, 3 vols. (Paris: A. Franck, 1855-66); *The Guide of the Perplexed*, Shlomo Pines, tr. (Chicago: University of Chicago Press, 1963), with introductions by Leo Strauss and Shlomo Pines. The quotations in this paper are from Pines' translation, with references to his page numbers.
[4] Cited by Pines, tr., *ibid.*, in his introduction, pp. lix-lx.
[5] See Cohen, tr., *Epistle*, Introduction, par. 1.
[6] *Ibid.*, p. xx.
[7] *Ibid.*, p. iii.
[8] *Ibid.*
[9] *Ibid.*, p. iv.
[10] *Ibid.*; cf. Daniel 7.
[11] *Ibid.*, p. viii, par. 1.
[12] *Ibid.*, pp. viii-ix.
[13] Qur'an 7:156.
[14] *Guide*, "Introduction to the First Part," in Pines, tr., *Guide*, pp. 5-6.
[15] *Guide,* "Epistle Dedicatory," in Pines, tr., *Guide*, pp. 3-4.
[16] *Guide* 1:71 in Pines, tr., *Guide*, pp. 176-79.
[17] Leo Strauss, *Persecution and the Art of Writing* (Glencoe, Ill.: Free Press, 1952).
[18] *Guide* 2:32, in Pines, tr., *Guide*, pp. 360-61.
[19] *Ibid.*
[20] This interpretation helped to prove the Qur'an's refutation of the accusation made against the Prophet by the Jews in Madīna, that he had read the Bible stories. Modern Western scholars, however, have generally accepted the interpretation of Nöldeke that *ummī* in the Qur'an refers to a person or people who lack a scripture, T. Nöldeke and F. Schwally, *Geschichte des Qorans* (Leipzig: T. Weicher, 1909), 14.

[21] *Guide* 2:32, in Pines, tr., *Guide*, p. 360.
[22] *Guide* 2:39, in Pines, tr., *Guide*, p. 380.
[23] *Guide* 2:40, in Pines, tr., *Guide*, pp. 381-85.
[24] *Guide* 2:40, in Pines, tr., *Guide*, p. 382.
[25] *Ibid.*
[26] *Guide* 2:40, in Pines, tr., *Guide*, p. 383.
[27] *Ibid.*
[28] *Guide* 2:40, in Pines, tr., *Guide*, p. 384.
[29] *Guide* 2:32, in Pines, tr., *Guide*, p. 360.
[30] *Guide* 3:29, in Pines, tr., *Guide*, p. 515.
[31] *Guide* 1:71, in Pines, tr., *Guide*, p. 178.
[32] *Ibid.*
[33] *Guide* 1:71, in Pines, tr., *Guide*, p. 182.
[34] *Guide* 1:71, in Pines, tr., *Guide*, p. 177.
[35] *Guide* 1:71, in Pines, tr., *Guide*, p. 179.
[36] *Ibid.*, pp. cxxiv-cxxxi.
[37] *Ibid.*, pp. lxxviii-xcii; Lawrence V. Berman, "Maimonides, Disciple of Alfārābī," *Israel Oriental Studies* 4 (1974): 154-78.
[38] Al-Fārābī, from *Ārā' Ahl al-Madīna al-Fāḍila*, F. Dieterici, ed. (Leiden: Brill, 1895), translated in Fazlur Rahman, *Prophecy in Islam* (London: Allen and Unwin, 1958), 37:

> When the imaginative faculty is very strong and perfect in a man . . . the imaginative soul figurizes the intelligibles bestowed upon it by the Active Intelligence in terms of visible symbols. These figurative images, in their turn, impress themselves on the perceptual faculty.
>
> Now, when these impressions come to exist in the *sensus communis*, the visual faculty is affected by them and receives their press. These impressions are then transmitted through the visual ray to the surrounding air filled with light and when they thus come to exist in the air, they come back and impinge upon the visual faculty in the eye and are transmitted back to the imagination through the *sensus communis*.

Maimonides, in *Guide* 2:36, in Pines, tr., *Guide*, p. 370:

> Thus He, may He be exalted, has informed us of the true reality and quiddity of prophecy and has let us know that it is a perfection that comes in a *dream* or in a *vision* [*mar'eh*]. The word *mar'eh* derives from the verb *ra'oh* [*to see*]. This signifies that the imaginative faculty achieves so great a perfection of action that it sees the things as if it were outside, and

> that the things whose origin is due to it appears to have come from it by the way of external sensation.

39 *Guide* 1:74, in Pines, tr., *Guide*, p. 221.

40 *Guide* 2:9, in Pines, tr., *Guide*, p. 268.

41 *Ibid.*, pp. xciii-ciii.

42 *Guide* 2:36, in Pines, tr., *Guide*, p. 371.

43 *Ibid.*, p. lx.

44 *Ibid.*, p. lix.

45 It is surprising that he does not mention al-Fārābī's celebrated commentary on the *Metaphysics*. Perhaps it was no longer in general circulation by the twelfth century, and only al-Fārābī's commentaries on the *Organon* were being used.

46 L. Strauss, "How to Begin Study," in Pines, tr., *Guide*, p. xiv.

47 *Guide* 2:16, in Pines, tr., *Guide*, p. 294.

The Toleration of Ethics and the Ethics of Tolerance in Judaism and Islam[1]

Alfred L. Ivry

The ethical traditions of Judaism and Islam—as of Christianity—are the adornments of these faiths, or rather part of their essential natures, for these are religions characterized as representatives of ethical monotheism. God's concern for the welfare of His creatures is reflected in the commandments urging them toward ethical behavior. This behavior is "ethical" in that it conforms, mostly, to standards which we deem to be such, standards which are implicit in the Bible and the Qur'an. There is, after all, no formal or explicit investigation of the nature of the good in these sacred writings. When Cain asks God, "Am I my brother's keeper?"[2] the Lord does not deign to answer the question directly. It is understood that man has certain obligations toward his fellowman, even as God is regarded as Creator, sustainer, and judge of all living beings.

The underprivileged in society are of particular concern to the God of the Bible, and it is toward them—toward the poor, the orphaned, the widowed, and the outsider—that divine compassion is often explicitly addressed.[3] Scripture legislates various ways for society to provide for the disadvantaged and dispossessed, both allocating to them certain rights in the fields of others more fortunate,[4] and envisioning the restoration of their entire patrimony in the Jubilee year.[5] The concept of the Jubilee perhaps best expresses the biblical ideal ethic, a view of society in which the wrongs of the past—the failures, the inequities, the enslavements—are redressed, and all people in the House of Israel are allowed to begin over again, on a sound and equal economic footing: "And you shall proclaim liberty throughout the land, to all its inhabitants."[6]

The Pentateuch does not, however, wait for the Jubilee year to implement its ethical vision, even it if must compromise, as it were, with its ideal in legislating for a normative reality. Thus slavery, injustices, and inequalities of various sorts are accepted as a fact of life, harsh realities which Mosaic legislation attempts merely to mitigate.[7]

The prophets are not prepared to tolerate what others would have seen simply as an imperfect society, and they inveigh against the evils they perceive as momentous and ubiquitous, on both social, economic, and political levels. Their uncompromising attitude led them inexorably toward apocalyptic and messianic visions, fearsomely militant constructions of an ultimate reckoning in which the ethical as well as ideational components of the faith emerge triumphant.

As the Qur'an indicates, the Prophet of Islam was initially drawn to the apocalyptic motif, the imminence of *yawm al-dīn*, the Day of Judgment.[8] Proper behavior as well as confession of belief in the One God were the conditions stipulated for inclusion among those to be saved and rewarded in Paradise. As Muhammad's mission succeeded, the social ethic received more detailed attention, and normative relations for the community were spelled out in the middle and later sūras of the Qur'an,[9] with the oral *ḥadīth* literature attributed to Muhammad amplifying this ethical concern still more.[10]

Thus Islam, like Judaism, was established as a realistic as well as visionary community, one to be guided politically by ethical norms. Both faiths did not—and do not—merely tolerate ethical behavior, but actively, even zealously, pursued it.

I make these well-known and presumably uncontroversial remarks in order to establish an appropriate perspective for the investigation of a concept which is at the heart of contemporary political theory in the West, a concept which reflects an ethical value quite foreign to the Bible and to the Qur'an, as traditionally understood. This is the concept of tolerance in its radical sense, that which entails the separation of religion from government, or, as it is usually called, the separation of church and state.[11] "Tolerance" alone does not require such a move, it should be noted, if we understand tolerance with Webster as a "sympathy or indulgence for beliefs or practices differing from or conflicting with one's own."[12] This indulgent attitude has appeared historically in both Judaism and Islam. It has taken the form politically of "toleration," which, again with Webster,[13] is defined as "a government policy of permitting forms of religious belief and worship not officially established"; i.e., presumably forms of belief and worship not established as the official religion of the state. Toleration of this sort has been the norm in the Islamic world vis-à-vis Judaism and Christianity. The *ahl al-dhimma* have been "tolerated" by Muslims and historically for the most part afforded legal protection and economic opportunity in *dār al-Islām*.[14]

It is, nevertheless, *dār al-Islām*, the Islamic world, which has been tolerant of its non-Muslim members, and that fact alone has led to unequal civil, social, and economic status for the *dhimmī*.[15] "Toleration" thus has been accompanied historically by discriminatory legislation and by social as well as religious prejudice, for all the official "acceptance" of the beliefs and practices of non-Muslims.

This attitude, however condescending and demeaning, was benign in comparison to the treatment accorded nonmonotheists, apostates and those regarded as heretics.[16] Islam, to put it mildly, has not been tolerant of religious dissent in its midst. In this it has followed biblical and rabbinic attitudes toward dissenters and those perceived as opponents of the faith,[17] even as medieval rabbinic Judaism paralleled Islam in its toleration of other monotheistic creeds;[18] with the difference that for Judaism the tolerance was more a theoretical rather than a practical issue.

Both Judaism and Islam, then, have practiced and preached a measure of tolerance, and Islam has exhibited a marked degree of political toleration of Jews, Christians, and others perceived as monotheists. Neither Judaism nor Islam, however, formulated a concept of tolerance which obviated the need for toleration by disestablishing religion as a political institution. The very notion of this is foreign to Judaism and Islam, both conceived originally as political entities.[19] Indeed, the political fortunes of the Jewish people are part and parcel of the history of Judaism, an intertwining of faith and politics which is also characteristic of Islam. If Islam is not entirely identified with the Arab people, it is only paradoxically because of its great political success, a success which could only strengthen the identification in theory of temporal and spiritual power.[20]

Muslims were to bear witness to God's presence on earth in every domain of life, including, in particular, the public and political sphere.[21] Islam was conceived to be in a state of perpetual enmity with the non-Muslim world, the *dār al-ḥarb*, that "realm of the sword" in which actual or potential warfare is the appropriate, even required, religious posture.[22] The initial military and political successes of the Arab armies only confirmed this attitude for the jurists and masses of believers, and all subsequent Islamic history, with its factionalism, internecine quarrels, and qualified political achievements, did not appreciably alter this perception.[23] Yet to the discerning Muslim the contrast between the promise and the reality of living in a world which he owned, or at least managed, must have been striking and disconcerting. For many people it must have seemed that, in contrast to the pagan times of the *Jāhiliyya*, everything had changed and nothing had changed. However much the bedouin Arabs may have become the new aristocracy of the Middle East, with new-found wealth and power, for most members of the new faith—and for the pious particularly—the vision of a better world, of a just society that would be appreciably different from what they had previously experienced, was seen through a glass darkly, if at all. For most Muslims, the personal material benefits to be derived from the political successes of Islam, like the spiritual blessings which were to follow immediately upon conversion, had to be deferred to an afterlife, even as the Day of Judgment was itself deferred and its immediacy blunted with the development of a normative *fiqh*, particularly in Sunnī Islam. In the meantime, *ḥadīth* and *fiqh* literature both taught that obedience to a Muslim ruler, however nominal his faith and suspect his morality, was mandatory.[24] It must have seemed to many thoughtful Muslims that one had to be a believer in spite of the successes of Islam, as much as because of them.

For this reason and others, Ṣūfism was originally in large part a response to and repudiation of the political, legalistic formulation of Sunnī Islam and of its call—and of the call of Shī'ī Islam as well—to collective, militant action.[25] The Ṣūfī turned this dimension of the faith inwards, making the individual fight the enemy within himself, struggling against his own soul's tendency to succumb to those very temptations of the world which were regarded now as evil. In this denial of material success the Ṣūfīs for a long time eschewed the quest for political office and advantage, leaving it to Allah to redeem the world through spiritual and not martial means.[26] In so doing, the Ṣūfī masters and their considerable mass of followers abandoned the political field to those who had a taste for government.[27] That is, the mystic orders did not pose a serious political threat to the princes of Islam for quite a while; not, in fact, until well into the fourteenth century in Persia.[28] The implicit rejection of the politicized religiosity of Sunnī and Shī'ī Islam remained until then politically just that—implicit, and relatively quiescent, politically.

Ṣūfism thus did not develop an ethic of tolerance beyond that already found in nonmystical circles. While the implications of mystical belief in the oneness of all being and the superficiality of differences may have led *ahl al-*

taṣawwuf to an essentially tolerant attitude to all mankind,[29] no specific political articulation of this viewpont emerged from these circles; perhaps because it would have been too political in its very neutrality. The mystics, cautious of being accused of antinomianism and indifference to the external structures of Islam,[30] were not prepared to express themselves unambiguously on God's love for the non-Muslim as such.

Medieval philosophers are a separate class of Muslims who offered yet another distinctly apolitical interpretation of their religious heritage, locating it in a nonnational, even universal framework. A philosopher like al-Fārābī presented his ideas of the virtuous state without specific references to Islamic institutions or history,[31] while Avicenna and Averroes are only slightly more accommodating.[32] Even in such a sensitive area as prophecy and revelation, the accommodation made by these philosophers to the particularities of the Islamic experience is minimal, on the whole. Indeed, the integration of the prophetic experience into a normative epistemology is one of the outstanding features of medieval philosophy, subscribed to by all the Islamic philosophers.[33] Though this theory is not devoid of divine assistance, through the mechanism of emanation (particularly from the celestial "Agent Intellect"), it is generally not earmarked to any one prophecy or revelation.

It is in the development of Aristotle's idea of "quick wit" or sagacity, the ability to hit upon the middle term of a syllogism in an instant,[34] that room could be seen as having been made not only for philosophically unenlightened prophets in general, but for the admittedly uneducated Prophet of Islam in particular. Avicenna develops this capacity of immediate intuition to include apprehension of all the terms of a syllogism, that is, of the whole body of knowledge affirmed by a proposition; and this without any external sensory source. This is seen as the intuitive gift of the prophet, though derived from the Holy Spirit, *al-rūḥ al-qudsī* (or as the Latin *Shifā'* has it, the *intellectus sanctus*), i.e., the universal Agent Intellect.[35] With its aid the individual prophet can dispense with sensory experience and with the normal stages of learning, that is, with induction and deduction; indeed, the prophet can dispense with and be innocent of education in general, and yet know all. Moreover, it is also this emanated endowment, extending beyond the intellect to the imagination, which is regarded as stimulating that faculty to represent the universal truths intuited in symbols easily comprehended by all, and in this way the whole body of revelation is brought into the philosophical corpus without losing its popular appeal or authority.[36]

This notion is ideally suited for attributing prophecy as well as political and intellectual perfection to Muhammad. It is, consequently, important to note that Avicenna refrains from making this connection explicit, and that he does not make any specific allusions to the Prophet of Islam in this connection. He thus does not develop an obvious identification of the general theory to his particular religious and political reality.

This distancing himself from his own tradition, no doubt for reasons of philosophical credibility, is present to some degree even in Avicenna's more apologetic and theologically oriented work, the short treatise called *On the Proof of Prophecies*.[37] This work is somewhat unique for Avicenna, in that, as the title indicates, he attempts to prove in it the existence of prophecy, as contrasted with merely describing it, his usual method. The proof is couched in general terms, using the key Avicennian concepts of essential (i.e., necessary) and accidental existence, in addition to standard Avicennian structures of emanation and conventional relationships between the spheres and individual intellects.

It is not our concern here to offer a critique of Avicenna's proof, but merely to point out that here, too, in his most rigorous attempt to justify the necessary occurrence of prophecy, there is little specifically Islamic about Avicenna's proof. This is not immediately apparent, perhaps, for Avicenna's subsequent discussion and the bulk of this short treatise is devoted to showing the congruence of Qur'anic statements and those of philosophy, particularly through an exegesis of Sūra 24:35, which speaks of God's light. This section is a good illustration of traditional philosophical exegesis, even if it is not philosophically compelling. Between the first and second parts of the opuscule, however, there is the following statement:

> This then is the summary of the discourse concerning the affirmation of prophecy, the showing of its essence, and the statements made about revelation, the angel, and the thing revealed. As for the validity of the prophethood of our prophet, of Muhammad (may God's prayers and peace be on him), it becomes evident to the reasonable man (*al-'āqil*) once he compares him with the other prophets, peace be on them. We shall refrain from elaboration here.[38]

Avicenna thus acknowledges the validity of the prophethood of Muhammad specifically, but only in comparison with that of other prophets. All the true prophets are accounted for by the general theory of prophecy. Muhammad compares very well, of course, but there are, according to this view at least, no philosophically unique claims about him or the faith he founded. For Avicenna, as for his fellow Muslim and Jewish philosophers, by and large, prophecy, as other areas of human experience, was a subject of scientific concern only as a universal phenomenon. True prophecy was considered as legitimate whenever certain conditions were or would be met, and it was the philosopher's job to analyze these conditions and to put them within a universal metaphysical/political framework. It was not the philosopher's job to determine whether these conditions had in fact been met in any particular case, i.e., whether prophet *a* was a true prophet and prophet *b* a false prophet.

Among Muslim and Jewish philosophers of the period, Maimonides stands out for his attempt to present rational arguments for the uniqueness of a particular person's—Moses'—prophecy,[39] and any sophisticated reader of his *Guide* could see that his arguments were all of a dialectical and rhetorical kind, philosophically inconclusive. Avicenna, as other Muslim philosophers, simply takes it for granted for the most part that the reader knows he is assuming Muhammad to be the ideal true prophet, and this tacit premise allows for both the integration of philosophy and religious beliefs and for their independence of each other.

If in political philosophy, which encompasses ethics as well, the philosophers were not essentially parochial, they were even less so in their physical and metaphysical teachings. There is no distinctly Islamic prime matter, or separate intelligences of the heavens, or even human rational faculty. There is just matter, form, and the combinations thereof. True, there was an attempt in Shī'ī thought, expressed in part in the *Rasā'il Ikhwān al-Ṣafā'*,[40] to establish a racial and spiritual superiority for themselves, at least for their leaders, to elevate them from the mass of mankind and bring them closer to the divine realm. The specific formulations of this Eastern, Baṣran-based view of Islam were apparently adopted by Judah Halevi in Spain and adapted to Judaism,[41] though he also drew on rabbinic sources to emphasize the unique and exalted nature of his people. Yet the remarkable point is that Halevi's *Kuzari* remained an isolated and relatively uninfluential work in Jewish philosophical circles until modern times, even as the philosophers of Islam did not follow up on the lead in this issue given by the *Ikhwān al-Ṣafā'* and their Ismā'īlī counterparts.

Particularly if we compare the *falāsifa* with the *mutakallimūn* or theologians of Islam are we struck with the objectivity that the philosophers bring to their understanding of nature and of the human condition, a condition which must include that of all peoples, Christians and Jews included. The autonomy of human reason and of physical nature was to the philosophers a necessary condition for any meaningful talk about Allah and His creation. *Kalām* occasionalism and the fatalism it engendered were regarded by the philosophers as self-contradictory and self-destructive positions, God representing for the philosophers the very essence of intelligibility.[42] These thinkers were prepared to admit that man's intellect was too limited to comprehend the Divine intellect in its totality, but they were convinced that man could be sure of the ultimate rationality of that intellect, a rationality that was in principle comprehensible to man, and was in effect communicated to him.

It is this shared intelligibility or rationality, this commonality of ideas in the divine and human realm, which is also the basis for the philosophers' adoption of originally Greek models of perfection, rather than for the theologically inspired notion that the idea of the good is dogmatically derived from revealed actions, however reasonable they may seem. The philosophers and the theologians agreed in practice on most examples of ethical behavior, as well as on the ultimate source of the good, the "Pure Good" as God was sometimes called; but they differed on the extent to which revealed actions and commandments were to determine the conceptualization of ethical behavior. In ethics as in other areas of rational inquiry, the philosophers were convinced that God had granted man an autonomous, or semiautonomous, reason. For the philosophers (as for the mystics), the revealed word of God was not to be understood literally, and any value system that embraced the word uncritically was naive and, worse, conducive to misbelief.

This is one of the lessons Averroes teaches in his famous study, *Kitāb Faṣl al-Maqāl,* translated by the late lamented George Hourani as *Averroes on the Harmony of Religion and Philosophy.* It is a lesson which philosophers had been teaching ever since Philo Judaeus, but which became highly characteristic of medieval philosophy, both Islamic and Jewish.[43] It is the lesson of allegorization, *ta'wīl*, the understanding of the word of God on a nondenotative level, where words do not mean what they say, but what they do not say, what they would say if revelation was not intended for everyone, i.e., for the uneducated masses, and so has to be presented in a popular, metaphorical manner.[44] These metaphors are to be understood, however, as allegories representing abstract truths; the divine attributes, actions, and anthropomorphisms of various sorts symbolizing a conception of God essentially different from what first seems to be the case.

For Averroes, as equally for Maimonides, as he explains in the *Guide*,[45] the allegorization of philosophical truth is the way revelation is transmitted. We can say that God's prophets, if not God Himself, are inspired artists, and the philosopher is merely turning the poetry into prose, interpreting popular and poetic discourse in a rigorous and scientific way.

The Qur'an and Bible are seen by Averroes and Maimonides respectively, as by their fellow philosophers, to command this sort of activity, this philosophical exegesis of Scripture, and, in the hands of such accomplished exegetes the God of Moses and of Muhammad does indeed become a deity whom Aristotle and Plotinus would have recognized. Yet, as Averroes points out in the *Faṣl al-Maqāl*, the exegetical approach to Scripture is not unique to philosophy. He as much as says that the categories of *fiqh*, the extensive legal system of Islam, are based on an interpretation of the Qur'an which is not self-evident in the original written and oral traditions attributed to Muhammad.[46] We can easily extrapolate from Averroes' remarks and see that for him every aspect of post-Qur'anic Islam may be said to be the product of man's interpretation of God's will; and that will as expressed in revelation is something which God has indicated He wants interpreted.

Man is thus commanded to use his reason in approaching the Book of God, and the institutions of religion, as well as the articles of faith, are filtered through, and interpreted by, human understanding. There is for Averroes, moreover, no time when a qualified man abdicates his right to use his reason, to have an opinion, no occasion when religious law or practice can block individual understanding and interpretation. Not even the consensus of the community—the revered *ijmā'*—can be invoked to freeze rationality and individual effort.[47] Islam for Averroes has to allow tacit, when not explicit, *ijtihād*, personal reasoning. Undoubtedly for him it is the divine will and the nature of man to encourage such a use of the rational faculty, and revelation has not been meant to, nor is it even capable of, stopping this process.

In this manner Averroes rather explicitly presents a relatively open-ended understanding of religion, one which encourages continued interpretation of the faith, in accordance, presumably, with current philosophical understanding of the nature of being and truth. The introduction of new ideas and conceptualizations of the faith is thereby legitimized, while at the same time the hermeneutic principles adopted ensure that one keeps to the original formulations found in God's book. The sacred texts of the community remain just that, the institutions largely remain in place, even while new interpretations are given to the words of the texts and new symbols attached to the institutions. At no time is *bid'a*, real innovation, acknowledged, for true reasoning is seen as always disclosing the original intentions of the faith only.

This is a process which rabbinic Judaism had initiated long before the advent of Islam without explicitly propounding it; and it is of course the process of change and adaptation which all religions undergo to adapt to changing conditions. Yet it was only in the Middle Ages that an Averroes was bold enough to articulate this process and to elevate it to a virtue. As Islamic and Jewish society turned defensive and conservative following the twelfth century, this liberal appreciation of revealed religion did not find many advocates. Law and mysticism combined to choke philosophical formulations of religion and the liberal approach that accompanied them.

I do not wish to exaggerate the liberal thrust of philosophy in this period, for part of its wisdom was to remain conservative, as I have noted. Certain issues were best finessed—as the doctrine of creation vs. eternity and God's knowledge of particulars—and others, such as resurrection and the afterlife, were best avoided, as much as possible. Avoided too were actual political issues and radical interpretations of the law. Here many of the philosophers donned their other hat, that of *qāḍī* or *dayyān*, and in that capacity functioned traditionally, i.e., conservatively, for the most part.

Thus, for example, Averroes' chapter on the *jihād* in his legal handbook, *Bidāyat al-Mujtahid*,[48] mostly written upon his assuming the role of *qāḍī* in 1167, betrays no disquiet with the institution of religious war, conceived of in traditionally literal terms. Such warfare, Averroes says in the name of a practically unanimous tradition, is an obligation for the community, commanded by the Prophet.[49] The only indication in the chapter of possible dissatisfaction with warfare as the preferred posture of the Islamic state may be found in Averroes' survey of differing opinions concerning the conditions for negotiating a truce.[50] According to Averroes, the overwhelming majority opinion in Islamic law is that a truce may be concluded when the ruler (the "Imām") feels it is in the community's interest, even if it is not absolutely necessary. This view is supported by Qur'anic citations[51] and by the example of the Prophet himself. Averroes does not actually recommend this view, but neither does he disassociate himself from it; he has simply brought to the reader's attention—and to the attention of the ruling class—an effective and sanctioned alternative to religious war and physical coercion.

A second message which Averroes communicates in this chapter, and throughout the handbook, is that Islamic law is not monolithic, and that the different schools of law indeed differ on their interpretation of Qur'anic verses and statements of the Tradition. As the translator of this chapter has remarked,[52] Averroes' originality in this treatise lies in his analysis of the conflicting interpretations, showing the priorities and with which each school resolved conflicting sources. Averroes' deconstruction of the legal tradition (whatever its historical accuracy) thus emphasizes both the diversity of the law and the diverse attitudes and initiatives of its leading spokesmen.

This is not the impression Maimonides wants to leave with his readers in his classical compendium of Jewish law, the *Mishneh Torah.* For the most part, *the* law is given on any particular issue, and the varying and conflicting interpretations and their underlying rationales are not brought out.[53] Yet this more dogmatic approach, for all its methodological severity, probably has a liberal purpose. Maimonides may well have wanted to acquaint the reader of his work solely with the conclusions of the rabbinic tradition in order to free him to engage in non-Talmudic pursuits, and in this way to make time in the day for science and philosophy. It is knowledge of the latter subjects which finally brings one into God's presence for Maimonides, and which is the ultimate condition for achieving immortality.[54] Thus the law, however strictly Maimonides applies it and however deeply he is committed to it, is not of ultimate significance for him, any more than the practical life which it regulates and the sociopolitical issues which it addresses. Maimonides can endorse the law in all its coercive force because, paradoxically, he and those philosophers like him are not adversely affected by it, any more than they are affected by the evil in the world.[55] Moreover, the philosophers as everyone else benefit from the salutary effects of law and order, the law being recognized as a necessary condition for the well-being of everyone in society.[56]

The law, then, for both Averroes and Maimonides, may be seen as having dimensions which mitigate the severity with which they expound its coercive nature. It would, however, be vastly excessive to claim that either man secretly disavowed the authority and mandate of religious law as traditionally understood. Maimonides certainly has no qualms in advocating the death penalty for dissidents from the rabbinic tradition, as well as for entire categories of enemies,[57] and in endorsing religious war and the subjugation of other peoples.[58] It would be anachronistic to expect more "tolerance" from him, and given the mentality of his day, perhaps he should be congratulated rather for whatever positive attitudes he occasionally expressed toward non-Jews, as in his remark that the non-Jew who, on the basis of deliberate observance and acknowledgment of the seven "Noahide" laws only, is vouchsafed immortality.[59] The separation of religion from the state is, accordingly, a concept which cannot be read back into the legal traditions of Islam or Judaism as a theoretical issue, and it is only the *de facto* separation of the two historically, both in mystical and philosophical circles as well as in the actual management of the state, from the Ummayad period on for Islam and from Roman times on for Judaism, that can serve as historical precedents for the idea. These precedents are very significant, however, and it is thus fair to say that Islam, as Judaism, has witnessed movements which have implicitly offered alternatives to the political formulations of their faiths. The mystical and philosophical currents in these traditions have been added on to the legal and political frameworks, and have found room within the latter structure.

This process has now to be expanded to include modern notions of personal freedom, religious tolerance, and individual rights. These concepts are not to be formally pitted against antithetical notions to be found in these traditions, but are to be placed alongside the earlier views, and viewed as their sequels.

Admittedly, it could be argued that accepting an ethic of radical tolerance would completely explode the traditional structure of both Islam and Judaism.[60] The experience of modern Turkey and of secular movements elsewhere in the Islamic world may be adduced in this regard,[61] and the opposition to the Turkish model in the Arab world shows the difficulties a proposal for the separation of religion and state would encounter. Yet our survey of the medieval experience of Judaism and Islam establishes the grounds for such a move and indicates the possibility of interpreting these faiths in new ways that may yet be seen as authentic and legitimate.[62] There have been a few attempts to do this in modern times, but they have not been sufficiently or widely appreciated, particularly not in traditional circles. Yet it is these very circles which most need to study and develop the kinds of modernist interpretations of their faith which have emanated from orthodox believers in their midst.

Within Judaism, Moses Mendelssohn still stands out, since the very beginning of the Enlightenment, as a bold and daring advocate of the separation of religion and state, a view that he clearly enunciated in his famous treatise *Jerusalem, or, On Religious Power and Judaism.*[63] Convinced of the need for separation, for both political and religious reasons, Mendelssohn found authority for it in the Bible, in the Israelites' desire for a king and for the institution of monarchy, rather than for a direct relation with God as king, and prophets such as Samuel his spokesmen.[64] For Mendelssohn this turn toward monarchy in ancient Israel, at the very beginning of its political coming of age, spelled the end of the ideal theocracy originally proclaimed by God. Henceforth, Mendelssohn argued, Judaism was a religion that foreswore coercion, even as with the fall of the Temple it relinquished political authority and the perquisites of power.[65] Judaism thus was able to conform to Mendelssohn's ideal model of voluntaristic religion, its original theocratic uniqueness, as he believed, abandoned.

This radical interpretation of biblical history and theology is breathtaking in its audacity and disregard for historical fact.[66] For our purposes, however, it is instructive to see how a learned and observant Jew could reinterpret the basic document of his faith to accommodate a modern ethical desideratum. The orginal theocracy is seen as of limited duration, the people having forced God, as it were, to change His mind on how to affect people's lives through religion. The new political vision is thus seen as already established in the earliest period of Israel's history, and given there a legitimacy which precludes it from being regarded as an alien implant in the tradition.

At the core of Mendelssohn's understanding of religion is the idea of a God of love, whose will cannot be achieved through coercive means.[67] Religion and compulsion are seen as antithetical terms,[68] a modern sensibility that Mendelssohn believed was already present in the Hebrew Bible.

This same sensibility, located in the Qur'an, was keenly felt by 'Alī 'Abd al-Rāziq, an Egyptian jurist and scholar, and an al-Azhar graduate in the first quarter of this century.[69] His interpretation of the Qur'an's call to faith left little room for militancy in religion,[70] and he boldly denied, on religious grounds, the institutional necessity of the caliphate.[71]

Al-Rāziq felt there was a clear division within Muhammad's own mission, and certainly in subsequent Islamic history, between religious and political issues; and that the latter were wrongly integrated with the former by the later rulers of Islam, for selfish reasons.[72] The future health of Islam and of Muslim peoples depended, in his view, on the separation of these two forces and on the responsiveness with which Muslims could relate to modern political forms of expression.

Al-Rāziq was not alone in calling for a reevaluation of the political institutions of Islam,[73] though the strong reaction to his views, in his time and since,[74] has no doubt contributed to the paucity of such voices in the Islamic world. In both Islam and Judaism, the orthodox camps mostly remain wedded, theoretically, to views which ignore or reject the modern notion of tolerance.

It may be argued, however, that classical rabbinic Judaism affirms a *de facto* separation of religion and state, and that it need not have moved or need not continue to attempt to move Judaism into an active political mode. That is, orthodox Judaism need not view current history in a messianic perspective that obliges political activism. This perspective and the claims made in its behalf have only antagonized others to the right and left religiously, and its proponents have discredited themselves both politically and religiously.

It is only slightly harder to urge the pious of Islam not to press for the implementation of Islamic law in Muslim countries. Such a plea might well seem ludicrous today. Yet the actual separation of civil and religious law in many of these countries, and the uses and abuses Islamic law has been put to by the rulers of these countries, makes such a plea not entirely quixotic. It is, moreover, the best chance such countries have for introducing truly democratic procedures, and the best chance Islam has to form a modern religious ethic. This ethic need not be viewed as essentially modern; it may be located in the richness of past Islamic experience by the historian and the theologian. I leave such a task to the modern exegete. May he—or she—soon appear.

NOTES

1 A shorter version of this article was given at the 1985 Denver meeting of the Institute for Islamic-Judaic Studies. I wish to thank the participants of that meeting, and particularly Dr. Vera Moreen, for their helpful comments.

2 Gen. 4:9.

3 Ex. 22:20-26; Deut. 15:7-15.

4 Lev. 19:9-10, and cf. Ruth 2.

5 Cf. Lev. 25:8-55.

6 Lev. 25:10.

7 Cf., e.g., Ex. 21:2-11, 20-27.

[8] Cf. Qur'an 74:8-10 and 84:1-12 in particular, and see W. Montgomery Watt, *Muhammad at Mecca* (Oxford: Oxford University Press, 1965), 64-66.

[9] W. Montgomery Watt, *Muhammad at Medina* (Oxford: Oxford University Press, 1966), 261-302.

[10] Cf. A. Guillaume, *The Traditions of Islam* (Oxford: Oxford University Press, 1924), 99-107.

[11] This article is not the place to analyze this concept itself or to trace its long and complicated development. Alexander Altmann, among others, has devoted a number of studies to the subject, and cf. the many references throughout his commentary to Moses Mendelssohn's *Jerusalem*, vol. 8, in Moses Mendelssohn, *Gesammelte Schriften. Jubiläumsausgabe: Schriften zum Judentum II* (Stuttgart-Bad Cannstatt: F. Fromann, 1983); abridged English version, *Jerusalem, or, On Religious Power and Judaism*, A. Arkush, tr. (Hannover: University Press of New England, 1983), 143-240. Cf., too, Altmann's article, "Gewissensfreiheit und Toleranz: Eine begriffsgeschichtliche Untersuchung," *Mendelssohn Studien* 4(1979): 9-46. In the present article I do not seek to justify or argue for the concept of tolerance, but take it as a given of modern civilization and a self-evident virtue.

[12] Cf. *Webster's Ninth New Collegiate Dictionary* (Springfield, MA.: Merriam Webster, 1984), 1241.

[13] *Ibid.*

[14] Cf. most recently on this subject, A. Khoury, *Toleranz im Islam* (München: Kaiser, 1980), 138-76. See too M. Khadduri, *War and Peace in the Law of Islam* (Baltimore: Johns Hopkins University Press, 1955), 175-201. Cf. further in English, the jurists' texts translated by P. Fenton in Bat Ye'or, *The Dhimmi: Jews and Christians under Islam*, D. Maisel, P. Fenton, and D. Littman, trs. (Rutherford, N.J.: Farleigh Dickinson University Press, 1985), pp. 161-204.

[15] Cf. Khoury, *War and Peace in the Law of Islam*, p. 177. The negative, dehumanizing aspects of the experience, treated primarily from a politico-social viewpoint, have been emphasized by Bat Ye'or, *Dhimmi*, pp. 51-77, 140-52, and cf. particularly the translations of historical documents reflecting the social and historical condition of the *dhimmīs*, pp. 205-388. The unfortunate effects of this legislation should not blind us from the realization that Jewish *halakhah* is strikingly similar to the Islamic *sharī'a* in this area, however much it was relegated to theory by actual circumstances. Cf. Maimonides, *Mishneh Torah*, "The Book of Judges, Kings," ch. 6 (Jerusalem: Ulamoth, 1965), 8:1863; English translation by A. Hershman in *The Code of Maimonides, Book Fourteen: The Book of Judges* (New Haven: Yale University Press, 1949), 220f.

[16] Cf. Khoury, *Toleranz*, pp. 29-43, 110-16. See, too, J. Kraemer, "Apostates, Rebels and Brigands," *Israel Oriental Studies* 10(1980): 34-73.

[17] Cf. below for rabbinic attitudes, as enunciated by Maimonides. For biblical attitudes cf., for example, Ex. 32:27; Lev. 17:3-9, 24:16; Deut. 27:15, 28:15; Ez. 38-9. The biblical attitude to the pagan "stranger" and even to paganism itself is actually more tolerant, relatively speaking, than often realized, if we exclude those peoples—the Canaanites and Amalekites—with whom the Israelites actually clashed. Cf. Ex. 22:20; Lev. 19:33-34, 24:22; Deut. 10:18;

Jer. 7:5-7; Micah 4:5. With the spread of the concept of a universal monotheism in rabbinic times, there arose, paradoxically, a concomitant intolerance of paganism. Cf. the opening section of the paper of David Novak in this volume, "The Treatment of Islam and Muslims in the Legal Writings of Maimonides," pp. 233-35. See, too, A. Altmann, "Tolerance and the Jewish Tradition," *Faces of Judaism* (Hebrew, Tel Aviv, 1983), 217-22.

18 Cf. *ibid.*, pp. 224-30, and see the remainder of Novak's article, "Treatment of Islam and Muslims," pp. 235-46 in this volume. The evolving position of European Jewry on this issue, and the pivotal role played by R. Menaḥem Meiri (1249-1306), has been recounted by J. Katz, *Exclusiveness and Tolerance* (Oxford: University Press, 1961), 51, 114, and elsewhere. Cf. in this regard ha-Meiri's *Bet ha-Beḥirah 'al Masekhet 'Avodah Zarah*, rev. ed., A. Sopher, ed. (Jerusalem: [N.S.], 1964), comments to pp. 10, 20, and 57 (pp. 19, 46, and 214 respectively). Rabbinic attitudes in the Middle Ages can be seen as rooted in earlier, Mishnaic times, with the majority of the rabbis of that period prepared for acquiesence in even pagan government (*dina dimalkhuta dina*), accepting thereby a *de facto* division of powers between civil government and religious authority. This position was not only one of pragmatic tactics, but for many it was an expression of the religious priority of peace and the requisite tolerance of opposing religious views. Cf. for example, T. B. Perek ha-Shalom 59a-b (The Chapter on Peace), translated by M. Ginsberg in *The Minor Tractates of the Talmud*, A. Cohen, ed. (London: Soncino Press, 1965), 2:597-602. See also in particular the teaching of R. Eliezer in *Midrash Agur*, edited by H. G. Enelow in *The Mishnah of R. Eliezer* (Hebrew, New York: Bloch Publishing, 1933), 67-78. I wish to acknowledge with gratitude the research assistance here provided by two graduate students at Brandeis, Rabbis S. Klatzkin and M. Gopin.

19 Muhammad saw himself as a leader of the Arab *umma* or people, to whom he was bringing a *dīn*. The political welfare of his community was from the beginning a primary "religious" concern for him, and pronouncements toward his enemies established forever after Islam's negative attitude to non-Muslims. Cf. Khoury, *War and Peace in the Law of Islam*, pp. 23, 68.

20 In practice, however, the *de facto* separation of religious and "civil" (i.e., governmental) authority very soon became the rule, their identification the exception. For a recent study of the earliest expression of this reality, cf. I. Lapidus, "The Separation of State and Religion in the Development of Early Islamic Society," *International Journal of Middle East Studies* 6(1975): 363-85.

21 Cf. Khoury, *War and Peace in the Law of Islam*, pp. 105, 177f. Islamic law (like Jewish law) has been predicated on this assumption, making it traditionally mandatory, where circumstances permit, that religious law be the law of the state.

22 Cf. the extensive literature on *jihād* assembled by Khoury, *ibid.*, p. 103, note 2, and p. 107, note 12, and see, too, Khoury's own discussion, pp. 103-24. It should be noted, however, that the requisite state of enmity between the Islamic and non-Islamic worlds did not preclude the development of alternative peaceful relations sanctioned, in however delimited a fashion, by Islamic law. Cf. Khoury, *ibid.*, pp. 109, 125.

[23] Some voices, and notably that of Ibn Khaldūn, were, however, raised already in the Middle Ages over the abuse of the authorities in waging war in the name of religion. Cf. M. Khadduri, *The Islamic Conception of Justice* (Baltimore: Johns Hopkins University Press, 1984), 173, 187.

[24] Cf. Guillaume, *The Traditions of Islam*, pp. 44-46. The very existence of these traditions and law is proof of the challenges, both pacific and militant, which were mounted against this idea. As is well known, the militant defiance of authority in the name of religious zeal (whatever other socio-economic factors were also involved) has been practically continuous in the history of Islam from the Khārijite revolt on.

[25] Cf. I. Goldziher's classic study, *Vorlesungen über den Islam* (Heidelberg: C. Winter, 1910), now translated and updated as *Introduction to Islamic Theology and Law*, A. and R. Hamori, trs. (Princeton: University Press, 1981), 130-38, 147, 155. There were, however, pietistic ascetics of Muhammad's time and immediately thereafter who participated in the wars waged, even while rejecting the personal material gains which then were their due. Cf. *ibid.*, p. 127f. The tendency among Ṣūfīs, nevertheless, was to view physical fighting with another person as "the lesser *jihād*," with "the greater *jihād*" being the struggle against one's own desires. Cf. M. Smith, *Al-Muḥāsibī: An Early Mystic of Baghdad* (London: Sheldon Press, 1935), 76. Sufyan b. Unayma al-Hilālī al-Kūfī (d. 814) is reported to have said the "*jihād* consists of ten parts, one of which is fighting against the enemy of Islam, and nine parts of which is fighting against the self."

[26] Cf. the brief biographies and sayings of eighth-century Ṣūfī masters collected by M. Smith, *ibid.*, pp. 60-82. Note, too, the attempt to avoid any involvement in political or juridicial issues, together with the appearance of orthodox belief, in the *Kitāb al-Ta'arruf li-Madhhab Ahl al-Taṣawwuf* of the tenth-century Abū Bakr al-Kalābādhī, translated by A. J. Arberry in *The Doctrine of the Sufīs* (Cambridge: University Press, 1935), 5-12, 51-57, 79f. Of course, presentations such as these did not always convince Islamic rulers of the Ṣūfī's political reliability.

[27] This is not to deny that even early Ṣūfism, once it became a popular movement, had a political dimension, often despite itself; and that it was often perceived as a threat by its opponents, for religious and "secular" reasons. Cf. Goldziher, *Introduction*, pp. 119f., 129; see, too, C. W. Ernst, *Words of Ecstasy in Sufism* (Albany: State University of New York Press, 1985), 97-116, for an analysis of the trials endured by Nūrī, Ḥallāj, and 'Ayn al-Qudat.

[28] This politicization of Ṣūfī orders in the East, leading to the political rule of the Safavids and other dynasties, had a great deal to do with the merger of Ṣūfī and Shī'ī beliefs and practices. Cf. S. A. Arjomand, *The Shadow of God and the Hidden Imam* (Chicago: University of Chicago Press, 1984), 67, 77.

[29] Cf. Goldziher, *Introduction*, pp. 151-53.

[30] *Ibid.*, p. 156.

[31] Al-Fārābī does use certain terms which resonate with religious associations for Muslims, though they are not intended to be limited to the Islamic tradition. Cf. particularly his use of "imām" for the ideal leader, in *Kitāb Ārā' Ahl al-*

Madīna al-Fāḍila, A. Nadir, ed. (Beirut: Dār al-Mashriq, 1959), 105; *Taḥṣīl al-Sa'āda*, tr. by M. Mahdi in *Alfarabi's Philosophy of Plato and Aristotle* (Ithaca: Cornell University Press, 1969), 46.

32 Many of Avicenna's recommendations for the ideal state are actually custom-suited to the Islamic pattern, but are proffered in a way that does not identify them completely with that pattern. Cf., e.g., Avicenna's condoning of challenges to caliphal authority in the name of "practical judgment" and "political management," on the one hand, and his reluctance to condone *jihād* against cities with "praiseworthy laws" on the other, in *Al-Shifā': Al-Ilāhiyyat*, I. Makdour, ed. (Cairo: Organisme Générale des Imprimeries Gouvernmentales, 1960), 2:452f.; partially translated by M. Marmura in R. Lerner and M. Mahdi, eds., *Medieval Political Philosophy: A Sourcebook* ([New York]: Free Press of Glencoe, 1963), 108f. Averroes' views on this subject may be gleaned from his paraphrase of Plato's *Republic*. Cf. R. Lerner's discussion of Averroes' deviations from Islamic norms of a politico-religious sort, in the introduction to his translation of the text, *Averroes on Plato's Republic* (Ithaca: Cornell University Press, 1974), xvi-xxviii.

33 Among the many examinations of this theme, cf. F. Rahman, *Prophecy in Islam* (London, 1958), 11-45, for al-Fārābī's and Avicenna's views, while for Averroes, see my article, "Averroes on Intellection and Conjunction," *Journal of the American Oriental Society* 86(1966): 84f.

34 Cf. *Posterior Analytics* 1:34, 89b 10f., and see Rahman, *Prophecy*, pp. 30-36.

35 Cf. *Al-Shifā'*, *De Anima*, F. Rahman, ed. (London: George Allen and Unwin, 1959), p. 248f., and the parallel *Al-Najāt* (Cairo: Maṭba'at al-Sa'āda, 1912), 2:272. Rahman has translated this section from the latter text, and cf. *Avicenna's Psychology* (Oxford: University Press, 1952), 36.

36 Cf. Rahman, *Prophecy*, pp. 36-45.

37 Edited by M. Marmura, *Fī Ithbāt al-Nubuwwāt* (Beirut: Dār al-Nahār wa'l-Nashr, 1968); Marmura's translation appears in Mahdi and Lerner, eds., *Medieval Political Philosophy*, pp. 113-21.

38 Marmura's trans. in *ibid*., p. 115; Arabic version in Marmura, ed., *Fī Ithbāt*, p. 47.

39 Cf. the *Guide* 2:32-36, in *The Guide of the Perplexed*, S. Pines, tr. (Chicago: University of Chicago Press, 1963), 363f. See also K. Bland, "Moses and the Law According to Maimonides," in J. Reinharz et al., eds., *Mystics, Philosophers and Politicians: Essays in Jewish Intellectual History in Honor of Alexander Altmann* (Durham: Duke University Press, 1982), 49-53.

40 Known in English as "The Epistles of the Sincere Brethren," though as yet untranslated into this language. Cf. F. Dieterici, *Thier und Mensch vor dem König der Genien* (Leipzig: J. C. Hinrichs, 1879), 60-61.

41 Cf. I. Goldziher, "Mélanges Judeo-Arabes," *Revue des Études Juives* 50(1905): 34ff., and see H. Wolfson, "Hallevi and Maimonides on Prophecy," in I. Twersky and G. Williams, eds., *Studies in the History of Philosophy and Religion* (Cambridge: Harvard University Press, 1977), 2:101-03.

[42] Cf. my article, "Averroes on Causation," in S. Stein and R. Loewe, eds., *Studies in Jewish Religious and Intellectual History Presented to Alexander Altmann* (University, Ala.: University of Alabama Press, 1979), 143-56.

[43] Allegorical interpretation of the scriptures is not, of course, limited to philosophical circles, being widespread in mystical circles as well. Cf. Goldziher, *Introduction*, p. 138, for Ṣūfism.

[44] Cf. G. Hourani, *Faṣl al-Maqāl* (Leiden: Brill, 1959), 12ff. English translation by Hourani in *Averroes on the Harmony of Religion and Philosophy* (London: Luzac, 1961), 49ff.

[45] Cf., e.g., Maimonides' introductory remarks to the *Guide*, in Pines, tr., *Guide*, p. 9.

[46] Hourani, ed., *Faṣl*, p. 7f.; English tr. in Hourani, *Averroes*, p. 46.

[47] Hourani, ed., *Faṣl*, p. 15; English tr. in Hourani, *Averroes*, p. 52.

[48] Averroes, *Bidāyat al-Mujtahid* (Cairo: al-Azhar, 1966), 1:390-400; translated by Rudolph Peters in *Jihad in Mediaeval and Modern Islam* (Leiden: Brill, 1977), 9-25.

[49] Averroes, *Bidāyat*, p. 391; Peters, *Jihad*, p. 9.

[50] Averroes, *Bidāyat*, p. 398; Peters, *Jihad*, p. 22.

[51] Qur'an 8:61.

[52] Peters, *Jihad*, p. 6.

[53] Cf. the introduction to Maimonides, *Mishneh Torah*, 1:9; English tr. by M. Hyamson, quoted by I. Twersky in *A Maimonides Reader* (New York: Behrman House, 1972), 40.

[54] Cf. Maimonides, *Guide* 3:54, in Pines, tr., *Guide*, p. 635. The *Guide*, written after the *Mishneh Torah* and all his other major works, should be seen as expressing Maimonides' final position on issues which he may handle differently in his other writings.

[55] *Guide* 3:12, in Pines, tr., *Guide*, pp. 441ff.; *Guide* 3:51, in Pines, tr., *Guide*, p. 625.

[56] *Guide* 3:27, in Pines, tr., *Guide*, p. 510.

[57] Cf. the *Mishneh Torah*, "The Book of Judges, Rebels," vol. 8, 1:2, 2:4, 3:2, pp. 1828ff.; English translation by A. Hershman, *Book of Judges*, pp. 138ff.

[58] *Mishneh Torah*, "Kings," 5:1, 4, 6; 6:4, pp. 1862-63; A. Hershman, tr., *Book of Judges*, pp. 217, 220.

[59] *Mishneh Torah*, "Kings," 8:11, p. 1867; A. Hershman, tr., *Book of Judges*, p.230. The liberality of this view notwithstanding, just what Maimonides meant by promising immortality here is problematic for a variety of reasons, one being the condition for immortality of intellectual achievement mentioned above; see also note 53.

[60] Cf. e.g., W. Montgomery Watt's considered opinion, "The Significance of the Theory of Jihad," in A. Dietrich, ed., *Akten des VII Kongresses für Arabistik und Islamwissenschaft* (Göttingen: Vandenhoeck und Ruprecht, 1976), 394.

[61] The record of the Turkish experience, as that of other movements in the Islamic world which embraced secularism, is not, however, unambiguous in its relation to religious tradition. It is definitely unfortunate that Ziya Gökalp, the ideologist of Turkism in the early part of this century, rendered *laïque*, "secular," as *lā-dīnī*, literally "irreligious," a term, which has more negative connotations

than necessarily intended by the Young Turks. Political opposition, rather than theoretical principles, gave their movement the impression of greater antagonism to religion *per se* than was the case. Cf. B. Lewis, *The Emergence of Modern Turkey* (Oxford: University Press, 1961), 397, 406.

62 The attempts of Mustafa Kemal and others to disestablish religion politically were not, in this view, sufficiently oriented towards establishing the policy on Islamic grounds, even when a positive vision of an enlightened Islamic faith was held. Cf. N. Berkes, *The Development of Secularism in Turkey* (Montreal: McGill University Press, 1964), 484, 497.

63 Cf. note 11 above. Reference will be to the English tr. by Alan Arkush.

64 Cf. 1 Sam. 8, and see Mendelssohn, *Jerusalem*, p. 132.

65 *Ibid.*, p. 130.

66 As Altmann says, *ibid.*, p. 232, "Mendelssohn's assertion that punitive measures by Jewish courts ceased after the loss of political independence does not fully correspond to the facts."

67 *Ibid.*, p. 121f. God's love is identified in classical Jewish style with the "thirteen attributes" announced at Sinai, Ex. 34:6-7.

68 *Ibid.*, pp. 43f., 57f.

69 Al-Rāziq's famous work is *Al-Islām wa-Uṣūl al-Ḥukm* (Cairo, 1925). This book was translated in French by L. Bercher as "L'Islam et les Bases du Pouvoir," *Revue des Études Islamiques* 7(1933): 353-91, 8(1934): 163-222. A second edition of the Arabic text, with a modest commentary by M. Ḥaqqi, appeared in Beirut in 1966. It is this latter edition, together with the French translation which is utilized in the following notes. Thus, the verses from the Qur'an that are cited in support of the view that Muhammad's religious mission was essentially peaceful—Qur'an 2:255, 3:19, 16:124, 87:21—are given in Ḥaqqi, ed., *Al-Islām*, p. 117, Bercher, "L'Islam," 8(1934): 175. A. Hourani, *Arabic Thought in the Liberal Age 1798-1939* (Oxford: University Press, 1967), 184-88, has offered a summary of the work as well, as has E. I. J. Rosenthal, *Studia Semitica* (Cambridge: University Press, 1971), 2:188-97.

70 Ḥaqqi, ed., *Al-Islām*, p. 116, though cf. the difficulties al-Rāziq has in explaining Muhammad's battles, *ibid.*, p. 154, Bercher, "L'Islam," p. 199.

71 Ḥaqqi, ed., *Al-Islām*, p. 120, Bercher, "L'Islam," p. 177.

72 Ḥaqqi, ed., *Al-Islām*, p. 199, Bercher, "L'Islam," p. 220.

73 Muhammad Iqbal is another, and even a more major figure in modern Islamic thought, who attempted to interpret Islam in contemporary terms, seeing it as a dynamic faith compatible with current science and philosophy. Cf. his well-known work, *The Reconstruction of Religious Thought in Islam* (Lahore: Muhammad Ashraf, 1960), 133, 138. As most other modernist reformers, however, he was not prepared for the radical kind of political proposals 'Ali 'Abd al-Rāziq suggested in the name of the faith. Nor most certainly was Muḥammad Rashīd Riḍā, the Egyptian modernist and disciple of Muḥammad 'Abduh, whose objections to al-Rāziq are quoted in translation by M. Kerr, *Islamic Reform: The Political and Legal Theories of Muhammad 'Abduh and Rashid Rida* (Berkeley: University of California Press, 1966), 179f. Cf. also Rosenthal, *Studia Semitica*, pp. 175-88.

[74] Cf. Kerr, *Islamic Reform*, p. 180, note 92, and see A. Hourani, *Arabic Thought*, pp. 188-91.

Rejecting Moral Virtue as the Ultimate Human End

Raphael Jospe

Aristotle's definition of the ultimate human end (Greek: *telos;* Arabic: *ghāya ākhira;* Hebrew: *takhlit aḥaronah*) in his *Nicomachean Ethics* 1:7, 1098a, 3-4, as "an active life of the element that has a rational principle"[1] poses an immediate difficulty: what is the relationship between rational virtue and moral virtue? To what extent, for example, is rational virtue entirely theoretical, and to what extent does rational virtue necessarily entail practical wisdom? W. F. R. Hardie suggests that Aristotle confused two concepts.[2] On the one hand, Aristotle treats rationality as a "dominant end" or "supreme end," to the exclusion of other human activity: only philosophy, as the most "godlike" of human activities, is worthy of constituting the ultimate human end. On the other hand, Aristotle also treats rationality as an "inclusive end"; rational action entails not only theory, but also practical intelligence and moral virtue. Hardie criticizes Aristotle for failing to make explicit this "inclusive end" and argues that "what is common and peculiar to man is rationality in a general sense, not theoretical insight, which is a specialized way of being rational."[3] Contemplation remains the "dominant end" even for a statesman, since his activity makes possible the life of contemplation.[4] But only contemplation, for Aristotle, is desired for itself alone, and thus is a higher end than those ends desired both for themselves as well as for their effects. As Hardie observes, "It is, so to say, beneath the dignity of the most godlike activities that they should be useful."[5]

At this point we should note that Maimonides explicitly rejects such reasoning in his discussion of the purpose of the commandments of the Torah—*ṭa'am ha-mitzvot.* To claim that God's actions, and thus God's commandments for humans, have no useful purpose, but only express his will, is to render them frivolous or futile. God's law, like his actions, conforms to wisdom as well as will, although humans are not always able to discern that wisdom.[6]

The fact that God's law must thus be "useful," however, does not necessarily imply that, for Maimonides, the ultimate human end must or should be defined in terms of social utility. In a famous discussion at the end of the *Guide of the Perplexed,*[7] to which we will return later in greater detail, Maimonides explicitly rejects moral virtue as the human end:

> This perfection regarding moral habits is, as it were, only the disposition to be useful to people; consequently, it is an instrument for someone else. For if you suppose a human individual alone, acting on no one, you will find that all his moral virtues are in vain and without employment and unneeded, and that they do not perfect the individual in anything. (Shlomo Pines translation)

Only contemplation, accordingly, expresses the true purpose of man as a rational being, rationality being the essential human characteristic constituting the "image of God."

Adam and Theoretical Perfection

The point is not entirely hypothetical. Maimonides argues forcefully at the very beginning of the *Guide of the Perplexed* that the divine *ṣelem* (image) in which the human being was created truly refers to the human intellect, which is man's "natural form, I mean to the notion in virtue of which a thing is constituted as a substance and becomes what it is."[8]

By this standard, of course, it is a mistake to interpret *ṣelem* as physical appearance or shape (for which Maimonides argues there are other Hebrew terms), and presumably the ceiling of the Sistine Chapel depicts not man in the divine image, but God in the image of man.

In the next chapter Maimonides interprets the story of Adam in the Garden of Eden in light of this insight.[9] If Adam was created in God's image, meaning that he was endowed with rational capacity, why does he acquire knowledge (presumably a rational function) only after his rebellious eating of the fruit of the "tree of knowledge of good and evil"? Maimonides' fascinating solution to this problem is his suggestion that Adam was initially endowed with a perfect theoretical intellect, i.e., the ability perfectly to distinguish true from false, and that this perfect theoretical intellect was, in fact, the divine image in which he was created. But Adam was not endowed with the practical ability to distinguish "generally accepted things," in other words, to make moral judgments of good and evil. (In sharp contrast to Adam, Maimonides attributes moral excellence, but not intellectual perfection, to Job.)[10] Such practical reason, which Adam lacked, is distinctly inferior to theoretical reason, for it deals with conventional truths ("generally accepted things" in the Shlomo Pines translation; "Right and wrong are matters not of reason but of repute" in the Lenn Evan Goodman translation; cf. F. Rahman's "commonly accepted opinions concerning actions" in Ibn Sīnā).

As Professor Lawrence Berman describes it:

> The fall of man consisted in a change of priorities, from an interest in the things of the mind to becoming interested in the things of the body; from being a philosopher, a master of his passions, to becoming a beast in human form, mastered by his passions; from being a solitary thinker, to becoming a ruler of cities, being informed by the imagination only. . . . Action, . . . the goal of choice between good and evil, cannot be qualified by truth and falsity, but only by good and evil. . . . Theory is the realm of fact in which one can seek whether one opinion is valid and another invalid; the sphere of action is that

> of value, which by its very nature is subjective. . . . Previous to the fall, Adam was not concerned with matters relating to values but only with the truth.[11]

Maimonides' view that Adam lost perfect intellectual apprehension, but gained moral judgment, is extended by Shem Tov ibn Falaquera. Since the rational truth, which is the basis of man's immortality, was abandoned in favor of conventional truth, man was now condemned to mortality.[12]

Adam thus did suffer a loss. He lost his perfect theoretical reasoning ability. What he gained in its place, practical reason, is a lower function, because it deals with a different, and lower level, of truth. But there is another factor in this loss.

Adam, at the beginning of the *Guide of the Perplexed,* had no prior need for practical reason, because Adam was in fact the hypothetical "man alone" of the last chapter of the *Guide* for whom the moral virtues are meaningless! Adam truly embodied the "image of God," because prior to his rebellion, for all practical purposes, he, like God, was alone, a perfect theoretical intellect, engaging in sublime self-contemplation. Despite his consistent insistence throughout the *Guide* that God is in no way analogous to any creature, and that the term "knowledge" applied to God is purely equivocal,[13] Maimonides states:

> Now when it is demonstrated that God . . . is an intellect *in actu* and that there is absolutely no potentiality in Him . . . it follows necessarily that He and the thing apprehended are one thing, which is His essence. Moreover, the act of apprehension owing to which He is said to be an intellectually cognizing subject is in itself the intellect, which is His essence. Accordingly, He is always the intellect as well as the intellectually cognizing subject and the intellectually cognized object. It is accordingly also clear that the numerical unity of the intellect, the intellectually cognizing subject, and the intellectually cognized object, does not hold good with reference to the Creator only, but also with reference to every intellect. Thus in us, too, the intellectually cognizing subject, the intellect, and the intellectually cognized object, are one and the same thing whenever we have an intellect *in actu.*[14]

Adam is thus the "man alone," with a perfect theoretical intellect, possessing the ultimate human perfection which constitutes the divine image. "Man alone" has no need for moral virtues, which accordingly cannot perfect him in any way. In all these ways, Adam resembles God, in whose image he was created. For in God, as in man, there is an essential identity of the actual intellectual subject (*'aql, sekhel*), act (*'āqil, maskil*), and object (*ma'qūl, muskal*). God and His knowledge are identical, and perfect Adam, alone like God, engages only in contemplation; one God, and one man in His image. The ultimate end of man, in the last chapter of the *Guide*, is to return to solitary theoretical perfection of the first man, in the beginning of the *Guide*.

The Ethical Dimension

But this is only one aspect of Maimonides' thought. For the fact is that God did not remain alone: God brought the world into being, and endowed it with useful laws in conformity with His wisdom. Adam, too, did not long stay alone, for out of his being came woman, and thus the human became a social being, for whom moral virtue and practical reason are not only relevant (whereas previously they had been of no value or meaning), but essential. God had created a world, which required cosmic governance; Adam and Eve would now create a society, which would similarly necessitate moral virtue and governance.

The confusion in Aristotle between the "dominant end" of contemplation, to the exclusion of all other "useful" activities, and the "inclusive end" of a balanced human life, requiring moral virtue and necessitating practical reasoning, is thus paralleled by a dynamic tension in Maimonides' own thought, between the ideal of solitary contemplation, as symbolized by Adam, created alone and perfectly rational, in the divine image, with the social-political ideal of the prophet as philosopher-king, an ideal necessitated by Adam's transformation into a social being with Eve, and brought to its perfect fulfillment in Moses.[15]

This tension in Maimonides' thought reflects his rich and eclectic use of diverse sources, as he attempted a Jewish synthesis, based on these biblical archetypes, of opposing tendencies in Greek thought (Plato vs. Aristotle) and Islamic philosophy (al-Fārābī vs. Ibn Bājja).

These tensions and opposing tendencies in Maimonides' thought and sources have been discussed and documented by various scholars. For example, in his "Translator's Introduction: The Philosophical Sources of the *Guide of the Perplexed*,"[16] Professor Shlomo Pines has shown the influence on Maimonides of al-Fārābī's view of the prophet as philosopher-king, and of Ibn Bājja's emphasis on solitary contemplative asceticism. Similarly, Professor Alexander Altmann[17] has shown that Maimonides' position on ultimate human perfection[18] is based on Ibn Bājja, and that this position has its source in Aristotle's *Nicomachaean Ethics*. Maimonides' synthesis or combination of al-Fārābī's Platonic politics with Ibn Bājja's Aristotelian ethics has been the subject of extensive study by Professor Lawrence Berman.[19]

Given these inherent tensions within Maimonides' own thought, it is not surprising that we find that the synthesis breaks down for some later Jewish philosophers. For example, as Dr. Aviezer Ravitzky has shown,[20] Samuel ibn Tibbon in the thirteenth century rebels against the Maimonidean synthesis by rejecting al-Fārābī's social-political role of the prophet, in favor of Ibn Bājja's emphasis on solitude.

What is perhaps more surprising is that another thirteenth-century Jewish philosopher, Shem Tov ibn Falaquera, finds it possible to reaffirm Maimonides' synthesis, while at the same time increasing dramatically the internal tension in that synthesis, by polarizing both trends (al-Fārābī and Ibn Bājja) in

Maimonides, and carrying them to an extreme. According to Falaquera, the prophet has a social-political role, as in Maimonides and al-Fārābī, and yet his negation of moral virtue as the ultimate human end is extreme, in comparison with Maimonides and even Ibn Bājja. His extremism (and, based on it, his explicit tendency toward asceticism and misogyny), is unusual both in traditional Jewish thought and in Aristotelian philosophic thought, both of which value ethics in much more positive terms.[21]

Falaquera's polarization or stretching of the Maimonidean synthesis may therefore help us understand better the inherent dynamic tensions, if not overt contradictions, within Maimonides' own thought, by pushing them to an extreme, and then by outflanking his master at his own ingenious reconciliations of opposites.

Let me note that I do not intend to survey here Falaquera's views on ethics in general, as I do in my forthcoming book on his life and philosophy, for, by and large, his views on ethics and the prophet as philosopher-king are not original and tend to be based on Aristotle and Maimonides. His contribution to Jewish ethics is not a result of originality.[22] In general, Falaquera's importance to the history of Jewish thought often lies in his lack of originality and in his careful preservation of other sources. Similarly, in ethics, his main contribution, importance, and influence lie in his bringing philosophical material to the people in a popular framework, in the Hebrew language, and in a clear style—old wine in a new flask.

Apropos the question of Falaquera's originality and language, it should be noted that Leopold Zunz[23] showed that the term *yeṣiri* as an adjective meaning "moral" or "ethical" is unique to Falaquera. We find, for example, that all the citations of the term *yeṣiri* in Klatzkin's *Oṣar ha-Munaḥim ha-Pilosofiyim* are taken from Falaquera's writings. As Professor Pines has explained, Falaquera's term is based on a literal translation of the Arabic root *khalaqa* (Hebrew *yaṣar,* "create" or "form"), which in the form *khulqī* means "moral" or "ethical," and thus we have *yeṣiri.*[24]

Nevertheless, in my opinion there is a "new" element in Falaquera's ethics, at least in degree, namely the extent of his negation of moral virtue as ultimate human perfection and a positive emphasis on asceticism and solitude.

In these two areas, Falaquera tends toward an extremism which is unusual in the context of the more moderate Jewish norm, which usually accepts asceticism only as a temporary antidote in certain circumstances, but which generally rejects asceticism as incompatible with the Torah. The Torah, in the words of Judah Halevi's *Kuzari,*[25] "did not obligate us to asceticism, but to the median path, giving each of the faculties of the soul and body its portion." In the words of Maimonides, asceticism is the error of fools who believe that "by this a person approaches God, as if God hated the body and sought its destruction."[26] This is not to say that asceticism finds no occasional expression among these and other Jewish thinkers, but that Falaquera's views on the subject are more consistent and extreme.

Rejecting Moral Virtue as the Ultimate Perfection

In his discussion at the end of the *Guide of the Perplexed*[27] cited above, Maimonides rejects the perfection of possessions (*kamāl al-qunya; shelemut ha-kinyan*) and bodily perfection (*kamāl al-binya wa'l-hay'a; shelemut gufanit*) as the human end. However, the perfection of ethical virtues (*kamāl al-faḍā'il al-khulqiyyāt*; *shelemut ma'alot ha-middot*) is also rejected.

> But this species of perfection is likewise a preparation for something else and not an end in itself. For all moral habits are concerned with what occurs between a human individual and someone else. This perfection regarding moral habits is, as it were, only the disposition to be useful to people; consequently it is an instrument for someone else. For if you suppose a human individual is alone, acting on no one, you will find that all his moral virtues are in vain and without employment and unneeded, and that they do not perfect the individual in anything; for he only needs them and they again become useful to him in regard to someone else. The fourth species is the true human perfection; it consists in the acquisition of the rational virtues—I refer to the conception of intelligibles (*al-faḍā'il al-nātiqiyya a'anī taṣawwur ma'aqūlāt; ha-ma'alot ha-sikhliyot roṣeh lomar ṣiyyur ha-muskalot*) which teach true opinions concerning the divine things. This is in true reality the ultimate end; this is what gives the individual true perfection, a perfection belonging to him alone; and it gives him permanent perdurance; through it man is man. (Shlomo Pines translation)

This does not mean, of course, that moral virtue has no value. Clearly ethics perfect a person, but this perfection is not his ultimate perfection as a human being. Not only does moral virtue have a value as the means to ultimate perfection (for example, "the moral virtues are means to the rational virtues"),[28] but they have intrinsic value. According to Aristotle, the good is desirable in itself.[29] Moreover, ethics are obviously necessary from a social perspective. Therefore, according to both Aristotle and Maimonides, ethics are clearly not absolutely negated, but are only rejected as the ultimate perfection of man *qua* man, in relation to intellectual perfection. Moreover, Maimonides' acceptance of al-Fārābī's Platonic view of the prophet only increases the value of ethics. Maimonides can still argue that the individual perfection of the prophet is intellectual, but "after the ascent and attaining of certain rungs of the ladder that may be known comes the descent . . . with a view to governing and teaching the people of the earth."[30] Therefore:

> It is clear that the perfection of man that may truly be gloried in is the one acquired by him who has achieved, in a measure corresponding to his capacity, apprehension of Him, may He be exalted, and who knows His providence extending over His creatures as manifested in the act of bringing them into being and in their governance as it is. The way of life of such an individual, after he has achieved this apprehension, will always have in view loving-kindness, righteousness, and judgment, through assimilation to His actions, may He be exalted, just as we have explained several times in this Treatise.[31] (Shlomo Pines translation)

As is known, Maimonides resolves the inconsistency between the prophet's social-political role (which requires ethical involvement) and his individual perfection by suggesting that

> there may be a human individual who, through his apprehension of the true realities and joy in what he has apprehended, achieves a state in which he talks with people and is occupied with his bodily necessities while his intellect is wholly turned toward Him, may He be exalted, so that in his heart he is always in His presence, may He be exalted, while outwardly he is with people,

and that this is the rank of Moses and the Patriarchs.[32]

A Stronger Rejection of Ethics

In Falaquera's thought, as we shall see, since the negation of ethics is more fundamental, consistent, and absolute than it is in the thought of Aristotle and Maimonides, there is also a more pronounced tendency toward asceticism, and even misogyny. Accordingly, Falaquera was forced to go farther in his conception of the prophet, a conception which affirmed the prophet's social-political role but combines this role with aspects of Ibn Bājja's *Governance of the Solitary* (*Tadbīr al-Mutawaḥḥid*).

Since ethical perfection does not constitute the ultimate and true human perfection, Falaquera says, in the words of the "Seeker" to the pious person (*ḥasid*) who had mastered moral virtue (*ba'al ha-ma'alot ha-yeṣiriyot*):[33] "You are perfect in every virtue, but you lack the highest virtue which is the virtue of intellect and wisdom." And in response to the Seeker's eighth question, the ethicist does not even know "to which of the soul's faculties good and bad actions are to be attributed."[34] Therefore, "when the Seeker had completed his discussion with man who possessed the moral virtues, which are connected to the body and are considered foreign to a person when he attains the true intellectual virtues. . . . For as much as he investigated the previous felicities, he found that they perish with the body, and are shared with animals."[35] Similarly, "whoever is satisfied with moral qualities is satisfied with someone else's existence. . . . Therefore, satisfaction with moral virtues cannot constitute the ultimate virtue."[36]

Thus far we have seen that ethical perfection does not constitute ultimate human perfection since it does not perfect the person *per se,* but is a means of relating to others, and because ethics pertain to bodily existence and are even a quality of some animals. This view, that moral virtue can be attributed to animals, at least equivocally[37] (and thus is not a distinctively human perfection), is also expressed in the Ibn Bājja's *Governance of the Solitary*[38] and *Letter of Farewell* (*Risālat al-Wadā'*).

The passage in the *Letter of Farewell* is quoted by Falaquera in his *Moreh ha-Moreh* (Commentary on the *Guide of the Perplexed*), and also by Joseph ibn Kaspi in his commentary *'Amudei Kesef:*

Joseph ibn Kaspi, *'Amudei Kesef*[39]	Falaquera, *Moreh ha-Moreh*[40]	Ibn Bājja, *Letter of Farewell*[41]
והגיע למעלה הנכבד שבבעלי חיים שאינם מדברים, עד שתהיה כמו האריה בגבורה וכתרנגול בנדיבות.	והדומה בעל המעלות היצירויות לבעלי חיים שאינו מדבר שהוא בעל התכונות הנכבדות, כאריה בגבורה והתרנגול בנדיבות.	וידמה בעל מעלות המדות לבעלי חיים בלתי מדברים בעלי תכונות נדיבות, כאריה בגבורה ותרנגול בנדיבות.

> The person who possesses moral virtues resembles the non-rational animals which possess honorable qualities, such as the lion in courage and the cock in generosity.

It is thus clear that moral virtue is not a distinctively human perfection. But Falaquera goes further. Not only do ethics not perfect a person, but occasionally ethics may even constitute an obstacle in the way of his intellectual perfection and true felicity. Thus, in his treatise on the *Perfection of Actions*, in a passage based on the *Nicomachean Ethics* 10:8, 1178ab:[42]

כל המעלות היצירויות יצטרכו לסבות מחוץ מהם ולפעולות מחולפות רבות. ובעל החירות יצטרך אל הממון כדי שיעשה עמו פעולת החירות. וכל המעלות היצירויות אין להם קיום אלא בגופים ובנפשות ובמה שהוא חוץ מהם יותר. אבל המעולה החכם המצליח עושה העצה והחכמה והשכל. ובעוד שהוא עושה המעלות היצירויות ימנעוהו מעשות עצתו באמת. וכשיעזוב אותן ולא ישתמש בהן יהיה ניצל מטורח הטבע וכליו והנפש וכחותיה וחושיה ומכל העסקים האנושיים, ויהיה עם השכינות האלהיות בשמחה וששון

וטובות אלהיות. ההצלחה השלמה היא לאלוה ית' ויתי' ואחר כך למלאכים האלהיים. ואין צריך שניחס אל המלאכים המעלות היצירויות, ולא יאמר שהם ישרים, כי אין ביניהם משא ומתן ולא השבת פקדונות ולא סחורות שיעשו הישר בהן, ולא ייוחס אליהם פעולות הגבורה כי אין ביניהם מלחמות. . .וכשנמנה כל פעולות המעלות היצירויות הן קטנות ואינו מההוגן שיהיו נאמרות על המלאכים.

> All the moral virtues require external causes and have many functions. The liberal man needs money in order to be liberal with it. All the moral virtues only exist in bodies and souls and what is more external than them. But the excellent, wise, and felicitous person engages in contemplation (*'eṣah*),[43] wisdom, and intellect. As long as he engages in moral virtues, they prevent him from engaging in his contemplation in truth. When he abandons them and does not employ them, he is saved from the trouble of nature and its utensils, and the soul and its faculties and senses, and from all human occupations, and then will be with the divine presences in joy and happiness and divine favors. Perfect felicity belongs to God, and then to the divine angels. But we need not attribute moral virtues to the angels, and one cannot say that they are honest, for they have no commerce, nor return of deposits, nor dealings by which they might be honest, nor can one attribute to them courageous actions, for they have no wars . . . And when we take into account all the actions of moral virtues, they are insignificant and should not properly be attributed to the angels.

We should note here that Falaquera departs from the words of Aristotle. Aristotle merely claimed that ethical actions require what Falaquera called *ha-sibbot huṣ me-hem,* external causes (*ektos choregias*)[44] such as money, and that these external goods or causes can present an impediment (*empodia*) to contemplation (*theoria*). But Falaquera goes further. He does not merely claim that the external causes present an impediment to contemplation; rather, he claims, the trouble or bother (*ṭoraḥ*) of human ethical involvement itself prevents a person from continual contemplation:

> As long as he engages in the moral virtues, they prevent him from engaging in his contemplation in truth. When he abandons them and does not employ them, he is saved from the trouble of nature, etc.

We have seen above that Falaquera attributes moral virtues to animals (so that ethics are no longer distinctively human), and here that moral virtue cannot be attributed to the angels, who enjoy continuous intellectual felicity and who have no ethical involvement which might detract from this felicity. Therefore, to the extent that a person engages in his external needs, which necessitate ethics, he resembles somewhat the animals. But to the extent that a person overcomes his external bodily needs, including ethics, and engages in continuous contemplation, he resembles the angels who have no use for ethics.[45]

Emphasis on Asceticism and Solitude

Asceticism and solitude thus play an important part in Falaquera's thought. Of course, this asceticism is not absolute, "because the felicitous person cannot be felicitous and choose the best as long as he is solitary, for the felicitous person needs someone to benefit. Man is political by nature, and acquires for his friend what he could not acquire by himself."[46]

Nevertheless, friends can often be harmful,[47] and therefore one should become friends with only one friend. "It seems to me that the (sages') saying, 'Acquire a friend' (Avot 1:6) and not 'friends' means that the true friend whose intention is the absolute good, can only be one."[48] Now there is probably no escape from a certain degree of social involvement, but as we have seen, that involvement impedes the attainment of true perfection.

The excellent man, i.e., the perfect prophet, can overcome this problem, because, as Maimonides wrote, the intellectual communion of such prophets as Moses and the Patriarchs was not interrupted when they were occupied with the external needs of society and ethical activity, as we have seen.[49] Falaquera accepted Maimonides' view, but again added to it. These prophets, and perhaps also the "solitary pious ones" (*ḥasidim mitbodedim*) who are below them in rank,

> are called strangers (*gerim*) in the words of the sages, for even when they are in their homes, among their brothers and families, they are strangers in their opinions (*gerim be-de'oteihem*), going in their thoughts to other levels which are their residences. Thus said the one speaking by divine inspiration (*ruaḥ ha-qodesh*): "I am a stranger in the land" (Exodus 2:22, 18:3), meaning, I was estranged to my brothers and alien to the children of my mother.[50]

Falaquera's "strangers in their opinions," who are alienated from their society despite the need to govern it and participate in its affairs, have their source in Ibn Bājja's concept of the solitary individual who attains perfection in an imperfect society:

> These are they whom the Ṣūfīs mean when they speak of "strangers," for, say they, even in their own

> countries and among their fellows and neighbors they are strangers in their opinions (*ghurabā'u fī ārā'ihim*) and travel in their thoughts to other levels which are, as it were, their own countries.[51]

This, of course, is the rank of the prophets, and perhaps also the pious, for Falaquera. Only these people succeed in maintaining the continuity of communion without stopping their bodily functions. Thus Falaquera interprets Isaiah 42:18-20:

> This is what the prophet alluded to by saying: "Hear, you deaf, and look, you blind, that you may see." He meant the deaf in the sensation of the ear, who do not pay attention to the vanities of the world . . . are the ones who hear the word of God. The blind in the perception of the eye, who do not watch and look at the vile pleasantries, see His glory. Therefore (the prophet) said, "Who is blind as one who is complete, and deaf as the messenger I send?", for it is well known that whenever the activity of the senses is strengthened, the activity of the intellect and intellectual contemplation are weakened. . . . (The prophet) alluded to this by saying, "Seeing many things but not observing," for when a person is occupied with the senses, he does not perceive any intelligible. Therefore the prophets did not halt any faculty whenever they prophesied, and thus is the way of the perfect.[52]

However, it is clear that most people, even the sages, do not reach this rank, and cannot maintain continuous intellectual communion, and cannot even attain communion in the presence of all the bodily and social impediments. Therefore Falaquera recommends: "The seeker of perfection should completely keep away from anyone possessing a bad quality or corrupt opinion, and should distance himself from association with him,"[53] for "Your separation from people will earn you hatred, but your closeness to them will acquire you a bad friend, and bad friends are more harmful than enemies' hatred."[54] Therefore, "clothe yourself in asceticism and solitude."[55]

Of course, Falaquera understood that not everyone has the capacity for asceticism and solitude, for as difficult as it is to overcome external, social impediments, it is even more difficult to overcome the internal impediments, i.e., the appetites.

> The existence of this perfection of a solitary individual (*mityaḥed*) is most difficult, except in old age, with continuous contemplation together with abandonment of most of what people deem important.

> An even greater condition is that he have no false belief. Many people attain such perfection when they are separated from this existence, for this perfection is the opposite of bodily perfection.[56]

The seeker of perfection must thus both isolate himself from external society and insulate himself from the internal appetites and bodily senses. Only after he attains the rank of perfect solitude can he function within a social framework without harming his communion, as we have seen.

The subjugation of the senses and appetites essential for the liberation of the person from bodily enslavement, to free him to attain felicity, is a central theme in Falaquera's ethical writings. Falaquera finds rabbinic support for his position: "What should a person do that he may live? Let him kill himself" (T.B. Tamid 32a). Falaquera explains:

> They meant that by killing his bad appetites and by subjugating his evil inclinations he makes himself live. For by subjugating the appetites, the rational soul can activate its particular functions. But when a person makes evil inclination live, and when his bad appetites become dominant, he kills his soul, for his being flooded with the bestial appetites darkens the light of the soul, so it cannot intelligize what it has the potential to intelligize, so that it perishes along with the body. This is true death.[57]

In this respect a person's body is his enemy:

> If you labor for your body, not your mind/
> You will be laboring for your enemy, not yourself.[58]

Similarly, Falaquera consistently condemns sexual relations as the quality of pigs, and claims that the wise do not marry, for sexual relations are an impediment to wisdom.[59] Therefore, whoever refrains entirely from sex is called holy.[60] Misogyny also finds sharp expression in Falaquera's books and poetry. Thus:

> Let your soul not trust a woman/
> Who is a spread net and pit.
> How can we believe in the honesty/
> Of a woman, who was made from a rib?[61]

In the best instance, a good woman serves her husband's bodily and material needs. In the very best instance, if "a perfect man should happen to have a virtuous wife (*eshet ḥayil*) she will not prevent him too much from attaining perfection."[62] Then, of course, Falaquera proceeds at length to describe the woman possessing evil qualities.

Conclusions

It seems to me that Falaquera understood the need to moderate and balance somewhat his tendency toward asceticism. In the *Book of Degrees* (*Sefer ha-Ma'alot*)[63] he quotes a whole section from Ibn Bājja's *Governance of the Solitary*.[64] In this section, Falaquera justifies his position in terms of Ibn Bājja's statement that "this does not contradict what has been said in political science that asceticism is entirely evil; rather it is essentially evil but accidentally good, as occurs with many natural things," such as certain foods which benefit the healthy and harm the sick, and drugs which harm the healthy and benefit the sick.

We have thus seen that Falaquera is extreme in his rejection of moral virtue as ultimate human felicity, and in his extremism he exceeds both Aristotle and Maimonides; not only does moral perfection not constitute the true human end, as in Maimonides, Ibn Bājja, and Aristotle, but ethical involvement *per se* impedes contemplative felicity. Falaquera therefore consistently concludes that it is preferable to choose the life of asceticism and solitude, and to avoid ethical involvement. Nevertheless, Falaquera retains Maimonides' and al-Fārābī's view of the prophet as philosopher-king. Therefore, like Maimonides, Falaquera had to bridge the gap between the prophet's social-political involvement and his solitude to attain his individual intellectual perfection, following Ibn Bājja's suggestion that the perfect person is a "stranger in his opinions," alienated and cut off spiritually from his society, while remaining physically involved, a condition Falaquera attributes to Moses and finds an allusion to in Isaiah. Falaquera's extremism in negating moral virtue as ultimate human felicity polarizes and thus exemplifies the internal, dynamic tension in Maimonides' own theory.

Addendum

A difficulty arises in the passage from Aristotle's *Nicomachean Ethics* 10:8, 1178b, 4-5, cited above. What is it that Aristotole calls an "impediment" to contemplation? On the one hand, since the gods (or angels) are above ethics, to the extent that a person wishes to devote himself to godlike contemplation, any other human activity, including ethics, can be construed as a diversion, or even an impediment. On the other hand, much of this discussion relates to the "external goods" requisite for ethics, and contextually, therefore, Aristotle can be understood as saying that these external goods can become impediments to contemplation.

The former view, that Aristotle regards ethical activity *per se* as the impediment, has grammatical basis in the Greek text, and was suggested to me by Professor Lawrence Berman, who kindly provided me with several versions, and is also supported by Professor Shlomo Pines. The latter view, that the impediment is the external goods, and not ethics as such, seems to me contextually more appropriate, given Aristotole's lengthy treatment here of the external goods, before and after these lines. In any event, this seems to be the general interpretation of various translations and versions.

I read the Arabic version as saying: "The more and nobler the activities are, the more he needs. But one who engages in contemplation (*al-ra'y*) does not need any such thing. . . . Rather, it can be said that this (*dhālika*) prevents engaging in contemplation." The Hebrew version of Ibn Rushd's *Middle Commentary* (L. Berman, ed.) is less clear: "The more and better the activities are, the more they require external things (*devarim mi-huṣ*). However, one who employs contemplation (*sevara 'iyyunit*) does not need any of these things (*davar me-elu ha-devarim*) for his activity. Rather, one can say that this prevents him from doing his unique activity, I mean doing the other virtuous activities." If "this" refers to "doing the other virtuous activities," Ibn Rushd would support the Pines-Berman interpretation of Aristotle, that ethics as such are the impediment to contemplation. ("This" could refer to "any of these things," in which case Ibn Rushd would support the alternate view, that the external goods are the impediment, but it is then unclear what he means by "I mean," etc.)

The Latin version of the *Summa Alexandrinorum* has: "Virtutes vero speculatine non indigent in complemento suarum actionum rebus extrinsecis, immo fortissime potius impediuntur ab ipsis: hominis perfectissimi considerato statu atque dignitate,"[65] which I translate as: "The virtues of the speculating man do not require for the completion of their actions external things; they even can be impeded by these: considering the status and dignity of the most perfect man." Here, too, "ipsis" modifies "rebus extrinsecis," so the impediment lies in the external things, not in the ethics *per se*.

The Hebrew version of 5165 (=1405) with a commentary by Isaac Satanow[66] and the modern Hebrew version of M. Shulbaum[67] and J. Liebes[68] all explicitly support the latter interpretation (that the external things, not ethics, are the impediment) as do the English translations of W. D. Ross and D. P. Chase. H. Rackham is most explicit: "On the contrary, worldly goods may almost be said to be a hindrance to contemplation."

Whichever interpretation of Aristotle is correct, Falaquera's approach is unusual and extremist. If the former view (of Pines, Berman, and possibly Ibn Rushd) is correct, then Falaquera correctly picked up on Ibn Rushd's nuance, and makes the rejection of ethics more explicit and consistent, unlike the other versions which then misunderstood Aristotle. Conversely, if Aristotle really only meant what most of the versions understood him to mean, then Falaquera's consistency and extremism in rejecting moral virtue as the ultimate human end place him outside the Aristotelian norm.

NOTES

[1] Aristotle *Nicomachean Ethics* 1:7, 1098a, 3-4. Translation by Sir David Ross (Oxford: Oxford University Press, 1961), 13. The translation by Martin Ostwald (Indianapolis: Bobbs-Merrill, 1962), 16, has "an active life of the rational element."

[2] W. F. R. Hardie, "The Final Good in Aristotle's Ethics" in J. M. E. Moravcsik, *Aristotle: A Collection of Critical Essays* (New York: Anchor Books, 1967), 297-322.

[3] *Ibid.*, p. 302.

[4] *Ibid.*, p. 305.

[5] *Ibid.*, p. 306.

[6] Maimonides, *Guide of the Perplexed* 3:25 and 3:26. An action which is futile (Arabic: *'abath*; Hebrew: *hevel*) is one which aims at no real end. An action which is frivolous (Arabic: *la'ib*; Hebrew: *seḥok*) is one which aims at some low end. Cf. *Introduction to the Mishnah*, Arabic and Hebrew edition, Y. Kafiḥ, ed. (Jerusalem: Mosad ha-Rav Kook, 1972), 1:39: "Every existing thing must have some end (*ghāya, takhlit*) for the sake of which it exists, for there is nothing whose existence is futile (*'abath*)."

[7] *Guide* 3:54.

[8] *Guide* 1:1.

[9] *Guide* 1:2. Cf. the interesting interpretation of this chapter in Lenn E. Goodman, *Rambam: Readings in the Philosophy of Moses Maimonides* (New York: Viking Press, 1976), 208-20.

[10] *Guide* 3:22.

[11] Lawrence V. Berman, "Maimonides on the Fall of Man," *Association for Jewish Studies Review* 5(1980): 8-9.

[12] Falaquera, *Moreh ha-Moreh* 1:2, M. L. Bisliches, ed. (Pressburg, 1837), 11; reprinted in *Sheloshah Kadmonei Mefarshei ha-Moreh* (Jerusalem: n.p., 1961). Falaquera's reference in this passage is to Ibn Sīnā's *Kitāb al-Najāt*. Cf. F. Rahman, *Avicenna's Psychology* (Oxford: Oxford University Press, 1952), 32-33.

[13] Cf. Maimonides' discussion of attributes in *Guide* 1:47-60, and of God's knowledge in *Guide* 3:16-21 and the end of ch. 8 of his *Eight Chapters on Ethics* (*Shemonah Perakim*), Joseph Gorfinkle, ed. (New York: Columbia University Press, 1912).

[14] *Guide* 1:68. See Professor Pines' discussion of this apparent fundamental contradiction in Maimonides' thought in his "Translator's Introduction: The Philosophic Sources of the *Guide of the Perplexed*," in Shlomo Pines, tr., *Guide of the Perplexed* (Chicago: University of Chicago Press, 1963), xcviii. Cf. Aristotle, *Metaphysics* 12:9, 1074b-1075a.

[15] Cf. Berman, "Maimonides on the Fall of Man," p.8, n. 22: "Thus Adam and Moses were identical, the difference being that Adam, before the Fall, represents the ideal for man not living in society, while Moses represents the ideal for man living in society."

[16] Pines, tr., in *Guide*, pp. lvii-cxxxiv. A Hebrew translation of this "Translator's Introduction" appeared in Pines' *Bein Maḥshevet Yisrael le-Maḥshevet ha-'Amim* (Jerusalem: Mosad Bialik, 1977), 103-73.

[17] Alexander Altmann, "Ibn Bājja on Man's Ultimate Felicity," in *Studies in Religious Philosophy and Mysticism* (Ithaca: Cornell University Press, 1969), 73-107; originally published in the *Harry A. Wolfson Jubilee Volume*, 2 vols. (Jerusalem: American Academy for Jewish Research, 1965), 1:47-87; and "Maimonides' Four Perfections" in *Israel Oriental Studies* 2(1972): 15-24.

[18] *Guide* 3:54.

[19] See Lawrence V. Berman, "Ibn Bājjah and Maimonides: A Chapter in the History of Political Philosophy" (Unpublished Ph.D. dissertation, Hebrew University, Jerusalem, 1959; in Hebrew with English summary); "The Political Interpretation of the Maxim: The Purpose of Philosophy is the Imitation of God," *Studia Islamica* 15(1961): 53-61; "Maimonides, the Disciple of Alfārābī," *Israel Oriental Studies* 4(1974): 154-78; "Maimonides on the Fall of Man" (Abstract in Association for Jewish Studies *Newsletter* 17(June 1976), and *Association for Jewish Studies Review* 5(1980): 1-15; "Maimonides on Political Leadership," in Daniel Elazar, ed., *Kinship and Consent: The Jewish Political Tradition and Its Contemporary Uses* (Ramat Gan/Philadelphia: Turtledove Press, 1981), 113-25.

[20] Aviezer Ravitzky, "Yesodo ha-Musari Shel ha-Pilosof: Ibn Tibbon ke-Neged ha-Rambam" (Lecture at the Fifth Inter-University Conference Departments of Jewish Thought, Hebrew University, February 1983).

[21] An example of the traditional attitude toward asceticism may be found in the commentaries to Numbers 6:11. The verse refers to the defiling of the Nazirite by his coming into contact with a corpse, but it literally says: "And he shall atone for him because of his having sinned on account of the soul (*nefesh*)." In the Talmud (Nedarim 10a), several of the rabbis are cited as concluding that the Nazirite himself is a sinner. The question is asked: on account of which soul did the Nazirite sin? The answer given is that he sinned against himself (his own soul) by refraining from such pleasures as drinking wine. "And thus all the more so: if this one (the Nazirite) is called a sinner for making himself sorry on account of wine, how much more so is one who causes himself sorrow on account of everything." An opposing point of view may be found in Ta'anit

11a: "Rabbi El'azar said, Whoever sits and fasts is called holy, etc." Maimonides' interpretation in the *Eight Chapters on Ethics* (*Shemonah Perakim*), chap. 4, is based on the first, and dominant view, as is his condemnation of asceticism in the *Mishneh Torah*, Sefer Mada', "Hilkhot De'ot" 3:1: "This is a wicked way, and it is forbidden to go on it." We should note, however, that Nahmanides' interpretation of Numbers 6:11 is diametrically opposed to that of Maimonides. Nahmanides sees the Nazirite as sinning aginst his soul by completing the period of his vow, and returning to an ordinary life of impurity, and leaving his higher state of purity as a Nazirite. Nahmanides thus identifies "holiness" (*qedushah*) with asceticism (*perishut*); cf. Nahmanides' commentary on Leviticus 19:2 and 21:6. See the discussion of Maimonides' attitude toward asceticism in Isadore Twersky, *Introduction to the Code of Maimonides* (New Haven: Yale University Press, 1980), 459-68.

22 Seven of Falaquera's 17 extant works deal with ethics, either directly or indirectly, including *Iggeret ha-Musar*, A. M. Haberman, ed. (Jerusalem: Qoveṣ 'al Yad, 1936); *Iggeret ha-Ḥalom*, H. Malter, ed., in "Shem Tob ben Joseph Palquera. II. His 'Treatise of the Dream (Iggeret ha-Ḥalom)'," *Jewish Quarterly Review* 1(1910-11): 451-501; *Batei Hanhagat ha-Nefesh Batei Hanhagat Guf ha-Bari*, I. Ḥadash-Chodos, ed., in *Ha-Rofeh ha-'Ivri* 10:2(1937): 150-70; 11:1(1938): 113-25; 12:1(1939): 52-64; *Reshit Ḥokhmah*, M. David, ed. (Berlin: n.p., 1902), reprinted (Jerusalem: Mekorot, 1970); *Sefer ha-Mevaqqesh*, M. Tamah, ed. (Hague: Lev Zussmensh, 1778), reprinted (Jerusalem: Mekorot, 1970), English tr. in M. H. Levine, *Falaquera's Book of the Seeker* (New York: Yeshiva University Press, Department of Special Publications, 1976); *Sefer ha-Ma'alot*, L. Venetianer, ed. (Berlin: S. Calvary Co., 1894) reprinted (Jerusalem: Maqor, 1970); and *Shelemut ha-Ma'asim* . All except the last have been published. My forthcoming book, *Torah and Sophia: The Life and Thought of Shem Tov ibn Falaquera* (Cincinnati: Hebrew Union College Press), includes a critical, annotated edition of *Shelemut ha-Ma'asim* (*The Perfection of Actions*). The work includes ten chapters. The first six chapters are basically a selective paraphrase of Aristotle's *Nicomachean Ethics*, but they bear no relationship to the Hebrew versions of Ibn Rushd's *Middle Commentary on the Nicomachean Ethics* published by Lawrence Berman (Jerusalem: Israel Academy of Sciences, 1981), either in terms of the content or linguistically. As far as I can tell, Falaquera translated this text directly from some Arabic version, and did not rely on someone else's translation, but he only translated those selections which interested him in particular, as he did when translating afresh those sections of the *Guide of the Perplexed* covered in his commentary (*Moreh ha-Moreh*) and when translating selections of the Ibn Gabirol's *Fons Vitae* (*Meqor Ḥayyim*). The last four chapters (ch. 7-10) of *Shelemut ha-Ma'asim* are not related to the *Nicomachean Ethics*, and occasionally are obscure; they contain various ethical maxims and parables. Approximately half of them are based directly on Ḥunayn ibn Isḥāq's *Adab al-Falāsifa*, but again, Falaquera's translation or paraphrase is independent and is not related to Judah al-Ḥarizi's translation, *Musarei ha-Pilosofim*.

23 Leopold Zunz, *Gesammelte Schriften* (Berlin: n.p., 1876), 3: 279.

24 Falaquera's *yeṣiri* additionally involves a play on the ethical connotations of the biblical and rabbinic usages of *yeṣer* (cf. Genesis 6:5 and 8:21).

25 Judah Halevi, *The Kuzari* 2:50. Cf. *Kuzari* 3:1-5 and Plato *Republic* 4:427-44.

26 Maimonides, *Eight Chapters on Ethics* (*Shemonah Perakim*), ch. 4. Cf. Twersky, *Introduction to the Code of Maimonides*, pp. 467-68, for a different emphasis.

27 *Guide* 3:54, Hebrew, p. 70a; Arabic ed., S. Munk, ed., (Jerusalem: Sifriyah Pilosofit, J. Junovitch, 1929), 467-68.

28 *Guide* 1:34.

29 *Nicomachean Ethics* 10:6, 1176b.

30 Maimonides, *Guide* 1:15. Cf. *Guide* 1:54: ". . . 'And see that this people is your nation' (Ex. 33:13), that is, that I must govern by performing actions in the same way as you govern them."

31 *Guide* 3:54.

32 *Guide* 3:51.

33 Falaquera, *Sefer ha-Mevaqqesh*, p. 41.

34 *Ibid.*, p. 48.

35 *Ibid.*, p. 51 (Levine, *Falaquera's "Book of the Seeker,"* p. 73). Cf. *Iggeret ha-Ḥalom*, p. 477.

36 *Sefer ha-Ma'alot*, p. 39.

37 On the other hand, in *Shelemut ha-Ma'asim*, ch. 1, p. 4 (based on *Nicomachean Ethics* 1:9, 1099b-1100a), Falaquera says: "One cannot say that a horse or a child is felicitous, because a horse or the child do not engage in this supreme activity."

38 Cf. Ibn Bājja, *Tadbīr al-Mutawaḥḥid* (*The Governance of the Solitary*), edited by Miguel Asín Palacios (Madrid: Escuelas de Estudios Arabes de Madrid y Granada, 1946). A partial English translation by Lawrence Berman may be found in Ralph Lerner and Muhsin Mahdi, eds., *Medieval Political Philosophy: A Sourcebook* (Ithaca: Cornell University Press, 1978), 122-33. Moses Narboni wrote a Hebrew paraphrase in his commentary on Ibn Tufayl's *Ḥayy ibn Yaqẓan*, which was published by David Herzog (Berlin: n.p., 1896), in which the relevant passage may be found in ch. 5, p. 13.

39 Joseph ibn Kaspi, *'Amudei Kesef* 3:54, S. Werbluner, ed. (Frankfurt, 1848); reprinted in *Sheloshah Kadmonei Mefarshei ha-Moreh*, pp. 144-45.

40 Falaquera, *Moreh ha-Moreh* 3:54, pp. 137-38.

41 Ibn Bājja, *Letter of Farewell* (*Risālat al-Wadā'*), Asín Palacios, ed., in *Al-Andalus* 8(1942): 32ff. The Hebrew version by Ḥayyim ben Judah Bibas was published by M. Schreiner, *Mimisrach Umimaarabh* (Vienna, 1895, and Berlin, 1898). The parallel passage appears on p. 32.

42 Falaquera, *Shelemut ha-Ma'asim*, ch. 6, pp. 20-21. The same passage, with slight variations, is partially quoted in Falaquera's *Moreh ha-Moreh* 3:51, p. 135.

43 The term *'eṣah* is translated here as "contemplation." Its common meaning is "counsel" or "advice." The term is used several times elsewhere in *Shelemut ha-Ma'asim* as well: ch. 4, p. 13, 1.6; ch. 6, p. 20, 1.11, 17, 18; ch. 6, p. 21, 1.8, 11. The translation of *'eṣah* as "contemplation" is based on Falaquera's

comment following the (partial) parallel citation of this passage in *Moreh ha-Moreh* 3:51, p. 135 (middle):

והחכם המצליח משתמש בעצה ובחכמה ובשכל. . . ושמוש המחשבה בדברים השכליים הנקרא עצה, והוא ראי בערבי, והוא הציור בשכל.

"The felicitous philosopher employs contemplation, wisdom, and intellect. . . . The employment of thought for intellectual things is called contemplation (*'eṣah*), which in Arabic is opinion (*ra'y*), which is intellectual conception." This is borne out by the Arabic version of the *Nicomachean Ethics* 10:, 1178b, 4-5, Badawi, ed. (1979), 353, which has *ra'y* at this point. Ibn Rushd's *Middle Commentary*, L. V. Berman, ed., has *ha-sevara ha-'iyyunit*. The reference is to *theoria* (contemplation). Cf. several meanings of *'eṣah* in Jacob Klatzkin, *Oṣar ha-Munaḥim ha-Pilosofiyim*, 4 vols. (New York: Philip Feldheim, 1968), 3:152-53.

44 Gr. *ektos choregias*. D. P. Chase translates this as "external goods," whereas W. D. Ross and H. Rackham translate it as "external equipment." Ibn Rushd, *Middle Commentary*, Berman, ed., has *devarim mi-ḥuṣ* (external things).

45 Cf. Maimonides, *Introduction to the Mishnah*, Kafiḥ, ed., p. 41: "Man's ultimate end (*ghāya, takhlit*) is one activity; his other activities only are to enable him to exist, so that this one activity might be perfected, namely the apprehension of intelligibles and the knowledge of the truth. . . . All his other activities are common to him and to the other species of animals. Cf. also Thomas Aquinas, *Summa Theologica*, First Part of Second Part, Q. III, Fifth Article: "Thirdly, it is again evident from the fact that in the contemplative life man has something in common with things above him, viz., with God and the angels, to whom he is made like in happiness. But in things pertaining to the active life, other animals also have something in common with man, although imperfectly."

46 *Shelemut ha-Ma'asim*, ch. 5, p. 17. Cf. *Nicomachean Ethics* 9:9, 1169b. Cf. also Falaquera, *Reshit Ḥokhmah*, p. 17, and al-Fārābī, *Attainment of Happiness* 18. This passage by al-Fārābī was translated by Falaquera in *Reshit Ḥokhmah*, p. 65, l. 14.

47 Falaquera, *Iggeret ha-Musar*, p. 9; *Batei Hanhagat ha-Nefesh*, p. 65.

48 *Moreh ha-Moreh* 3:51, p. 136. Cf. *Sefer ha-Mevaqqesh*, p. 46.

49 *Guide* 3:51, cited above.

50 *Moreh ha-Moreh* 3:51, pp. 136-37.

51 Ibn Bājja, *Tadbīr*, Asín Palacios, ed., p. 11; Dunlop, ed., Arabic p. 68, English pp. 77-78; Lawrence Berman, ed., in Lerner and Mahdi, eds., *Medieval Political Philosophy*, p. 128; Hebrew ed., M. Narboni, ed., p. 9. Cf. Berman, "Ibn Bājjah and Maimonides," p. 57.

52 Falaquera, *Sefer ha-Ma'alot*, p. 41.

53 *Ibid.*, p. 32.

54 *Sefer ha-Mevaqqesh*, p. 45.

55 *Ibid.*

56 Falaquera, *De'ot ha-Pilosofim* 6.2.3. Ms. Parma f. 186b; ms. Leiden f. 299a.

[57] *Sefer ha-Ma'alot*, p. 40. Cf. *Shelemut ha-Ma'asim*, ch. 9, p. 31: "Whoever loves life for his soul, kills it." Cf. Ḥunayn ibn Isḥaq (Judah Al-Ḥarizi, tr.), *Musarei ha-Pilosofim* 2.87: "Whoever wishes to make his soul live should kill it."

[58] *Batei Hanhagat ha-Nefesh*, p. 60.

[59] *Iggeret ha-Musar*, p. 39. Cf. *Sefer ha-Mevaqqesh*, p. 25; *Iggeret ha-Ḥalom*, pp. 471-73; *Batei Hanhagat Guf ha-Bari*, pp. 28-30; *Batei Hanhagat ha-Nefesh*, p. 76.

[60] *Iggeret ha-Ḥalom*, pp. 471-73. Cf. the position of Nahmanides, note 21 above.

[61] *Iggeret ha-Musar*, p. 24. Cf. Proverbs 1:17, 22:14. Cf. also *Shelemut ha-Ma'asim*, Ch. 8, p. 29; *Sefer ha-Mevaqqesh*, pp. 7, 30, 69; *Sefer ha-Ma'alot*, p. 59; *Reshit Ḥokhmah*, p. 2.

[62] *Sefer ha-Ma'alot*, p. 59.

[63] *Ibid.*, pp. 49-50.

[64] Ibn Bājja, *Tadbīr*, Asín Palacios, ed., p. 78. Ed. L. V. Berman, in Lerner and Mahdi, eds., *Medieval Political Philosophy*, p. 132. Hebrew ed., Moses Narboni, ed., end of ch. 7, pp. 17-18.

[65] *Summa Alexandrinorum*, C. Marchesi, ed., (Rome, 1904), lxxxiv.

[66] (Berlin, 1790; reprinted Jerusalem, Fisher, 1984), 53b.

[67] (Lemberg, 1877), 144.

[68] (Jerusalem: Schocken, 1973), 254-55.

The Rule of Law and the Rule of Wisdom in Plato, al-Fārābī, and Maimonides[1]

Jeffrey Macy

Introduction

The influence of Greek philosophic thought on al-Fārābī's political philosophy and the influence of both Greek and Islamic philosophy on Maimonides have been well documented in both medieval and modern sources. Al-Fārābī wrote commentaries on Plato's *Laws* and *Republic* and repeatedly made reference to the philosophic corpus of both Plato and Aristotle; he certainly was familiar with the contents of most of Plato's political writings as well as with almost all of Aristotle's works—with the possible exception of the *Politics*.[2] Likewise, Maimonides exhibits great knowledge of the works of Plato and Aristotle as well as the writings of many of Aristotle's later commentators.[3] Maimonides also makes reference to a number of Islamic philosophers and, in particular, he praises most highly the writings of al-Fārābī. Regarding al-Fārābī, Maimonides wrote in a well-known letter to Samuel ibn Tibbon, the Hebrew translator of the *Guide of the Perplexed*: "All his writings are faultlessly excellent. One ought to study and understand them; for he is a great man."[4] Indeed, the influence of al-Fārābī's writings on aspects of Maimonides' philosophic and political thought has been analyzed by a number of twentieth-century scholars.[5]

In this paper I will attempt to analyze the issue of "the rule of law" versus "the rule of wisdom" in the political thought of Plato, al-Fārābī, and Maimonides. In this manner I hope to contribute to the understanding of Plato's influence on al-Fārābī's political thought and of al-Fārābī's influence on Maimonides' political thought—particularly in the area of their philosophies of law.

"The Rule of Law" versus "The Rule of Wisdom" in Plato and al-Fārābī

The question of who or what is sovereign in a political regime provides an important key to the character of that regime, as well as highlighting the locus of political power. In his discussions of who should rule in the virtuous political regime and whether the "rule of law" or the "rule of wisdom" should be the regime's ultimately sovereign element, al-Fārābī was influenced strongly by Plato's political writings.

In general, for Plato and al-Fārābī the "rule of law" is a central characteristic of the *second-best* regime and it is perceived as inferior to the "rule of wisdom," which is the central characteristic of the best regime. Al-Fārābī is in fundamental agreement with Plato's analysis of the problematic character and lower status of the "rule of law." According to Plato, law is fixed and can thus be changed or adapted to deal with new circumstances only with great difficulty.[6] Further, such tampering with the law carries with it the implicit danger of undermining (in the eyes of the masses) the authority and legitimacy of the preexisting legal code—which at least in part continues to exist in the new legal code—as well as placing into question the authority of legal codes *per se*.[7] In addition, as law by its nature deals with the general case, it therefore is not infrequently unable to deal in a just manner with specific cases, each according to its particular merits.[8]

In contrast to the "rule of law," the "rule of wisdom" is flexible and dynamic, dealing with changes of circumstances according to an evaluation of each situation. Further, when wisdom or wise rule deals with each case according to its merits, the authority of an "unchanging" wise ruler is not undermined by changes, modifications, or special applications which *he* makes to the general principles of the regulative, but nonsovereign law—law which he, himself, and/or his equally wise predecessors and successors[9] have laid down (or will lay down). The best regime, according to Plato (and al-Fārābī), is the regime in which the wise man rules according to the dictates of his (theoretical and practical) reason and not according to the general or specific dictates of a preexisting legal code. The best regime is one in which the wise philosophic ruler is superior to the law—even in the case where that law is as good an imitation of wisdom as is possible.[10]

However, as both Plato and al-Fārābī recognized—to varying degrees in their different writings—the ideal of a philosopher-king ruling in a virtuous city is, to say the least, not always realizable. On the one hand, a philosopher-king is rarely if ever to be found.[11] On the other hand, Plato (on this point in partial contrast to al-Fārābī) emphasizes that the establishment of a regime where the rule of such a man will be accepted by the rest of the populace is difficult to envision without radical changes being made in every regime which exists or is known to have existed.[12] Further, at least according to Plato's Socrates—in this case in complete contrast to al-Fārābī[13]—it is not clear that a philosopher would wish to be a king (i.e., to rule).[14]

The difficulty in bringing about the rule of a philosopher-king in a virtuous city provides a suitable introduction to the statements which Plato makes in some of his writings about the positive aspects of law and the "rule of law" in second-best regimes—statements which are reflected in some of al-Fārābī's discussions of this subject.[15] In the absence of a philosopher-king and the best possible regime, well-constructed laws protect men from the arbitrary or unjust rule of those who do not possess superior philosophic wisdom: only the possessors of philosophic wisdom can act based on objective, rational knowledge, whereas nonphilosophic rulers will be directed in their actions by subjective evaluations, selfish interests, and corrupt values unless they are bound by a fixed law.[16] Thus, according to Plato (in the *Statesman*), in all regimes other than the one ruled by the philosopher-king, the presence of the sovereign "rule of law" makes the regime superior to any regime which is ruled by a ruler (or rulers) who either is not bound by the law or who rules in the absence of law.[17] In speaking about the positive aspects of a fixed and supremely sovereign law in the absence of rule by a philosopher-king, Plato goes so far as to say that in such regimes there should be a rule "that none of the citizens may venture to do any act contrary to the laws, and that if any of them ventures to do such an act, the penalty is to be death or the utmost rigor of punishment. This is the justest and most desirable course as a second-best when the ideal we have just described [the rule of a philosopher-king] has been set aside."[18]

In Plato's writings there are three different formulations of the desirability and viability of the "rule of law" versus the "rule of wisdom." The first formulation, in the *Republic*, finds expression in Socrates' attempt to found a city "in speech" based on the standard of absolute justice and according to the principle that the rule of the city should be entrusted only to those individuals who embody the ultimate human perfection in the attainment of wisdom. The ruler who is chosen on this basis is a philosopher-king, who may be said to be "the living law" in the city.[19] In the *Republic*, Plato leaves no room for the "rule of law," at least not as an ultimately sovereign element in the regime. He places exclusive emphasis on the need for ultimate sovereignty to be based on the "rule of wisdom" by the philosophers.[20]

A second formulation is found in its fullest form in Plato's *Statesman*, which includes a comparative analysis of the relative strengths and weaknesses of the "rule of law" versus the "rule of wisdom" (i.e., the rule of the philosopher-king). In this dialogue Plato continues to support the possibility of bringing about the best regime (ruled by the philosopher-statesman-king), but, in addition, he examines the possible character of relatively good regimes (or adequate and acceptable regimes) whose existence is desirable in the absence of such a ruler.[21] It is here that Plato argues that "the justest and most desirable course as a second-best"—when the regime ruled by a philosopher-king is put aside—is that the law should rule and be acknowledged as the regime's supreme authority.[22] The sovereignty of the law—which is an imitation of wisdom—replaces the sovereignty of a human ruler, and anyone who tries to tamper with the law or who disobeys the law must be punished with the utmost severity. While the "rule of wisdom" is preferable to the "rule of law," in the absence of a philosopher-king and his wisdom as a "living law," written law, which should be an imitation of the philosopher's wisdom, insofar as this is possible, is preferable to all other sovereigns and rulers.

A third formulation of the issue is set forth in Plato's *Laws*. The *Laws* presents a regime which is founded on the basis of an absolutely sovereign "divine" law.[23] The regime constructed in the *Laws* is intended to spell out the practical application of the principle of the "rule of law," which Plato had already suggested in general terms in the *Statesman*. The "rule of law" is presented as the best implementable regime,[24] and the practical dimensions of such a regime are explored in detail.[25] Nevertheless, in the *Laws*, the actual critique of the possibility of rule by a philosopher-king is brief and somewhat inconclusive,[26] and Plato's commitment to a pure form of the "rule of law" is far from absolute. To mention the most important limitation which he places on the ultimate sovereignty of the "rule of law," the Nocturnal Council plays an essential role not only in guarding the laws, but also in discussing the character and content of the laws (and of law *per se*) with the express aim of reinterpreting, redirecting, and changing those "divine" laws.[27]

Al-Fārābī, like Plato, presents different formulations of his position on the "rule of law" versus the "rule of wisdom" in his various writings. Further, the writings of these two philosophers display similar, although not identical, changes of emphasis and perspective on this issue.

In all of his writings al-Fārābī, like Plato (particularly in the *Republic* and the *Statesman*), maintains that the best regime is ruled by the wise philosopher who retains the authority to reinterpret, modify, or change the law whenever and however he deems fit.[28] In some of his writings, al-Fārābī, like Plato in the *Statesman* and *Laws*, suggests the possibility of a second-best regime where the existing law, which was laid down by a wise philosopher-lawgiver, will be supremely sovereign over the human rulers—when it is not possible to find a true philosopher to rule.[29] Occasionally, al-Fārābī, like Plato in the *Laws*, is prepared to call such laws divine, and by so doing to affirm the sovereign authority of the law by ascribing its origin to divine revelation and by linking it to the religious beliefs of the inhabitants of the regime.[30] While, as in Plato's political writings, al-Fārābī's presentation of the "rule of law" is never so unqualified as to negate the role of wisdom as a necessary regenerative master element for periodically updating and improving the "supremely sovereign" law of the second-best regime, this subject is treated differently in al-Fārābī's various political works.[31] In order to illustrate al-Fārābī's position on the "rule of law" and the "rule of wisdom" in more detail, it will be helpful to analyze his *Aphorisms of the Statesman (Fuṣūl al-Madan ī)*, pointing out cases where similar or variant positions are presented in other of al-Fārābī's writings.

In *Fuṣūl al-Madanī*, al-Fārābī describes the best type of rule as the rule of the true king (or supreme ruler).[32] Essentially, al-Fārābī's true king is a philosopher who also is capable of being a legislator, a political ruler, and a military leader. He is a philosopher-king who is ready and able to do battle on philosophical, political, and military grounds in order to defend his regime and polity from decay or from internal or external attack.[33] The relationship between the true king and the existing law follows the principle set down by Plato in the *Republic* regarding the relationship between the philosopher-king and the law: "He in whom all these things are united is the *living law*.[34]. . . He is the one whose words and commands[35] are to be accepted and it is this man who should rule according to what he thinks right and however he wishes."[36] If one man cannot be found who possesses all the necessary qualities which must be united in the true king, a group of men—each one possessing one of these qualities—may together rule the city. In such a case this group as a whole takes the place of the true king (and would not appear to be subordinate to the existing law any more than was the true king).[37]

In both of the above regimes it is necessary that a philosopher be present and that he take an active part in the ruling of the polity—either as the supreme ruler or as one of the virtuous rulers. When a philosopher is not present[38] to participate in the ruling of the polity, a different type of ruler must rule and his relationship to the existing law will resemble the relationship between a loyal subject (the ruler) and his sovereign (the law).[39] This ruler (or ruling group) must be no less in possession of practical wisdom and the political and military virtues than was the philosophic ruler, but in place of and in contrast to the true king's theoretical wisdom, the "king according to the law" (*malik al-sunna*) must acknowledge and possess knowledge of the existing (ancient) laws and of the "spirit" of those laws. Thus, the first three conditions which must coexist in such a ruler are listed by al-Fārābī as follows:

> [1] That he is one who acknowledges the ancient laws and traditions which the first religious leaders (*a'imma*)[40] gave and by which they ruled the cities; [2] furthermore, that he possesses excellence in discrimination of the places and circumstances in which it is necessary that those traditions be employed, according to that which was intended in these things by the first [religious leaders]; [3] further, that he possesses the ability to derive that which is not found explicitly in the ancient traditions, both oral and written, imitating in that derivation the model of the ancient traditions.[41]

On the basis of these three conditions it would appear that in the absence of a philosophic ruler, the "rule of law" is to be preferred to all other types of rule.

Al-Fārābī's apparent preference for the "rule of law" in the absence of a philosophic ruler is modified somewhat by the next quality which he establishes as a prerequisite for the "king according to the law." The inclusion of this quality highlights al-Fārābī's concern about the natural limits of the "rule of law," and this in a way which reminds one of the corrective function which is filled by the Nocturnal Council in Plato's *Laws*:

> [4] Then, that he possesses excellence of opinion [or independent judgment] (*ra'y*)[42] and practical wisdom concerning each of the above-mentioned cases which vary from that which is found in the ancient ways of life—all this in order that by these means he may preserve the thriving of the city.[43]

Thus, the ruler (or rulers) "according to the law" in almost all cases bases his rule on the established precepts of the (religious-political) law or on the logical extension of these precepts that allow him to deal with new situations within the spirit of what was intended by the original lawgivers. However, by means of the fourth condition which must coexist in the rule of the "king according to the law," al-Fārābī makes provision for those situations where such a king must use his own ideas (or independent judgment) and practical wisdom in a way which may vary from that which is found in the ancient ways of life and from that which is contained in the law and traditions, both oral and written. In such situations the somewhat imperfect judgment of a relatively, if not supremely, wise king is preferable to the inadequacy of the law; this is because the existing law is unable to preserve the thriving of the city without the extralegal direction provided by the ruler's independent judgment and practical wisdom—which are not grounded in that law and which could not be explained to the inhabitants of the regime on the basis of that law (except by means of innovative interpretations).[44]

While, according to *Fuṣūl al-Madanī*, the imperfect "king according to the law" can act in an extralegal manner to preserve the city from the inherent limitations of the law, nevertheless this king and his second-best regime are inferior to the true king and his truly virtuous regime. Hence, the question is raised whether a king (or rulers) "according to the law" can deal successfully with all of the problems faced by the city, including all those problems that supreme rulers and true kings succeed in resolving based on the fundamentals of their theoretical wisdom—fundamentals which are not possessed by the "king according to the law" and which transcend the principles contained in the traditional law. Put differently, if the city is to continue to survive and thrive is it a necessity, at least periodically, that a supreme ruler and true king assume the rule of the city, or can the king (or rulers) "according to the law" continue to maintain the polity's health and strength for an indefinite period of time? Is there a period of time after which a "king according to the law" will not continue to be successful in making the necessary adaptations and changes in the existing laws and traditions—when this king's lack of (true or theoretical) wisdom will lead to the weakening or even destruction of his regime? In his *Fuṣūl al-Madanī*, al-Fārābī places no limit on the length of time a second-best regime may continue to exist and thrive; indeed, there is no reference made to a possible need for the periodic appearance of a true king in order to rejuvenate and/or preserve the regimes whose rulers rule "according to the law."[45]

The deemphasis of the possible inability of second-best regimes to continue to exist without the reappearance of a true philosopher-king is also a characteristic of al-Fārābī's *The Political Regime* (*Al-Siyāsa al-Madaniyya*). In this treatise al-Fārābī states:

> If it does not happen that a man exists with these qualifications [i.e., the qualifications of the true king or supreme ruler], then one will have to adopt the laws prescribed by the earlier ones, write them down, preserve them, and govern the city by them. The ruler who governs the city according to the written laws received from the past "imams" (*a'imma*) will be the king according to the law (*malik al-sunna*).[46]

The position that al-Fārābī takes in the above two texts is consistent with Plato's position in the *Statesman* and *Laws*: these writings do not emphasize the difficulties involved in the continued existence of the less-than-perfect, second-best regime, which is based on the (more or less) sovereign "rule of law" rather than on the wise rule of a philosophic ruler. In contrast to this, al-Fārābī, in his treatise *The Opinions of the Inhabitants of the Virtuous City* (*Arā' Ahl al-Madīna al-Fāḍila*), states explicitly that in the second-best regime the sovereign rule of the laws and of the rulers "according to the law" is a situation that cannot long endure.

> But when it happens, at a given time, that philosophy has no share in the regime, though every other condition may be present in it, the virtuous city remains without a king, and the city will be on the verge of destruction. And if it happens that no philosopher can be found who will be attached to the actual ruler of the city, then, after a certain interval, this city will undoubtedly perish.[47]

Thus, according to the *Virtuous City*, without periodic infusions of the "rule of wisdom" (i.e., rule by a true king or supreme ruler), the "rule of law" and rule by those rulers who are subordinate to the law will be inadequate to preserve the city, and it will undoubtedly decay and perish.[48]

To conclude, throughout all of al-Fārābī's political writings a consistent position can be discerned regarding the proper relationship which should exist between the "rule of law" and the "rule of wisdom." This position maintains that only a wise philosopher may become a supreme ruler and true king, and that all nonphilosophic rulers are inferior to this king. Only the supreme ruler is not subject to the "rule of law": he rules by the "rule of wisdom" and retains the authority and ultimate sovereignty to reinterpret, modify, or change the law whenever and however he deems fit. In the absence of a philosophic ruler, the replacement "ruler(s) according to the law" must accept the ultimate sovereignty of the law (although in certain extreme situations these rulers may also modify the law on the basis of their own judgment in order to respond to new situations which have no precedent in the traditional law and the ancient ways of life). Thus, when a wise philosopher is not the ruler of the city, the established law is the sovereign principle or sovereign "ruler" in the regime. Regarding the possibility of long-term continued existence for a regime which is based on the "rule of law," al-Fārābī's position varies—at least in emphasis—in his various writings; in the *Virtuous City* he predicts the eventual destruction of such a city, but elsewhere he does not evidence such pessimism.[49]

Maimonides on "The Rule of Law" and "The Rule of Wisdom"

A significant difficulty is encountered in examining and analyzing Maimonides' views on the "rule of law" versus the "rule of wisdom." Despite the overabundance of textual material in Maimonides' various writings regarding his philosophy of law, Maimonides' comments concerning certain "sensitive" aspects of law's efficacy are few, as well as being brief and elliptical in character. Among these "sensitive" issues are the question of the Jewish Law's unconditional sovereignty (including possible limitations on the "rule of law," in theory and in practice) as well as the respective claims of Jewish Law and of philosophic wisdom to lead individuals to the attainment of ultimate human perfection.[50] I believe that insights into Maimonides' treatment of these "sensitive" issues can be gained by comparing his discussions of these issues with similar discussions in al-Fārābī's political writings.

Before examining the above-mentioned issues, it is important to note a striking characteristic of Maimonides' discussion of law—particularly in the *Guide of the Perplexed.* In the *Guide*, there are at least four distinct meanings of "law" to which Maimonides makes reference. These different meanings must be identified and defined in order to arrive at an accurate understanding of Maimonides' position on the various issues and problems which he discusses.

The most readily apparent distinction between the different usages or categories of law in Maimonides' writings is the difference between "*the Law*," or the Jewish Law (a uniquely Jewish category), as opposed to "law"—that is, law as a general phenomenon which exists in all (or almost all) communities. Law as a general phenomenon may often include Jewish Law, although occasionally all non-Jewish law is contrasted with Jewish Law.

The secondary distinction is one of scope: is the Jewish Law or the general category of law analyzed in an overarching, "macro," and often theoretical manner, or is it examined in a "micro," case-by-case, and specific fashion?[51]

It should be noted that Maimonides' discussion of law frequently has unexpected implications. Sometimes, what appears to be a discussion of law in general may have important ramifications on Jewish Law.[52] Sometimes a discussion which appears to contrast Jewish and non-Jewish law is far less clear-cut when it is studied closely.[53] Sometimes what appears to be a purely Jewish issue in legal interpretation has implications beyond the seemingly narrow Jewish legal topic, and it may be necessary to clarify such discussions by making reference to a wider philosophic or political frame of reference.[54]

One of the most notable statements of the great importance which Maimonides attributes to law (including the Jewish Law) can be found in *Guide* 2:40. Here Maimonides emphasizes that law is necessary in human communities in order to establish norms and create common practices that will be accepted by all as binding on the community as a whole. In this way law provides a fundamental—almost natural—framework for the maintenance of order in the community. Maimonides writes:

> Now as the nature of the human species requires that there be those differences among the individuals belonging to it and as in addition society is a necessity for this nature, it is by no means possible that his society should be perfected except—and this is necessarily so—through a ruler who gauges the actions of the individuals, perfecting that which is deficient and reducing that which is excessive, and who prescribes actions and moral habits that all of them must always practice in the same way, so that the natural diversity is hidden through the multiple points of conventional accord and so that the community becomes well ordered. Therefore I say

> that the Law, although it is not natural, enters into what is natural.[55]

Maimonides nowhere contradicts the position that law is necessary in human communities so that men's "natural diversity [will be] hidden through the multiple points of conventional accord and so that the community [will become] well ordered."[56] Yet, in other passages in the *Guide*, Maimonides makes a point of noting some intrinsic limitations of law and the "rule of law." Echoing Plato's and al-Fārābī's remarks about the nonspecificity and inflexibility of law, Maimonides writes: "[Law] is directed only towards things that occur in the majority of cases and pays no attention to what happens rarely or to the damage occurring to the unique human being because of this way of determination and because of the legal character of the governance."[57] Further, Maimonides contends that "it also will not be possible that the laws be dependent on changes in the circumstances of the individuals and the times, as is the case with regard to medical treatment, which is particularized for every individual in conformity with his present temperament."[58] Emphasizing both the limitations of law as well as its proper function, Maimonides continues:

> On the contrary, governance of the Law ought to be absolute and universal, including everyone, even if it is suitable only for certain individuals and not for others; for if it were made to fit individuals, the whole would be corrupted and you would make out of it something that varies. For this reason, matters that are primarily intended in the Law ought not to be dependent on time or place; but the decrees ought to be absolute and universal. . . . However, only the universal interests, those of the majority, are considered in them, as we have explained.[59]

Maimonides' position on the strengths and limitations of the "rule of law" can be seen to parallel Plato's and al-Fārābī's positions. As in those writings of Plato and al-Fārābī which emphasize the positive aspects of the "rule of law," Maimonides argues that law (including the Jewish Law) is—and must be, or at least must appear to be—absolute and universal (or "the whole would be corrupted and you would make out of it something that varies").[60] Further, in agreement with Plato and al-Fārābī, Maimonides also points to the fact that law (including the Jewish Law) occasionally must be updated and changed—and that this process is extremely dangerous and should be undertaken with utmost circumspection, being entrusted to an official body which is composed of a few wise and trustworthy individuals.[61] All other individuals should be forbidden to tamper with the Law—or even to disagree publicly with its official interpretation. This matter is especially sensitive since, according to Maimonides, the law in question is divinely revealed. In *Guide* 3:41, Maimonides expounds at length on the problem of updating and changing the Jewish Law:

> Inasmuch as God, may He be exalted, knew that the commandments of this Law will need in every time and place—as far as some are concerned—to be added to or subtracted from according to the diversity of places, happenings, and conjunctures of circumstances, He forbade adding to them or subtracting from them. . . . For this might have led to the corruption of the rules of the Law and to the belief that the latter did not come from God. Withal He permitted the men of knowledge of every period, I refer to the "Great Court of Law," to take precautions with a view to consolidating the ordinances of the Law by means of regulations in which they innovate with a view to repairing fissures, and to perpetuate these precautionary measures. . . . Similarly they were permitted in certain circumstances or with a view to certain events to abolish certain actions prescribed by the Law or to permit some of the things forbidden by it; but these measures may not be perpetuated, as we explained in the Introduction to the *Commentary on the Mishnah* in speaking of "temporary decisions." Through this kind of governance the Law remains one, and one is governed in every time and with a view to every happening in accordance with what is happening. If, however, every man of knowledge had been permitted to engage in this speculation concerning particulars, the people would have perished because of the multiplicity of the differences of opinion and the subdivisions of doctrines. Consequently He, may He be exalted, has forbidden all the men of knowledge with the single exception of the "Great Court of Law" to undertake this, and has those who disagree with [this Court] killed. For if it could be opposed by everyone who engages in speculations, the intended purpose would be annulled and the usefulness of these regulations abolished.[62]

Regarding a point which already been noted, Maimonides—in language similar to Plato and al-Fārābī—argues that law by its nature deals with the general case and, unlike medicine (or the "rule of wisdom"), it is unable to be particularized for every individual and circumstance. Maimonides hints at the conclusion which Plato and al-Fārābī drew explicitly: law (including the Jewish Law) is not always able to deal with a particular individual or situation in a totally just or perfect manner. The unique individual[63] will not be addressed uniquely by the Law. Maimonides emphasizes that the Law pays no attention to the damage occurring to the unique individual because of its concern only with the things which occur in the majority of cases, and because of the fundamentally legal (rather than rational or philosophic) character of the governance.[64] This raises the question of whether observance of the Law (or living according to the "rule of law") is sufficient to lead the most perfect individuals to ultimate human perfection. Maimonides' answer to this question is crucial for those individuals who are perplexed regarding the compatibility of living according to the dictates and principles of the Jewish Law and living according to the dictates and principles of reason.

An important aspect of Maimonides' response to this issue is found in his comparison between Jewish Law and all other laws. Maimonides argues that man needs political life in order to attain perfection and that without law it would be impossible to maintain well-ordered political communities. Yet not all laws are the same. Maimonides distinguishes between divine law and human laws (*nomoi*) according to the legal code's compatibility with the attainment of ultimate human perfection, and he expresses the opinion that the Jewish Law conforms to the requirements expected of a divine law.[65] In addition, throughout the *Guide*, Maimonides discusses the superiority of the Jewish Law over all other laws—and particularly over the pagan laws which were in existence at the time that the Jewish people received their Law.[66] Among its numerous qualities, the Jewish Law has done away with incorrect and pernicious beliefs and actions which were an integral part of many if not all of the pagan laws. This was true in Moses' lifetime and it continues to be true to a greater or lesser extent in Maimonides' lifetime as well. According to Maimonides, the activities and beliefs that the Jewish Law requires are conducive to man's attainment of his ultimate perfection; further, at least in a summary way (through the commandment "To love the Lord"),[67] the Law calls upon men to accept all correct opinions concerning the whole of being—the knowledge of which is a necessary condition for the attainment of human perfection.[68]

It would appear that the Jewish Law provides the basis for the attainment of ultimate human perfection. However, there are limitations to what even the Jewish Law discusses and makes known regarding correct opinions. Maimonides maintains:

> In regard to the correct opinions through which the ultimate perfection may be obtained, the Law has communicated only their end and made a call to believe them in a summary way—that is, to believe in the existence of the Deity, may He be exalted, His unity, His knowledge, His power, His will, and His eternity. . . . With regard to all other correct opinions concerning the whole of being—opinions that constitute the numerous kinds of all the theoretical sciences through which the opinions forming the ultimate end are validated—the Law, albeit it does not make a call to direct attention

> toward them in detail . . . does do this in a summary fashion by saying: "To love the Lord."[69]

It should be noted that, according to Maimonides, there is a fundamental difference between believing in correct opinions and being able to validate or invalidate opinions on the basis of one's own rational investigation.[70] The theoretical sciences are able to provide the basis for true, demonstrable knowledge—to the extent that such demonstrable knowledge is attainable by human beings and to the extent that a particular individual is able to perfect his rational faculties. Indeed, man's ultimate perfection, as it is described by Maimonides, cannot be attained on the basis of believing in correct opinions which are contained in a legal code, but only on the basis of acquiring true knowledge concerning the whole of being (at least insofar as such knowledge is within human capacity) and this by means of rational investigation and speculation. Maimonides states:

> [Man's] ultimate perfection is to become rational *in actu*, I mean to have an intellect *in actu*; this would consist in his knowing everything concerning all the beings that it is within the capacity of man to know in accordance with his ultimate perfection. It is clear that to this ultimate perfection there do not belong either actions or moral qualities and that it consists only of opinions toward which speculation has led and that investigation has rendered compulsory.[71]

However, rather than dwelling on the limitations of Jewish Law, it is a consistent characteristic of Maimonides' discussion of the Law to highlight its outstanding qualities. Among the most notable achievements of the Jewish Law in comparison to the laws of other nations is its purposefulness. According to Maimonides: "It is the doctrine of all of us [Jews]—both of the multitude and of the elite—that all the Laws have a cause."[72] While Maimonides explains that the specific details of certain commandments have no particular reason and "were given merely for the sake of commanding something," he holds that "the generalities of the commandments necessarily have a cause and have been given because of a certain utility."[73] Maimonides attempts to show that the Jewish Law provides a supremely virtuous foundation for the continued existence of the Jewish people and for its well-ordered political, legal, and social structures. The causes which led to the giving of the various Jewish laws—and the beneficial results which are derived from those laws—are classified as falling into at least one of three twofold categories:

> Every commandment from among the six hundred and thirteen commandments exists either with a view to communicating a correct opinion, or to putting an end to an unhealthy opinion, or to communicating a rule of justice, or to warding off an injustice, or to

> endowing men with a noble moral quality, or to warning them against an evil moral quality. Thus, all [the commandments] are bound up with three things: opinions, moral qualities, and political civic actions.[74]

The discussion of the causes or reasons for specific laws should be seen as part of Maimonides' attempt to argue that the Jewish Law is as perfect an example of law as can be attained—considering the restrictions imposed by human nature and by the continued existence of the large number of the "masses" in any political community. Thus, even though the Law does have limitations, and even though it may only point to the end rather than itself being the end, the "perplexed" Jewish thinker should appreciate law's necessity and the Jewish Law's virtue and utility.

In the light of Maimonides' treatment of the importance of law in general and the Jewish Law in particular, it may be possible to appreciate his untiring efforts in the preparation of his codification of the Jewish Law. The writing of the *Mishneh Torah* and his many Responsa are examples of Maimonides' efforts to preserve and defend the Jewish Law, as well as to actively apply the Law to the conditions which existed in his own day. Maimonides emphasizes the importance of this undertaking in the "Introduction" to the *Mishneh Torah.* Here Maimonides traces the transmission of the Jewish Law, and emphasizes that the redactors of the Mishnah and the Talmud were led to commit the Oral Law to writing in order to ensure the preservation of the Law and in order to make knowledge of the contents of the Law more easily accessible to all Jews. In similar fashion, Maimonides reflects on his own times and on the reasons which led him to prepare his codification of the Jewish Law and to commit it to writing. Maimonides states:

> In our days, severe vicissitudes prevail and all feel the pressure of hard times. The wisdom of our wise men has disappeared; the understanding of our prudent men is hidden. Hence, the commentaries of the Gaonim and their compilations of laws and responses, which they took care to make clear, have in our times become hard to understand so that only a few individuals properly comprehend them. Needless to add, such is the case with the Talmud itself—the Babylonian as well as the Palestinian—the Sifra, the Sifre, and the Tosefta, all of which works require, for their comprehension, a broad mind, a wise soul, and considerable study, and then one can learn from them the correct practice as to what is forbidden or permitted, and the other rules of the Torah.
>
> On these grounds, I, Moses the son of Maimon the Sefardi, bestirred myself, and, relying on the help of

> God, blessed be He, intently studied all these works, with the view of putting together the results obtained from them in regard to what is forbidden or permitted, clean or unclean, and the rules of the Torah—all in plain language and terse style, so that thus the entire Oral law might become systematically known to all . . . so that all the rules shall be accessible to young and old.[75]

Human societies require law if they are to be well ordered; moreover, law must be clear and well-known if it is to serve as a unifying force in those societies, providing the basis for individual and collective action. Only if the Jewish Law is known and properly observed will the Jewish religious community be able to maintain itself, particularly in the face of its dispersion and the lack of any universally recognized, central political institutions. It may not be unfair to suggest that for Maimonides the overriding need to preserve and defend the Law often takes precedence over the less pressing question of whether the "rule of law" or the "rule of wisdom" should be dominant in the political-religious community (or whether there are particular circumstances when the "rule of wisdom" should be dominant over the "rule of law"). Yet, as has been shown, Maimonides does not ignore this issue in his writings. Indeed, even in his *Commentary on the Mishnah* and *Mishneh Torah*, Maimonides discusses the (theoretical) question of the powers of the prophet versus the powers of the collective assembly of "wise men" (*ḥakhamim*), and in this context states that the extraordinary supralegal powers of the prophet are limited to *temporary* suspension of or addition to laws, without any power to permanently change the Law or authoritatively reinterpret it against the considered judgment of a majority of the *ḥakhamim.*[76] Only collective action by the *ḥakhamim* who are members of the Great Court of Law together with the prophet who is alive in a given time can bring about permanent additions or changes in the Law.[77]

The sovereign powers of a king in Israel also are discussed by Maimonides. He emphasizes that, according to the Jewish Law, the king's sovereignty is subordinate to the "rule of law"—although the king has extraordinary powers "if the exigency of the hour demands it . . . in order to insure the stability of the social order." Indeed, in contrast to the Court, "he may put to death many offenders in one day, hang them, and leave them hanging for a long time, in order to put fear in the hearts of others and break the power of the wicked."[78] However, there is no question that the sovereignty of the king is subordinate to the ultimate sovereignty of the Law. Maimonides writes:

> Whoever disobeys a royal decree because he is engaged in the performance of a religious commandment, even if it be a light commandment, is not liable [to punishment], because [when there is a conflict] between the edict of the Master [i.e., God] and the edict of the servant [the king], the former takes precedence over the latter. It goes without

> saying that if the king issues an order annulling a religious commandment, no heed is paid to it.[79]

Further, in most vivid fashion, the king is constantly reminded that his rule must be subordinate to the "rule of law" which is contained in the Torah:

> As soon as the king ascends the throne, he must write a scroll of the Law for himself, in addition to the one(s) which his ancestors left him. He is to have it corrected by the court of seventy-one from the scroll in the Temple Court. If his father left him no scroll or it was lost, he must write two copies. . . . When he goes forth to war, it shall be with him; when he returns [from war] it shall be with him; when he sits in judgment, it shall be with him; when he sits down to eat, it shall be before him, as it is said: "And it shall be with him, and he shall read therein all the days of his life."[80]

To conclude, it is Maimonides' concern to defend and preserve the Jewish Law that most sharply sets his treatment of law apart from al-Fārābī's treatment of law. Al-Fārābī is content to examine law in theory and to declare its obvious inferiority to the "rule of wisdom" of a philosophic "supreme ruler"—a ruler who acts as the "living law" and who possesses the sovereign authority to change existing legal and religious systems whenever and however he deems fit. In his analysis of law *per se* and Jewish Law, Maimonides incorporates much of al-Fārābī's theoretical treatment of the law, but he also remains committed to the continued existence of the Jewish Law. Thus, Maimonides' discussions of the "rule of law" versus the "rule of wisdom" are presented in a cautious manner. The centrality of Jewish Law in Jewish communal and religious life makes any overt impugnment of the Law also an attack on all Jewish beliefs and practices that are dependent upon the divine sanction of the Law for their binding authority. If the divine and sovereign character of the Jewish Law were to be undermined, the continued existence of the Jewish community would itself be placed in jeopardy. Maimonides is outspoken regarding the danger of undermining Jewish Law and is clearly opposed to any activity which could irresponsibly lead to such an occurrence. Nevertheless, Maimonides' caution is not inconsistent with analytical rigor. His position points to certain intrinsic limitations of all law, including the Jewish Law—particularly when it is viewed in light of Plato's and al-Fārābī's critiques of the limitations of law (and the "rule of law"). Further, while Maimonides is consistent in the emphasis which he places on the need for law, this does not contradict his equally consistent position on the superiority of the rational faculty of the human soul (and human wisdom, which is based on the attainments of this faculty) over all other faculties of the soul, and it does not undermine Maimonides' insistence on the necessity for attaining rational perfection in order to reach the level of the prophets and attain human perfection.

Maimonides' position is not inconsistent with the positing of the superiority of rational investigation and speculation—over belief in and acceptance of the tenets of the Law—as the necessary medium and ultimate arbiter in man's quest to attain human perfection. In this regard, a man who seeks to rule himself on the basis of wisdom will benefit from the existence of a virtuous law in his political community, and he will undoubtedly do his best to uphold and strengthen that law.

NOTES

[1] This article was written during my tenure as a Rothschild Fellow and while affiliated as a research fellow at the Harvard University Center for Jewish Studies. I wish to thank both institutions for their generous support. In addition, I wish to acknowledge a research grant from the Memorial Foundation for Jewish Culture which helped to defray the costs of preparing this article for publication.

[2] Al-Fārābī's *Commentary on Plato's Laws* is extant; the Arabic text has been edited and published by F. Gabrieli, *AlFarabius Compendium Legum Platonis* (London, 1952); an English translation of the Introduction and the first two Discourses of the text has been published by Muhsin Mahdi in Ralph Lerner and Muhsin Mahdi, eds., *Medieval Political Philosophy: A Sourcebook* (New York: The Free Press, 1963), 83-94. Al-Fārābī's *Commentary on Plato's Republic* has not been recovered by modern scholars, but it is cited by many medieval sources. In addition to his commentaries on Plato's dialogues, al-Fārābī also wrote a number of commentaries on the writings of Aristotle. For a general survey of the writings of Plato and Aristotle which were translated into Arabic and which al-Fārābī undoubtedly knew, as well as references to al-Fārābī's commentaries on Aristotle's writings, see Majid Fakhry, *A History of Islamic Philosophy*, 2nd ed. (New York: Columbia University Press, 1983), esp. pp. 4-18 and 109-28. See also Richard Walzer, *Greek into Arabic* (Oxford: Bruno Cassirer, 1962), esp. pp. 18-23, 29-37, and 243-47, and M. Steinschneider, *Al-Farabi: Des Arabischen Philosophen Leben und Schriften* (St. Petersburg, 1869). It should be obvious to the reader of al-Fārābī's *The Philosophy of Plato* that not every work which was cited by al-Fārābī was known by him—the description of Plato's writings often being quite fanciful. For references to Aristotle's *Politics* in medieval Arabic philosophy, see Shlomo Pines, "Aristotle's *Politics* in Arabic Philosophy," *Israel Oriental Studies* 5(1975): 150-60. Pines points to a number of passages in al-Fārābī's writings which strongly suggest that al-Fārābī did have knowledge of the contents of Aristotle's *Politics*, perhaps in the form of "a paraphrase or abridgement of a part of the *Politics* composed in the Hellenistic or Roman period," *ibid.*, p. 160.

[3] The most important general study which has been published on the classical and medieval philosophic sources which were referred to or utilized by Maimonides is contained in Shlomo Pines, "Translator's Introduction: The Philosophic Sources of *The Guide of the Perplexed* ," in Maimonides, *Guide of the Perplexed,* Shlomo Pines, tr. (Chicago: The University of Chicago Press, 1963), lvii-cxxxiv.

[4] Maimonides' letter to Samuel ibn Tibbon has been published by Alexander Marx in "Texts by and about Maimonides," *Jewish Quarterly Review* N.S. 25(1935): 378-80; the quotation here is from p. 379.

[5] See, for example, the following articles and books: Lawrence Berman, "Maimonides, the Disciple of AlFārābī," *Israel Oriental Studies* 4(1974): 154-78; Lawrence Berman, *Ibn Bājja and Maimonides: A Chapter in the History of Political Philosophy,* Ph.D. dissertation, Hebrew University of Jerusalem, originally submitted May 1959, reprinted (Tel Aviv: Jacob Twersky, 1977); Herbert Davidson, "Maimonides' *Shemonah Perakim* and AlFārābī's *Fuṣūl al-Madanī,*" *Proceedings of the American Academy for Jewish Research* 31(1963): 33-50; Emil Fackenheim, "The Possibility of the Universe in Al-Fārābī, Ibn Sīnā and Maimonides," *Proceedings of the American Academy for Jewish Research* 16(1947): 39-70; Miriam Galston, "Philosopher-King v. Prophet," *Israel Oriental Studies* 8(1978): 204-18; Zev (Warren) Harvey, "Comparing Political Thought and *Halakhah* in Maimonides' Teaching" (Hebrew), *'Iyun* 29(1980):198-212; Joel L. Kraemer, "Alfārābī's *Opinions of the Virtuous City* and Maimonides' *Foundations of the Law,*" *Studia Orientalia: Memoriae E. H. Baneth Dedicata* (Jerusalem: Magnes Press, 1979), 107-53; Jeffrey Macy, "The Theological-Political Teaching of Maimonides' *Shemonah Perakim,*" *Proceedings of the Eighth World Congress of Jewish Studies* (Jerusalem, 1982), Division C:31-40; Shlomo Pines, "The Limitations of Human Knowledge According to Al-Fārābī, Ibn Bājja and Maimonides," in Isadore Twersky, ed., *Studies in Medieval Jewish History and Literature,* (Cambridge, Mass.: Harvard University Press, 1979), 82-109; Shlomo Pines, "Translator's Introduction: The Philosophic Sources of *The Guide of the Perplexed,*" in Pines, tr., *Guide* (Chicago: University of Chicago Press, 1963), especially pp. lxxviii-xcii; Leo Strauss, "The Literary Character of the *Guide of the Perplexed,*" in *Persecution and the Art of Writing* (Glencoe, Ill.: The Free Press, 1952), 38-94; Leo Strauss, "Quelques remarques sur la Science Politique de Maimonide et de Farabi," *Revue des Études Juives* 100(1936): 1-37; Leo Strauss, "How to Begin to Study *The Guide of the Perplexed,*" in Pines, tr., *Guide*, pp. xi-lvi; Leo Strauss, "Maimonides' Statement on Political Science," in *What Is Political Philosophy? and Other Studies* (New York: The Free Press, 1959), 155-69.

[6] See, for example, Plato *Statesman* 294b-c: "But we find practically always that the law tends to issue just this invariable kind of rule. It is like a self-willed, ignorant man who lets no one do anything but what he had ordered and forbids all subsequent questioning of his orders even if the situation has shown some marked improvement on the one for which he originally legislated." See also Plato *Statesman* 295b-296a.

[7] For an interesting and relevant comment on this issue by a medieval Christian thinker, see St. Thomas Aquinas, *Summa Theologica*, Question 97, Article 2 ("Whether human law should always be changed when something better offers itself").

[8] See, for example, Plato *Statesman* 294a-b and 294e-295a: "Law can never issue an injunction binding on all which really embodies what is best for each: it cannot prescribe with perfect accuracy what is good and right for each member of the community at any one time. . . . We must expect that the legislator who has to give orders to whole communities of human creatures in matters of right and mutual contractual obligation, will never be able in the laws he prescribes for the whole group to give every individual his due with absolute accuracy. . . . But we shall find him making the law for the generality of his subjects under average circumstances. Thus, he will legislate for all individual citizens, but it will be by what may be called a 'bulk' method rather than by individual treatment; and this method of 'bulk' prescription will be followed by him whether he makes a written code of law or refrains from such a code, preferring to legislate by using unwritten ancestral customs." In addition to the above passages, see, in general, Plato *Statesman* 294a-300e.

[9] All of whom, according to al-Fārābī, are like *one* ruler and *one* soul. See al-Fārābī, *Political Regime*, in Fauzi Najjar's edition of the Arabic text, *Al-Siyāsa al-Madaniyya* (Beyrouth: Imprimerie Catholique, 1964), 80-82; in the English translation by Fauzi Najjar in Lerner and Mahdi, eds., *Medieval Political Philosophy*, pp. 37-38. This passage appears to be al-Fārābī's explanation of (or commentary on) the relationship of one philosopher-king to another in the political regime described by Socrates in Plato's *Republic*.

[10] In Plato's writings see: *Republic* 497c-d, 473c-e, 499b-d (and 488a ff.); and *Statesman* 293a-300e—especially 293a-e, 295e-297b, and 300c-e.

[11] See, for example, Plato *Laws* 875a-d and 711d-e, or *Republic*, 498d-499d.

[12] See, for example, Plato *Republic* 487b-489b (the parable of the true ship's pilot); 496a-e (the claim that the philosophers are "just like a human being who has fallen in with wild beasts and is neither willing to join them in doing injustice nor sufficient as one man to resist all the savage animals; . . . taking all this into the calculation, he keeps quiet and minds his own business—as a man in a storm, when dust and rain are blown about by the wind, he stands aside under a little wall"); 497a-c ("Which of the current regimes is suitable for it?" "None at all." I said, "but this is the very charge I'm bringing; not one city today is in a condition worthy of the philosophic nature"); 501a: ("They would take the city and the dispositions of human beings, as though they were a tablet," I said, "which, in the first place, they would wipe clean. And that's hardly easy. At all events, you know that . . . [they would] not be willing to take either private man or city in hand or to draw up laws before they receive it clean or themselves make it so); and also 540d-541a. Al-Fārābī would appear to be somewhat more optimistic about the possibility of bringing about such a regime, although he recognizes that such regimes will not always occur even when a supreme ruler is present. Cf. al-Fārābī, *Attainment of Happiness (Taḥṣīl al-Sa'āda)* (Hyderabad, 1345 A.H.), 46; see Muhsin Mahdi's English translation in *AlFarabi's Philosophy of Plato and Aristotle*, Muhsin Mahdi, ed.

and tr., rev. ed. (Ithaca, New York: Cornell University Press, 1969), par. 62, p. 49. See also *Fuṣūl al-Madanī, faṣl* 32 according to the numbering of the Najjar ed., published as *Fuṣūl Muntaza'a* (Beirut: Dar al-Mashreq, 1971), 49-50, and al-Fārābī's *Commentary on Plato's Laws*, p. 8 in the Arabic text, Gabrieli, ed., *AlFarabius Compendium*—in Mahdi's English translation found in Lerner and Mahdi, eds., *Medieval Political Philosophy*, pp. 83-94, First Discourse, par. 14, p. 88.

13 See, in particular, *Attainment of Happiness*, on the difference between the true philosopher and the defective philosopher. In most, if not all, of his political writings, al-Fārābī holds the position that the philosopher desires to rule and that he is unable to attain supreme happiness if he does not possess the ability to rule.

14 My comments here are not meant to deny that there is also an opposite trend in Plato's thought, which argues that the philosopher might indeed desire to rule —see, for example, *Republic* 497a; however, it appears to me that there is far more aversion to rule than willingness to rule which can be found in the Platonic description of the philosopher. The greatest example of the Platonic philosopher's unwillingness to rule can be found in the "myth of the cave," in Book 7 of the *Republic*, especially 516c-517d and 520b-521b.

15 See below, pp. 208-11.

16 On this point see Plato's *Statesman* 293a-303c, *Laws* 711d-715e, and the general argument of the *Republic*, especially in contrast to the description of the nonvirtuous regimes in Books 8 and 9. Note that, according to Plato, the nonphilosophic regimes echo the flaws of their nonphilosophic rulers, particularly when these rulers are not limited by a fixed constitution. See especially the discussion of this point in the *Statesman*; in the *Republic*, the relative merits of a nonphilosophic regime with a fixed set of laws in comparison to a nonphilosophic regime without such a fixed set of laws are not discussed.

17 Plato *Statesman* 300e-303c.

18 *Ibid*., 297d-e; cf. 300b-d.

19 The philosopher is the "living law," inasmuch as he is the ultimate authority for everything which the law contains and inasmuch as he can change or modify that law whenever and however he deems necessary. Al-Fārābī attempts to utilize the concept of the philosophic ruler as "the living law" in his treatment of the supreme ruler (*al-ra'īs al-awwal*); see, in particular, *Fuṣūl Muntaza'a, faṣl* 58, p. 66, and al-Fārābī's description of the supreme ruler, including his use of the term *al-dustūr*. See below, p. 208 and note 34.

20 The distinction between virtuous regimes ruled by a philosopher and second-best regimes ruled by law should not be understood to imply that there will be no laws when a philosopher rules, but rather than any such law will appear fixed or even inviolable only to nonphilosophers, while the philosopher will recognize the salutary character of the law as well as his sovereign right and duty to change, modify, or reinterpret it however and whenever he deems fit. Cf. J. B. Skemp, "How Political Is the *Republic*," *History of Political Thought* 1(1980): 1-7.

21 This possibility is not entertained in the *Republic*.

[22] See above, pp. 206-07 and note 18. In accordance with this position, Plato confers the status of the best of the imperfect regimes on those regimes that are ruled on the basis of the laws (i.e., monarchy, aristocracy, and "constitutional" democracy), and the worst of the imperfect regimes on those regimes that are ruled in defiance of the established laws and/or on the basis of the ignorance and passions of the ruler(s) (i.e., tyranny, oligarchy, and "nonconstitutional" democracy). Cf. *Statesman* 301a-303b.

[23] See *Laws* 712b ff., 762e, 803c-804b, and especially all of Book 10; nevertheless, note the role of the legislator (or the Athenian stranger) in designing the laws, and the role of the Nocturnal Council in changing or (re)interpreting the laws.

[24] Despite the popular distinction between Plato's *Republic* as a nonimplementable utopian work, and Plato's *Laws* as a practical attempt to build an improved political society, it does not appear to me that the regime which Plato presents in the *Laws* is a model which is realistically possible to implement. Among other problems, the basis for changing the law which resides in the Nocturnal Council is less than consistent with the law-bound horizon within which the citizens grow up and flourish. In many respects, the city which is created in the *Laws* is a "city in speech," even if the speech in the mouth of the Athenian stranger is less revolutionary than the speech which Socrates utters in the *Republic*.

[25] See, in particular, Books 4-12 of the *Laws*.

[26] See, for example, *Laws* 709e-712a and 875c-d.

[27] See *Laws* 899-909 (passim), and, in particular, 949e-953e and 960c-969d.

[28] See above, p. 207 and note 19, and below, p. 208. See also the description of the supreme ruler in al-Fārābī's *The Political Regime*, *Attainment of Happiness*, and *Virtuous City*.

[29] See above, p. 207, and below, pp. 208-10. On the use of the term "*malik al-sunna*" to describe the king whose rule is circumscribed and guided by the existing law, see below, note 46.

[30] In *The Opinions of the Inhabitants of the Virtuous City*, Arabic text, F. Dieterici, ed. (Leiden: Brill, 1895), 58, al-Fārābī characterizes the process by which the philosopher-king attains knowledge and legislates the laws of the city as "divine revelation." Compare with the passages from Plato's *Laws* which are cited above, in note 23. See, also, al-Fārābī's comments in *Attainment of Happiness, Hyderabad ed.*, p. 44; Mahdi's English trans. in *AlFarabi's Philosophy*, par. 59, p. 47.

[31] See below, pp. 208-11.

[32] See, for example, *Fuṣūl Muntazaʻa,* Najjar, ed., *fuṣūl* 4, 5, 12, 30-32, and especially 58. He must possess "(theoretical) wisdom, perfect practical wisdom, excellence in persuasion, excellence in producing an imaginative impression, capacity to fight in battle in person, and there should not be anything in his bodily condition that would prevent him from pursuing matters which require effort and diligence" (*faṣl* 58, p. 66). (*Al-ra'īs al-awwal* is translated as "the supreme ruler," and *al-malik fī al-ḥaqīqa* is translated as "the true king.")

[33] In this context it is interesting to note that in the *Republic*, Plato does not place emphasis on the philosopher's physical or military qualities—qualities

which al-Fārābī sees as essential prerequisites for the supreme ruler. The philosopher's use of persuasion rather than physical force is emphasized in the *Republic*; further, physical and military qualities are discussed within the context of the education of the warrior class. This may be the result of the historical fact that Socrates, Plato's model of the philosopher *par excellence*, was a "man of discussion" and not a "man of violent action," although Plato's position in the *Republic* may also reflect the ultimate difference between being a philosopher and being a king. In the *Statesman*, Plato does emphasize the compulsion which the true statesman may have to use; see *Statesman* 293a-e, 296b-297b and 304e-305a.

[34] I have translated the term *al-dustūr* as "the living law." Al-Fārābī's use of this term is noteworthy as this may be the earliest documented use of *dustūr* in Arabic. [The use of *dustūr* in *Kalīla wa-Dimna* may stem from a later recension of the text—cf. *The Encyclopedia of Islam*, New ed. (Leiden: E. J. Brill, 1965), 2:638 and *ibid.* (1978), 4:503 (especially the comments on Ibn al-Muqaffa''s Arabic edition of *Kalīla wa-Dimna* and the corruption of its contents which occurred in its transmission). There is no extant manuscript of *Kalīla wa-Dimna* which predates the lifetime of al-Fārābī.]

It appears to me that by his use of *al-dustūr* al-Fārābī is attempting to coin a phrase, based on this Persian loan-word, which will capture the Platonic concept of the philosopher-king as the "living law." According to Edward William Lane, *An Arabic English Lexicon* (London: Williams and Norgate, 1867), 1:879, the meaning of the original form of the Persian word *dastūr* is: "The copy, or original (of the register, as will be seen from what follows), which is made for the several classes (of the officers and servants of the government), from which their transcription is made, . . . and in which are collected the rules and ordinances of the King; . . . Hence, the great 'wazīr' to whom recourse is had (by the King) with respect to what he may prescribe to the people, because he is the possessor of the register so called." Thus, al-Fārābī may have attempted to use this word to describe the supreme ruler in an attempt to point out his being like the register of the laws made by the king—as it were, an embodiment of the law. If the supreme ruler is like this law book, his thoughtful and "living" word would be the law for all those in his polity. This meaning is clearly consistent with the idea that al-Fārābī is trying to put forth: "it is this man who should rule according to what he thinks right and however he wishes."

Despite thc aptness of al-Fārābī's idiomatic usage of *dustūr*, it would appear that his use of this term did not become established in the terminology of the succeeding generations of Islamic philosophers.

[35] Or: "His words and his commands . . ."

[36] Najjar, ed., *Fuṣūl Muntaza'a, faṣl* 58, p. 66.

[37] *Ibid.* A parallel to this virtuous group rulership can be found in Plato's *Laws* 710c-d, and in Plato's own attempts to become an advisor to Dionysus, the tyrant of Syracuse. In addition, see al-Fārābī's *Opinions of the Inhabitants of the Virtuous City,* F. Dieterici, ed., p. 61.

[38] Najjar, ed., *Fuṣūl Muntaza'a, faṣl* 58, p. 67. See below, pp. 210-11, for al-Fārābī's somewhat different statements of this problem in *The Political Regime* and *Virtuous City*.

[39] Compare this with the similar statement of the problem in Plato's *Statesman*; see above, pp. 206-07 and note 18.

[40] The meaning which al-Fārābī ascribes to the term imām is not necessarily the same as the meaning of this term in traditional Shī'ī or Sunnī Islam; nevertheless, his use of this traditional term is not without significance. Cf. *Attainment of Happiness*, p. 43; Mahdi's English translation in *AlFarabī's Philosophy*, par. 57, pp. 46-47.

[41] Najjar, ed., *Fuṣūl Muntaza'a, faṣl* 58, p. 67.

[42] Cf. *ibid., faṣl* 45, p. 59: "Excellence of opinion [or independent judgment] *(ra'y)* is that a man should have opinions or excellent opinions—that is, that a man should be good or virtuous in his actions, then that he should have opinions—and that [this man's] words, opinions, and counsel should have been tested many times and found sound and right, bringing the man, when he employs them, to approved results, and that his words should therefore have come to be welcomed—I mean because of the truth(fulness) which is commonly witnessed in him—*so that his well-known virtue, sound judgment and counsel can dispense him from having to say or point out anything by way of argument or proof.* Evidently, when this man gets the right opinion and takes into account the propriety of it [in a given situation], *he does so only by practical wisdom.* This, then, is a kind of practical wisdom" (emphasis mine).

[43] *Ibid., faṣl* 58, p. 67.

[44] As a result of this king's above-mentioned qualities, the inhabitants of his regime will accept his innovation or his attempt to resolve a new problem because "his well-known virtue, sound judgment, and counsel can dispense him from having to say or point out anything by way of argument or proof." Cf. the passage from Najjar, ed., *Fuṣūl Muntaza'a, faṣl* 45, cited above in note 42.

[45] However, see below, pp. 210-11 and note 47, for a different position on this subject which al-Fārābī expresses in *The Opinions of the Inhabitants of the Virtuous City*. Perhaps understandably, on the subject of the potential longevity of political regimes which are ruled by "ruler(s) according to the law," Maimonides may be said to be far more in agreement with the position which al-Fārābī presents in *Fuṣūl al-Madanī* and in *The Political Regime* than he is with the position set forth in *Virtuous City*. Nevertheless, even in Maimonides' case, there is a recognition that occasionally it may be necessary to modify elements of the legal code, or to temporarily override the injunctions of the law for the sake of preserving the religion (or political community). Maimonides' position on this issue is examined below.

[46] Al-Fārābī, *The Political Regime*, Arabic ed., Najjar, ed., p. 81; English translation by Najjar in Lerner and Mahdi, *Medieval Political Philosophy*, p. 37. On the use of the term *malik al-sunna* in al-Fārābī's writings, it should be noted that D. M. Dunlop is incorrect in his contention that this term occurs only in *Fuṣūl al-Madanī*—see Dunlop's edition of *Fuṣūl al-Madanī* (Cambridge: University Press, 1961), p. 88 (lines 23-28).

[47] Dieterici, ed., *The Opinions of the Inhabitants of the Virtuous City,* see p. 61.

[48] This position resembles Plato's teaching in the *Republic*, where the absence of philosopher-kings inevitably leads to the four-stage process of decay in cities which is outlined in Book 8. One possibly significant difference between Plato's account in the *Republic* and al-Fārābī's comments in *Virtuous City* is that al-Fārābī suggests the possibility of periodic change from rule by a true king to rule by the law (and vice versa). In Plato's thought, the structural differences which exist between the regime based on "the rule of wisdom" and the regime based on "the rule of law" would seem to be so great that easy and periodic movement from one type of regime to the other is difficult if not impossible to imagine.

[49] Although limitations of space do not permit the examination of the following aspect of al-Fārābī's discussion of law, it is worthy of note that in some of his writings al-Fārābī refers to the origins of the law in the regime as being "divine" or "revealed," and that he links such law to the religion which is invented by the wise lawgiver and which is followed by the nonphilosophic "mass of men" who are inhabitants of the city. See, for example, *Attainment of Happiness*, p. 44; Mahdi's English translation in *AlFārābī's Philosophy*, par. 59, p. 47. In this paragraph al-Fārābī claims that the philosopher-legislator invents the images and persuasive arguments of religion—or, in other words, that the contents of the prophetic revelation is of the philosopher's invention. Consider al-Fārābī's remarks in Najjar, ed., *The Political Regime,* Arabic text, pp.79-80 and 85-86; Najjar's English translation in Lerner and Mahdi, eds., *Medieval Political Philosophy*, pp. 36-37 and 40-41. See also al-Fārābī's *On Religion*: "Religion consists of opinions and actions, determined and limited by conditions, which their supreme ruler lays down to the group, seeking to achieve a specific goal which he has, either in them or by means of them, through their active utilization of these opinions and actions." This passage is cited in Lawrence Berman, "Maimonides, the Disciple of Alfārābī," *Israel Oriental Studies* 4 (1974): 159.

The meaning of "divine revelation" is far from being unambiguous in al-Fārābī's thought. In some passages (cf. Dieterici, ed., *Virtuous City*, pp. 58-59, Najjar, ed., *The Political Regime*, Arabic text, pp. 78-80—Najjar's English translation in Lerner and Mahdi, *Medieval Political Philosophy* , pp. 36-37), the highest human attainment, which is attained only by the philosopher, is described as divine revelation (*waḥī*). In other passages (cf. Najjar, ed., *Fuṣūl Muntaza'a, faṣl* 94, pp. 98-99), al-Fārābī emphasizes that the philosophic process is totally different from divine revelation, and he makes no mention whatsoever of revelation as the process by which knowledge of the highest truths and first principles is attained by the supreme ruler (who is a philosopher). On the ambiguous status of prophecy and divine revelation as a characteristic of the lawgiver or supreme ruler, see also, *Averroes' Commentary on Plato's "Republic"*, E. I. J. Rosenthal, ed. and tr. (Cambridge: Cambridge University Press, 1956), 61.

[50] To be sure, these "sensitive" issues are alluded to or discussed in many of Maimonides' writings, including his so-called "legal writings"; yet, the

discussion of these issues often is brief, incomplete, and scattered throughout a large body of material. The analysis contained in this paper emphasizes passages from Maimonides' *Guide of the Perplexed*, but it should be noticed that important discussions of these issues also occur in the *Mishneh Torah* and *Commentary on the Mishnah*, as well as in other of Maimonides' works. The mere fact that a discussion of these issues occurs in one of Maimonides' halakhic writings should not be interpreted, *ipso facto*, as implying that the position expressed is "less philosophic" in content; each passage must be judged on its own merits.

[51] On the basis of these distinctions, the four different usages or categories of law which can be distinguished in Maimonides' writings are as follows:

1. The Jewish Law in a general sense—including the fundamentals of Jewish belief as well as the content of the corpus of traditionally accepted Jewish writings. (A variant usage, the examination of which is beyond the scope of this paper, is Maimonides' distinction between what is contained in the Torah and what is contained in the Oral Law or other traditional Jewish sources.)

2. The specific laws of the *halakha* or Jewish Law. This includes the reasons for specific commandments and prohibitions, as well as the categorization of specific laws into classes (e.g., *ḥuqqim* and *mitzvot* or *mishpaṭim*).

3. Law as a general or universalizable phenomenon. This category can include Jewish Law as part of a wider phenomenon, although, on occasion, Jewish Law may be juxtaposed against all other law in order to highlight a general principle. Here, specific laws as such are not discussed; the focus is law in general or the fundamental types of law. An example of a fundamental and universal typology of law which Maimonides discusses is his distinction between laws that are *nomoi* and laws that are divine.

4. Law meaning specific laws (or groups of specific laws) which are not particularistically Jewish. Indeed, in most cases this usage of the term "law" pertains to specific laws of corrupt, pagan nations which are contrasted to specific Jewish laws (category 2, above)—the Jewish laws being singled out for their superiority and virtue, while the pagan laws are exposed for their inferiority and corruption.

[52] See, for example, Maimonides' discussion of the limitations of law (in general) and the fact that law should not vary: *Guide* 3:34. See below, pp. 213-15.

[53] See, for example, the distinction which Maimonides makes between "divine law" and "nomos": *Guide* 2:39 and (especially) 40. Here, rational (philosophic) criteria are used to distinguish between these two categories, and careful consideration of these criteria make it far from clear that only the Jewish Law can have a claim to be "divine" according to this standard.

[54] An example of this is Maimonides' discussion of *ḥuqqim*, *mitzvot* or *mishpaṭim*, and rational laws. (Elsewhere, I have examined this case—Jeffrey Macy, "The Theological-Political Teaching of *Shemonah Perakim*," especially pp. 34-38—and I am currently preparing a more comprehensive article on the subject of "rational," "conventional," and "particularistic" laws in medieval Jewish thought.) Regarding Maimonides' treatment of these categories of

Jewish Law, it is most helpful to compare his three-fold categorization with al-Fārābī's comments on laws accepted by a particular community or group, "generally accepted" laws, and rational or truly virtuous laws. Cf. especially *Shemonah Perakim*, ch. 6, and *Guide* 3:26, together with al-Fārābī's *Attainment of Happiness*, par. 33, 40, 44, 45, and 50.

55 *Guide* 2:40—in Munk's edition of the Judeo-Arabic text, edited with variant readings by Issachar Joel (Jerusalem: J. Junovitch, 5691 (1930/31), 270; in Pines, tr., *Guide*, p. 382.

56 Maimonides' concern that law be maintained to preserve order in the community is highlighted by his own efforts in writing a compilation of Jewish law—the *Mishneh Torah*. See Maimonides' comments in his "Introduction" to the *Mishneh Torah*—in *Sefer Hamada'* of the *Mishneh Torah*, Moses Hyamson, ed. (Jerusalem: Feldheim Publishers, 1971), 4b.

57 Munk/Joel, eds., *Guide* 3:34, p. 391; in Pines, tr., *Guide*, p. 534.

58 *Guide* 3:34.

59 *Ibid.*; in Pines, tr., *Guide*, pp. 534-35.

60 See above, pp. 206-10. In particular, compare Maimonides' comments with the passage from Plato's *Statesman* which is cited above in notes 18 and 22. On the possibility that Maimonides qualifies his position on the absolute and universal character which must be possessed by law (and the Jewish Law), see below, pp. 214-15, 218, and notes 61 and 62.

61 Cf. above, note 27 as well as al-Fārābī's comments on the *malik al-sunna*. Regarding the individuals or groups which should be entrusted with responsibility for temporarily or permanently changing or modifying the laws, Maimonides discusses this issue in a number of places. In addition to what follows in the body of the text, and the passages referred to below, in notes 62 and 76, see also Maimonides' comments in the Introduction to his *Commentary on the Mishnah* on the "special virtue" (*faḍīla*) of the prophet. In the Introduction to the *Commentary on the Mishnah* (as well as in the *Mishneh Torah*, "Hilkhot Yesodei ha-Torah," chapter 9), Maimonides emphasizes that the prophet can order the temporary suspension of a commandment or temporary addition to the commandments, but under no circumstances is he to be followed if he orders any permanent change in the Law; indeed, if the prophet orders permanent changes to be made in the Law or if he asserts that he has received a new authentic interpretation of the Law (which conflicts with the interpretation of the *ḥakhamim*), he is to be put to death as a false prophet. Maimonides' comments in the Introduction to the *Commentary on the Mishnah* should be compared with his statements in the *Mishneh Torah*, where temporary changes are made by the wise men or the court—cf. "Hilkhot Mamrim," chapters 1 and 2—or by the prophet—cf. "Yesodei ha-Torah," ch. 9, sections 3-4. In a passage from the "Introduction" to the *Mishneh Torah*, referred to in note 62, Maimonides states that permanent additions to the Law have been made by the Court (wise men) together with the prophet living at the time. Cf. below, p. 218.

62 Munk/Joel, eds., *Guide* 3:41, pp. 412-13; in Pines, tr. *Guide*, pp. 562-63. See also the references to the "rebellious elder" in the *Mishneh Torah*, especially

in "Hilkhot Mamrim," as well as Maimonides' interpretations in his *Commentary on Mishnah Avot*, 1:11 and 3:11.

That the Jewish Law has been updated in the past is clear from comments which Maimonides makes in a number of places in his writings. One illustration can be found in his "Introduction" to the *Mishneh Torah*, where the issue of nonscriptural commandments is examined. Maimonides comments:

> These are the six hundred and thirteen commandments which were orally transmitted to Moses at Sinai, together with their general principles, detailed applications, and minute particulars. All these principles, details, particulars, and the explantion of every commandment constitute the Oral Law, which every court received from its predecessor. There are other commandments which were innovated after the giving of the Torah, which the prophets and the *ḥakhamim* instituted, and which became accepted throughout Israel, such as reading the *Megillah* [on Purim], [lighting] the Chanuka lights, the fast of the Ninth of Av, [washing] the hands [before meals] and *'Eruvin*. . . . We are required to accept and observe all these newly established commandments, as it is said: "You shall not turn aside from every thing" ["You shall not turn aside from the sentence which they shall declare to you, neither to the right hand nor to the left"] (Deut. 17:11). They are not an addition to the commandments of the Torah. Regarding the warning of the Torah, "You shall not add to it, nor take away from it" (Deut. 13:1), this was in order that a prophet would not have the authority to innovate something, saying that the Holy One, blessed be He, commanded him to add this commandment to the commandments of the Torah, or to abrogate one of the six hundred and thirteen commandments. But if the Court, together with the prophet who is living at that time, add a commandment as an ordinance (*takanah*), judicial decision (*hora'ah*) or decree (*gizerah*), this is not [considered] an addition [to the Torah]. For they did not say that the Holy One, blessed be He, commanded the making of an *'Eruv*, or reading of the *Megillah* at its appointed time. Had they done this, they would be adding to the Torah. However, we say that the prophets, together with the Court, enacted this ordinance and commanded to read the *Megillah* at its appointed time to proclaim the praises of the Holy One, blessed be He, and [to remind us of] the salvation which he brought us, and

> that He was near [when] we cried for help, and in order that we should bless Him and praise Him and inform future generations that what He promised us in the Torah is true, "For what great nation is there that has God so close to it" (Deut. 4:7). In this way each and every commandment instituted by the Scribes (*mi-divrei sofrim*) should be understood, whether it is a positive or negative [commandment].

In his Introduction to the *Commentary on the Mishnah*, Maimonides also comments on the role of the *ḥakhamim* in the interpretation and updating of the Jewish Law; see Maimonides' *Commentary on the Mishnah*, Judeo-Arabic ed., Joseph Kafiḥ, ed., 7 vols. (Jerusalem: Mossad Harav Kook, 1963-68), 1:14-23. See also, *Mishneh Torah*, "Hilkhot Mamrim," chapters 1 and 2. In addition to the above passages, consider also Maimonides' comments in *Guide* 3:32.

63 See, for example, ch. 5 of *Shemonah Perakim* as well as Maimonides' comments in the Introduction to his *Commentary on the Mishnah*, Judeo-Arabic ed., Joseph Kafiḥ, ed., 1:42-44. In the *Guide*, consider Maimonides' comments on the "perfect man" (who, on occasion, is described as living in solitude)—see, for example, *Guide* 1:34 (end), 2:36, 3:51, 54.

64 Cf. *Guide* 3:34.

65 *Guide* 2:39, 40. Another way of stating the difference between divine laws and *nomoi* is that the aim of the divine law is consistent with the attainment of true human perfection, while the aim of a *nomos* is merely the achievement of political order, without any attention being paid to the perfecting of men's rational faculty.

66 See, especially, *Guide* 3:29-32, 2:39, and the discussion of the "reasons for the commandments" in 3:35-50.

67 Cf. *Guide* 3:28.

68 Cf. *Guide* 2:39-40, 3:25-34.

69 Munk/Joel, eds., *Guide* 3:28, p. 373; Pines, tr., *Guide*, p. 512.

70 See, for example, *Guide* 1:50.

71 Munk/Joel, eds., *Guide* 3:27, p. 372; Pines, tr., *Guide*, p. 511.

72 Munk/Joel, eds., *Guide* 3:26, p. 368; Pines, tr., *Guide*, p. 507.

73 Munk/Joel, eds., *Guide* 3:26, p. 370; Pines, tr., *Guide*, p. 508. Cf. *Mishneh Torah*, "Hilkhot Me'ilah," 8:8. On Maimonides' discussion of the *ḥuqqim* and *mishpaṭim* or *mitzvot*, see also *Shemonah Perakim*, ch. 6; cf. above, note 54.

74 Munk/Joel, eds., *Guide* 3:31, p. 383; Pines, tr., *Guide*, p. 524. Elsewhere Maimonides points to the interrelationship between the last two categories—moral qualities and political civic actions; both contribute to "the welfare of the conditions of the city, which is achieved through two things: abolition of reciprocal wrongdoing and acquisition of excellent (moral) characters" (Munk/Joel, eds., *Guide* 3:28, p. 374; Pines, tr., *Guide*, p. 513).

75 Hyamson, ed., *Mishneh Torah*, Introduction, p. 4b.

76 See, in particular, the general Introduction to Maimonides' *Commentary on the Mishnah*, Kafiḥ, ed., 1:4-14. See also the citations referred to above, in notes 61 and 62.

[77] See the citations from Maimonides' writings which are referred to above in notes 61 and 62.

[78] *Mishneh Torah*, "Hilkhot Melakhim" 3:10. See also Maimonides' description of the extraordinary powers of the king in "Hilkhot Melakhim" 3.8 and throughout Chapter 4. Maimonides summarizes the reasons for the appointment of the king in "Hilkhot Melakhim" 4:10: "His sole aim and thought should be to uplift the true religion, to fill the world with righteousness, to break the arm of the wicked, and to fight the battles of the Lord. The prime reason for appointing a king was that he execute judgment and wage war."

[79] *Mishneh Torah*, "Hilkhot Melakhim" 3:9.

[80] *Ibid.*, 3:1; the closing quotation is from Deut. 17:19.

The Treatment of Islam and Muslims in the Legal Writings of Maimonides

David Novak

Introduction

When dealing with the specific questions concerning the status of Islam and Muslims for Judaism, Maimonides had behind him the development of the overall treatment of other religions in Jewish legal tradition (*Halakhah*). It was this tradition to which he was bound as his religious heritage, and it was this tradition that he himself developed in such a way that it was never quite the same after him. Thus, in order to understand the significance of Maimonides' treatment of these specific legal questions, we must take a brief look at how that tradition developed and the options it gave an halakhist as gifted and subtle as he. Moreover, we must look at Maimonides' philosophic work to understand the full significance of the method employed in the legal decisions he made in this area especially. Elsewhere I have argued against the view that Maimonides' legal and philosophic interests were separate and distinct.[1] Certainly in legal questions such as these, where the theological issue of belief so quickly enters the picture, one can hardly ignore the fact that the same philosophic concerns which permeated his theology also permeated his treatment of this theologically charged area of law.

In biblical Judaism, religion—any religion—is seen as inextricably intertwined with national existence and culture. At this level the worship of the One God (YHWH) was seen as the unique covenant between the One God and the nation of Israel. Other nations had their own respective covenants with other gods.[2] Israel is monotheistic; every other nation is polytheistic.[3] For this reason nowhere in the Hebrew Bible was any non-Israelite, any gentile, faulted for the practice of polytheism, including the cult of idolatry.[4] This being the case, Israel's relations with these other nations were not based on specifically theological criteria inasmuch as these other nations were all taken to be polytheists, but they were not all to be treated the same way by the people of Israel. As such, they were differentiated by other criteria.

Some nations were regarded as the inherent enemies of the people of Israel, in particular the seven nations of Canaan and the Amalekites.[5] They were regarded as incorrigibly antagonistic to Israel, lacking any human compassion and decency, even among themselves.[6] The fact that they were designated as "not fearing God (*Elohim*)" is not an indictment of their polytheism as much as a moral indictment of their way of life which seemed to place no restrictions on their cruelty and lack of trustworthiness, especially but not exclusively to Israel.[7] For this reason, primarily, they were to be destroyed by Israel.

Other nations, with whom Israel was able to conduct stable political relations, were primarily judged by the political criterion of reciprocal trustworthiness.[8] Indeed, trustworthiness (*emunah*) is the most basic criterion for the judgment of any interpersonal relationship in the Hebrew Bible, be that relationship between man and man or between God and man.[9] In the case of those nations who were subjugated by Israel, the basic criterion of judgment was their faithfulness to Israelite suzerainty and Israel's faithful guarantee of their rights as vassals.[10] The same was the case for non-Jews domiciled in Israel (*gerim*).[11]

Only in the case of certain unusual individual gentiles was the rejection of polytheism something considered praiseworthy, but still not mandatory.[12] Nevertheless, it was realized that even such unusual gentile monotheists would have to practice public idolatry in their own societies.[13] The notion of non-Israelite monotheistic communities was not considered by the authors of the Hebrew Bible. The acceptance of monotheism by any large group of gentiles was considered only in the context of their becoming part of the covenant with Israel. In postexilic biblical texts this was envisioned as an item on the messianic agenda.[14]

In the rabbinic writings we see a rather radical development in terms of Judaism's treatment of other religions. With the emergence of the doctrine of the "seven commandments of the children of Noah"—a doctrine I have elsewhere argued emerged late in the second century of the Common Era[15]—a universal ban on polytheism and idolatry came to be accepted in Judaism. Just as Jews are prohibited to hold polytheistic beliefs or to practice idolatry, so are gentiles.[16] Although there are traces in the early rabbinic writings of the older notion that every gentile is *ipso facto* an idolator, the distinction between polytheistic gentiles and monotheistic gentiles was more and more emphasized.[17] Unlike the biblical writings, where a gentile monotheist was regarded as an anomaly, acting above and beyond what is expected of him, in the rabbinic writings gentile monotheism was regarded as the norm, at least *de jure*, even though it was recognized that public idolatry was still common *de facto*.[18] It was recognized that polytheism was becoming less and less a matter of personal conviction for gentiles and more and more a cultural vestige. Gentiles were now judged by theological criteria. Despite this, however, the notion of a community of gentile monotheists, separate and distinct from the Jewish people, was something of which the rabbis were unaware. Thus some obvious rabbinic polemics against the new religion of Christianity were directed against what were perceived as Christianity's compromise of Jewish monotheism, specifically through its corrupt use of the Hebrew Bible.[19]

The recognition of the fact of individual gentile monotheists is something which was already found in the Hellenistic Jewish writings. There we find the notion that these gentile monotheists are in fact potential Jews. It was recognized that the rejection of idolatry and its ideological basis in polytheism is the first step towards the eventual adoption of full Jewish identity and full Jewish responsibility for all the commandments of the Mosaic Torah.[20] In the rabbinic writings we find two disparate views about whether or not gentile monotheists are potential Jews. One view holds that gentiles are obligated for seven commandments and no more.[21] The other view holds that gentiles should observe more and more of the commandments, which of course means that they are to do so and become eventually absorbed into Judaism altogether.[22]

Thus Maimonides inherited a number of options as regards Jewish treament of a non-Jewish religion: (1) the biblical option primarily based on political and moral criteria; (2) the rabbinic option primarily based on theological criteria; (3) the one rabbinic view that gentile monotheists are potential Jews; (4) the other rabbinic view that gentile monotheists have a sufficient religious and political life without any attachment, actual or even potential, to Judaism and the Jewish people. We shall see how he orders these options and how this ordering is philosophically determined.

Judaism and Islam

Maimonides lived his entire life under Muslim rule, and despite his eventual rise to high position under the Muslim rulers of Egypt, his view of that rule as regards Jews was often quite negative. He and his family were forced by the Almohad persecutions to leave their native Córdoba in Spain in the middle of the twelfth century (Maimonides always signed his name "Moses son of Rabbi Maimon the Spaniard") and had to roam throughout the Maghreb until eventually settling in Fuṣṭāṭ, the old city of Cairo. In his famous *Epistle to Yemen*, written early in his career, where he attempted to comfort a Jewish community being persecuted by Muslims, he wrote

> Remember, my co-religionists, that on account of the vast number of our sins, God has caused us to fall in the midst of this people, the Arabs (*Yishma'el*), who have persecuted us severely, and passed baneful legislation against us. . . . Never did a nation molest, degrade, debase and hate us as much as they . . . . We have acquiesced, both old and young, to inure ourselves to humiliation. . . . All this notwithstanding, we do not escape this continued maltreatment which well nigh crushes us.[23]

At the end of this epistle Maimonides recognized that he was taking a political risk in attacking both the Muslims and the claim of Islam that it is superior to Judaism. Nevertheless, his concern for the downtrodden Yemenite Jewry took precedence over his concerns for his own safety and security.[24]

However, what is important to note, even in this highly polemical work, is the fact that Maimonides only criticized Muslim charges against the veracity of the Hebrew Bible and Jewish tradition in general. He did not criticize Islam *per se*. This should be contrasted with his treatment of Christianity. Maimonides asserted that although Jesus, unlike Muhammad, never intended to found a new religion, Christianity was still considered to be a form of idolatry.[25] No doubt he regarded its doctrine of the Trinity to be a basic compromise of the monotheism required of all persons, gentiles as well as Jews.[26]

Such is not the case with Islam. The important thing to bear in mind is that despite the political persecution of the Jews by Muslims in Maimonides' lifetime, a persecution he himself experienced and to which he himself responded more than once, Islamic monotheism was what ultimately determined his halakhic treatment of Muslims. As we have seen, the whole political criterion for determining the status of gentile emphasized in the Hebrew Bible was played down by Maimonides.[27]

This comes out in his treatment of the question of gentile wine (*stam yenam*). According to the Talmud Jews are not to drink wine prepared by gentiles or derive any monetary benefit from it. In the Talmud two distinct reasons are given for this prohibition: (1) It was assumed that all gentile wine has been dedicated to idolatry, even if this is not verifiable in every case.[28] (2) Gentile wine is not to be drunk in order to minimize social contact with gentiles, which was seen as leading to intermarriage and perhaps to idolatry as well.[29] Now it would seem that if a gentile is not an idolator, this prohibition should no longer apply according to this first Talmudic reason.[30] The ban on intermarriage, on the other hand, applies whether the gentiles were monotheists or polytheists.[31] In the second case the prohibition is clearly more extensive but weaker, and it was this tendency in *Halakhah* that Maimonides followed in dealing with the wine of Muslims. Although a Jew may not drink the wine of a Muslim, he may derive monetary benefit from it. He wrote:

> A resident-alien (*ger toshav*), that is one who has accepted upon himself the seven commandments, as we have explained, it is prohibited to drink his wine, but it is permitted to derive monetary benefit (*muttar be-haniyyah*) from it. . . . And so it is with any gentile who does not practice idolatry (*'avodah zarah*) like these Muslims (*Yishma'elim*): their wine is prohibited for drinking but permitted for monetary benefit. And so rule all the *geonim*.[32]

Furthermore, in a responsum that was probably written before the publication of his great code, the *Mishneh Torah* (in 1178), Maimonides stated concerning the wine of Muslims:

> These Muslims are not far from idolatry as you mentioned. . . . Ultimately all of the *geonim* of the West [Spain] were lenient concerning their wine. It should be permitted to derive monetary benefit from it but no more. Permitting the drinking of it is something that has not been heard from any halakhic authority (*ba'al hora'ah*). This is accepted practice (*halakhah le-ma'aseh*) in the presence of all the *geonim* of the West: when it happens that a Muslim touches our wine with a touch that could entail religious significance (*nissukh*), they prohibited drinking it but permitted selling it, just like Muslim wine itself.[33]

Thus, even though Maimonides regarded many of the folk practices of Muslims to be largely of pagan origin, he nevertheless held that Islam had removed the idolatrous intent which would make articles associated in any way with these practices idolatrous accessories.[34] This being the case, the only reason for the continuation of the ban is the rabbinic goal of limiting Jewish-gentile social intercourse, and that could be fulfilled by a prohibition on drinking gentile wine alone.

To appreciate the significance of Maimonides' ruling here, a ruling which was widely disputed,[35] we must examine the key terms he used in it. The resident-alien (*ger toshav*) refers to a gentile who was given the right to dwell in the Land of Israel and to be protected by Jewish civil and criminal law. The Talmud indicates that the *ger toshav* ceased to be a real political status with the destruction of the Second Temple in Jerusalem in 586 B.C.E.[36] However, the Talmud did discuss anyway what was the criterion for becoming a *ger toshav*. The minimalist view was that one had to renounce idolatry; the maximalist view was that one had to adopt the whole Torah with the sole exception of the ban on eating improperly slaughtered meat (*nevelot*). The view which Maimonides accepted, however, is that the criterion for becoming a *ger toshav* is the acceptance of the seven Noahide commandments.[37] Now the acceptance of these commandments is a universal obligation irrespective of time and place. Thus one who accepts these commandments is often referred to by Maimonides as a *ger toshav* or "like a *ger toshav*" because the obligatory character of these commandments remains even though the political privileges they entailed have been bracketed by history.[38]

How ironic that Maimonides should speak of Muslim wine inasmuch as it is well-known that the Qur'an explicitly prohibits Muslims from drinking any alcohol.[39] That, however, is an internal Islamic matter, something with which Jews and Judaism need not be concerned. Clearly, many Muslims violated this Qur'anic prohibition rather openly. What is important to note is that Maimonides regarded Muslims to be monotheists who could not be judged to be those who make wine an accessory to idolatry. Furthermore, both in the responsum and in the *Mishneh Torah* Maimonides invoked the Talmudic rule that wine not fit to be used on the Temple altar (*she-eno ra'uy 'al gabbei ha-mizbeaḥ*), that is, wine with some admixture of honey or leaven, that this wine is exempt from the status of wine which one may not drink with a gentile.[40] Thus we can see that he even played down the whole rationale for this prohibition, namely a bar to Jewish-gentile socializing. There seems to have been no reason to ban social contacts with Muslims.

Maimonides' Response to a Muslim Convert to Judaism

We have seen that in the rabbinic writings there are two views regarding non-Jewish monotheists: (1) they are in fact potential Jews; (2) their monotheism is a fully actual relationship with the One God and is, therefore, sufficient for them from the standpoint of Judaism. Elsewhere I have argued that the first view is the older one and the latter is later, a view largely formulated after the rise of Christianity and its separation from Judaism and the Jewish people.[41] We shall now see how Maimonides, as much as possible within the limits of *Halakhah* as it developed up until his time, returned to the older view about gentile monotheism being in fact potential Judaism.[42] As a philosopher largely influenced by Aristotle, Maimonides used the Aristotelian ontological scheme of potency-act in his halakhic treatment of the relation between gentile and Jewish monotheism.[43]

A certain Rabbi Obadiah ('Abdullāh?), a Muslim who had converted to Judaism, wrote to Maimonides complaining that his Jewish teacher said that Muslims are idolators. The curious thing about Maimonides' response, one which a student of the the *Halakhah* would immediately notice, is that even if the charge about Muslims were true, the teacher of Rabbi Obadiah was transgressing the rabbinic rule about taunting a convert about his pagan past.[44] However, instead of even mentioning this, Maimonides immediately made a long statement denying the charge altogether.

> These Muslims are not idolators (*'ovdei 'avodah zarah*) at all. It has already been cut off from their mouth and mind. For they are totally and properly committed to the One God (*yiḥud ke-ra'uy*) without deceit (*dofi*). . . . And if someone says that the house that they praise [*al-Ka'ba*] is an idolatrous shrine and an idol is hidden in it which their ancestors used to worship—what about it? Those who worship in its direction today, their thoughts are only for God (*en libbam ella la-Shamayim*). . . . So it is with these Muslims today, all of them, even children and women, idolatry is cut off from their mouth.[45]

Maimonides did not give unqualified acceptance to every Islamic practice. Some of them he called "their error and their foolishness" (*ve-ṭa'utam ve-ṭippeshutam*), refusing to elaborate lest Jewish informers report him to the Muslim authorities. Nevertheless, concerning the most fundamental theological doctrine, the existence and unity of God, Maimonides argued that Islam is totally committed to it and that this commitment can be taken for granted even among the simplest Muslim believers.

If this is the case, then Islam is clearly as monotheistic as Judaism. In the case of Rabbi Obadiah, the former Muslim, his conversion to Judaism did not entail the nullification of any polytheistic belief or the abandonment of any idolatrous practice. It would seem that for Maimonides Judaism and Islam are both equally monotheistic and that monotheism is the foundation of all true religion.[46] Is Islam, then, more than potential Judaism but the equal of Judaism? If so, then what is the significance of Rabbi Obadiah's conversion altogether? What has he actually gained?[47]

The answer to these questions seems to lie in Maimonides' view of the superiority of Mosaic prophecy whose product is the Torah. Mosaic prophecy is superior to any other prophecy, whether Jewish or non-Jewish, on two accounts.

First, Mosaic prophecy is the full expression of original monotheism. All other true prophecy, and here "true" and "monotheistic" are synonyms, is derived from it in the sense that it can only reconfirm it. Any contradiction with this original monotheism would render the subsequent prophecy false.[48] Thus Rabbi Obadiah's conversion from Islam to Judaism is a movement from derivative monotheism to the original source. Ultimately, all monotheistic persons and peoples will return to their Jewish origins. In his treatment of Jewish messianism in the *Mishneh Torah* (a part removed by the Christian censors), Maimonides wrote about both Christianity and Islam (after some rather negative comments about both Jesus and Muhammad) in the following way:

> But there is no power in man to apprehend the thoughts of the Creator of the world. . . . Thus these words of Jesus of Nazareth and this Arab who came after him were only to prepare the way for the Messiah-King and to order (*le-taqqen*) the whole world to serve the Lord altogether, as it says in scripture, "For I will unite all the peoples into pure speech, all of them to call upon the name of the Lord and to serve Him with one shoulder."[49]

In this concept of derivative monotheism, especially in the case of Islam (I shall discuss the distinction between Islam and Christianity later in this paper), Maimonides followed the lead of the earlier Spanish Jewish theologian, Rabbi Judah Halevi. In his dialogue, *Kuzari*, Halevi depicted a pagan king—already a philosophical monotheist—who attempts to find the true religion. He ultimately chooses Judaism over both Christianity and Islam because the latter two religions are at best derivative and, therefore, the original monotheism is no doubt the most authentic—and that is Judaism.[50] In so arguing, ha-Levi, and after him Maimonides, reversed the successionist claims of both Christianity and Islam. Succession is not improvement but dilution of the original revelation.

Second, the test of the most effective monotheism is not only the purity of its belief—a point where Islam is not inferior to Judaism—but, also, the unified political and personal order it creates and which is singularly monotheistic in its intentionality.[51] Here Maimonides was convinced of the practical superiority of the Torah over any other form of revealed legislation. In addition, Judaism has the longest experience as a monotheistic community. Thus he continued his discussion of how Christianity and Islam prepare the way for the Jewish Messiah-King and his exalted reign, how they prepare for it but are by no means equal to it.

> How is this so? The whole world is already filled with the words of [their] messiah and the words of the Torah and the words of the commandments, and these words have spread to the farthest islands and among many obstinate (*'arelei lev*) peoples, and they discuss

> these words and the commandments of the Torah. They say, "These commandments were true (*emet hayu*), but are already invalid (*baṭlu*) today, and are not to be perpetual (*nohagot le-dorot*)." . . . But when the true Messiah arises and will triumph and be uplifted and exalted, all of them will immediately return and comprehend that their ancestors inherited falsehood (*sheker*) and their prophets and ancestors misled them.[52]

The error of the Christians and the Muslims, for Maimonides, is that they assume that the Torah is passé and that a monotheistic community can be constituted without it. Yet, despite their political power—as contrasted with the political impotence of the Jewish people—they have not been able to bring about the social and political unity and harmony which should be the practical outcome of monotheism. It is important to note that Maimonides regarded the Messiah-King as a political ruler who will be able, without supernatural intervention, to effect universal monotheism by putting the Torah into full practice. He seemed convinced that if the Jews had the necessary political power, monotheism would become the pervasive practical force that it is now in belief the world over.[53] The messianic failure of both Christianity and Islam is something which indicates that their monotheism (real in the case of Islam; imaginary in the case of Christianity) cannot effect a unifed and harmonious world order. Hence they have not superceded Judaism, as they claim, but have rather diluted its message and missed its great monotheistic strengths. In the days of the Messiah all the peoples—certainly all the Christian and Muslim peoples—will see Judaism as the purest and most comprehensive practical monotheism and will accept it. In the meantime there will be certain insightful Christians and Muslims who will anticipate this messianic reality. The convert Rabbi Obadiah was one such Muslim and Maimonides thus addressed him with the greatest personal respect as well as voicing an appreciation of how his former Islam was in effect potential Judaism, an anticipation of the true messianic realm.

Circumcision and Islam

Maimonides not only regarded Islam as an unambiguously monotheistic religion, but he also saw certain Islamic practices as actually being mandated by Judaism. Concerning the practice of circumcision he wrote:

> Our sages said that the sons of Keturah, who are of the seed of Abraham, who came after Ishmael and Isaac, are obligated to be circumcised. And because today the sons of Ishmael have assimilated (*ve-nit'arvu*) with the sons of Keturah, all of them are obligated to be circumcised on the eighth day.[54]

To understand the significance of this ruling in Maimonides' great code of Jewish law, the *Mishneh Torah*, one must be aware of the fact that he used the term *Ishmaelite* somewhat ambiguously in his legal writings. On the one hand, *Yishma'elim* or *benei Yishma'el* refer to Muslims who are adherents of Islam, a universal religion, irrespective of ethnic background. On the other hand, however, the only Muslims who are literally *Yishma'elim* are the Arabs. Moreover, although Maimonides was certainly aware of the fact that there are many non-Arab Muslims, nevertheless, his own experience seems to have been limited to Arabs. Therefore, when he spoke about the actual doctrines of Islam, *Ishmael* refers to an abstract theology, whereas when he spoke of the practices of Muslims *Ishmael* refers to a real present cultural community. This distinction is important to bear in mind because Maimonides' high estimation of Islamic doctrine was not matched by a similarly high estimation of many of the Muslim practices he actually saw in his own time and place. In fact, as we have seen, one of his main arguments for the superiority of Judaism over Islam was that Jewish practice is more consistent with pure monotheism than Muslim practice is. An exception to this general tendency, however, is the Islamic practice of circumcision, a practice he saw among the Arabs with whom he lived and worked. Maimonides traced this practice to the literal descent of the Arabs from Ishmael who became assimilated with the Keturites. As an extant ethnic group the Keturites no longer exist. Therefore, the only non-Jewish descendants of Abraham are the Ishmaelites/Arabs. In fact, according to one rabbinic opinion, Keturah is another name for Hagar, the mother of Ishmael, whom Abraham took back and remarried after the death of Sarah, the mother of Isaac.[55] Thus, it seems, Maimonides saw the Islamic practice of circumcision, most prevalent among Muslim Arabs, as coming from Judaism and something which Judaism sees as a requirement for Arabs, and a requirement not originally Islamic. It is important to note that Muslim circumcision is not prescribed in the Qur'an, a fact undoubtedly known to Maimonides.[56]

This ruling of Maimonides caused a number of serious problems for later commentators because it seemed to contradict a number of Talmudic rulings, rulings which are supposed to be authoritative for subsequent halakhists, including Maimonides.[57]

The contradictions are as follows:

1. The Talmud explicitly states that Noahides, that is, all monotheistic, law-abiding non-Jews, are to practice seven commandments as binding according to Jewish criteria. Anything else which they practice, even if it is not in violation of these seven commandments, still does not partake of their revealed character.[58] For one group of Noahides and a large and important one at that, Maimonides has, however, designated an eighth commandment, circumcision, an eighth commandment every much a part of the divine law for them as the other seven.

2. The Talmud refers to the phenomenon of the "circumcised Arab" (*'Aravi mahul*).[59] There is a debate in the Talmud about symbolic circumcision (*haṭṭafat dam berit*) of a convert to Judasim who was circumcised already prior to his conversion. (This symbolic circumcision consists of drawing a drop of blood from that place on the male organ where the foreskin had been connected

to it.) Although one version of this debate reports that the Hillelites—the school of rabbinic legal opinion whose view is almost always taken to be normative—as ruling that symbolic circumcision is not required, nevertheless, the other version of this debate reports unanimity of rabbinic opinion about the requirement of this symbolic circumcision.[60] Clearly the Talmud was aware of the widespread practice of circumcision among the pre-Islamic Arabs and, yet, did not see any Jewish religious significance in it. Circumcision was only a religious act within the context of the covenant of Israel.[61] Moreover, elsewhere in the *Mishneh Torah* Maimonides codified this view.[62] If so, then why does he in the *Mishneh Torah* passage we just examined now see a Jewish religious significance in this fact? Why should an Arab convert to Judaism, whose previous circumcision as a Muslim did have a religious significance—in a religion Judaism (for Maimonides anyway) regards as a perfectly valid monotheism—be required to undergo another symbolic circumcision upon converting to Judaism? Surely a Muslim convert to Judaism would not have to reaffirm his opposition to idolatry since he had never been an idolator even in his former religion.[63]

3. The fact that the Keturites are now considered by Maimonides to have become indistinguishable from the Arab people raises another problem with Talmudic tradition. The Talmud ruled that in most cases of doubt one is to assume that what obtains for the majority obtains for the whole (*zeel batar rubba*).[64] Thus, for example, if a family whose members are barred from marrying with other Jews because of a strain of bastardy (*mamzerut*) became assimilated into the whole Jewish people, then the Talmud rules that their problematic background is to be forgotten.[65] Why, then, according to Maimonides, do the majority Arabs now have the obligation of circumcision of the minority Keturites? Why are the Keturites not regarded as having lost this obligation because of their assimilation with the Arabs?[66]

These are the contradictions with Talmudic tradition one can see in this ruling of Maimonides regarding Arab circumcision. However, they can all be resolved, I think, if we remember that Maimonides regarded Islam as having totally permeated the belief and most of the practice of the Arabs, who are related to the Jewish people by literal Abrahamic descent.

1. As we saw earlier concerning gentile observance of the commandments of Judaism, namely, the later view is that this observance must be confined to the seven Noahide commandments only; and the earlier view (with Hellenistic Jewish precedents) is that monotheistic gentiles are in fact potential Jews and should observe as many of the commandments of the Torah as possible, as their potential Judaism. Now although the later view became the normative one, the earlier one—like so many other overruled opinions in *Halakhah*—could not be totally and permanently suppressed.[67] Clearly Maimonides himself was partial to it and ruled that in anything short of actual religious syncretism, gentiles could practice Jewish commandments and receive transcendent rewards for such practices.[68] The fact that the Muslim Arab practice of circumcision in his day—as contrasted with the pre-Islamic, pagan Arab practice of circumcision known in Talmudic times—the fact that this practice was based on Islamic monotheism seems to have enabled Maimonides to regard it as an acceptable

practical application of the Islamic monotheism he so admired in theory. The fact that he could assign an Abrahamic origin to this practice through the Keturites enabled him, it seems to me, to once again emphasize to Jews and Muslims alike the true Judaic source of all that is truly valid in Islam.

2. There is no doubt that as a halakhist Maimonides could not always follow the practical conclusions of his philosophically conceived theology. In the case of symbolic circumcision of all previously circumcised converts to Judaism he had a long tradition behind him, going back to the post-Talmudic *geonim*, a tradition which required this symbolic circumcision irrespective of what the circumstances of the gentile circumcision were.[69] This is not the only case where Maimonides as a halakhist had to place tradition before theology in terms of practical rulings. Thus, for example, even though he codified the one Talmudic view that gentiles who keep the seven Noahide commandments as divine law are admitted to the world-to-come,[70] he nevertheless codified another Talmudic view—one which is undisputed—that one must tell all prospective converts to Judaism that the world-to-come is for Israel alone.[71] However, the important thing to remember, in looking at Maimonides' treatment of the question of the Muslim Arab practice of circumcision, is that despite the fact that it should have followed from his theological premises that circumcised Muslims do not require circumcision symbolically when they convert to Judaism, despite the fact that he had to codify the tradition which said otherwise, Maimonides still regarded Islam *per se* as being different and superior to any other non-Jewish religion. This difference is something of which he makes Jews, and no doubt Muslims as well, aware.

3. If one understands Maimonides' regard for Islam and its salutory influence on at least some of the practices of the Arabs who are now Muslims, perhaps an explanation of his rather strange view of the assimilation of the Keturites and Ishmaelites can emerge. If this assimilation is simply seen in quantitative terms, then the Keturites should be regarded as having disappeared into the Ishmaelites. However, what if the source of Arab monotheism, the overwhelming and enthusiastic Arab acceptance of Islam, is the result of the *influence* of Abraham through the Keturites? Whereas Islam traces its roots in Abrahamic monotheism through Ishmael,[72] rabbinic tradition regarded Ishmael as an idolator.[73] It is the children of Keturah who like the children of Isaac and Jacob—the Jews—are monotheists. Therefore, it would seem that Maimonides regarded the Keturites as those who converted the Ishmaelites to the monotheism which subsequently became Islam. The Keturites may have become Ishmaelites ethnically and politically. But in spiritual terms—and for Maimonides this is far more important than ethnicity—the Ishmaelites became Keturites as evidenced by Islam and the Muslim practice of circumcision as a religious rite.[74] Unlike Isaac and his seed, the children of Keturah were the children of a concubine.[75] As such, their status is Abrahamic but clearly lower than that of Isaac and his seed. Here again, it seems to me, Maimonides took the opportunity to show his regard for Islamic monotheism and consistently monotheistic Islamic practice, while at the same time refuting any Islamic supercessionist claims of being a superior and final revelation in relation to Judaism.[76]

Islam and Christianity

In his treatment of Islam, Maimonides emphasized that it is a complete monotheism. Christianity, on the other hand, was considered by him to be in effect polytheistic and, therefore, a form of idolatry (*'avodah zarah*). It would thus seem that Maimonides ranked Islam higher than Christianity. Nevertheless, in one specific area at least, Maimonides expressed a preference for Christianity over Islam. When asked whether or not the Talmudic ban on teaching gentiles any more of the Torah than the seven Noahide commandments[77] still obtained with contemporary gentiles, Maimonides answered strongly in the affirmative, but then he continued

> It is permitted to teach the commandments (*ha-mitzvot*) to Christians (*Noṣrim*) and to draw them to our religion, but this is not permitted with Muslims because of what is known to you about their belief that this Torah is not divine revelation (*enah min ha-Shamayim*). When you will teach them something from Scripture, they will find that it contradicts what they have devised (*she-badu hem*) from their own minds according to the confused stories and incoherent doctrines which have come to them, and this will not be a proof to them because they possess error (*she-ṭa'ut be-yadehem*), . . . but the uncircumcised ones believe that the version (*nusaḥ*) of the Torah has not changed, only they interpret it with their faulty exegesis. . . . But when these scriptural texts will be interpreted with correct exegesis (*'al ha-perush ha-nakhon*), it is possible that they will return to the good. . . . There is nothing that they will find in their Scriptures which differs from ours.[78]

Now it is clear from the question which prompted this response that Maimonides meant that *anything* in the Hebrew Bible may be taught to Christians. The question states: "Is every Jew obligated to refrain from teaching anything (*davar*) from the commandments (*min ha-mitzvot*) except the seven commandments or what is based on them, or not?"[79] Furthermore, "correct exegesis" seems to encompass much of postbiblical Jewish teaching as well. Muslims, as opposed to Christians, having rejected the Hebrew Bible as authentic revelation *per se*, will not be moved by scriptural proofs as would Christians. Moreover, Maimonides explicitly stated that the purpose in teaching Scripture to Christians is to attract them to Judaism, namely, that it is "likely" (*efshar*) that they will convert to Judaism if exposed to such proper teaching.

Maimonides, as we have seen, regarded both Christians and Muslims as paving the way for the coming of the Messiah, which is the full restoration of Jewish political sovereignty, the full hegemony of the Torah, and the final triumph of monotheism in human history. In the *Mishneh Torah* Maimonides spoke of the divinely mandated duty of Jews "to force" (*la-kof*) all humanity to accept the commandments given to the Noahides.[80] On the other hand, however, he emphasized there that only those "who want to convert" (*kol ha-roṣeh le-hitgayyer*) are to be accepted as converts. Whereas the acceptance of the Noahide commandments can be seen as a political necessity which Jews should enforce when they have the power to do so, conversion to Judaism can only be a matter of inner conviction. Maimonides in this responsum also emphasized that when Jews have political power over gentiles, study of the Torah by them should be contingent upon conversion. That can be enforced, but conversion itself can only be a matter of persuasion. Now it is clear that for Maimonides the conversion of both Christians and Muslims to Judaism is a desideratum, something which Jews ought to encourage and facilitate as much as possible.[81] However, it is only with Christians that study of the Hebrew Bible, what is their "Old Testament," could be an appropriate means to this end. With Muslims, conversely, it would do more harm than good. And the fact that these Christians are not pure monotheists as are the Muslims did not seem to detract from Maimonides' high esteem for their biblicism.

One could, of course, simply leave the matter at this point and conclude that in terms of his philosophical theology Maimonides preferred Muslim monotheism over Christian trinitarianism, but in terms of what we might term his historical theology, he preferred the Christian canonization of the Old Testament over the Muslim rejection of it and the total replacement of it with the Qur'an.[82] Nevertheless, I think one can infer even here a unified Maimonidean approach. This inference on my part is admittedly conjectural, but I think it is a conjecture that is not inconsistent with the overall *Tendenz* of his thought.

As far as Maimonides is concerned, the study of Scripture in and of itself is no guarantee of the philosophically demonstrable monotheism he considers the foundation of all true religion. For the nonphilosophical study of Scripture leads one to accept its anthropomorphism literally and Maimonides thought that anthropomorphism is the ideational corollary of polytheism, a limiting of the authentic transcendence of God.[83] Now Christianity is the prime example of the error of such anthropomorphism in its original doctrine of the incarnation and the closely related doctrine of the Trinity. As such, the study of Scripture only has immediate practical value, but on the theoretical level it requires a philosophical hermeneutic to reveal its esoteric truth (*sitrei Torah*).

This difference between practice and theory can be applied to the difference between Christianity and Islam for Maimonides. On the theoretical level, Islamic monotheism is clearly superior to Christian trinitarianism and, for Maimonides, although historical revelation enabled the people of Israel to emerge as the original monotheistic community, historical revelation is not the *conditio sine qua non* of monotheism. Monotheism being *ratio per se* is something which can be attained by philosophical means, although in the sense of *ratio quod nos* most people not being philosophers will require an historical revelation.[84] Therefore, if Muslims are pure monotheists, then it is ultimately unimportant that they derived their monotheism from historical sources other than the Hebrew Bible. Their potential for Judaism, then, must be seen in theoretical, philosophical terms rather than in practical, scriptural ones. Christians, on the other hand, are not true monotheists, but they have accepted the practical monotheism of the Hebrew Bible. In their case proper scriptural exegesis will bring them to Judaism. Here again we see how for Maimonides Judaism is ultimately superior to both Christianity and Islam. It is superior to Islamic monotheism because it is the earliest monotheism and one which entails a far more consistent monotheistic practice than that of Islam, and certainly than the folk practices of most Muslims.[85] It is superior to Christianity and its biblicism because it has the correct, monotheistic, exegesis of scripture based on a theology which rejects philosophically untenable incarnationism and trinitarianism. However, since philosophy is superior to biblical literalism,[86] and since Islam does entail many acceptable practices in the light of monotheistic criteria, even this responsum, despite its preference for Christianity's biblicism, does not, it seems to me, contradict the clear conclusion emerging from looking at many of Maimonides' writings: he regarded Islam as indeed the closest religion to Judaism.

NOTES

1 D. Novak, *The Image of the Non-Jew in Judaism: An Historical and Constructive Study of the Noahide Laws* (New York and Toronto: Edwin Mellen Press, 1983), 275ff.

2 See, e.g., Mic. 4:5.

3 See, e.g., Ps. 96:5; 1 Chron. 17:20-24.

4 See Novak, *The Image of the Non-Jew in Judaism*, 108ff.

5 See, e.g., Deut. 20:16-18, 23:4-9, 25:17-19.

6 See, e.g., Gen. 13:13, 18:20ff.; Ex. 17:8-13; Lev. 18:24-25; 2 Kings 23:10.

7 See, e.g., Amos 1:3ff.; Mal. 2:10ff; 1 Kings 15:19; Hab. 2:4.

8 See Gen. 21:22ff., 31:44ff.; 2 Kings 5:21ff.

9 See, e.g., Amos 1:3ff.; Mal. 2:10ff.; 1 Kings 15:19; Hab. 2:4.

10 See Deut. 20:10ff.; Josh. 9:15ff.; 2 Sam. 21:1ff.

11 See, e.g., Ex. 22:20; Lev. 24:22.

12 See, e.g., Josh. 2:1ff.; Job 1:1ff.

13 See 2 Kings 5:15ff.

14 See, e.g., Is. 2:2-3, 19:25, 56:7; Mic. 4:5; Zeph. 3:9; Zech. 14:1ff.; Novak, *The Image of the Non-Jew in Judaism*, 111ff.

15 *Ibid.*, 23ff.

16 T. 'Avodah Zarah 8:4; T. B. Sanhedrin 56a-b.

17 See T. B. Giṭṭin 45b and parallels; also, T. B. Yevamot 61a.

18 See T. B. Ḥullin 13b.

19 See, e.g., Ecclesiastes Rabbah 4:13.

[20] See Josephus *Antiquities* 14:110; Philo *De Vita Mosis* 2:14; cf. Juvenal *Satires* 14:96; Tacitus *History* 5:5.

[21] T. B. Sanhedrin 58b-59a.

[22] T. Y. 'Avodah Zarah 2:1/40c; T. B. Ḥullin 92a-b.

[23] Maimonides, *Epistle to Yemen*, A. S. Halkin, ed.; English translation by B. Cohen (New York: American Academy for Jewish Research, 1952), xviii.

[24] *Ibid.*, p. xx and n. 22 thereon.

[25] *Ibid.*, p. iv; *Mishneh Torah*, "Hilkhot 'Avodah Zarah" 9:4.

[26] See *Moreh Nevukhim* 1:50.

[27] See Maimonides, *Mishneh Torah*, "Hilkhot Melakhim" 6:1ff., where the acceptance of the Noahide laws, over and above making peace with Israel, is the *sine qua non* for Jewish tolerance of any gentile nation, including Canaan and even Amalek. See the note of Rabad thereon. Maimonides' rabbinic source is T. Y. Shevi'it 6:1/36c; but there the acceptance of the Noahide laws is not mentioned. Cf. B. Giṭṭin 46a, Tos., s.v. "*kevan*."

[28] T. B. 'Avodah Zarah 29b. See Tos., s.v. "*yayin*."

[29] T. B. 'Avodah Zarah 36b.

[30] T. B. 'Avodah Zarah 57a.

[31] T. B. Kiddushin 68b re Deut. 7:4 and T. B. 'Avodah Zarah 36b.

[32] Maimonides, *Mishneh Torah*, "Hilkhot Ma'akhalot Asurot" 11:7. Anything associated with idolatry, even if practiced by Jews, is not to be used for any monetary benefit. See M. 'Avodah Zarah 5:8; T. B. Makkot 22a; T. Y. 'Avodah Zarah 5:12/45a re Deut. 13:18; Maimonides, *Mishneh Torah*, "Hilkhot 'Avodah Zarah" 7:2.

[33] *Teshuvot ha-Rambam*, no. 269, J. Blau, ed. (Jerusalem: "Miqqiṣei Nirdamim," 1960), 2:515-16.

[34] See above, n. 28.

[35] See *Teshuvot ha-Rashba* 1, nos. 717, 813; 4, no. 149; *Teshuvot ha-Ribash*, no. 180; *Teshuvot Tashbaṣ* 2, no. 168; *Teshuvot ha-Radbaz* 1, no. 2.

[36] T. B. 'Arakhin 29a.

[37] T. B. 'Avodah Zarah 64b.

[38] See Maimonides, *Mishneh Torah*, "Hilkhot 'Avodah Zarah" 10:6 (and the note of Rabad thereon); "Hilkhot Millah" 1:6; "Hilkhot Issurei Biah" 14:7; "Hilkhot Melakhim" 8:10-11.

[39] Qur'an 5:93-94. See F. Rahman, *Islam*, 2nd ed. (Chicago: University of Chicago Press, 1979), 51.

[40] T. Y. Terumot 8:3/45c.

[41] See Novak, *The Image of the Non-Jew in Judaism*, pp. 26ff.

[42] Maimonides, to be sure, codified the later Talmudic bans of gentiles practicing basic Jewish rites such as Sabbath observance and Torah study (*Mishneh Torah*, "Hilkhot Melakhim" 10:9 re T. B. Sanhedrin 58b-59a; T. B. 'Avodah Zarah 3a). He wrote: "The essence of the matter is that we do not allow him to innovate a religion (*le-ḥaddesh dat*) and to make up commandments from his own mind. Either he should become a full convert *(ger ṣedeq)* and accept all the commandments, or he should remain in his own Torah—neither adding to it nor detracting from it." Nevertheless, he also wrote immediately afterwards ("Hilkhot Melakhim" 10:10): "If a Noahide wants to

practice any other commandment from the commandments of the Torah in order to receive transcendent reward, we do not stop him from doing so according to its proper halakhic procedure" (see the note of Radbaz thereon). See his comment on M. Terumot 3:9 (cf. T. B. Bava Kama 38a). The point that emerges out of this seems to be that if the gentile observance of Jewish practices is part of an actualizing process of moving towards Judaism in stages, then it is acceptable. If, however, it is part of diluting Jewish practices for the sake of some sort of syncretism, then it is unacceptable. It all depends on the intent, and intent is clearly a teleological criterion; see Aristotle *Nicomachean Ethics* 3:2, 1112a, 15.

[43] Thus in the *Mishneh Torah* he refers to the Mosaic Torah (613 commandments) as "completing (*ve-nishlamah*) the seven Noahide commandments" ("Hilkhot Melakhim" 9:1).

[44] M. Bava Meṣia 4:10; T. B. Sanhedrin 94a.

[45] *Teshuvot ha-Rambam*, no. 448, 2:726. See, also, his "Iggeret ha-Shemad" in *Iggrot ha-Rambam*, Rabinowitz, ed. (Jerusalem: Mosad ha-Rav Kook, 1960), 44. No doubt something like the Muslim practice of throwing pebbles at certain shrines (see *Islam from the Prophet Muhammad to the Capture of Constantinople*, B. Lewis, ed. and tr., 2 vols. [New York: Harper and Row, 1974], 2:29) reminded many Jews of the rabbinic description of this as a pagan practice in honor of the god Mercury (M. Sanhedrin 7:6). The Talmud rules that this practice is considered unacceptable whether done reverently or even irreverently (T. B. Sanhedrin 64a) and Maimonides codified this (*Mishneh Torah*, "Hilkhot 'Avodah Zarah" 3:5). However, if the act was no longer connected with pagan worship at all, then it would seem, for Maimonides, that it assumed a different character altogether (see T. B. Sanhedrin 64a, Tos. s.v., "*af-'al-gav*"). Intentionality, not historical origin, ultimately determines the character of any act. Similarly, Maimonides removed (in another responsum to R. Obadiah the Convert) any restrictions on a convert from reciting the liturgical formula "God of our fathers." *Teshuvot ha-Rambam* no. 393, 2:548-50. See *Mishneh Torah* , "Hilkhot Bikkurim" 4:4 re Y. Bikkurim 1.4/64a à la Gen. 17:5. Cf. also I. Twersky, *Introduction to the Code of Maimonides (Mishneh Torah)* (New Haven: Yale University Press, 1980), 485-86.

[46] See *Mishneh Torah*, "Hilkhot Yesodei ha-Torah" 1:1 and *Moreh Nevukhim* 2.33.

[47] However, conversion from Judaism to Islam—even if Islam is not polytheistic—is clearly prohibited in that it entails a Jew abandoning Mosaic revealed law. Such a person, for Maimonides, is an *apiqoros*, viz., one who rejects Mosaic prophecy. Also, he is a *kofer*, viz., one who denies the full divine revelation (*Mishneh Torah*, "Hilkhot Teshvuah" 3:8). Maimonides advocated rather harsh punishment for such deviants (*Mishneh Torah*, "Hilkhot 'Avodah Zarah" 10:1). Clearly he follows the rabbinic view which enabled gentile admission to Judaism (see T. B. Yevamot 22a), but denied Jews the right to exit from Judaism (see T. Demai 2:4; T. B. Yevamot 47b). When conversion was forced, however, he was rather lenient concerning the legal consquences. See "Iggeret ha-Shemad," *passim*; cf. also H. Soloveitchik, "Maimonides' Iggeret Ha-Shemad: Law and Rhetoric," in the *Joseph Lookstein Memorial Volume* (New York: Ktav Publishers, 1980), 281ff.

48 See *Mishneh Torah*, "Hilkhot Yesodei ha-Torah" 8:3.

49 *Mishneh Torah*, "Hilkhot Melakhim" 11, end, uncensored version, ed. Rabinowitz (Jerusalem: Mosad ha-Rav Kook, 1962), 416, citing Zeph. 3:9. Maimonides' use of Zeph. 3:9 as his prooftext is significant because this verse was also the prooftext for the rabbinic view which advocated growing gentile observance of the commandments of the Torah as potential Judaism (see above, n. 22). See *Moreh Nevukhim* 3:29.

50 *Kuzari*, 1:4, 9-11. For Islamic charges of Jewish corruption of true revelation, see Qur'an 2:87-89, 106-08.

51 See *Moreh Nevukhim* 2:40 for the integration of theoretical and practical elements as the evidence of divine law.

52 *Mishneh Torah*, Rabinowitz, ed., "Hilkhot Melakhim," p. 417. See *Commentary on the Mishnah*, Y. Kafiḥ, ed. (Jerusalem: Mosad ha-Rav Kook, 1965), Sanhedrin, chap. 10, prin. 9, p. 144 and n. 77 thereon.

53 *Ibid.*, 12.1ff. See D. Novak, "Maimonides' Concept of the Messiah," *Journal of Religious Studies* 9:2 (Summer 1982): 42ff.

54 *Mishneh Torah*, "Hilkhot Melakhim" 10:8.

55 Genesis Rabbah 61:4.

56 See D. S. Margaliouth, "Circumcision: Islam," in J. Hastings, ed., *Encyclopedia of Religion and Ethics*, 13 vols. (New York: Charles Scribners Sons, 1951), 3:677-79.

57 See, e.g., R. Judah Rozanis, *Mishneh le-Melekh* on "Hilkhot Melakhim," 10:7; R. Aryeh Leib of Metz, *Shaagat Aryeh*, no. 49.

58 T. B. Sanhedrin 58b-59a; T. B. 'Avodah Zarah 3a.

59 T. B. Shabbat 135a. See M. Nedarim 3:11 and Epistle of Barnabas 9:6.

60 See T. Shabbat 15:9; T. B. Shabbat 135a, Tos., s.v. "*lo*"; *Behag*, ed. Hildesheimer (Jerusalem: Miqqiṣei Nirdamim, 1971), 1:205, 216; *Alfasi: Shabbat*, ed. Vilna, 53b-54a.

61 See T. B. 'Avodah Zarah 27a; T. B. Nedarim 31b; T. Y. Nedarim 3:9/38a-b; Maimonides, *Mishneh Torah*, "Hilkhot Millah" 2:1 and Karo, *Kesef Mishneh* thereon.

62 Maimonides, *Mishneh Torah*, "Hilkhot Issurei Biah" 14:5.

63 *Ibid.*, "Hilkhot 'Avodah Zarah" 8:9.

64 T. B. Ḥullin 11a re Ex. 23:2.

65 T. B. Kiddushin 71a; Maimonides, *Mishneh Torah*, "Hilkhot Melakhim" 12:3; cf. also M. Yadayim 4:4; *Pirqei de Rabbi Eliezer*, chapter 44.

66 Thus Rashi (living in Christian eleventh-century France) only saw the obligation of circumcision as applying to the sons of Keturah herself (B. Sanhedrin 59b, s.v. "*le-rabbot*") mentioned in Gen. 25:2, not to their descendants who assimilated and lost their Keturite identity. For Rashi it is clear that the Keturites were a one-generation phenomenon as far as Judaism is concerned. See D. Novak, *Law and Theology in Judaism*, 2 vols. (New York: Ktav Publishers, 1974-76), 1:67-68; 2:221-22.

67 See, e.g., T. B. Berakhot 9a and parallels.

68 See *Teshuvot ha-Rambam*, no. 148, 2:282-84 (and *Mishneh Torah*, "Hilkhot Melakhim" 10:10). Maimonides permitted a Jew, no doubt for this reason, to circumcise either a Christian or a Muslim who wants this for a religious

purpose, even though he was not converting to Judaism. Cf., however, T. 'Avodah Zarah 3:12; T. B. 'Avodah Zarah 26b.

[69] See *Sheiltot de-Rab Ahay Gaon*, ed. Kenig (Jerusalem: n. p., 1948), 26d and 10a.

[70] Maimonides, *Mishneh Torah*, "Hilkhot Melakhim" 8:11.

[71] *Ibid.*, "Hilkhot Issurei Biah" 14:4 re T. B. Yevamot 47a-b. Actually the extant text of the Babylonian Talmud does not present this problem. Maimonides' text apparently read: "The world-to-come is only in store for the *righteous and they are Israel.*" The extant text of the Babli reads: "The world-to-come is only made for the righteous; *but Israel at this time* is unable to receive too much good" (Italics mine), and see the note of R. Zvi Hirsch Chajes thereon.

[72] Qur'an 2:125-27; 19:54-55.

[73] See Targum Yerushalmi on Gen. 21:9; Genesis Rabbah 53:11.

[74] For Maimonides view of circumcision as a means of unifying believers, see *Moreh Nevukhim* 3:49.

[75] See Gen. 25:6.

[76] See above, n. 50.

[77] See above, n. 58.

[78] *Teshuvot ha-Rambam*, no. 149, 1:284-85.

[79] *Ibid.*, p. 284.

[80] Maimonides, *Mishneh Torah*, "Hilkhot Melakhim" 8:10.

[81] For Maimonides endorsement of what seems to be proselytizing gentiles, see *Sefer ha-Mitzvot*, pos. no. 9.

[82] See D. Novak, "Review-Essay of Paul van Buren's *Discerning the Way: A Theology of the Jewish-Christian Reality*," *Judaism* 31:1 (Winter 1982): 116.

[83] See, esp., Maimonides, *Mishneh Torah*, "Hilkhot Teshuvah" 3:7 (cf. Rabad's note thereon); also, "Hilkhot Yesodei ha-Torah" 1:7ff.; *Moreh Nevukhim* 1:35.

[84] See *Mishneh Torah*, "Hilkhot Shemiṭṭah ve-Yovel" end, and *Qoveṣ Teshuvot ha-Rambam ve-Iggrotav*, ed. Lichtenberg (Leipzig: n. p., 1859), 2:23b-24a; also, S. Atlas, *Netivim be-Mishpaṭ ha-'Ivri* (New York: n. p., 1978), 13-14; Novak, *The Image*, pp. 302-04.

[85] See *Moreh Nevukhim* 2:33.

[86] See *ibid.*, 2:22, 25.

Indexes

I. Index of Names, Subjects, and Foreign Terms

II. Index of Passages

Jewish Authors and Works

Pseudepigrapha

Early Christian Authors and Works

Classical Authors and Works

List of Contributors

Mahmoud M. Ayoub
Centre for Religious Studies
University of Toronto

William M. Brinner
Department of Near Eastern Studies
University of California, Berkeley

Joshua Halberstam
Department of Philosophy
Long Island University

*George F. Hourani
Department of Philosophy
State University of New York

Alfred L. Ivry
Department of Near Eastern and Judaic Studies
Brandeis University

Raphael Jospe
Center for Judaic Studies
University of Denver

Hava Lazarus-Yafeh
Institute for Asian and African Studies
Hebrew University of Jerusalem

Jeffrey Macy
Department of Political Science
Hebrew University of Jerusalem

* deceased

Gordon D. Newby
Department of History
North Carolina State University

David Novak
Department of Philosophy
Baruch College, City University of New York

Stephen D. Ricks
Department of Asian and Near Eastern Languages
Brigham Young University

Andrew Rippin
Religious Studies
University of Calgary

Stanley M. Wagner
Center for Judaic Studies
University of Denver

Marilyn R. Waldman
Department of History
Ohio State University

Farhat J. Ziadeh
Department of Near Eastern Languages and Civilization
University of Washington

BROWN JUDAIC STUDIES SERIES

Continued from back cover

140040	*Israeli Childhood Stories of the Sixties: Yizhar, Aloni, Shahar, Kahana-Carmon*	Gideon Telpaz
140041	*Formative Judaism II: Religious, Historical, and Literary Studies*	Jacob Neusner
140042	*Judaism in the American Humanities II: Jewish Learning and the New Humanities*	Jacob Neusner
140043	*Support for the Poor in the Mishnaic Law of Agriculture: Tractate Peah*	Roger Brooks
140044	*The Sanctity of the Seventh Year: A Study of Mishnah Tractate Shebiit*	Louis E. Newman
140045	*Character and Context: Studies in the Fiction of Abramovitsh, Brenner, and Agnon*	Jeffrey Fleck
140046	*Formative Judaism III: Religious, Historical, and Literary Studies*	Jacob Neusner
140047	*Pharaoh's Counsellors: Job, Jethro, and Balaam in Rabbinic and Patristic Tradition*	Judith Baskin
140048	*The Scrolls and Christian Origins: Studies in the Jewish Background of the New Testament*	Matthew Black
140049	*Approaches to Modern Judaism*	Marc Lee Raphael
140050	*Mysterious Encounters at Mamre and Jabbok*	William T. Miller
140051	*The Empire and the Subject Nations: The Middle Eastern Policy of Imperial Rome*	Eliezer Paltiel
140052	*Sparda by the Bitter Sea: Imperial Interaction in Western Anatolia*	Jack Martin Balcer
140053	*Hermann Cohen: The Challenge of a Religion of Reason*	William Kluback
140054	*Approaches to Judaism in Medieval Times I*	David R. Blumenthal
140055	*In the Margins of the Yerushalmi: Glosses on the English Translation*	Jacob Neusner
140056	*Approaches to Modern Judaism II*	Marc Lee Raphael
140057	*Approaches to Judaism in Medieval Times II*	David R. Blumenthal
140058	*Approaches to Ancient Judaism VI*	William Scott Green
140059	*The Commerce of the Sacred: Mediation of the Divine Among Jews in the Graeco-Roman Diaspora*	Jack N. Lightstone
140060	*Major Trends in Formative Judaism I: Society and Symbol in Political Crisis*	Jacob Neusner
140061	*Major Trends in Formative Judaism II: Texts, Contents, and Contexts*	Jacob Neusner
140062	*A History of the Jews in Babylonia. I: The Parthian Period*	Jacob Neusner
140063	*The Talmud of Babylonia: An American Translation. XXXII: Tractate Arakhin*	Jacob Neusner
140064	*Ancient Judaism: Debates and Disputes*	Jacob Neusner
140065	*Prayers Alleged to Be Jewish: An Examination of the* Constitutiones Apostolorum	David Fiensy
140066	*The Legal Methodology of Hai Gaon*	Tsvi Groner
140067	*From Mishnah to Scripture: The Problem of the Unattributed Saying*	Jacob Neusner
140068	*Halakhah in a Theological Dimension*	David Novak
140069	*From Philo to Origen: Middle Platonism in Transition*	Robert M. Berchman